GRAMMAR TECHNICAL SCHOOL
WOLVERHAMPTON

Session 1965—— 1966

PRIZE

For 4 G Form Prize

awarded to

Marilyn C.A. Smith

Headmaster

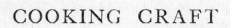

COOKING CRAFT

COOKING CRAFT

A PRACTICAL HANDBOOK FOR STUDENTS IN TRAINING FOR COOKERY AND FOR THE HOMEWORKER

BY

S. ELIZABETH NASH

Examiner for the National Council for Domestic Studies
Late Member of Staff, National Training College of Domestic
Subjects; Also Late Member of Staff, Battersea Training
College of Domestic Science

FIFTH EDITION

REVISION FOR FIFTH EDITION BY
M. M. BEGG

Formerly Senior Cookery Lecturer, The National Training College
of Domestic Subjects

LONDON
SIR ISAAC PITMAN & SONS LTD.

Fifth edition 1963
Reprinted 1966

SIR ISAAC PITMAN & SONS Ltd.
PITMAN HOUSE, PARKER STREET, KINGSWAY, LONDON, W.C.2
THE PITMAN PRESS, BATH
PITMAN HOUSE, BOUVERIE STREET, CARLTON, MELBOURNE
20–25 BECKETT'S BUILDINGS, PRESIDENT STREET, JOHANNESBURG

ASSOCIATED COMPANIES
PITMAN MEDICAL PUBLISHING COMPANY Ltd.
46 CHARLOTTE STREET, LONDON, W.I
PITMAN PUBLISHING CORPORATION
20 EAST 46TH STREET, NEW YORK, N.Y. 10017
SIR ISAAC PITMAN & SONS (CANADA) Ltd.
(INCORPORATING THE COMMERCIAL TEXT BOOK COMPANY)
PITMAN HOUSE, 381–383 CHURCH STREET, TORONTO

MADE IN GREAT BRITAIN AT THE PITMAN PRESS, BATH
F6—(E.6149)

AUTHOR'S NOTE

THE object of this book is not to increase the already large collection of recipes, but to provide instruction with regard to such important matters as the relative nutritive and economic values of foodstuffs, the principles based upon scientific data which underlie all culinary methods and processes used in the preparation of food and in its storage and preservation in the home, and manipulative skill in handling different preparations and in carrying out the different processes.

As illustrations or examples, simple typical or basic recipes have been selected, for a system of standardization is the only practical method of collecting information either for household use or for class work. This can be supplemented as opportunity and experience permit, and at the same time it fosters initiative and resourcefulness.

Since new standards of living have completely revolutionized the general estimate of comparative values, the conservation of energy, physical and mental, by economy of time, labour, material, and money, has become superlatively the keynote to " efficiency " in all occupations, and in none more than in the teaching and practice of the craft of Cookery. The intelligent and successful worker, whether in the home or in the class, brings all her experience and knowledge to aim at efficiency. The very fact of efficiency divests the daily work of some of its inevitable monotony and tedium, and affords to the worker the additional satisfaction of knowing that the provision of wholesome well-cooked food, which builds up the physique of a nation, is one of the greatest assets in that nation's economy.

The author takes this opportunity of expressing her indebtedness to the work of Dr. Hutchison upon *Food and the Principles of Dietetics*, and to Messrs. Edward Arnold for permission to reproduce diagrams from this work ; also grateful acknowledgment to Messrs. Jones Bros. and the Davis Gas Stove Company for the use of blocks illustrative of culinary utensils and requisites.

S. E. N.

CONTENTS

CHAPTER 8

CHAPTER 9

CHAPTER 10

CHAPTER 11

CHAPTER 12

CHAPTER 13

CHAPTER 14

CHAPTER 15

CHAPTER 16

CHAPTER 32

Sterilizing outfit—General directions for bottling fruit—Simple methods without use of sterilizing outfit—Fruit pulp—Bottling of vegetables—Pickles—Deep freezing—Accelerated freeze-drying

CHAPTER 33

Selection of breakfast and supper dishes—Construction of the menu—How to estimate quantities and portions for the family's meals—Cooking utensils for small households of 4–6 persons

ILLUSTRATIONS

COOKING CRAFT

CHAPTER 1

THE DOMESTIC WORKSHOP

THE domestic workshop, or kitchen, is the centre of activity of the House Craft Worker, the intelligent capable housewife, whose object is the health and welfare of the family, a social unit of immense value. Therefore its equipment for effective administration is of the utmost importance, its most obvious function being perhaps to provide environment for economic and hygienic catering and cooking of food, although kitchen activities do not stop there. The key to success is to be found in the principle of *conservation*, that is, making the most of everything available for the purpose in hand : there is involved the sound business proposition—maximum efficiency and no waste—no waste of energy, physical or mental, of time or money. A knowledge of costing and of time and motion study is as invaluable to the organizer of the home as to the house of business. This proposition presupposes thoughtful and wise location and planning of the kitchen ; a " short walking circuit " to save unnecessary steps, for over-fatigue of workers lessens efficiency and shows faulty method ; judicious selection and arrangement of equipment suited to the requirements of the house-hold ; a realization of values, comparative and relative, so that non-essentials may be subordinated to essentials ; and a clear idea concerning the style and manner of life preferred by or necessary to the family under consideration. Light and ventilation, dust and dirt-repelling surfaces for floors, walls, woodwork, and ceiling are of the first importance, almost as vital as a good water supply ; but details concerning these matters are outside the scope of this book. The modern kitchen-scullery is an example of efficient economy as to space, equipment, and labour.

EQUIPMENT

The scientific grouping of equipment, permanent and fixed, or small and portable, that is, grouping of articles in co-ordination with their purpose, is of enormous value in reducing the *walking circuit*.

Fixtures should be placed in a good light, and the relative location of shelving (at a convenient height), cupboards, stove, table, and sink, is especially important, because of the constant passage from one to another, and the spaces between them should permit of easy and quick movement. The position of stove and sink must obviously be determined by that of the flues and water-pipes, etc.

A solid fuel cooker, electric or gas stove should be fixed in a good light if possible and not in a draughty position, otherwise there is loss of heat and unequal heating and, from a gas stove, escape of fumes of consumed gas and danger of gas being blown out.

The grouping of small equipment is no less valuable in minimizing fatigue and loss of time. Shelving should be fixed near to stove, sink, and table, as convenience may suggest, for holding utensils and things in daily, and almost hourly, use.

Scientific grouping can be adapted to the construction and requirements peculiar to any kitchen, and a little thought and small expenditure may transform the most badly planned and constructed kitchen into a useful, if not a perfect, workshop. The height of surfaces for working upon is important, as much unnecessary muscular strain and fatigue can be prevented if the height is suitable, particularly as regards stove (oven), sink, and table. It is not practicable to lay down special measurements, but a well-calculated average should be chosen.

An adequate supply of equipment is desirable, and its life is lengthened by care in handling and thorough cleanliness.

Sufficient storage is essential. Cupboards and shelves should be judiciously placed, space being economically used ; they must be easy of access and not too high ; shelves shallow rather than deep are the more convenient. A kitchen cabinet is useful.

Drawers and cupboards are convenient for articles that are not in constant use, but shelving within easy reach is preferable for things that are frequently in hand, except that, where there is much dust, shelving may not be satisfactory. Saucepan shelves should be arranged to allow free circulation of air.

The sink should be beneath a window, of some material that does not absorb grease and moisture—such as glazed earthenware, stainless steel, or Fibreglass—7 in. to 9 in. deep, and fitted with a removable grid and plug. It should be fixed on cantilever brackets, with a clear open space beneath, easy to keep clean and dry, the sink itself sloping slightly towards the plug. There should be a good supply of cold water, and also of hot water, if possible. The absolute cleanliness of the sink is very important; if neglected, it is a very fertile breeding ground for bacteria.

Selection of Equipment. In the selection of equipment, either fixed and large, or portable and small, suitability as to type, size, or capacity for the specific requirements of the household and the available accommodation, is of primary importance.

Large or superfluous equipment uselessly occupies air, floor, and shelving space, serving also as dust-traps, hampering easy movement, and necessitating more labour in cleaning.

Bear the following points in mind when planning purchases—

1. An adequate supply economizes time and labour ; a superfluity is wasteful of both. Insufficient or indifferent equipment does not make for efficiency.

2. Cheapness without efficiency and durability is no economy, the wear and tear of small equipment especially being constant and particularly heavy.

3. The inclusion of *practical* labour- and time-saving appliances.

4. Selection of easily cleaned utensils where labour is limited ; avoid much bright metal.

Cooking Pots. (1) Choice: metal of good quality, seamless, and sufficiently thick for the pan to last a reasonable time and to bear constant use and exposure to the extreme heat of cooking stoves without risk of damage to pan or its contents. (2) Closely-fitting lids to prevent loss of heat and evaporation. (3) Handles, preferably insulated, are an advantage. (4) Lining perfectly smooth and pan rounded at the junction of sides and bottom, thereby less risk of contents "catching," and ease in stirring and cleaning. Cheap enamel-lined pans chip readily and are dangerous. (5) For electric stoves a special pan is made; the bottom is turned so that the pan comes into immediate contact with the hot-plate, and there is no loss of heat and therefore less expenditure of fuel (current). (6) One or more double-lipped small pans useful for sauces.

Types of Pans. (1) The old somewhat heavy iron pot has been superseded by the modern cast-iron or pressed steel pan of lighter design, a variety of which has a silicate enamel lining, with the outside enamel-coated and polished. (2) Aluminium pans made of poor and thin metal quickly burn, bruise, warp, buckle, and get out of shape—result, loss of heat from stove and from pan, with evaporation of its contents. (3) Steel tin-lined. These also must be of good quality to be efficient and durable. (4) The copper pan is the most durable, but the most expensive and difficult to keep bright: verdigris poisoning is apt to occur if the tin lining becomes worn ; it must be renewed as soon as this happens. (5) Fireproof earthenware, flameproof ware, French glazed china, and fireproof glass are indispensable utensils now in the modern kitchen. They are not only ornamental, the food being served in them, but by their use fuel, food, and labour can be economized. See Use of Fireproof Earthenware and Glassware (p. 32).

Cooking Stoves. *A perfectly reliable stove is an absolute essential to good cooking.*

Whatever the type, whether the simplest or the most improved pattern of its kind, its full efficiency is made possible only by absolute cleanliness, and by skilful management with the minimum expenditure of fuel. Provided the stove be really well made, the intelligent housewife will soon understand how to manage it to a nicety.

The type and class must be determined largely by the nature of the fuel supply; gas, electricity, coal, smokeless fuel and oil are all available in urban districts, but in an entirely rural locality, where neither gas nor electricity may be installed, coal is often largely supplemented by wood, or by the useful oil cooking stove, or by a cooker using gas from a cylinder. Stoves may vary, but *the cardinal tests of efficiency are the same.*

1. Cost as low as possible to be consistent with efficiency.
2. Capacity sufficient for requirements of household.
3. Durability with strength, and easy replacement of worn or of movable parts.

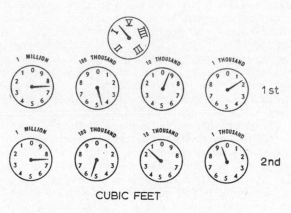

CUBIC FEET

FIG. 1. How to Read a Gas Meter

4. Conservation of heat by closely fitting parts, by lagging of oven (coal, gas, and electric).
5. Simplicity of design, affording ease in working, ready access to parts requiring cleaning, and rapid heating of oven.
6. Ventilation of oven; means of carrying off fumes of cooking and of combustion of fuel (gas stove).
7. Economy of fuel and labour in cleaning. For the latter plain surfaces and a minimum of tarnishable bright parts.

How to Read Gas and Electricity Meters. As gas and electric stoves have now practically superseded the coal range in most modern households, it is necessary to know how to read the meters, so that wasteful consumption of gas or current may be checked.

This is quite an easy matter. Begin with the dial at the left-hand, note the lower of the figures between which the hand on each of the four dials appears and add 2 ciphers—this gives the reading in cubic feet, 751,900. It is assumed that the previous reading was 749,100 c. ft.; subtract this from the present reading to ascertain the consumption in the interval: 751,900–749,100 = 2,800 c. ft.

The small dial on top indicates any defect ; if it remains stationary when no gas is being consumed the supply and the meter are in order.

Conversion of Cubic Feet into Therms. The charge for gas is now on the basis of its heating value, which has to be declared from time to time. The unit measure of heat is called the British Thermal Unit (B.Th.U.), and is the amount of heat required to raise 1 lb. of water through 1 degree in temperature (Fahrenheit). A Therm consists of 100,000 of these units. The declared heating value of a certain company's gas is, say, 510 B.Th.U. per cubic foot.

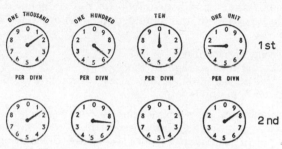

FIG. 1A. HOW TO READ AN ELECTRICITY METER

The calculation of gas consumed in Therms is easily ascertained by this formula—

$$\frac{\text{Current consumption of gas in c. ft.} \times \text{declared heating value of gas in B.Th.U.}}{100,000 \text{ B.Th.U. (1 Therm)}}$$

$$= \frac{2,800 \times 510}{100,000} = 14 \cdot 28 \text{ Therms.}$$

The price of gas supplied by the company is about 2s. per Therm ; therefore the cost of 2,800 c. ft. of gas consumed as registered by the meter would be 14·28 × 2s. = 28s. 6d.

Electricity is charged so much per unit. The above illustration shows the four indicating dials on the meter, which resemble those of the gas meter, the alternate dials working anti-clockwise. The dial to the extreme right registers units of electricity, while the three on the left register tens, hundreds, and thousands respectively. To read the meter subtract the first reading 1,602 units from the second, which is 1,748 units; the difference gives the amount of electricity used, viz. 146 units.

CHAPTER 2

MANAGEMENT OF THE DOMESTIC WORKSHOP ON BUSINESS LINES

THE application of the " Science of Costing " to this branch of home organization is indispensable to the economical expenditure of that portion of the family budget allowed for food, and includes—

(a) Keeping of accounts.
(b) Marketing and storage of food.
(c) Records of all kitchen activities : in relation to cookery, those of recipes, methods, etc.

Keeping accounts economizes time, prevents much unnecessary worry, and requires no elaborate system of book-keeping. This subject is dealt with fully under Domestic Calculations. With reference to expenditure upon food, it is an excellent plan to keep these items entirely separate, this being an aid to the housekeeper in spending to the utmost advantage every penny allowed.

Marketing. The selection of foodstuffs in relation to good results in cooking is very closely allied, their purchase requiring the exercise of sound common sense, forethought, and discrimination. The amount of the weekly allowance for food only must influence the housewife in her selection, but the smaller the amount, the greater the need for spending it to the greatest advantage.

Points essential to best results in marketing—

1. Familiarity with the current prices and their fluctuations, and the practice of reading the notices in the daily Press as to food supplies : comparison of price lists of local shops with others before final selection of a reliable tradesman.

2. Knowledge of the qualities and nutritive properties of various foods, which determine their suitability and economical use in relation to particular culinary methods. Some foods differing greatly in price and quality are equally nutritive, but to be digestible and easily assimilated must be cooked by different processes. Also cheap food is often not only no economy, but wasteful on account of, e.g., excess of bone and of fat as in meat, of skin and bone in fish, of blemished parts or thickness of skin in fruit and vegetables, or of stale or over-dry pieces, as in pulse and dried fruits.

3. Purchase preferably where trade is brisk, as here one can depend on a rapid turnover and consequent freshness of goods,

and from shops or markets conducted under clean and sanitary conditions. Self-service stores, where all goods are displayed for personal selection, are now open throughout the country. The state of the food before use in the home is of vital importance, danger from bacterial contamination and transmission of disease by handling being great, especially to foods eaten in a raw state.

4. *Personal Selection* is without doubt the most economical and most satisfactory method of shopping, more particularly as regards perishable food, such as meat, fish, vegetables, and fruit, the supplies of which vary considerably in price and quality from day to day, owing to climatic and other conditions. In this way, the purchaser obtains exactly what she desires as regards weight, cut, and quality (a matter involving much economy), the tradesman understands the requirements of his customer, and there is also afforded an opportunity to other and younger members of the household of gaining valuable experience in purchasing food.

5. Consideration of the season of the year, and of the size and needs of the family and storage accommodation, particularly that of the larder.

6. Selection of food in season : it is then at its best and usually cheapest.

7. Before purchasing fresh supplies, arrange the day's menu so as to utilize " left-overs " in the larder.

8. Shop or send orders early in the day ; perishable food is then freshest, and food necessary for the midday meal is less likely to be late in dispatch and arrival.

Purchasing in Bulk. The purchase of perishable food in larger quantities mainly concerns establishments where its consumption is rapid and larder accommodation is extensive. The capacity for storing frozen foods in a refrigerator, or in a domestic deep freezer, may also influence the purchase of these foods in bulk. The buying, however, of non-perishable food and household commodities in quantity is an economy common to every household, for certain dry goods, etc., if purchased in bulk, are generally cheaper and some improve by storage. The capacity of the housekeeping purse and storeroom accommodation are important determining factors in regard to the amount purchased.

Records. Recipes, menus, and records of the activities undertaken in the management of the kitchen should be kept in some form easy to refer to, and decipherable at once.

The Card Index System solves all difficulties, the file being simple and easy to make. Some correspondence cards, a few indicator cards to differentiate and to separate the classes or sections of information, and a strong cardboard or wooden box to hold them, are the only requirements. In the application of this system to cookery recipes, one recipe is entered on each card, the items

being noted as in specimen card below, the method on the reverse
side.   The first card in each section should give the standardized

Dish Type		Method
Fruit Pie Short Pastry		
Ingredients *Cost*		
No. of portions		
Time		*Remarks*
Preparation		
Cooking		

FIG. 2. CARD INDEX FILE

recipe for the type, this having been carefully tested before being
entered.

CHAPTER 3

PRINCIPLES OF NUTRITION

To supply food which is nutritious and suitable to the needs of the human body some knowledge of the composition of the principal foods and their functions in the body is required. Blood, muscle, bone, teeth, nails, sinew, nerve, all organs and tissues, secretions and body fluids are built up from the nutrient constituents of food.

The body is composed of compound substances which are formed by the combination of the primary elements, the chief of which are oxygen, hydrogen, carbon, calcium, phosphorus, potassium, sulphur, magnesium, iodine, and iron. The various foodstuffs are likewise composed of similar substances, which are combinations of these same elements, and when taken into the body provide material for its growth, for tissue repair, and for the maintenance of health.

The functions of food, therefore, are—

(*a*) To build up the body structure and to repair and renew the tissues.

(*b*) To supply energy as muscular and nervous power for its work, and heat to keep it warm. For the maintenance of the health of the human body, a *mixed diet* of food, which is of good quality and containing the following nutrients, is necessary.

Nutrients Necessary for Growth and Repair.	Nutrients Necessary for Energy.	Nutrients Necessary to Regulate Body Processes.
Proteins Mineral Elements Water	Fats Carbohydrates Proteins	Vitamins Mineral Elements Water Some proteins

Energy Foods. Proteins, fats, and carbohydrates supply energy. All contain carbon, hydrogen, and oxygen, but *nitrogen* is present *only* in the *proteins*. They alone are essential to the life of every body tissue.

These food substances are obtained from animal and plant life, and man is either directly or indirectly dependent upon the vegetable kingdom for them. Animals which provide us with food feed upon plant life, and these green plants derive their colour from the chlorophyll present, which substance under the influence of

9

sunlight enables the plant to use the carbon dioxide, water, nitrogen, and mineral matter which they have derived from the air and soil and to combine them so as to form organic living matter upon which the animals which supply us with food are fed.

Proteins—Tissue Builders. The primary and chief function of the proteins is the building up, replacing, and repair of the body tissue. They also furnish the body with energy, but while surplus protein can be used to produce energy, fats and carbohydrates cannot take the place of protein and do its special work. Proteins are found more or less in most foods, and these nitrogenous compounds are the most important constituents of food, nitrogen being absolutely necessary for body-building, for replacing and repair of the tissues. As proteins are very abundant in muscle tissue, they have been termed flesh- and muscle-formers.

Proteins are present in both animal and vegetable foods, but are more abundant in the former; vegetable protein is less stimulating and also less digestible, as this substance is enclosed in cells of a fibrous nature (cellulose).

Proteins in animal foods are found in meat, fish, eggs, milk, and cheese; in vegetable food as *legumin* in legumes (beans, peas, lentils), and in a smaller quantity as *gluten* in some cereals, such as wheat, rye.

Animal Proteins—
Myosin in muscle of meat and fish.
Albumen in white of egg.
Casein in milk.
Gelatine in connective tissue of meat and fish.

Vegetable Proteins—
Legumin.
Gluten.

The proteins are extremely complex in composition, consisting of bodies termed "amino-acids," each containing nitrogen, and certain of these amino-acids are essential to the growth and development of the body and its tissues. As many as eighteen to twenty different amino-acids are found in the common proteins and as few as three or four in others; the number, nature, and combination of these bodies determine the relative value of the different proteins as to their power in building up and repairing particular body tissues. Compared with the vegetable proteins, those of animal origin are of much higher value biologically as they are able to yield up most readily those amino-acids necessary to the body for tissue formation. Of these vitally essential amino-acids there are eight, but in some proteins they are not all present or are deficient, e.g. in gelatine and in some vegetable proteins, which on this account are unable alone to sustain life and to build up body tissue.

The essential amino-acids are present in most of the proteins used in an ordinary mixed diet composed of meat, fish, eggs, milk, vegetables, and such will supply an adult with the protein necessary for the body.

Fats and Carbohydrates—Chief Sources of Energy. These contain the elements carbon, hydrogen, and oxygen, and both supply energy to the body, in the production of which the proteins also assist, but in a less degree.

Fats are highly valuable energy foods. They supply more energy than any other food substance, and the reserve of fuel fat is stored in the body as adipose tissue, which also protects delicate internal organs.

Being richer in carbon than carbohydrates, they are not as easily digested. Carbon is present in a very concentrated form in fat, which is, however, not the cheapest source of this food substance; hence the diet of the poor is, on account of expense, too frequently deficient in fat and overburdened with carbohydrates.

In a diet these two food substances can be substituted one for the other to a certain degree, but not entirely. Fats are of both animal and vegetable origin, and are compounds of fatty acids and glycerol, three of the fatty acids occurring most widely being stearic acid, palmitic acid and oleic acid; their relative proportions in any fat determine its melting point and consistency or firmness. In a hard fat, such as mutton fat, the proportion of stearic acid to the other fats is high and the melting point correspondingly high; in the softer fat, butter, palmitic acid and oleic acid are present in higher proportions than stearic acid, and the melting point is consequently lower; in olive oil, a fat which is liquid at the ordinary temperature, a very high percentage of oleic acid is present. Fats occur chiefly in animal foods: meat, oily fish, milk and its products; in some cereals, such as maize and oats, and in nuts and vegetable oils.

Animal fats: Suet, lard, dripping, butter, cream, cod liver oil.

Vegetable fats: Olive and cotton seed oils, margarine, nut butter, cocoa butter.

APPROXIMATE PERCENTAGE OF FAT PRESENT IN VARIOUS FOODS

Skimmed milk.	.	0·4–0·5	Cheese .	.	. 33
Whole milk	.	. 3·5–4·5	Cream (ordinary)	.	41
Maize	.	. 5	,, (centrifugal)	.	82
Oatmeal .	.	. 7·2	Nuts .	.	. 50–60
Herring .	.	. 8	Lard (pure)	.	. 100
Medium fat mutton	.	19·5	Olive oil .	.	. 100
,, ,, pork	.	26·2			

Carbohydrates. These are also composed of carbon, hydrogen, and oxygen, but the two latter elements are present in the same proportions as in water. Carbohydrates constitute about two-thirds of the food in the ordinary daily diet. They are an abundant and relatively cheap source of energy, and are quickly and easily digested; in the process of digestion they become chemically changed and are absorbed by the tissues, and with fat and protein supply the body with energy. By chemical action in the body, the carbohydrates can also be changed into fat, and this with the surplus fat from fat foods is stored in the body as reserve to be drawn upon for supplementary fuel when there is a deficiency in the food supply.

With the exception of *lactose* (milk sugar) and *glycogen*, found in the liver of animals, carbohydrates are obtained entirely from the vegetable kingdom.

CLASSES OF CARBOHYDRATES

1. Starches.	3. Sugars.
2. Dextrins.	4. Roughage (cellulose).

1. *Starches* are most abundant in and found largely in cereals and their products, in tubers, mostly in potatoes, and in small and varying amounts in other vegetables.

2. *Dextrins.* Starch when subjected to heat becomes "dextrinzed"; that is, changed into a form of carbohydrate termed "dextrin," which is sweetish in flavour, for example the crust of a baked loaf.

3. *Sugars* are found chiefly in fruits and in root vegetables. Such are *cane sugar* present in the sugar cane, maple tree, beetroot, carrot, and parsnip; *glucose* or *grape sugar* in honey and fruits; *maltose* or *malt sugar* in malted barley; *lactose* or *milk sugar* in milk.

Sugar is very soluble and is easily digested. As a food it is wholesome if taken in moderation and is a good preservative.

4. *Roughage* or *cellulose*, the fibrous substance forming the framework of plants is present in fruits and vegetables and in the husks of cereals. Roughage is valuable and essential in the diet, it gives bulk, and, on account of its indigestible nature, it incites the churning (peristaltic) action of the alimentary tract and so assists digestion and prevents constipation.

Extractives. These also contain nitrogen, but they differ greatly from the proteins, as they can neither form tissue nor supply energy, but they are valuable in the diet as appetizers and stimulants, thus indirectly aiding digestion by stimulating the flow of the digestive juices. They are so called because they are extracted by boiling water and are in solution in meat juices, the minute differences as to amount and kind giving the characteristic flavour to different meats. The sapid bodies (*osmazome*) are more developed in roast or baked meat than in that which is cooked by moist heat, and are more abundant in the flesh of fully grown than immature animals, hence the usual accompaniments with roast lamb and veal and boiled meats. Substances similar to the meat extractives are present in vegetables, such as asparagine in potatoes.

Mineral Matter. In small quantities this is absolutely essential to the structure of the body and to the maintenance of health and makes up about 5 per cent of its weight. It is present chiefly in the bones and teeth, also in the body tissues and fluids. Mineral salts are compounds of an acid and a metal, some of which are sodium, magnesium, calcium, potassium, and iron. Mineral matter is present in all foods, the largest proportion being found in vegetables and fruit; it is also present in yolk of egg, in milk as calcium salts, and in cereals, hence the value of such food in the diet, especially for children.

Phosphorus and calcium are essential to bone formation and to teeth; iron is necessary for the red corpuscles of the blood, and both it and phosphorus are elements indispensable in the structure of body cells.

Water. This is most essential to the health of the body. A human being cannot live for long without water, but he is able to exist for quite a considerable period upon water alone. Water assists in regulating the body temperature, it holds matter in solution in the body fluids and transmits it to the tissues, and facilitates the removal of waste through the excretory organs. Water is present in all solid foods, largely in fruits and green vegetables, but the chief source of supply is beverages. In addition to the water present in food, the adult requires from 2½–3 pt. of water daily.

Water present in dried legumes (peas, beans) . . . 10–12 per cent
  ,,   ,,   vegetables and fruit . . . . 80–90 ,,
  ,,   ,,   meat (with average amount of lean and fat) 75·77 ,,

Vitamins. In addition to the nutrients, mineral matter, and water, there are the vitamins, or so-called accessory food factors, which are present in very minute quantities in various foods. These are chemical substances *essential* to life, the amount needed being so minute that it is almost negligible, but their presence in the diet is of vital importance to nutrition and they are indispensable to the growth and development of the body tissues, to the maintenance of health, and as a protection against infection and disease. A diet lacking or deficient in vitamins is the cause of conditions or disorders which affect the joints, nervous system, mucous tissue, growth of teeth and bone, and general development. The result of a deficiency or absence of vitamins in a child's diet shows itself very quickly, and may prove serious or even fatal. Vitamins are found in many foods, but very few contain all the classes which are known up to the present, and one vitamin cannot be substituted for another as is the case with carbohydrates or fats. The human body is unable to manufacture some of these in the body, but some are stored by it in its tissues and all are derived from animal and vegetable food, which is obtained in the first place from plant life, sunlight being an important factor in the production of certain vitamins. Each class is essential, and a mixed diet of good food, which includes fruit and vegetables, will supply all the vitamins necessary to the maintenance of health of the normal adult.

Vitamins are affected by heat in the presence of air, by heat under pressure, and by the loss of freshness. Drying is harmful to some, and certain vitamins are destroyed by the use of soda in cooking.

Of the known vitamins, the following are the most important for the housewife to provide in the diet. There should be no deficiency of others in a good mixed diet.

Vitamin A (Fat Soluble). Vitamins of this class are essential to human life, to the adult and child, but the former requires less than the growing child. These vitamins promote growth and development and are a protective against infection ; a deficiency in a child's diet arrests development, is the cause of loss of weight, of low resistance to infection, and of eye trouble ; in an adult a deficiency is the cause of a form of night blindness.

Found mainly in animal fats, beef and mutton (not in pig fat—lard), in milk and its products in a greater degree when animals are pasture fed ; in oily fish, largely in cod liver oil ; also as carotene in green-leaved vegetables, tomato and the yellow part of carrot. It is stable to the ordinary temperature of cooking, but is destroyed by prolonged heating or in the presence of air.

Vitamin B Complex. In this class, several types have been separated ; these are *soluble* in *water*.

Thiamine—Vitamin B1. Necessary for the utilization of carbohydrates ; a deficiency causes a check in the growth of children, loss of appetite, fatigue and irritability. Severe deficiency causes beri-beri.

Found chiefly in cereals, in the germ, which is particularly rich in it, and in the husk ; in the seed of legumes, peas, and beans, and largely in yeast and in its manufactured products, e.g. marmite ; also in the internal organs of animals and in egg yolk.

Riboflavin. Also concerned with the utilization of carboydrates ; deficiency may check growth, and may cause irritation of the eyes. Sources are dairy produce, eggs, yeast extract, meat extract, liver, meat, whole-grain wheat, wheat germ.

Nicotinic Acid. Necessary for the processes in the body involving utilization of proteins, fats and carbohydrates. Severe deficiency causes the disease pellagra, characteristics of which are diarrhoea, dermatitis and mental disorder. Lesser deficiency may cause one or more of these symptoms. Good sources are fish, meats, liver and kidney, yeast, yeast extract.

Vitamin C (Ascorbic Acid) is also soluble in water. It is necessary for the formation of collagen, dentine and cartilage, and it is also considered necessary to assist in the absorption of iron. A deficiency of Vitamin C increases susceptibility of gums and mouth to infection. Scurvy occurs in severe cases of deficiency.

Present in fresh fruits, particularly of the citrus class—lemons, grape fruit, oranges ; fresh vegetables and in green salad plants, also in tomatoes. Vitamins of this class are most affected by cooking and are unstable even in moderate heat in the presence of air, therefore uncooked fruits and raw vegetables are of much greater value in the diet than those which are cooked or dried. The vitamins in green vegetables are destroyed by the use of alkali and exposure to great heat.

Vitamin D is another fat soluble. It is termed antirachitic, as it wards off rickets and, in conjunction with calcium and phosphorus is essential to the growth of bone and teeth. Without it calcium cannot be deposited. It is not considered essential to include it in an adult's dietary.

Present in oily fish, in fish fats (cod liver oil), vitaminized margarine and, in a lesser degree, in dairy produce. It can also be produced by the action of the sun on ergosterol, a fat substance present in some fats.

Spices and Condiments do not supply the body with building material and energy, but are useful adjuncts in the diet by rendering insipid and flavourless food appetizing; they incite the flow of the digestive juices and so assist indirectly in digestion.

Refuse or Waste. Food as purchased, after preparation, and even when served, contains inedible parts, such as bone of meat and fish, shell of egg, skin, and seeds of fruit and vegetables, the composition of which is similar to the edible portions. This is of importance in considering the real cost of the food and in the economical planning of meals.

Measurement of Muscular Power and Heat supplied by Food.

The Calorie. As coal is burnt in a furnace in the presence of oxygen, its latent energy being transformed into heat and power, so food, consumed and oxidized in the body, produces energy for the performance of its physical and mental work. Just as different kinds of coal have various fuel values, which are estimated by the energy produced per ton, in the same way the nutrients of food give off different amounts of energy, varying also in their fuel or calorific value. This is measured by a Calorie or fuel unit; that is, the amount of heat required to raise 1 kilogramme (about 1¾ pints) through 1° Centigrade; or, if transformed into mechanical power, it would raise 1 ton through 1·54 ft.

To Find the Fuel Value of any Food. The fuel value of a food depends upon the actual proportion of nutrients present, especially upon the amount of fat it contains.

To ascertain the calorific value of a particular food, multiply the percentage present of protein and also of carbohydrate by 4·1, and of fat by 9·3, the total being the number of Calories in 100 parts of that food.

A milk containing in every 100 grammes 2 per cent of protein, 4 per cent of fat, and 6 per cent of carbohydrates, will yield 70 Calories—

Protein	.	.	.	.	$2 \times 4·1 = 8·2$
Fat	.	.	.	.	$4 \times 9·3 = 37·2$
Carbohydrate	.	.	.	.	$6 \times 4·1 = 24·6$

Total fuel or calorific value $= 70·0$ Calories

Conservation of Energy. Of food taken into the body in excess, more or less of the surplus may be stored in the body as fat (fuel). Proteins can be transformed into carbohydrates and fats, carbohydrates changed into fats, and these, with that derived from various foods, are stored as reserve fuel to be used as necessity demands.

True Nutritive Value of Food. It is not the *amount* of food consumed, but that which is *digested* and *absorbed* into the system, that nourishes the body. The food is digested by the ferments secreted by the digestive juices, and undergoes a number of chemical changes in its passage through the alimentary canal ; this begins in the mouth by the action of the saliva upon starches, in the stomach by the gastric juices upon the proteins, and in the intestines by the pancreatic juice upon proteins, fats, and carbohydrates.

Digestion is aided by the fine division of the food in the process of mastication and by the churning or peristaltic action of the stomach and intestines, which mixes the digestive juices with the food. The digested food passes through the walls of the alimentary canal, undergoing further chemical changes, is absorbed into the blood stream, which is supplied with oxygen in the lungs and is distributed by the heart and large vessels to every part of the body, furnishing it with material and energy necessary for its maintenance and for the functions of its various organs.

Proteins are the least completely absorbed of all the three chief constituents. Fat in comparison with protein is very completely absorbed ; the absorption of carbohydrates is the most complete, sugars being assimilated to the minutest quantity. Dieticians vary greatly as to their proportions in the diet.

Individuals differ greatly as to the quantity and kind of food they require, consequently the amount and proportions of the above must vary slightly. Men as a rule require more food than women; women more than young children, and growing children and adolescents more than men or women; and old people and those of sedentary habits less than those of active habits and accustomed to heavy muscular work.

A Mixed Diet, so essential to maintain the body in health, is brought about by necessity, for no one article of food can furnish the nutrients in the correct proportions. Instinct, taste, and experience, with the knowledge of the composition of food and its nutritive properties, make the arrangement of a well-balanced diet no very difficult matter. With careful selection and adaptation of food to the individual requirements, the ordinary diet of most households usually supplies the body with sufficient energy and, with them, the necessary protein and vitamins, the excess of one constituent in a food being counterbalanced by its deficiency in another ; thus, milk puddings usually consist of milk, egg, and rice or bread, milk and egg being rich in proteins, and rice and bread in carbohydrates.

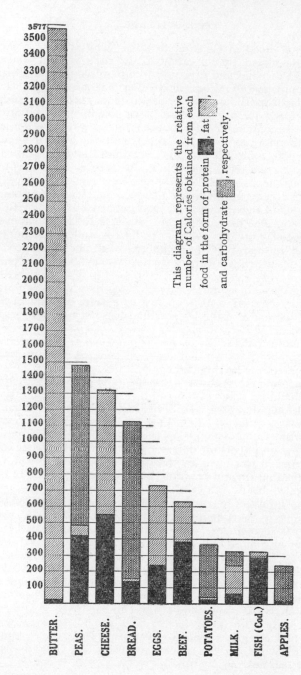

This diagram represents the relative number of Calories obtained from each food in the form of protein ▓, fat ▒, and carbohydrate ▒, respectively.

FIG. 3. FUEL VALUE OF ONE POUND OF SOME TYPICAL FOODS
(By courtesy of Messrs. Edward Arnold & Company)

Economy of Food in Relation to Cost. The price of a food is frequently regulated by its rarity, by caprice of the palate, by popularity in demand and difficulty of supply, and is no true estimate of its nutritive and economical value. This can be determined only by comparing the quantities of nutrients and energy supplied by certain foods for a given sum. For example, as a source of protein, cheese contains about 25 per cent, and raw lean beef under 20 per cent, therefore as cheese is about half the price of beef its food value as to protein is much greater than that of beef. Again, Stilton cheese costs twice as much as Cheddar, but contains about the same nutriment. The following facts relative to the three chief organic constituents of foods are of much practical importance in considering diets and the value of food nutrients in relation to cost.

Protein. (*a*) The most important and also the most expensive ; some variety of protein is essential to health, and this requires the most careful consideration, the economy being to use and to combine those varieties which will supply the necessary amount at the least cost.

(*b*) Animal protein is more easily digested than vegetable protein and it is therefore often an economy to expend more money for the required amount of the former than less for an equal quantity of the latter.

(*c*) The more that foods rich in protein, such as meat, eggs, and milk, are combined with other foods in cooking, the less are the former required as separate dishes.

(*d*) In choosing protein-rich foods, the amount of energy supplied by them should be taken into account, e.g. 1 lb. medium fat meat, 2 quarts of milk, and 8 eggs each yield about 2 ozs. of protein, but the meat has more fat, yielding three times as much energy as milk and nearly three times as much as the 8 eggs.

(*e*) There is an important difference in amount of protein present in cooked and in raw legumes and cereals ; in cooking, both take up a considerable amount of water, becoming more bulky and more dilute. Boiled beans will contain almost two-thirds less protein than as in the raw state ; and cereals from one-eighth to one-third less, according to the amount of water used in cooking.

Fats and Carbohydrates. (*a*) Of the two sources of carbon, the cheaper but also more bulky carbohydrates cannot be substituted for the more expensive and highly essential fats. However, the relative proportions of these necessary constituents of food vary with the individual, the climate, the season, and other conditions. Fat is the principal food of the Eskimo, while rice, deficient in fat and rich in starch, is the staple food of the Hindoo.

(*b*) Where cost is a ruling factor, fat must not be entirely eliminated or replaced by carbohydrates, but a less expensive fat, or food materials rich in fat, must be substituted, e.g. margarine, nut butter, oatmeal, maize, nuts.

The Day's Food. The matter of chief importance is the inclusion in each day's dietary of the necessary protein, fat, carbohydrates (sugar, starch, and cellulose), mineral matter, and vitamins.

The essentials for economic planning of the meals of a household, based upon a knowledge of the principles of nutrition are—

1. A combination of foods which, without waste of material, will daily supply all the needs of the body without overburdening any of its functions. An excess of food is often more harmful than a meagre supply.

2. Variety—an important factor in securing a well-balanced fare—is conducive to enjoyment of food and stimulating to capricious or jaded appetites.

3. Selection of foods pleasant to the palate ; one that is unpalatable, though highly nutritious, is often not so easy of digestion and of assimilation, since it does not stimulate the flow of the digestive juices.

4. Adaptation to the needs of individual members of the household, with regard to age, sex, build, size, occupation, and to the digestive idiosyncrasy of any member—for instance, some cannot digest eggs, shellfish, rhubarb, etc. All require protein and energy producers, but differ as to amounts and proportions, invalids and dyspeptics often needing a special diet.

5. Selection of foods according to climate, season, and weather.

6. The education of the household, particularly of children, in good food habits : wholesome and economical dishes should not be eliminated just for a mere whim or fancy.

7. Economical and careful cooking whereby the maximum amount of nutriment is retained.

CHAPTER 4

STORAGE OF FOOD IN THE HOME

MICRO-ORGANIC GROWTH IN RELATION TO FOOD

COOKING is not the only responsibility of the housekeeper in relation to food : its purchase, careful storage, and handling before and after it reaches the kitchen are of equal importance. Absolute cleanliness of the environment, utensils, and apparatus, and of the worker herself, is a *sine qua non* where cooking is concerned ; but in addition a knowledge of the causes of the " spoiling " of food and of means for its prevention, is also highly necessary. Deterioration of food is not only wasteful, but injurious to health, and often a menace to life itself. In former days food storage was a comparatively easy matter, but now, under the cramped and crowded conditions of present-day life, this problem is one of greater difficulty. Even before our food reaches the larder, " spoiling " or deterioration may have already commenced, in some cases retarded or checked by cold storage, in others developed during transit (if protracted and in unfavourable and unhygienic conditions), and also by exposure to sale in the dust- and germ-laden atmosphere of crowded thorough-fares.

This deterioration of food, which results finally in its putrefaction and decay, is brought about by the action of micro-organisms, by the constituents of dust; by contamination from the common house-fly and other germ-carrying household pests, also by the use of polluted water. The activities of most of these causes of deterioration of food can easily be prevented by the careful housewife, but micro-organic growth is so insidious and so incredibly rapid that arrest is very difficult. Her object is, therefore, to prevent its getting a start, to which end some knowledge of bacteriology is not only useful but an essential to efficient home organization.

Micro-organisms are microscopic forms of plant life, and those affecting food include *yeasts*, *moulds*, and *bacteria*. Being infinitesimally light they float about in and are distributed by the air, flourishing in the kitchen, larder, storeroom, pantry and cellar, and under favourable conditions multiplying with inconceivable rapidity. These tiny organisms live on organic matter, animal and vegetable, the bulk of them being comparatively harmless under normal conditions. Some are even useful in the preparation of certain foods, while others cause putrefaction of the food and the development of toxins.

Moulds belong to the fungus class. Conditions favourable to growth are moderate warmth, darkness, moisture and stagnation of air, all of which may obtain in an ill-constructed and ill-kept larder ; acidity of a food is also conducive to mould growth. On the other hand, light, ventilation, dryness and a low temperature (which are the basic conditions of cold storage), retard their growth.

The spore or reproductive body of a mould works from the surface, throwing a thread-like filament down into the substance of the food and growing rapidly where the air is stagnant and the material moist—as in food heaped together. Hence the growth of mould in

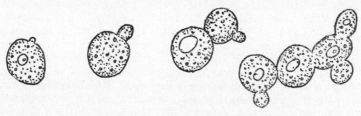

FIG. 4. MULTIPLICATION OF YEAST CELLS BY THE METHOD OF BUDDING

a pile of pieces of stale bread or on fruit and vegetables left in bags, which does not occur so readily if the bread be spread out and the fruit and vegetables placed on dishes or in racks. Moulds spoil the appearance and flavour of food. If they occur on the surface, they may be scraped off, leaving the inner part quite wholesome ; if the mould growth continues for a considerable time, it rapidly changes in colour, and the food attacked by it putrefies or decays.

Yeasts are also forms of microscopic plant life, the cells being not greater than $\frac{1}{2800}$ in. in diameter, originating in the soil, in decaying fruit and on the surface of ripening fruit. Reproduction

FIG. 5. MULTIPLICATION OF YEAST BY SPORES

is by two methods, by means of *buds* from the parent cell or by *spores ;* by the latter method the contents of the cell split up into several distinct bodies and, when the cell wall ruptures, these spores are released, and become air-borne natural agents of spontaneous fermentation.

Sugar, warmth and moisture are essential to the growth of the cells, which is extremely rapid, but extreme heat kills, while extreme cold retards their growth and the presence of a high percentage of sugar hinders it (see PRESERVATION of FRUIT). Yeasts are of two kinds—

(a) The wild yeasts floating about in the air—these cause the fermentation of bottled fruits and jams and jellies, from which air has not been entirely excluded.

(b) Commercial yeast used in breadmaking which is first prepared from wild yeasts freed from all impurities. These, when placed in contact with some pure food stuff and upon exposure to warmth, grow rapidly in great abundance and, after certain purifying processes, result in the dried or compressed yeast used for bread and cakes (see pages 247 and 248).

Bacteria. To the housewife bacterial growth is a very deadly foe, far more subtle and formidable than moulds, and fraught with enormous danger to health and life. Bacteria exist everywhere and in everything : in the air, water, soil, and in our own bodies. They are lighter than air, and, being much smaller even than the microscopically minute yeast cells, can be detected only with a microscope of very high power. Their growth is inconceivably rapid and prolific, reproduction being also by spores, which, unlike the yeast spores, can only be destroyed by submitting the food to a temperature of, at least, 240° F. for a considerable period. The presence bacteria in the earliest stage of attack is not perceptible ; only when the flavour and odour of the food are altering is their presence apparent, hence their great danger. Bacteria live on both animal and vegetable foods, but they flourish mostly on protein matter, which they decompose chemically ; a slight odour is developed and a flavour is imparted, which is rather pleasant than objectionable, as in game and soft cheeses ; but this stage rapidly passes, and as the growth continues and increases, putrefaction sets in. Bacteria require more moisture than moulds, e.g. moist raw meat does not mould easily, and foods in a dry state or artificially dried (if not exposed to a moist atmosphere) are not affected ; acidity conducive to mould growth (mould on lemons and oranges) is injurious to that of bacteria, while matter of an alkaline nature is a stimulant. These organisms flourish mostly in dark or dim corners. Most bacteria require moderate heat. They grow a at temperature of 70° to 75° F., more rapidly between 75° and 95°, from 125° to 140° they become inactive, while from 149° to 160° F., they are destroyed, with the exception of the spores. This powerful resistance to heat is frequently the cause of unsuccessful results in the preservation of food—the temperature not being sufficiently high nor maintained long enough to kill spores, as often happens in bottling vegetables— it is also the principle upon which the methods of pasteurization and sterilization of milk is based.

Flies and Dust. The common house-fly is a very active disease carrier, for it breeds and feeds upon the most offensive infected matter, distributing wherever it may settle. Dust, too, is productive of injury to food, for it contains yeast and mould spores and bacteria. Protection of food from flies and dust in kitchen and larder is most important, the only efficient method of removal of dust being a damp cloth, since the duster and brush only stir it up for part, and often most, of it to settle again in a few hours.

Water Pollution and House Pests. The use of water of doubtful origin for cleansing cooking utensils and in the preparation of food, especially of that to be eaten raw, e.g. salads, is a source of much danger ; hence the necessity of a good water supply to the sink. House pests are also carriers of disease, and should be exterminated at once where there is the slightest trace. The habit, too, of allowing household pets in the kitchen is not to be encouraged.

The Larder. The careful supervision of the larder is an important factor in kitchen economy, and the housewife with a knowledge of the causes of deterioration of food, their prevention and the danger and waste resulting therefrom, will make its daily visit one of her first duties. The necessary conditions of a good larder are plenty of light and air, coolness and good ventilation. One ideally planned has a N. or N.E. aspect, where little or no sun penetrates; ventilation by two windows on adjoining walls to secure a cross-current for the very necessary free and continuous circulation of air; and to exclude flies. Windows should not look out on to gullies or dust-bins.

Floors, walls, and ceiling with flat and smooth surfaces; the floor of bricks or tiles, walls of a non-absorbent and easily cleaned material. Shelves preferably of stone or of slate (one of the latter is useful for making pastry in hot weather). Scrupulous cleanliness of larder and of utensils is important.

Equipment for storage is small and of the simplest. A few earthenware and enamel utensils—plates and dishes, jugs and basins for liquids. A vegetable rack is a convenience; failing this, place vegetables on the stone floor or on shelf with a free circulation of air. A small safe is useful, but not necessary; one or more gauze meat covers. Muslin for covering food to protect it from dust and flies; wash and boil this frequently to ensure it is clean and fresh, and replace. Polythene bags and covers are also useful for protecting some foods.

Storage of Food in Larder. Remove food from paper or bags as soon as delivered, and put on clean plates or dishes. Place butter and milk on a shelf apart from any strong-smelling foods. To prevent souring in very hot weather, reheat liquids, such as milk, stock, soup, gravies, and sauces in which milk and vegetables are ingredients. Heat and cool rapidly; gradual heating and slow cooling promote bacterial growth.

Cleaning. Daily wipe shelves and floors with a clean, damp cloth; once a week remove all food; then every part of the larder—floor, shelves, etc.—should be washed and allowed to get perfectly dry before the food is put back.

A Refrigerator. It is used in many homes as a means of keeping perishable foods—uncooked and cooked. It may be run by gas or electricity but in either case its use and care are similar. Foods put into a refrigerator should be covered, e.g. placed in polythene bags or in containers with lids or other covers; containers are supplied with many refrigerators. Covering of foods is advisable to prevent evaporation and to prevent any odour from one food tainting another.

Circulation of air is essential, therefore foods must not be packed in too tightly.

A compartment for the storage of frozen foods is incorporated into many refrigerators, which is an advantage to a housewife.

The door of a refrigerator should not be opened too frequently, since warmer air enters and raises the temperature. The door must be firmly shut.

The temperature in a refrigerator is thermostatically controlled and instructions are usually given as to the setting of the thermostat to ensure efficient operation. The temperature in the cabinet is 40° F. (approximately), in the ice-making compartment 18° F. and in the compartment for storing frozen foods 0° F.

The refrigerator should be defrosted regularly according to instructions given by the makers.

CHAPTER 5

COOKING OF FOOD

Just as the nutritive value of a food depends upon its digestibility and absorbability, so its degree of ease of digestion and subsequent assimilation by the body is largely determined by the way in which it is cooked.

Cooking is no longer merely a household art, but a practical science, the outcome of traditional methods systematized after scientific tests. For this reason, success is more certain, failure can be reduced to a minimum, and conservation of material and avoidance of waste ensured.

The object in cooking food is—

(a) To render it pleasing to eye and palate by the decomposition of red colouring matter, such as *haemoglobin* in meat, and by development of new flavours and stimulating to the digestive juices.

(b) To sterilize it partially, and to render it easier to keep.

(c) To facilitate and hasten digestion by bringing about alteration in texture, thus assisting mastication, and by physical and chemical changes.

Heat, either moist or dry, essential to all cookery processes, is conveyed by radiation, convection, and conduction. It brings about changes, physical and chemical, in the condition of foods.

A Physical Change occurs when a substance changes its form, colour, or size, but still remains *the same substance* ; as when water turns to ice, and solid lead is melted.

A Chemical Change is effected when two or more substances combine so as to form an entirely new body.

These changes in food form the foundation for the principles upon which the various culinary processes are based.

Effect of Heat upon the Three Chief Constituents of Food. *Proteins* (a) The protein of meat (*myosin*), of egg (*albumen*), of wheat (*gluten*), of pulse (*legumin*), is coagulated by heat : if the temperature is raised much above 160° F. the protein hardens and shrinks, and the food becomes indigestible : as overcooked meat, and the white of hard-boiled egg.

(b) Connective tissue is converted into gelatine, which is soluble in water and rendered digestible.

Carbohydrates. (a) Starch in food is greatly affected by heat : by moist heat it is converted first into a soluble form, then by extreme heat into a new substance, sweetish in flavour—dextrin—as in the crust of bread. Moist heat causes the starch grains to swell, the cell coverings of cellulose rupture and the starch is released, gelatinizing at a temperature below boiling-point of water, the degree of heat varying with the kind of starchy food.

(*b*) Cellulose is softened by application of moist heat.

(*c*) Sugar when heated in water dissolves, then colours, and upon further heating, turns brown and becomes caramel, but does not crystallize.

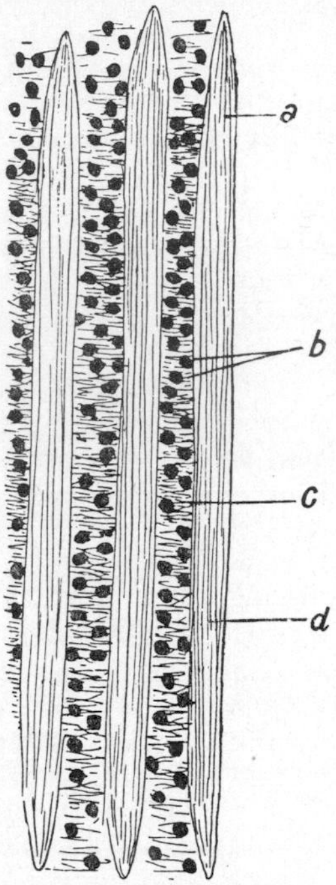

Fats are not so affected by heat as either proteins or carbohydrates, but if heated to a very high degree by a dry method of cooking, as in roasting, they undergo partial decomposition, and fatty acid substances are produced, acrid in odour and irritating to the digestive organs.

Methods of Cooking.

Roasting and Baking } By dry and
Broiling or Grilling } radiant heat.
Frying
Stewing
Boiling—Steaming } By moist heat.
Braising

All are suitable for cooking animal foods and for most of those derived from the vegetable kingdom. To carry out the more complicated and elaborate culinary processes, it is essential to have a good grip of the *simple methods* and their *application to meat* in particular, animal food being expensive, and the most important food as a body builder, the valuable nutrients of which are very easily dissipated in cooking or rendered indigestible.

Success in Cooking Meat depends largely upon the degree of heat employed and the method of applying it, which is determined by the object in view, whether

(*a*) to retain as far as possible all the nutritive and flavouring ingredients, as in roasting, baking, grilling, frying, boiling, stewing;

(*b*) to extract as much as possible of the nutrients and flavouring ingredients as in making stocks and soups.

To achieve this it is easier if the structure of lean meat is understood. The muscle (lean of meat) as looked at by the naked eye, consists of stringy fibres ; these, under the microscope, are seen to be composed of bundles of hollow tubes, or fibres, containing meat juice (both fibre and juice containing protein). The fibres

FIG. 6. DIAGRAMMATIC REPRESENTATION OF THE STRUCTURE OF MEAT

a, muscle fibres; *b*, fat cells; *c*, connective tissue; *d*, muscle juice.

(*By courtesy of Messrs. Edward Arnold & Company*)

are held together by a fine network of connective tissue (*collagen*), which is converted into gelatine in process of cooking: thus the fibres are more easily separated and the meat becomes tender and easy of mastication. Embedded in the tissue are particles of fat.

NOTE. (*a*) The shorter the fibre, the more tender the meat, the length of fibre varying in different kinds. Meat should be cut against the grain or across the long axis of the fibres ; this diminishes their length and renders them more accessible to the digestive juices. When the fibres are cut, the meat juice exudes, spreads over the surface of the meat, and hardens or coagulates when exposed to heat, thus partly sealing in the nutrients.

(*b*) After slaughter, the muscles become tense and the fibres of the meat harden (*rigor mortis* stage) ; when this has passed, they relax, certain acids are developed which aid in the gelatination of the connective tissue, and the meat becomes tender ; this is the reason for hanging meat before it is cooked.

(*c*) Connective tissue is denser and the walls of the fibres thicker in very mature animals, and in any part where there is much muscular activity; therefore such a part is tougher.

(*d*) Very fat meat is more difficult to digest than that which is moderately so, because the fat forms a coating round the fibres, and the former is not so easily penetrated by the digestive juices.

Flavour, Nutritive Value, and Digestibility.

Flavour. Depends upon amount and kind of extractives present, development of various acids, pasturage, and food.

Nutritive value depends upon the proportion of fat, fat replacing water, but *not* protein ; therefore fat meat is a better source of heat than lean meat, while not inferior as to body-building nutrients. Protein is present in a comparatively small bulk, and is easily digested.

Digestibility is determined by the period of *rigor mortis* and subsequent hanging, length of fibres, amount of connective tissue, fat and extractives present, and the nature of the latter.

Effect of Heat in Cooking Meat. Dry heat coagulates the surface protein, partly sealing in the meat juices and causes shrinkage, whereby some of the juices are squeezed out, water evaporated from them and flavour is concentrated; heat also ruptures the fat cells and fat escapes, and converts the connective tissue into gelatine. Prolonged cooking and intense heat harden the protein and gelatine, cause charring of the surface, decomposition of the fat with the production of acrolein, which gives off acrid fumes, evaporation of moisture, and shrinkage and falling apart of the fibres.

Moist heat at the ordinary temperature has a similar effect to dry heat, except that there is less concentration of flavour, and long cooking causes the gelatine to dissolve, the fibres to fall apart, more fat to be extracted, and the meat is "boiled to rags."

CHAPTER 6

METHODS OF COOKING

ROASTING AND BAKING

ROASTING or baking is cooking by the dry radiant heat of an oven. The meat is cooked (*a*) in the oven of a solid fuel cooker which is practically closed, permitting of the entrance of little air and of meagre ventilation, (*b*) in a gas or electric oven, the facility for entrance of air being much greater in the former, since more abundant ventilation also is absolutely essential to carry off not only fumes of cooking but products of gas consumption.

Essentials to Good Results in Roasting and Baking.

1. Quality of meat good. Sinewy, coarse-fibred and gelatinous meat is unsuitable for roasting and baking (dry heat). Large joints are more economical to roast (or bake) as there is less shrinkage in proportion to their size.

2. Alternative methods can be used—

(*a*) Subject meat to high temperature (450° to 475° F.) for 15 to 20 minutes, reduce meat to moderate (325° F.) and continue cooking. As a rule, losses are greater by this method.

(*b*) Cook meat at a moderate temperature (350° to 325° F.) which is maintained throughout.

(*c*) Cook meat at a low temperature (300° F.) throughout. More time is required for cooking—cheaper cuts can be cooked successfully by this method.

3. For roasting the ventilation of the oven is very important; **both oven and shelves must be scrupulously clean, otherwise the** flavour of the meat is impaired. A double baking tin may be used, **the lower to contain water, which prevents the over-heating and** burning of fat. Meat may stand on a meat rack to allow hot air to circulate freely round joint, or it may stand in the baking tin.

4. Where there is a layer of fat on meat, e.g. sirloin of beef, place the joint in the baking tin, fat side uppermost; during cooking the fat melts and bastes the joint. Very lean meat (veal), poultry and game, are covered with greased paper or with bacon, to protect from too rapid browning.

5. Turn once or twice.

6. Avoid piercing meat with a skewer or fork, which allows the juices to escape.

7. Time for cooking varies with the kind of meat, whether English or imported: quality, weight, thickness, shape, and proportion of bone. As heat penetrates slowly, it takes some time for the deeper

parts of the meat to reach the necessary cooking temperature, which must be allowed for in calculating time. Longer time is required for—

(*a*) *Solid* joints with little or no bone—topside of beef, leg of mutton.

(*b*) *Boned* meat, sirloin, or ribs of beef. The joint weighs less when the bones are removed, but it is more solid.

(*c*) *Lamb*, also veal, is the flesh of an immature animal; the fibres are fine, but very close, and the heat longer in penetrating. Underdone lamb and veal are insipid and unappetizing, the extractives present not being so fully flavoured as those of sheep and ox.

(*d*) *Pork*, too, requires longer time; its fibres are

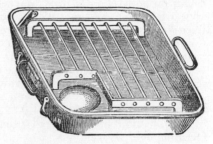

FIG. 7. DOUBLE BAKING TIN

very close, fat in large proportion. Pork must never be served underdone, otherwise there is a risk that parasites in the flesh are not destroyed.

As the joints, cuts, and texture of meat differ so much, the intelligent housewife soon learns to rely upon her own judgment and experience as to the time required. The following is a

TABLE OF APPROXIMATE TIMES FOR BAKING MEAT

Thin, small pieces of mutton with much bone (neck, loin, shoulder)	15 minutes to the pound and 15 minutes over	
Solid joints of beef and mutton	20 ,, ,,	20 ,,
Veal and lamb . .	20–25 ,, ,,	20–25 ,,
Pork . . .	30 ,, ,,	30 ,,
Poultry and game .	15 ,, ,,	15 ,,

GRILLING OR BROILING

Grilling or broiling is a very quick method, the high degree of heat applied being maintained practically throughout the process. It is also a method of cooking by radiant or direct heat on a hot grid: (*a*) over a glowing and smokeless fire; (*b*) beneath the glowing deflector of a gas or electric griller. This method, on account of the intense heat and rapid cooking, is only suitable for meat of the best quality; inferior meat would become tough and uneatable. Meat for grilling should not be fat. Meat grilled loses less juice than by any other method.

The principles underlying the method of grilling are the same as for roasting, but the former differs from the latter, for it is adapted to cooking *only small* and comparatively *thin* pieces of tender, juicy meat, which can cook quickly—steak, chops, cutlets; also kidneys, joints of game, and poultry; fish whole and in slices, and vegetables, such as mushrooms and tomatoes, are grilled.

Appearance of Grilled Meat.

A chop or steak successfully grilled is of an appetizing brown colour on both sides, is juicy and tender when cut, and has a puffy appearance due to the vaporization and expansion of the meat juices in the deeper parts, which are retained by the rapid coagulation of the surface protein, the result of the application of intense heat at once to the surface.

If sufficiently cooked, the surface of grilled meat is slightly elastic to the touch; it is spongy when raw, and hard if over-cooked.

Essentials to Good Results.

1. Protection of surface to prevent charring or scorching by brushing over with fat.

2. High degree of heat at commencement of the process.

3. Rapid coagulation of surface protein and evaporation of some water as shrinkage occurs—exposure of a *cut surface first* to heat for a minute, then turning; if both surfaces are cut, first one side for a minute, then the other.

4. Reduction of temperature after first few minutes to ensure all water is not evaporated—it is required for the gelatination of connective tissue.

5. Frequent turning to ensure uniform cooking without charring surface.

6. Prevention of escape of meat juices: avoid piercing with a skewer or fork, turn with two spoons.

7. Serve at once. (For details upon Grilling, see pp. 108–10.)

BOILING

The method of cooking food by the application of moist heat, which is conveyed by convection currents and by conduction, the food coming into direct contact with boiling water by immersion in it, the temperature of boiling water varying only slightly under certain normal conditions, e.g. the addition of salt. As compared with roasting and baking, boiling is a longer method, the cooking temperature being lower. The temperature of boiling water and of steam is the same, except when the latter is under pressure, but the difference affecting food by boiling is the amount of steam due to the rate of ebullition caused by the rapidity at which the water boils. With rapidly boiling water, there is no increase in degree of heat, the difference in the rate of cooking is because a greater volume of steam is passing off, which is water vapour partially condensed and visible. The term "boiled meat" is misleading, for its temperature while cooking is *not raised* to the boiling point of water, for the meat is not in contact with it for more than five minutes. When meat is exposed to the temperature of boiling water (212° F.) for a few minutes, the surface protein is coagulated and a thin coating is formed with the temporary retention of meat juices. Shrinkage occurs very shortly after the coagulation of the protein and some of the meat juices pass into the liquid. This rapid cooking is discontinued after five minutes. The heat of the water is then reduced to simmering point (about 180° F.); there is less ebullition, the steam coming off less rapidly, and the rate of cooking is reduced to an even and gentle degree. Meat may be put into cold water and brought to simmering point, in which case coagulation and shrinkage occur more slowly, but whichever method is used there is a comparable loss of soluble constituents, because of the shrinkage that inevitably takes place. If the surface of the water becomes quite still, the heat generated is insufficient thoroughly to cook the deeper parts by bringing them up to the necessary cooking temperature. Rapid boiling of the liquid for the whole of the time in relation to meat would harden the protein and gelatine, causing excessive shrinkage of fibres, and increased loss of nutrients and of flavouring matter, for water is a powerful solvent. For this reason, meat boilings should be used as a foundation for stock and soups. In addition to causing deterioration of food value, flavour and digestibility, rapid boiling breaks up the delicate texture of food, such as fish; and, unless there is an object, it is wasteful of heating power.

Boiling point must be maintained:—

1. For some culinary processes when the water in which the food is cooking must boil not only fairly rapidly, but very steadily the whole time, as in cooking vegetables, suet puddings, etc.

2. In reduction of liquids for making jams, syrups, etc.

Essentials to Good Results.

1. Use a minimum amount of water, the capacity of pan being suitable to bulk of food cooked. Add more boiling water as it evaporates.

2. To prevent evaporation, use pan with tightly-fitting lid, otherwise the cooking is retarded.

STEWING

Stewing is economical because the cheaper parts of meat can be used ; there is very little waste by evaporation ; the meat juices which escape from the meat in cooking are not lost, but are present in the liquid portion, which is served with the stew ; and the expenditure of fuel is comparatively small after the stewing process, that of gentle simmering, has commenced, for the contents of the stewpan can be kept at the correct heat on a gas or electric cooker or on the hot plate of a range.

Stewing, also a method of cooking by moist heat, is performed either in a stewpan on the cool part of the hot plate of a range, over a low gas or electric boiling ring, or in a casserole in a moderately hot oven. This method differs from boiling in (a) the comparatively small quantity of liquid used; (b) the prolonged action of uniformly low degree of moist heat, 180° F. to 200° F.

The aim in stewing is to render meat tender, and this method is suitable for any kind or part of meat, particularly for coarse, tough, and gelatinous meat, such as shin of beef, scrag end neck of mutton, sheep's head and feet, ox-tail, etc. The whole success of the cooking of such food depends upon not allowing the liquid to reach a high temperature. By the slow process of cooking and gentle heat, the connective tissue is converted into gelatine, so that the fibres fall apart easily and so become tender; the protein is coagulated without being over-hardened, and some of the soluble nutrients and flavouring constituents pass out into the liquid, all of which is served.

Essentials to Success.

1. Use of a casserole or stewpan with a well-fitting lid, to prevent evaporation.

2. Use of lean meat, and its division into neat pieces of a moderate size, if tough meat into small pieces, to expose as much surface as possible to the solvent action of the water.

3. Correct proportion of meat and water—approximately 1 lb. meat to ¾ pint water ; the gravy should not be poor and watery, but full-flavoured, a characteristic of a well-made stew.

4. Preliminary preparation. Very tough meat may be steeped for a few minutes in a little vinegar to soften it, or a meat tenderizer may be used. Meat of a better quality, such as steak for certain brown stews, is, after division into small pieces, fried slightly on both sides before stewing : this concentrates the flavour, as some water is evaporated from the meat, and the colour of a brown stew is improved. For stews of white meat, the meat is often not fried.

5. Skimming of brown stews to remove surface fat.

6. Slow, steady, and prolonged cooking to make the meat tender, but overcooking reduces it to " rags " and renders it tasteless, as most of the flavour has passed out into the liquid.

The time required varies, not with the quantity but with the quality and kind of meat. For very coarse and tough meat 3 to 4 hours may be necessary ; beef generally requires 2½ to 3 hours; mutton about 2 hours ; veal from 1¼ to 1½ hours.

Use of Flameproof, Fireproof and Glass Ware. A casserole made of any of these is particularly adapted to stewing. It has considerable powers of retaining heat, which is economical of fuel and its contents will cook slowly over a low heat without burning. Other advantages are—it is easy to keep clean, and it neither affects the colour nor the flavour of the food cooked in it, therefore a casserole is very suitable for white meats and vegetables, for farinaceous substances, for curries and for fruits; it is durable if handled with proper care. Fireproof dishes are generally for use in the oven; flameproof dishes can also be used on a boiling-ring. Food cooked in a casserole can be sent to table in it, hence the term "en casserole." The cost of such dishes varies; some are comparatively inexpensive; others, including the French fireproof casserole, are quite costly.

Care in Using the Casserole. Always heat a casserole gradually, particularly when new. To prevent a new one from cracking wash with warm water, fill with cold, add salt, heat gradually to boiling point, and boil gently for 10 to 15 minutes. Sudden extremes of temperature cause cracking; never fill a casserole with cold water immediately it has been emptied of hot food. On removal from top heat of stove or from oven, do not put casserole on a cold surface.

FRYING

Frying is a method of cooking food in heated oil or fat, and requires continuous and careful attention; therefore it is less easy to carry out than certain other methods. It is the quickest, since oil or fat can be raised to a very high temperature without burning, and the food coming into sudden contact with it is very rapidly heated and cooked, for which reason it is a method of cooking entirely unsuited to tough meat. The expression so often heard, "frying in boiling fat," is misleading and incorrect; most fats under ordinary atmospheric pressure decompose and burn at a considerably lower degree of heat than that required for them to boil; the bubbles seen on the surface of heated fat being either due to water present in the fat itself, or to the rapid conversion into steam of moisture given off from the surface of the fried food. Fats, however, can be heated to 350° to 420° F. without burning, a degree of heat far exceeding that of the boiling point of water, and undergo no change beyond the physical one of the conversion of the solid fat into its liquid state. The sudden exposure of the food (either meat or fish) to a very high temperature produces an almost instantaneous coagulation of the protein on the surface, and prevents the escape of soluble matter, while the temperature of the surrounding liquid is so high that the food is cooked very rapidly.

Methods of Frying.
1. Shallow Fat Frying.
2. French or Deep Fat Frying.

Shallow Fat Frying. This is the more popular method, but uniformly good results are not so easily obtainable as by frying in deep fat. The food is fried in a shallow pan with a small quantity of fat in the following ways—

(a) In sufficient fat to cover the bottom of the utensil and to prevent the food from adhering to it, the food being turned to cook evenly on both sides. Suitable for small pieces of meat—chops, steaks, cutlets, kidneys, liver, fish (whole, filleted or in slices), pancakes, omelets, eggs.

(*b*) Sautéing, derived from the French *sauter*, to jump, or toss. A small quantity of fat is used, generally oil or butter, just sufficient to be absorbed by the food cooked in it, the article sautéd being tossed lightly in it. The object of sautéing is threefold : to cook completely, as in sautéing kidneys or potatoes ; as a preliminary step in preparing vegetables for soups and sauces ; or to complete cooking and to flavour, as in the preparation of garnishes for dishes.

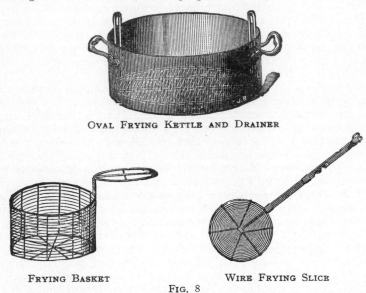

OVAL FRYING KETTLE AND DRAINER

FRYING BASKET   WIRE FRYING SLICE

FIG. 8

(*c*) Cooking in a heated pan without additional fat, e.g. bacon and pork sausages : the heat of the pan extracts from the food itself sufficient fat for frying. This is often called " dry frying."

French or Deep Fat Frying. Except for frying whole fish, sole and plaice, for which a vessel of a special shape is a convenience, an ordinary pan, about 4 in. deep and 7 in. to 8 in. in diameter, of some stout metal, iron or seamless steel (the intense heat chips enamel and burns tin) will answer the purpose. A wire frying basket, an inch less in diameter than that of the pan, is convenient and necessary to avoid much handling of food, and for its immersion in and removal from fat, also for draining ; failing this a perforated or wire slice.

There should be sufficient fat to fill two-thirds of the pan about,

4 lb. of fat being sufficient for a pan 7 in. to 8 in. in diameter. This method is more economical than shallow fat frying, notwithstanding the greater initial outlay for fat, for less is absorbed and therefore less is used ; if carefully treated, not allowed to burn and strained each time after use, the fat will last for a considerable time with small additions as the quantity diminishes. Meat, fish, vegetables, and sweet mixtures can be cooked in the same pan of fat, provided it is clean and is used at the correct cooking temperature, the various flavours being neither extracted nor absorbed by the fat. Neglect means that the fat soon becomes unfit for use.

Frying Oil and Fat. Fats and oils used as a cooking medium must be pure. They should not contain any extraneous matter such as water, protein, starch or salt—examples are vegetable oils, clarified beef and mutton fat and commercially prepared fats.

Butter, lard, and dripping are used for shallow fat frying.

Cooking Temperature of Fat Affected by Hazing temperature. Well fried food is golden or light brown in colour, free from grease, crisp and not difficult of digestion ; that which is badly fried being greasy, unappetizing in appearance and flavour, and most indigestible. Successful results depend upon the temperature of the fat ; if it is not sufficiently hot, it is absorbed by the food fried, which becomes greasy and sodden. Various fats, when heated sufficiently to give good results in frying, do not all show the same degree of temperature when tested, but those that have a hazing temperature of between 380° and 420° F. are the most suitable. Butter, which may be used for its flavour in shallow frying, must be clarified before use.

Average Frying Temperature. This varies from 320° to 400° F. The actual degree varies with the food fried—the kind, texture (whether solid or delicate), consistency, e.g. (croquette mixtures), thickness, raw or cooked, amount of surface moisture (fritters and batters).

Fritters	approximately	320°–360° F.
Fish	,,	340°–380° F.
Meat and food already cooked . .	,,	360°–380° F.
Whitebait and potato chips . .	,,	400° F.

Tests to Determine if Temperature of Fat is Suitable. The thermometer is the sure test, but experience soon teaches, with observation of the following—

(*a*) Quiescent state of fat. Bubbles indicate the presence of water, which must be driven off before the fat is ready for frying. When cold food is placed in hot fat, it cools down the fat and the surface becomes covered with bubbles, this being due to the moisture driven off from the surface of the food : the more bubbles, the hotter the fat ; the cessation of bubbling indicates the rapid reheating of the fat and cooking of the food.

(*b*) A slight blue haze rises from the surface, becoming thicker as the temperature rises : if fat is over-heating and burning, this vapour comes off rapidly, and is dense with an acrid odour.

(c) A small piece of dry bread, about 1 in. sq., if thrown into the fat causes bubbling, and it becomes crisp and golden in a minute if the fat is ready. When the fat is not sufficiently hot, there is little or no bubbling, and the bread remains pale in colour and greasy-looking.

Some vegetable oils do not show a haze when heated to a temperature suitable for frying, therefore a thermometer should be used, or the foregoing test made.

Protective Coverings for Fried Food. The object in coating certain foods is to protect the surface from the intense heat of the fat, to prevent the escape of the nutrient constituents of the food, and to modify the too rapid penetration of the intense heat.

These coatings are—

(a) Flour.

(b) Beaten egg and bread-crumbs, crushed vermicelli or commercially prepared crumbs.

(c) Pastry.

(d) Batter.

Essential Points for Good Results.

1. Absolutely clean fat ; strain each time after use and during use if necessary ; avoid burning.

2. Correct degree of heat of fat for kind of food cooked.

3. Careful draining, first in basket over the pan of fat, then on kitchen paper.

4. Frying only a few pieces at a time ; too large a quantity cools down fat, so that juices of meat and fish are not sealed in, and food is sodden ; also too much in the pan causes excessive bubbling and fat may flow over sides of pan, causing an accident.

5. Turning articles fried in shallow fat ; necessary also for some cooked in deep fat, such as fritters.

6. Food protected with egg and bread-crumbs, etc., or batter, must be evenly coated ; bread-crumbs pressed on well and batter allowed to drain off slightly; this to prevent loose crumbs and pieces of batter in the pan, which readily burn.

To Render Down Suet. Remove any discoloured parts or particles of meat, cut suet into small pieces, put these into a strong pan or baking tin, heat slowly until a faint haze rises. Strain off fat and return any solid pieces to pan; reheat until all fat has been extracted.

To Clarify Dripping for Frying and Other Purposes. Put the fat into a strong pan and just cover with cold water; bring slowly to boiling point and boil gently for 10 to 15 minutes. Allow to cool for a short time, then strain into a bowl in which there is a small quantity of cold water. Leave until a solid cake of fat has formed. Remove the cake of fat, scrape away any sediment beneath. Heat slowly in the pan to drive off any moisture, i.e. until a faint blue haze rises from the surface.

Fat which has been used for deep fat frying can be clarified in the same manner.

To Clarify Margarine or Butter. Heat very slowly in a pan until fat is quiescent, and salt and other solids have been precipitated. Strain.

STEAMING

Also a method of cooking by moist heat, but slower than that of boiling, being more gradual, as the food does not come into contact with the boiling water, but is cooked by (a) direct, or (b) indirect contact with steam, the vapour from boiling water.

Steamed food is lighter and more digestible than that cooked by other methods, therefore it is suitable for invalids and for persons with weak digestion. There is much less risk of over-cooking and of hardening the proteins of animal food ; the flavour of steamed meat is more delicate and the loss is less ; fish loses less of its very soluble ingredients, and vegetables less of their saline matter. All light egg mixtures (whether made with whole egg or with the white separated and whipped) which are cooked by moist heat are steamed, and more solid mixtures, such as puddings made with suet, bread-crumbs, etc., are lighter if steamed. Meat, both fresh and salted (tongue, ham, bacon, and poultry) are more tender and of fuller flavour if steamed rather than boiled.

(a) **By Direct Contact** with steam from boiling water, as in the ordinary steamer. This method is used for animal food : joints of meat, poultry, fish ; and for vegetables ; but as the steam comes into direct contact with the food, some of the soluble constituents passing out fall through the perforations into the water below, and are lost. It is most suitable for the light, and also the heavier, pudding mixtures enclosed in basin or tin, and for potatoes and other vegetables, except green vegetables.

(b) **By Indirect Contact.** The food is placed in a covered receptacle placed over or surrounded by steam from boiling water a method of cooking, by which the food is cooked in the steam of its own juices; it absorbs no water, and its full flavour and nutrients are preserved. This is carried out in a very simple way, by putting the food between two plates and placing this over a pan of boiling water, or by placing the food in a covered jar or basin inside a saucepan filled one-third full with boiling water.

Essential Points in Steaming Food.

1. The water in the lower vessel must be kept at boiling point, and must be maintained throughout the process ; the rate at which the steam passes off is due to the amount of ebullition and the rate

must depend upon the nature of the food cooked, e.g. for steamed *soufflés* only slight ebullition is necessary.

2. The steamer must be provided with a tightly-fitting lid, and whatever form it may take, it must fit the lower vessel closely to prevent escape of steam.

3. Small pieces of meat, fish, also puddings, should be covered with a greased paper to prevent condensed vapour from falling upon the food and rendering it sodden.

4. The rate of cooking and the time allowed is largely determined by the texture of the food and the kind—meat, fish, poultry, pudding mixtures. The time allowed for steaming food is on an average half as long again as for boiling.

5. When dishing do not waste the nutritive and flavouring juices of meat and fish, which have been extracted in cooking. Either pour the liquid over or around the food—chop or fillets of fish—or use it for making the sauce if one is served.

NOTE. Food steamed under pressure in a special apparatus is cooked in much less time, as the temperature is higher and no heat is lost. This method is used when food in bulk has to be steamed, as in hospitals, canteens, etc. There are several types of pressure cookers on the market suitable for household use.

CHAPTER 7

GLOSSARY AND MISCELLANEOUS HINTS

Au Gratin. A dish covered with sauce, coated with bread-crumbs, browned in the oven and served in the utensil in which it is cooked.

Au Maigre. Dishes prepared without either meat or meat stock, and suitable for Lenten fare.

Au Naturel. Food served raw, or plainly prepared and cooked.

Bain Marie. A large pan, square or oblong, with about 4 in. deep of boiling water, fitted with a set of small saucepans, in which sauces, etc., can be kept hot without burning or reducing.

Beignet. Fritter.

Bisque. A thickened soup made from shellfish.

Blanch. To put into cold water and bring to boiling point—object: to remove strong flavour, to whiten, to soften, or to cleanse, and to remove skins from nuts.

Bouillon. Beef broth unclarified.

Bouquet Garni. Bunch of herbs, usually bay leaf, parsley, thyme, and marjoram (tied in piece of muslin), with or without other flavouring ingredients.

Croquette. Mince of fish, meat, poultry or game, made into various shapes—coated and fried.

Croûte. Thick slice of fried bread upon which small birds and entrées are dished.

Croûtons. Small dice and fancy shapes of fried bread.

Larding. Method of inserting strips of fat bacon or pork into surface of lean meats.

Liaison. A binding or thickening for soups and sauces.

Macedoine. A mixture of various fruits or vegetables, cut into a variety of shapes.

Marinade. A kind of pickling medium consisting of vinegar or lemon juice, oil seasoning and flavourings. Meats, fish, etc., are steeped in it for a short time before cooking, to give additional flavour.

Marmite. Stockpot or soup.

Mirepoix. Foundation or bed of vegetables used in preparing braised food—soups, and sauces.

Panada. Mixture of flour, butter, and liquid used as a foundation for mixture of soufflé type, and for binding ingredients together.

Paprika. Red Hungarian pepper, less pungent than Cayenne.

Purée. Vegetables, meat, fruit, etc., reduced to a pulp by cooking and sieved.

Réchauffé. Any dish made with reheated food.

Rissoles. Mixture similar to that of croquette, enclosed in pastry and fried.

Roux. A thickening for soups and sauces, made of butter and flour and cooked over the fire to colour or not as required for white or brown soup or sauce.

Salpicon. A mince of meat, poultry, etc., enriched with other ingredients and used for croquettes, rissoles, patties, etc.

Tammy. A cloth through which sauces are pressed to make them smooth and glossy.

Zest. The rind of a lemon or orange grated or pared thinly without any pith.

HOMELY MEASURES

To ensure the best results in cookery, accuracy as to quantities is most essential; for some cooks, good judgment with experience may suffice, but the use of scales and of homely measures is necessary to most people.

Liquids

1 teacupful	= 1 gill or ¼ pint or 6 tablespoonfuls.
1 breakfastcupful or 1 tumbler	= ½ pint.
10 oz. liquid	= ½ pint.
½ fluid oz.	= 1 tablespoon.

Dry Ingredients

2 level tablespoonfuls (finely chopped suet, flour, moist sugar)	= approximately		1 oz.
2 level dessertspoonfuls	=	,,	½ oz.
2 level teaspoonfuls	=	,,	¼ oz.
1 level teacupful	=	,,	¼ lb.
1 breakfastcupful castor sugar or flour	=	,,	8 oz.
1 breakfastcupful rice or brown sugar	=	,,	7 oz.
1 breakfastcupful butter, lard or dripping (heaped)	=	,,	7 oz.
4 level tablespoonfuls breadcrumbs	=	,,	1 oz.
1 tablespoonful treacle or jam	=	,,	2 oz.
Piece of butter size of small hen's egg	=	,,	1¼ oz.
Piece of butter size of walnut	=	,,	½ oz.
8 large or 10 small eggs	=	,,	1 lb.
1 hen's egg	=	,,	1¼–2 oz.

Temperature Conversion. At present the Fahrenheit scale is used in stating temperatures of ovens and for indicating temperatures of water, etc., and it is used throughout this book. It is most probable that temperatures will eventually be given in degrees Centigrade and the following table states degrees Fahrenheit and their approximate equivalents in Centigrade degrees.

To convert degrees Centigrade into Fahrenheit, multiply the figure by 9, divide by 5 and add 32—

$$\frac{100° \text{ C.} \times 9}{5} = 180 \text{ plus } 32 = 212° \text{ F.}$$

To convert Fahrenheit to Centigrade degrees, subtract 32, multiply by 5 and divide by 9—

$$212° - 32 = 180 \times \frac{5}{9} = 100° \text{ C.}$$

CONVERSION—FAHRENHEIT TO CENTIGRADE

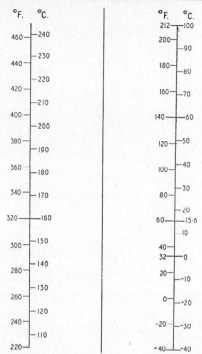

EXAMPLES OF OVEN TEMPERATURES IN °F. AND EQUIVALENTS °C.

°F.	°C.	°F.	°C.
240	115·5	380	193·3
265	129·5	400	204·4
290	143·3	425	218·3
310	154·6	445	229·3
335	168·3	470	243·3
355	179·5		

Oven Test. The thermometer, although very useful and absolutely essential for certain processes (e.g. sugar boiling), is not really practical for household cookery, a knowledge of the correct heat necessary for most culinary methods being soon acquired by experience. A homely test for the heat of the oven is that of a small

piece of thin white paper placed in the oven for 3 to 4 minutes. If
it does not colour, the oven is too cool, if it becomes dark brown
or black, it is too hot. A golden brown colour denotes the heat
is sufficient for bread, small cakes, and pastry ; a pale fawn for
large cakes, sponge cakes, and gingerbread. Almost without exception, ovens are now thermostatically controlled, but on occasions the
preceding test may be of use.

GAS OVEN CHART

Type of Food.	Thermostat Setting.	Approximate Temperature Centre Oven.	Heat of Oven.
Fruit bottling . . .	$\frac{1}{4}$	240° F.	Very cool
Stews	$\frac{1}{2}$	265°	
Custard and egg dishes .	1	290°	
Milk puddings . . .	1	290°	
Rich fruit cake . . .	2	310°	Cool
Slow roasting, shortbread .	3	335°	Warm
Madeira and plain fruit cakes	4	355°	Moderate
Biscuits	4	355°	
Queen cakes, sponges . .	5	380°	Fairly hot
Plain buns, plate tarts, short pastry	6	400°	Hot
Quick roasting, scones . .	7	425°	
Flaky pastry . . .	8	445°	Very Hot
Puff pastry	9	470°	

By kind permission of the Gas Council.

MOVEMENTS TO COMBINE INGREDIENTS

Deft and rapid manipulation is important ; this minimizes muscular exertion and *noise*, and although the use of the small and
practical labour-saving devices for chopping, mincing, whisking,
mixing, etc., should be adopted, it is essential to be able to be
independent of such means and to know the correct method of
carrying out these minor culinary operations, for the correct way
is both the quickest and the easiest. In combining ingredients
there are three ways—stirring, beating, and cutting and folding in,
all of which require dexterity of manipulation.

Stirring. The movement of the spoon, metal or wooden, is circular
the circle increasing until all ingredients are blended, e.g. in mixing
a batter.

Beating. The object is smoothness of the mixture and the introduction of air, the mixture being turned over continually, each time bringing the under parts to the surface, the whisk or spoon being in constant contact with the whole and drawing it away from the bottom and sides of the basin or bowl.

Cutting and Folding In. The object is to combine one ingredient of light texture, such as whipped white of egg, with another or mixture of ingredients. To do this move the spoon vertically as in cutting, and alternately with this use a turning-over movement until the whole is uniformly and smoothly blended. A metal spoon is used, as it cuts more sharply and prevents the escape of air already introduced in the whisked ingredients.

SEASONING AND FLAVOURING

The fine art of cooking is to develop the natural flavour of the food, the additional flavouring and seasoning being used to improve it, so that the food is thereby rendered more appetizing and more easy of digestion. In ordinary household fare, seasoning and flavouring are particularly important; by the judicious use of simple and varied ingredients of this class, many appetizing variations can be made from the same recipe. Seasoning and flavouring in excess is just as unpalatable as lack of it. Fresh or dried herbs and fresh vegetables are preferable to, and cheaper than, the manufactured sauces; spices, ingredients of a very pungent, strong or acid nature, and strong essences must be used with judgment—essences, being volatile, should be added at the last. Where a variety of flavourings are added, these must be well blended, e.g. tomato sauce. When using vegetables, herbs, etc., the quantity used must be left to personal discrimination.

DISHING AND GARNISHING

Dishing. Food should be not only attractive to the palate, but also to the eye, for if uninviting in appearance it is not as stimulating to digestive activity. Neat and smart dishing is important, it contributes greatly to the success of all dishes and to none more than to the very simple ones, which may look most uninviting if served in a slovenly or untidy fashion.

When dishing hot food—

(*a*) Both the dish and any accompaniments should be really hot and in readiness for the food to be sent " piping hot " to table.

(*b*) Dish quickly; grilled foods, *soufflés*, batters, omelets, and light, hot after-dinner savouries should be upon the table as quickly as possible after they are cooked.

(*c*) Remove any traces of spots of gravy from the rim of the dish with a cloth dipped into hot water.

Garnishing. The object of garnishing is either to supply some appropriate and suitable adjunct to a dish, e.g. chipped potatoes and *maître d'hôtel* butter with grilled meat or to make the dish more attractive in flavour and appearance, e.g. lemon and parsley with fish and white meats.

The choice and suitability of the garnish must be left greatly to individual judgment and taste ; for hot food the garnish should

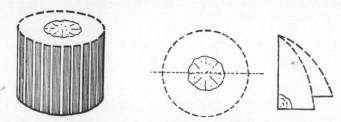

FIG. 9. HOW TO CRIMP CUCUMBER

be simple so that the food can be quickly dished ; for cold food that of a more elaborate nature can be used, but over-garnishing detracts from rather than contributes to the smart appearance of the dish. The following are simple and very generally used—parsley, lemon, cucumber, croûtons.

To Chop Parsley. Wash it well, remove the sprigs from the stalks and squeeze them as dry as possible in a cloth ; gather them up

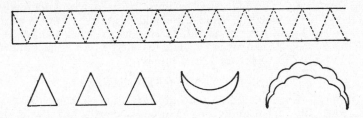

FIG. 10. HOW TO CUT CROÛTONS

into a bunch and cut them across several times, then chop finely. Keep the point of the knife on the board and work the handle up and down and forwards and backwards.

To Crimp Lemon. Cut thin slices, remove pips and with a small pointed knife serrate the edge. Cut each slice in half, and, for a more decorative effect, cut each half again nearly in half and arrange in butterfly shape.

To Crimp Cucumber. Crimped cucumber is an attractive garnish for cold entrées of fish and of meats.

For crimping, a straight cucumber with a smooth skin is necessary. With a sharp knife score the skin down in narrow strips about $\frac{1}{16}$ in. in depth, then remove every alternate strip of skin: this gives a striped appearance.   Cut the block in half lengthwise and cut each piece into *very* thin slices; pinch these up, as in Fig. 16.

Croûtons. Cut the bread, which should not be new, into slices about ¼ in. in thickness, the slices into strips, and the strips into diamond or triangular shapes, and for soup into dice; or stamp the slices of bread out into small shapes with a fancy or plain cutter. Fry in hot, deep fat.

HINTS UPON COOKING A MEAL

1. Attend to the oven if it is needed, so that the latter may be at the correct heat when required.

2. Collect all ingredients and utensils before beginning to work.

3. Weigh and measure accurately, be careful as to details in all methods and processes.

4. Begin with the dish that requires longest cooking; endeavour for the preparations to proceed simultaneously, this to avoid waste of time later on and to ensure that all the adjuncts and accompaniments to a dish will be properly cooked when they are required for dishing.

5. Be alert of eye and of ear, giving frequent attention to stove and to oven, and gauge the time for cooking accurately, not by guess-work.

6. Economize space in the oven and on the hot plate to allow each article of food to be cooked at the right heat.

7. Avoid waste of gas and electric current by not putting it on too soon and by turning it out when it is no longer needed. Do not use unnecessarily large utensils for boiling water, and avoid letting the water boil for a long time before it is required.

8. Clear and wash up as you go along, and put away any utensils or ingredients which have been used and are not again required.

9. Dish quickly and neatly and serve punctually. Serve all hot food very hot.

CHAPTER 8

STOCKS AND SOUPS

STOCK

STOCK is a liquid containing some of the soluble nutrients and flavouring constituents of food, which are extracted by prolonged and gentle simmering; such liquid is the foundation of soups, sauces, and gravies. The method of preparation is based upon (*a*) the solvent action of water, (*b*) the prolonged application of moist and moderate heat. The lean, gelatinous and sinewy parts of meat, with a certain proportion of bone, are most suitable. Much seasoning and flavouring are to be avoided, as these overpower the characteristic flavour of meat stock and that of the food to which it may be added. Herbs and spices are not generally used for meat stock, and should be added with discretion in fish and vegetable stocks. Vegetables must be fresh, not necessarily young and expensive, and trimmings and coarse stalks can be utilized; of the vegetables generally used, carrot, turnip, onion, and celery, no one flavour should predominate—celery and turnip, if old, are particularly strong, and should not be used. Vegetables, being very absorbent of meaty flavours, should not remain too long in the stock while it is cooking, and for the same reason they must not be left in it after cooking; neglect of removal in hot weather causes fermentation. In very hot weather it is advisable to omit the vegetables.

Household Stock. First stock, brown and white, is made only for special purposes, but a supply of household stock can be made when required. Bones, scraps and trimmings of meat and poultry, cooked and uncooked, giblets, and pieces of fresh vegetable can be utilized, but *everything must be perfectly fresh*, free from the slightest suspicion of taint, and suitable. Things which should *not* be put into the stock-pot are fat, cabbage, cooked vegetables, and any starchy matter, such as bread, thickened sauces, etc., which make the stock cloudy. A saucepan with a well-fitting lid should be used, of a size suitable to the quantity of stock being made. It must be scrupulously clean.

Stock should be made on the day previous to using it; it can, then, have the time necessary for cooking it, and fat can be removed when it has solidified on cooling.

To prevent stock from turning sour, which is very possible in mild or hot weather, strain off meat and vegetables as soon as stock is cooked; the vegetables are of no further use, being flavourless. When cold, remove the congealed fat from the surface; boil up daily in hot weather, and every second day in winter. The fat removed from the surface can be clarified and used for frying. Surplus stock can be boiled down for glaze.

VARIETIES OF STOCK

Kind.	Principal Ingredients.	Uses.
FIRST. (a) Brown (b) White	{ Fresh meat only, the first boiling of the meat. { Fresh flavouring vegetables.	For *Consommé*. For best white soups.
SECOND.	Meat strained from first stock with addition of fresh vegetables, sufficient water or meat boilings to cover.	General. *Purées*, etc.
BONE.	Fresh meat bones. Bones can be re-boiled once or twice before all the gelatine is extracted. Cooked meat bones afford a better flavour, but some of the nutrients have been already extracted. Stock is cooked until bones are dry and pitted with small holes.	General.
HOUSEHOLD or GENERAL.	The economical and " stand-by " stock. Scraps of uncooked and cooked meat and bones, pieces of fresh vegetables, giblets, carcases of birds, unthickened gravies. Meat boilings instead of water ; if salt it must be diluted.	General.
GAME AND POULTRY.	Carcasses and trimmings of game and poultry, cooked and uncooked, feet, giblets.	Game soups and dishes.
FISH.	Cheap white fish or heads, skin and trimmings (oily fish unsuitable). Additional flavourings, such as bay leaf, mace, etc.	Fish soups and dishes.
VEGETABLE.	Various vegetables, trimmings, and parings of fresh vegetables with herbs. Liquid in which vegetables (except cabbage), macaroni and rice have been cooked can be utilized. For white stock, vegetables, *sautéd* in butter, not coloured ; for brown, cooked until brown.	Vegetarian cookery.

Approximate Proportions of Chief Ingredients and Time for Cooking

Kind.	Foundation.	Water.	Time.
BROWN	Shin of beef 3lb.	4 qt.	4–5 h.
	Knuckle of veal 1lb.		
WHITE	Knuckle of veal 4lb.	,,	,,
BONE	Fresh bones 4lb.	,,	6–7 h.
FISH	White fish and bones 2lb.	3 qt.	¾ ,,
VEGETABLE	Various kinds 1½–2lb.	2 ,,	1–1½ ,,

Essential Points in Making Good Meat Stock.

1. Absolute cleanliness of utensil and freshness of ingredients.

2. Division of meat and bones to expose as much surface as possible to solvent action of water.

3. Steeping meat in cold water before application of heat, *cold* soft water having greater solvent action than *hot hard*.

4. Gradual heating to boiling point for easy extraction of meat constituents, followed by maintenance of gentle and uniform degree of heat.

5. Removal of white scum at the commencement of and during cooking, *not* of brown scum ; the latter is coagulated protein matter, the former consists of impurities. Stock is cloudy if not skimmed.

6. Use of vegetables whole if small, or cut into large pieces ; this to prevent pulping, which would make stock cloudy, and to prevent increasing their absorbent power.

BROWN STOCK (*First*)

Proportions.

3 lb. shin of beef.	Carrot, onion.
1 lb. knuckle of veal.	2 stalks of celery or ¼ teaspoonful celery
4 qt. cold water.	seeds.
1 teaspoonful salt.	

Method. 1. Wipe meat, remove any fat, and cut into 1 in. cubes, break bones and remove marrow. 2. Cover the meat and bones with water, add salt, and leave to steep for 30 minutes. 3. Bring slowly to boiling point and remove white scum. 4. After stock has been cooking about three hours, add cleaned vegetables. 5. Bring to boiling point again, simmer gently for 2 hours, skimming it occasionally. 6. Strain through a nylon sieve or colander to remove bones and vegetables, and when cold remove fat.

White Stock made as above with white meat, veal (knuckle, feet, head) and poultry ; richest white stock from knuckle of veal and fowl.

Meat Glaze. Surplus stock can be made into glaze. For this use any good brown stock and the second boiling from meat and bones. Remove every trace of fat, boil quickly with the lid off and skim frequently, reducing the liquid to about half a pint ; then reduce again until it is about the consistency of treacle or syrup, being very careful to keep it well stirred at this stage, as it burns readily. If not required for immediate use, pour into a small jar, cover the surface with melted lard and cover tightly. Used for coating meat and for enriching sauces and gravies.

NOTE. Both second stock and bone stock are boiled more rapidly than first stock ; this is to extract completely all the gelatine from the bones.

CHAPTER 9

SOUP-MAKING

THE principles governing the making of soups are the same as for stock, soup being a liquid which contains the soluble constituents of its ingredients : this may be thickened or not.

As an item in the daily diet, it is too frequently neglected, and should be eaten more generally for dietetic and economic reasons. Warm food is more stimulating than cold ; a soup is a suitable prelude to cold meat, particularly in winter. The utilization of stock and of remnants of food, animal and vegetable, with other additions, will supply some of the necessary nutriment for a meal, which otherwise must be derived from meat, the most expensive form of protein. Through the medium of soup, other foods of a tissue-forming and energy-producing nature pass into the system, for which reason a nourishing and stimulating soup is of considerable value in invalid dietary, being also easy of digestion.

Classification of Soups. The foundation liquid of soups is stock of various kinds, or water.

The enormous number of soups used may be grouped as follows—

Thin.	*Thick.*
1. Consommé (clarified or clear soups).	1. Purées.
2. Broths (unclarified).	2. Thickened (*potages liés*).
	(a) Brown, oxtail, mulligatawny, etc.
	(b) White, including the rich white cream soups.
	(c) Bisques.

Relative Food Values of Clear and Thick Soups. The value of soup as a food depends upon the type, that is, whether it is clear or thick. A clear soup (*consommé*) is prepared from first meat stock. In the process of making such stock a portion of the meat constituents is extracted into the liquid—some of the connective tissue is converted into gelatine (even a strong stock made with very gelatinous meat contains only a very low percentage, 1 per cent only of gelatine being sufficient to set the liquid), a considerable quantity of mineral matter and extractives, a small proportion of soluble proteins, and a small amount of fat, the latter being removed by skimming, and the coagulated protein by straining the stock before use ; the remaining liquid contains little but extractives and gelatine. A clear soup is therefore of little actual food value, but it *is* of *dietetic* importance, being a stimulant and aid to digestion, because its chief constituents, extractives, and gelatine, promote the flow of the digestive juices.

For a soup to be nourishing as well as stimulating, it must be thickened either by the retention of its ingredients finely divided as in mutton broth, or sieved as in lentil soup, or by the addition of nitrogenous matter such as eggs, milk, grated cheese, etc., or starchy food, as cereals and their products e.g. macaroni.

Thick soups are on this account of very considerable food value, and in combination with other foods will provide part of the nutriment necessary in a well-balanced meal.

In making soup, as in all other culinary processes, a reliable basic recipe for a particular type can be suitably varied, and the housewife with a knowledge of food values and the principles of soup-making is able to provide a considerable variety of nourishing household soups at a small cost.

Essentials of a Well-prepared Soup. 1. *Flavour.* Full and good, that of its chief and foundation ingredients being predominant ; minor flavourings well blended and not overpowering. Factors in determining flavour are—

(*a*) Correct proportion of ingredients—

> Approximately ½ lb. meat   to 1 pint liquid.
> „   1 lb. vegetables   „   „   „
> „   1 gill soaked pulse „   „   „

(*b*) Quality of stock. Perfect freshness, whatever its strength, first stock only for *consommés* and rich white soups.

(*c*) Fine division of ingredients, and steeping meat in cold water.

(*d*) Heating slowly to boiling point, then gentle and steady simmering to extract nutrient and flavouring constituents.

(*e*) Judicious use of flavourings, vegetables, herbs, and spices.

2. *Seasoning.* Sufficient, not in excess ; a soup should not require to be seasoned after it is sent to table ; salt added at commencement of cooking.

3. *Freedom from greasiness* by—(*a*) Use of stock free from fat, and removal of fat from soup meat.

(*b*) Careful sautéing of vegetables to ensure absorption of fat.

(*c*) Skimming at commencement of cooking after boiling point is reached, and at intervals afterwards if necessary.

4. *Consistency and Smoothness.* These refer to thick soups only. The consistency should be that of cream, not thick like porridge, nor as thin as milk : it varies with the type of soup, a *purée* being slightly thicker than a *potage lié* or thickened soup. Causes of variation in consistency are—

(*a*) Over reduction of liquid by too rapid cooking and by cooking in an uncovered pan.

(*b*) Insufficient cooking of ingredients and imperfect formation of the *liaison*, or thickening.

Smoothness is affected by careless addition of any starchy ingredient, causing lumps ; also by faults in sieving, and by not mixing sieved portion thoroughly with the liquid.

5. *Colour.* To ensure the colour of white and delicately coloured soups being good—

(*a*) A white-lined pan and wooden spoon should be used.

(*b*) Vegetables should be carefully cleaned, trimmed, and kept in cold water until required, particularly in the case of white vegetables —potatoes, artichokes, celery.

(*c*) Sautéd vegetables must not be allowed to colour.

For brown soups, use brown stock and brown roux : onion fried in the fat improves colour and flavour.

6. *Liaison*, from the French *lier*, to bind (hence the term *potages liés*), is a binding or thickening medium necessary in thick soups and serves two purposes—

(*a*) To afford consistency and to ensure smoothness of texture.

(*b*) To hold ingredients (sieved or not) in suspension, without which they would separate and settle at the bottom of the soup tureen—e.g. Lentil soup, Tapioca soup.

Varieties of Liaison. (*a*) Farinaceous : flour, cornflour, arrowroot *crème de riz*, tapioca, sago, semolina, etc.

(*b*) Roux, consisting of equal quantities of flour and fat.

(*c*) Yolks of eggs mixed with cream or milk, and used for the richer and more expensive white soups.

Addition of liaison. An absolute essential is thorough cooking.

(*a*) Farinaceous matter in powder form ; mix smoothly with a small amount of liquid, then add to the soup just before dishing, and boil for at least five minutes, stirring the whole time. If a small grain be used, such as crushed tapioca or semolina, this must cook in the soup until quite transparent, 15 to 20 minutes.

(*b*) Roux. This consists of equal quantities of fat and of flour, blended over heat for a sufficient time to colour or not, as required. To make the roux, melt the fat, draw pan aside from the heat, blend flour smoothly with fat, reheat, and cook slightly, being careful not to let it over-heat and become oily, or colour if required for a white soup or sauce. Draw the roux away from the fire and add liquid gradually, stirring it in gently (or the soup will be lumpy), and boil for at least 7 to 10 minutes. Over-cooking brown roux frequently happens unless care is exercised, causing the starchy matter to change chemically (dextrinize) and lose some of its thickening property; the fat separates from it, rising to the surface, the soup being thin and greasy.

(*c*) Yolks of eggs mixed with stock, milk, or cream, are added to the soup just before it is dished. Sufficient heat is necessary to coagulate the egg protein and to form the liaison, but the soup must not be at boiling point when it is added, or allowed to boil afterwards or it will curdle.

Approximate Proportions of Ingredients for Liaison.

¼–½ oz. flour   to 1 pint liquid.   For *purées* made of ingredients rich in starch. e.g. lentil *purée*.

¾–1 oz. flour   ,,   ,,   ,,   When ingredients contain little starch. e.g. tomato soup.

¼–¾ oz. cornflour ,,   ,,   ,,

Roux.

1 oz. fat }
1 oz. flour } ,, 1 qt.   ,,

1–2 yolks of eggs to 1 pint liquid.

¼ gill cream   ,,   ,,   ,,

CONSOMMÉ

A consommé or *clarified soup* is a clear bright liquid. It must be prepared from first meat stock with a full flavour, which is augmented by the addition of fresh vegetables and of meat juices. The stock, which must be perfectly free from fat and sediment, is cleared by the albumen of the egg white and meat, which rises to the surface carrying impurities with it, the crushed egg-shell acting as a filtering medium in the cloth through which the soup is strained. One white of egg and 4 oz. lean beef are sufficient for one quart of stock.

Cloudiness is due to use of stock poor in quality, stock that is greasy and not strained ; imperfect coagulation of clearing agent ; whisking after boiling point is reached, whereby the impurities mix again with the liquid ; not allowing the soup to settle before straining ; lack of cleanliness of pan or cloth—any trace of grease, soap, or starch will destroy brilliancy of *consommé*.

Garnishes. There is only one method of preparing a clear soup, but it is served under different names. A variety of ingredients are used as garnishes, the name of the *consommé* being that of the particular garnish added to it, e.g.—

Consommé à la Julienne	Garnish of shredded vegetables.
Consommé à la Brunoise	,, ,, dice of vegetables.
Consommé à la Royale	,, ,, steamed custard stamped
(See CUSTARDS)	out into fancy shapes.

Other garnishes are: asparagus points, French beans, quenelles, and Italian paste. All must be cooked before addition to the soup, and anything of a starchy nature, such as Italian *pasta*, macaroni, etc., washed after cooking to avoid making *consommé* cloudy.

Consommé à la Julienne.

1 quart first brown stock, or half brown and half white stock.
2 tablespoonfuls cold water.
Shell and white of 1 egg } clearing
4 oz. lean juicy beef } ingredients.
Carrot finely shredded }
Turnip ,, ,, } garnish.
Leek ,, ,, }

1 small onion }
½ small carrot }
10 peppercorns }
Small *bouquet garni* } flavourings.
Blade of mace }
1 clove }
1 tablespoonful sherry }

1. Scrape or chop the meat very finely and steep in the cold water for 30 minutes; clean vegetables and cut into thick pieces or

blocks ; remove fat from stock and strain through muslin ; wash and crush egg shell, whisk white slightly.

2. Put the stock into a clean, scalded saucepan and add all the ingredients, the herbs tied up in muslin : heat *gradually* and stir the contents until close upon boiling point, then remove spoon.

3. Bring the liquid to boiling point, and boil for three to five minutes to coagulate thoroughly the albumen, with which the impurities are entangled. Draw the pan aside, cover with a plate and leave by the side of fire or gas for 30 minutes to extract flavour of vegetables and to allow solid matter to settle.

4. Strain through a perfectly clean, scalded, fine linen cloth, pour the *consommé gently* through; repeat if the *consommé* is not quite clear.

5. Pass a piece of kitchen paper over the surface to remove minute specks of grease. Cook garnish in boiling salted water and drain.

6. Reheat ; season with salt if required, add garnish and wine if desired—1 tablespoonful sherry to 1 quart *consommé* is sufficient.

NOTE. When clear soup is frequently made a special soup stand is a convenience, but a cloth tied over the legs of an inverted chair answers all ordinary purposes (see STRAINING OF JELLIES, page 226).

BROTHS

A Broth is a *thin or unclarified* soup, and is of a very considerable food value that is very much higher than that of the *consommé* or that of clarified soup, for it contains all the soluble constituents of its ingredients, meat, vegetables, and cereals, none of these being removed by straining and clearing. Such a soup is both stimulating and nourishing and, if made with additional vegetables and cereal matter and eaten with bread or potatoes, will furnish a substantial dish in an economical two-course meal.

Mutton, beef, veal, chicken, cow-heel, and sheep's head all make excellent broth. The two latter must be blanched to cleanse them before use.

Mutton Broth.

1 lb. scrag-end or knuckle of mutton.	1 small leek.
2 pt. cold water.	Carrot, turnip, onion.
1 oz. rice or barley.	(1 teacupful).
1 teaspoonful chopped parsley.	1 teaspoonful salt.
	Pepper.

1. Wipe the meat, cut it away from the bone, removing marrow from the latter, and fat and skin from former ; divide meat into small neat pieces. Slice leek (if used) thinly, cut carrot, turnip, and onion into small dice ; wash rice or blanch barley—this is very necessary or broth will be very cloudy. 2. Put meat, bones, and one teaspoonful of salt into saucepan, bring slowly to boiling point

and skim ; add barley or rice and simmer for 1½ hours. 3. Add vegetables and continue cooking for another hour, skimming occasionally. 4. Strain through a fine sieve, and remove the bones and fat from surface of broth. 5. Return liquid and solid ingredients to pan, add parsley, season to taste, and boil up to remove raw flavour of parsley.

NOTE. Veal or chicken broth is prepared in the same way, half a chicken being used to 2 pints of water ; the substitution of crushed tapioca, sago, or arrowroot for rice or barley is preferable for invalids. In that case the omission of vegetables is often necessary, and the food value may be increased by a larger proportion of meat and by the addition of the yolk of an egg just before serving.

PURÉES

Purées. Of thick household soups the *purée* is one of the most economical and easy of preparation. The liquid (stock, milk, or water, or a mixture of two, or of all) is thickened by the retention of the solid ingredients. These are first sautéd in fat to soften and to impart additional flavour, and then by slow and thorough cooking reduced to a *purée* or pulp, which is sieved (sometimes pounded first as for a meat *purée*—kidney) and mixed with the liquid. To prevent separation of the *purée* from the liquid, to ensure smoothness of texture by preventing a granular appearance, and a proper consistency, the addition of a small quantity of starchy matter as a binding medium (*liaison*) is essential. Usually half an ounce of flour or cornflour to one pint of liquid is sufficient, but amount varies with quantity of starch present in the pulped ingredients.

Meat, poultry, game, fish, fresh vegetables, and pulse, are largely used as a foundation for these soups, the accompaniment being dice of toasted or fried bread. The addition of milk to vegetable *purées* increases their food value, enriches flavour, and improves the colour, and cream augments these qualities to a greater degree. Both milk and cream should be added quite at the last ; if boiled in the soup, their flavour is altered and there is a tendency to curdle.

Vegetable Purées are of three classes, being made with

(*a*) Pulse.

(*b*) Succulent vegetables, potatoes, artichokes, carrots, etc.

(*c*) Green and other vegetables of delicate flavour : spinach, green peas, sorrel, asparagus, tomatoes.

Pulse Purées. Pulse soups require *slow* and *very* thorough cooking, otherwise they have a raw starchy flavour. The time of preparation varies with the kind ; lentil about 1½ hours, pea 2 to 2½ hours, haricot (the longest time of all) 2½ to 3 hours or even more if the pulse is stale, stale pulse being very difficult to soften. The same method is used for haricot as for pea or lentil, but as this is a white soup, carrot is omitted and the use of a white-lined pan is necessary. For pea and lentil soups, pea and lentil flour may be substituted for the split peas or lentils (about 2½ oz. to 1 pint liquid), the flour being boiled in the soup for 15 to 20 minutes after the vegetables are tender. Tie herbs, when used, in muslin.

A small ham-bone is an improvement to pulse soups ; salt must be added carefully, if either it or salt meat liquor be used.

Pea or Lentil Soup.

6 oz. split peas or lentils.
2 pints cold water, ham or meat boilings, or vegetable stock.
1 large onion.
Carrot } 4–6 oz.
Turnip
2 sticks celery or ¼ teaspoonful celery seeds.

Small bunch of herbs.
1 oz. dripping.
Pepper and salt.
½ oz. flour.
¼ pint milk.
Dice of fried or toasted bread.

1. Wash pulse in cold water and soak overnight in the 2 pints of liquid to be used. 2. Strain off the liquid reserving it, slice vegetables thinly. 3. Heat the fat in the saucepan and in the hot fat sauté the pulse and vegetables. 4. Add the liquid, herbs, and salt, and bring to boiling point. 5. Skim and simmer till pulse is quite tender, stirring occasionally. 6. Rub through a nylon sieve and return to rinsed pan ; mix flour smoothly with milk, if used (if not, with a little stock or water), stir into soup, boil five minutes and season. Serve with fried or toasted bread and, in the case of pea soup, with dried and powdered mint, which is a digestive.

Potato Soup.

1 lb. potatoes.
1 onion (¼ lb.).
2 sticks celery, or ¼ teaspoonful celery seeds.
1 oz. butter or dripping.
Slice of bread.

1 pint second white or vegetable stock, meat boilings or water.
½ oz. flour } liaison.
1 gill milk
Pepper and salt.

1. Clean, prepare, and slice vegetables thinly, keeping sliced potatoes in water unless used at once, then dry well in a clean cloth. 2. Heat fat in a white-lined pan, sauté vegetables in it for five minutes without colouring, shaking pan occasionally to prevent sticking. 3. Add liquid, bring to boiling point, simmer till vegetables are tender, for 1 to 1½ hours, stir occasionally—a thick liquid burns readily. 4. Rub through a nylon sieve ; if sieve not available press out lumps against side of pan or rub through a colander. 5. Mix sieved portion and liquid smoothly together, and reheat in *rinsed* pan. 6. Blend flour smoothly with milk, add to soup, and boil for five minutes, stirring all the time. 7. Season and dish very hot ; serve with dice of toasted bread or fried dice of bread—bread served separately.

The use of good white stock and cream gives a rich potato *purée*.

Artichoke Purée. Use same method and proportions as for potato *purée*, but double amount of flour to thicken, as artichokes contain less starch than potatoes. This vegetable discolours very easily : wash and brush very thoroughly ; as they are peeled, throw into cold water to which a few drops of lemon juice have been added ; also, when slicing, keep in slightly acid water until required ; dry well in a cloth before sautéing.

Tomato Soup.

1 lb. tomatoes, or 1 pint canned tomatoes.
1 pint white stock or water.
1 oz. lean ham or small ham-bone.
1 carrot
1 onion } about 4 oz.
Celery
1 shallot.

½ oz. butter.
Small *bouquet garni*.
Salt, pepper, nutmeg.
¼ oz. cornflour } for binding.
½ gill milk
Sugar, if necessary.
Dice of toasted or fried bread.

1. Chop ham, slice vegetables and tomatoes, heat butter, and sauté these in it for fifteen minutes. 2. Add herbs, stock, and salt. 3. Simmer till tender, about 1 to 1½ hours, skimming occasionally, then rub through nylon sieve. 4. Mix cornflour with water or stock, add to soup, and boil for five minutes. Tapioca may be used instead of flour ; add to soup and boil till transparent, then add milk at the last. Boiling tends to alter flavour of milk and cream, and acid ingredients of soup cause them to curdle. 5. Season with pepper and grated nutmeg, a little sugar if necessary to counteract acidity, and serve with dice of toasted or fried bread.

Green Pea Soup.

¾ pint shelled peas.
1 handful pea-pods.
½ pint milk.
1 oz. flour.
6 spinach leaves.
1½ pints second white stock.

1 small onion.
3 or 4 sprigs of mint.
Small bunch of parsley.
1 teaspoonful castor sugar.
Pepper, salt.
2 tablespoonfuls cream (optional).

1. Rinse shelled peas in cold water. Tie one-third of the quantity loosely in a muslin bag, wash spinach (used to improve colour of soup), mint, and pea-pods. 2. Put stock in white-lined pan ; when boiling add salt and pea-pods and all the vegetables except peas in bag, and boil gently for 1 hour or till peas are quite soft ; cook peas in bag in soup till just tender ; then remove to use as garnish. 3. Rub soup through a nylon sieve. 4. Return to rinsed pan, mix flour with milk, add to boiling soup, cook for five minutes, stirring the whole time. 5. Lastly, add the garnish of peas, sugar, and additional seasoning, if required ; just before serving stir in the cream ; serve with fried or toasted dice of bread.

Kidney Soup.

½ lb. ox kidney, or	2 cloves.
4 sheep's kidneys.	1 bay leaf.
1 oz. dripping.	4 peppercorns.
1 onion (browned if necessary).	1 quart stock.
1 carrot, sliced.	Salt.
¼ turnip, ,,	1½ oz. cornflour.

1. Remove skin and core from kidney, wash and soak it for a short time. Dry and cut it into dice. 2. Fry quickly in the fat.

FIG. II. SIEVING SOUP

3. Add the stock, salt, vegetables and flavouring, tied in muslin; bring to boiling point and simmer for 2 hours. 4. Strain, remove vegetables. 5. Blend cornflour with water or stock, stir into soup, bring to boiling point and cook for 5 minutes. 6. Correct seasoning and consistency if necessary. 7. Add diced kidney, reheat and serve.

NOTE. Sheep's kidney cooks more quickly than ox kidney.

A soup made with sheep's or calves' liver substituted for kidney is excellent if well seasoned and flavoured.

To Sieve Soup or any Other Mixture. Use two spoons for sieving; stand the sieve with the narrow rim uppermost inside a basin. Pour a little of the soup or mixture on to the sieve and rub it through with the back of a spoon; if necessary, moisten the mixture with some of the liquid and with a clean spoon remove what is on the under side of the sieve. Mix the sieved and liquid portions well together before reheating the soup.

THICKENED SOUPS

To this class belong a large number of economical household and more expensive soups, brown and white, including those of the rich " cream " type. This class is also termed *potages liés* on account of the various *liaisons* used for thickening and binding purposes, such being—

(*a*) Some cereal in grain or granular form, such as rice or tapioca, added at the commencement, the starch thickening the liquid as the cooking proceeds, e.g. tapioca soup.

(*b*) Flour or cornflour mixed with a little liquid and added to soup shortly before dishing, e.g. white vegetable soup.

(*c*) Roux, brown or white, added before or after the ingredients are cooked in the liquid, e.g. oxtail, Hollandaise, and fish soups.

(*d*) *Liaison* of egg yolk mixed with cream or milk in addition to a thickening of some farinaceous matter—this, added just at the last, thickens slightly and enriches soup as to flavour and food value, e.g. tapioca soup.

Fish Soup. A fish soup is nutritious, very palatable if carefully flavoured and seasoned. It is also economical, for any cheap *white* fish is suitable, and every part, flesh, skin, and bone, can be utilized. Bones and trimmings alone, or a cod's head, make excellent fish stock—only oily fish is not suitable.

Proportions.

1½ lb. white fish—cod, hake, haddock, etc.	Pepper and salt.
1½ pints cold water.	1½ oz. flour | thickening.
1 small onion.	1 oz. butter |
1 small carrot.	1 gill milk.
Small bunch of herbs.	1 teaspoonful chopped parsley.
1 clove.	¼ teaspoonful lemon juice.

1. Scale fish if necessary, clean, remove eyes and viscera, wash thoroughly and cut into small pieces. 2. Put fish in a white-lined pan, cover with cold water, add salt, bring to boiling point, skim, simmer for 10 to 15 minutes, then remove a few neat pieces of fish to be served as garnish in soup later. 3. Slice the vegetables, add these and bunch of herbs, simmer for 1 hour. 4. Strain off the liquid, rub a quarter of the solid ingredients (being careful to remove bones) through a nylon sieve, add fish stock. Rinse pan, melt butter in it, add flour, mix smoothly, draw pan aside, pour liquid on to it, and stir until it boils; add chopped parsley and pieces of fish, and cook for 5 minutes; lastly add lemon juice, seasoning and milk, and serve very hot.

1 tablespoonful finely shredded carrot, cooked in boiling salted water and added just before serving, is a suitable additional garnish.

For an invalid. Use good fish stock only, thicken with sago, crushed tapioca or semolina, and enrich with one or two yolks of eggs or a little cream.

Mulligatawny Soup.

1 lb. scrag-end neck of mutton.	1½ oz. flour.
1 qt. second or household stock.	½ oz. curry powder.
1 small apple or stick of rhubarb.	1 teaspoonful curry paste.
Carrot ⎫	Salt.
Turnip ⎬ 4–6 oz.	1 teaspoonful lemon juice.
Onion ⎭	2–3 oz. Patna rice.
1 oz. dripping.	

1. Wipe meat, remove bones, and cut meat into small neat pieces, slice vegetables, and chop apple or rhubarb. 2. Melt fat and fry vegetables lightly, add curry powder to vegetables and fry slowly for 30 minutes, then add flour, meat, bones, curry paste and liquid, mixing well. 3. Bring to boiling point, skim, simmer slowly 2 to 2½ hours, skimming occasionally. 4. Strain through a fine wire sieve, reserving a few of the best pieces of meat to serve in soup, and rub the remainder through. 5. Reheat, add more salt if necessary, and lemon juice ; serve with rice carefully boiled and dried (see How to Boil Rice, page 115).

NOTE. Beef and tinned mutton are frequently used. Rabbit must be thoroughly washed and soaked for 30 minutes in cold water, then dried and cut into neat joints. Scraps of meat, game, poultry, and bones, cooked and uncooked, make excellent foundation for an economical mulligatawny soup.

Oxtail Soup.

One oxtail, medium size.	1 small onion.
2 qts. second stock.	*Bouquet garni.*
2 oz. dripping.	2 cloves.
2 oz. flour.	Blade of mace.
2 sticks celery or celery seeds.	Salt.
Carrot ⎫	20 peppercorns.
Turnip ⎬ 1 oz.	Garnish of small rounds or dice
	of cooked carrot and turnips.

1. Wash the tail, cut into joints, dividing the larger ones into two, remove superfluous fat, put into a pan, cover with cold water, bring to boiling point (blanching to cleanse), pour off water and dry the pieces. 2. Coat these with half the flour (1 oz.), melt half (1 oz.) the dripping in a pan, and when this is quite hot add pieces of oxtail and brown. 3. Add stock, bring to boiling point, skim thoroughly ; then add the vegetables cut into large pieces, herbs, spices, and salt ; simmer for 3 to 4 hours, skimming occasionally. 4. Strain soup through a nylon sieve, reserving some small joints for garnish. Remove every trace of fat from surface of stock (it is better to leave it to get cold, and if possible to make the day before using). 5. With the remainder of flour and dripping make a brown roux, add the

strained stock, bring to boiling point, season to taste, add the pieces of tail and simmer for a few minutes.   6. Just before dishing add the garnish of carrot and turnip previously cooked in boiling salted water, and wine if desired (1 tablespoonful sherry to 1 qt. soup).

White Vegetable Soup.

1¼ pints white stock or meat liquor.	Leek.
Onion.	Bunch of herbs.
Celery.	1 oz. butter.
Carrot.	1½ oz. flour.
Turnip.	¼ pt. milk.

1. Cut vegetables into thin strips about 1½ in. in length (half a pint when cut). 2. Melt butter and sauté vegetables in it. 3. Add liquid, herbs, and salt, simmer vegetables until tender, about ½ hour, and strain off vegetables. 4. Mix flour with milk, add to soup, and boil for five minutes. 5. Return vegetables to soup, season, and serve.

CREAM SOUPS

Tapioca Soup.

1 pint good white stock.	2 yolks of eggs.
½ oz. crushed tapioca.	½ gill cream. } *Liaison.*
Pepper, salt.	½ gill milk.

Put stock in white-lined pan, bring to boiling point, sprinkle in tapioca, simmer for 15 minutes until tapioca is quite transparent. 2. Mix yolks of eggs with cream and milk, strain into soup, which must be well below boiling point (or the liquid will curdle) ; or pour hot soup gently and slowly on to the *liaison*. 3. Reheat, but do not reboil, until the egg thickens and tapioca is suspended—great care is necessary to prevent curdling. 4. Season and serve.

Hollandaise Soup.

1 pint good white stock.	½ gill cream.
2 yolks of eggs.	1 tablespoonful green peas.
½ oz. flour.	1 tablespoonful cucumber.
½ oz. butter.	1 tablespoonful carrot.
¼ gill milk.	Pepper and salt.
1 teaspoonful chopped tarragon.	

1. Cut carrot and cucumber to the shape and size of the peas and cook them with the peas in boiling salted water. 2. Make a roux with the butter and flour. 3. Add the stock which should be strained and free from fat and boil for 10 minutes. 4. Cool slightly and then strain in the *liaison* (the yolks mixed with the cream and milk), and stir over a moderate heat until the soup thickens; do not let it boil. 5. Season, add the cooked vegetables, and serve in a hot tureen.

BISQUES

These are thickened soups made with shellfish.

Lobster Bisque.

1 lobster, medium size or	½ teaspoonful anchovy **essence**.
2 whiting.	Pepper, salt.
2 pints white or fish stock.	Lemon juice.
Carrot ⎱ 4 oz.	2 oz. butter.
Onion ⎰	2 oz. flour.
Bunch of herbs.	2 tablespoonfuls **cream**.

1. Remove meat from lobster, cut that of claws into neat pieces and reserve for garnish ; wash shell (about ½ lb.) thoroughly, and pound with the butter and remainder of the lobster. 2. Place this in white-lined pan, allow butter to melt before adding flour, fry slightly ; add stock, vegetables, and herbs, bring to boiling point, skim and simmer for ¾ to 1 hour. 3. Strain through a nylon sieve and return to the rinsed saucepan, bring to boiling point and skim. 4. Add the lobster meat, seasoning, few drops of lemon juice and anchovy essence, lastly the cream.

It is an economy to substitute whiting for the lobster meat, which can be used for another dish, e.g. lobster patties, cutlets, etc.

Soups which may be either Thick or Clear.   Certain thick soups, e.g. mulligatawny, ox-tail, tomato, or mock turtle, are often cleared. To prepare them, make a stock with the ingredients given for the particular soup, but be careful to omit any starchy ingredient, and not to brown either meat or vegetables. When the stock is cold, free from fat, strain, and follow directions given for clearing stock for making consommé.

CHAPTER 10

SAUCE-MAKING—FORCEMEATS—FLAVOURING BUTTERS

This is a most important item in cookery, simple or elaborate, for a dish to which sauce is an accompaniment is generally improved by this adjunct, the real success of a dish being not infrequently determined by its sauce. Its use is to supply additional richness or piquancy of flavour, sometimes to add actual nutriment to a dish by its food value, and also to counteract the richness of some food, e.g. apple sauce with roast pork, etc. Judicious seasoning and careful blending of its ingredients are essentials to a well-made sauce, which should be characterized by its own distinctive flavour and suitable to the dish it accompanies. Its addition to certain somewhat insipid and flavourless foods is to develop or to impart some fresh flavour, e.g. caper sauce with boiled mutton or parsley sauce with boiled cod. On the other hand, some meats, game, and poultry have strong characteristic flavours, which would be overpowered by a sauce over-seasoned or too strong in flavour.

A sauce is really a seasoning in some liquid form, thickened, as soups are, by the addition of some ingredients termed *liaisons*, those generally used being (*a*) roux, (*b*) eggs, (*c*) butter and cream, (*d*) farinaceous products. Of the hundreds of sauces used, a large proportion are more or less variations or elaborations and derivatives of certain types which may be classified thus.

CLASSES OF SAUCES

I. Those made with *roux*, including the foundation sauces, white and brown, of plain household and advanced cookery, with their derivatives.

Household.	Advanced.
White.	Béchamel ⎫
Brown.	Velouté ⎬ white.
	Allemande ⎭
	Espagnole brown.

II. Cooked Egg Sauces

(*a*) Custard type.
(*b*) Whipped egg.

III. Cold Sauces.

(*a*) Mayonnaise and derivatives—chief ingredients oil and egg.
(*b*) Chaudfroid—foundation of white or brown sauce with addition of aspic jelly—used for coating meats, etc.
(*c*) Some unclassified—ingredients, vinegar and others, e.g. horse-radish, mint, and simple salad dressings.

IV. Nondescript Sauces.

(a) Of *purée* type : tomato, bread, apple, and cranberry sauces.

(b) Fruit, syrup or jam sauces, made with fruit juice, fresh or tinned, boiled with sugar and thickened ; golden syrup, jam or marmalade diluted with water and boiled—lemon juice added.

(c) Made of milk or water only, simply thickened with flour, cornflour, or arrowroot, enriched often by addition of lump of butter just before serving.

The first group thickened with roux is of particular importance ; to it belong the foundation sauces, white and brown, of simple and more elaborate cookery, various additions giving a distinctive flavour and name to the sauce.

These additions may be incorporated in three ways—

(a) By simmering the flavouring ingredients in the sauce itself, e.g. ham, etc., in tomato sauce.

(b) With or without subsequent recooking, these being quite simple ingredients, e.g. yolk of egg, cream, capers, lemon juice.

(c) By cooking ingredients in wine, butter or vinegar to extract their flavour.

A thorough knowledge of how to make the simple white and brown sauces is the basis of all sauce making, the true secret of success being almost continuous attention until the sauce is finished.

PLAIN WHITE SAUCE

The Ingredients : butter, flour, and liquid suitable for food with which sauce is served. For savoury sauces, meat, fish or vegetable stock and milk ; for meat, half milk and half meat liquor ; for fish, half fish stock and half milk can be used. For sweet sauces, milk or water.

Essential qualities in a white sauce are : good colour, smoothness, and correct consistency

The roux consists of equal quantities of flour and butter, the proportion to liquid varying with purpose for which sauce is intended, viz. : (a) for coating, (b) for pouring round a dish or serving separately, (c) as a binding medium or panada.

Coating.	Flowing.	Panada.
1 oz. flour.	$\frac{3}{4}$ oz. flour.	2 oz. flour.
1 oz. butter.	$\frac{3}{4}$ oz. butter.	2 oz. fat.
$\frac{1}{2}$ pt. liquid.	$\frac{1}{2}$ pt. liquid.	$\frac{1}{2}$ pt. liquid.

Method. 1. Melt butter in a white-lined pan, draw aside, mix in flour smoothly with a wooden spoon and stir over gentle heat for 3 to 4 minutes without allowing roux to colour ; this is the preliminary step in cooking the flour, heat and moisture causing capsules enclosing starch to swell. 2. Draw pan aside again to cool roux slightly, add liquid gradually (particularly at first), mixing it in with the roux very smoothly. 3. Return pan to heat bring sauce to boiling point, stirring the whole time, continue to stir, and boil for at least 7 minutes to ensure thorough cooking of flour, otherwise sauce does not thicken properly and is not of the correct consistency, is raw in flavour, and lacks glossiness. 4. Season, and if too thick dilute with a little liquid, either milk or stock, and bring up to boiling point again, stirring the whole time.

Should the sauce be too thin, reduce by boiling rapidly, stirring continuously ; at this stage it is very apt to burn.

Lumps are the result of addition of flour to hot fat and of liquid to roux without allowing fat and roux to cool slightly by removal of pan from heat ; they also arise from failure to mix roux smoothly with milk and to stir continuously during process of blending roux and of making sauce.

If allowed to stand for a time over a moderate heat, a sauce made with roux will become thin, due to chemical change (dextrinization) in the flour.

A skin forms rapidly on a thick sauce if left to stand, due to evaporation from the surface : covering closely with a paper dipped in cold water, the wet surface being in immediate contact with the sauce, tends to prevent this ; then cover with saucepan lid.

To reheat a cold sauce, apply heat gently ; stir or whisk vigorously to prevent lumps from forming.

Additions to a White Sauce.

1. At commencement of cooking—

(a) Solid ingredients for flavouring only and not as a garnish, e.g. vegetables in Béchamel sauce.

(b) Ingredients to flavour milk when used as liquid for sauce must be boiled in the milk to extract flavour, e.g. lemon rind, vanilla pod, bay leaf, etc.

2. Immediately before serving without *reboiling* sauce. Butter, cream, eggs, sugar, essences, mild acids.

(a) *Butter.* About 1 oz. to ½ pt. sauce to enrich it : divide into small pieces, whisking or stirring in each separately and thoroughly, otherwise butter separates and floats on the surface, and sauce is oily in appearance—reboiling sauce after addition of butter has the same effect.

(b) *Cream.* Add gradually, stirring in carefully—boiling causes curdling and alters flavour of cream.

(c) *Eggs*, whole or yolks only. Heat of sauce well below boiling point is sufficient to cook the egg—reboiling of sauce causes curdling.

(d) *Essences* are volatile ; they easily evaporate if sauce reboils.

(e) *Minor acids* such as lemon juice, added drop by drop and only in small quantity to avoid curdling of sauce.

(f) Sugar burns readily ; therefore added to a sweet white sauce just before dishing.

3. Cold ingredients either already cooked or only requiring slight cooking, such as shrimps, lobster, capers, parsley.   Heat these in sauce for 5 to 10 minutes just before serving to reheat and to extract flavour.

Some Variations of the Standard Plain White Sauce. To *half a pint* of white sauce made (a) for meat with half milk and half meat stock or entirely of milk, (b) for fish, with half fish stock and half milk or entirely of milk, add the following ingredients and season to taste.

Parsley Sauce. 1 dessertspoonful finely chopped parsley, cook in sauce for 5 minutes just before dishing—a longer time causes it to turn brown.

Caper Sauce. 1 tablespoonful chopped capers. 1 teaspoonful caper vinegar. Cook capers in sauce for a few minutes, add vinegar at the last.

Egg Sauce. 1 hard boiled egg finely chopped—add to sauce to reheat egg.

Anchovy Sauce. 1 dessertspoonful anchovy essence and few drops of lemon juice added at the last.

Shrimp Sauce. Half a gill of picked shrimps and a few drops of anchovy essence. Cook shrimps in sauce for 5 to 10 minutes.

Mustard Sauce (with herrings and mackerel).   1 teaspoonful made mustard, 1 dessertspoonful vinegar. Add mustard to sauce, cook for 5 minutes, then add vinegar and cook a couple of minutes longer.

Cheese Sauce. 2 tablespoonfuls finely grated Parmesan or dry Cheddar. 1 oz. butter. Add cheese gradually just before serving, lastly butter in small pieces.

Brain Sauce (with sheep or calf's head). Brains of a calf or sheep. Blanch, remove the skin, cook gently in stock or water for 25 to 30 minutes, chop, and add to sauce.

Dutch Sauce (with fish). 1 raw yolk of egg or 1 whole egg, a few drops of lemon juice. Add to sauce just before serving.

Onion Sauce. ½ lb. onions. Blanch, then boil till tender, drain well, chop, add and cook for 2 or 3 minutes.

Fennel Sauce. 2 tablespoonfuls of chopped fennel. Wash the fennel well, remove stalks, cook in boiling water till tender ; drain, chop finely, and add to white sauce.

PLAIN BROWN SAUCE

The foundation is roux, the method for making the sauce being similar to that for a white sauce, except that the roux is cooked until it is light chestnut brown in colour. Although quite simple, the plain brown sauce requires particular and constant attention, otherwise it can be most unpalatable, either pale, greasy, and insipid, or very dark with a burnt, unpleasant flavour. Greasiness is a very common fault caused by (a) over-cooking of roux and separation of fat, (b) cooking at too high a temperature after the liquid is added (simmering is necessary to extract the flavour of the vegetables), which results in the flour yielding up some of the butter already absorbed, for which reason *skimming* of a brown sauce is very necessary. A brown sauce, after it is cooked, if left exposed to a low degree of heat will show a tendency to become " oily."

Uneven browning of flour gives sauce a speckled appearance.

Points Essential to Success.

(a) Sufficient and uniform browning of vegetables and roux.

(b) Thorough cooking, but not over-cooking, to extract full flavour and to cook flour.

(c) Freedom from greasiness.

Proportions—

¾ oz. flour
¼ oz. dripping } roux.
Carrot, turnip, onion.

½ pint second stock.
Pepper, salt.

Method. 1. Slice thinly carrot, turnip, and onion. 2. Heat dripping, add carrot and turnip, and fry until they shrivel; add sliced onion (this burns more readily than the other vegetables) and fry slightly; stir in the flour and fry all slowly over a low heat, stirring frequently until the roux is a good brown colour. 3. Draw the saucepan away from heat, add the stock and salt, mixing liquid smoothly with the roux. 4. Bring to boiling point, skim and boil for 30 minutes, stirring occasionally and skimming. 5. Just before dishing, skim thoroughly, season to taste, strain, and reheat for use.

Thin down with stock, or reduce before using if it is required.

Four Foundation Sauces of More Advanced Cookery

Sauce.	*Liaison* (roux).	Liquid.	Flavourings and Additions.
Béchamel	2 oz. butter 1½ oz. flour	1 pt. milk	1 shallot, 12 peppercorns, blade of mace, ½ bay leaf, bunch of herbs ; ¼ gill cream.

Method. Put vegetables and herbs in the milk, bring slowly to boiling point, cover pan and stand it aside for 10 to 15 minutes to extract flavour of vegetables ; strain off milk. Make the roux and proceed as for ordinary white sauce, boil for 10 minutes, season, strain or tammy,[1] reheat, and add cream.

Sauce.	*Liaison* (roux).	Liquid.	Flavourings and Additions.
Velouté	2 oz. butter 1½ oz. flour	1 pt. white stock (veal)	6–8 button mushrooms, 12 peppercorns, lemon juice, ¼ gill cream, piece of parsley, pinch of nutmeg.

[1] See Tammying on page 67.

Method.   Make white sauce with roux and stock ; when boiling add parsley, chopped mushrooms and peppercorns, simmer gently for 20 minutes, stirring and skimming frequently. Strain or tammy and reheat; add seasoning, pinch of nutmeg, cream, and lemon juice.

Sauce.	*Liaison* (roux).	Liquid.	Flavourings and Additions.
Allemande	1 oz. butter 1 oz. flour	½ pt. white stock (chicken)	1–2 yolks of eggs, ¼ oz. butter, 1 tablespoonful cream, nutmeg, lemon juice, pepper and salt.

Method.   Make white sauce with roux and stock, add pepper and salt and pinch of nutmeg, and let it simmer for 20 minutes, mix yolks of eggs with cream, add this *liaison* to soup, also butter in small pieces gradually, stir until sauce thickens ; *it must not boil.* Add lemon juice, strain or tammy, and reheat.

Sauce.	*Liaison* (roux).	Liquid.	Flavourings and Additions.
Espagnole	2 oz. butter 2 oz. flour	1 pt. good brown stock	2 oz. ham ⎫ Characteristic ½ gill sherry ⎬ flavourings. 2 tomatoes ⎭ 1 shallot, 1 small onion, bunch of herbs, small carrot, 6–8 button mushrooms.

Method.   1. Chop ham and vegetables, sauté ham in butter, add vegetables and fry slightly, add flour and brown the roux slowly until of a good brown colour. 2. Add stock and mushrooms, bring to boiling point, and skim. 3. Simmer for 30 minutes, skimming frequently ; add tomatoes and sherry, simmer for 10 minutes, skim, strain or tammy, season, and reheat.

These four sauces are not only the principal ones used in this class of cookery, but are also the basis of a very large variety of compound and more elaborate sauces, the latter being characterized by supplementary ingredients and flavourings.

Of the three white sauces, Allemande, made with chicken stock, is the richest and most expensive; Béchamel the cheapest, is more generally used, and is the basis of Chaudfroid and other sauces; Espagnole is the foundation of many rich brown sauces for meat, poultry, game, and fish.

Tammying.   It is necessary to strain all sauces in which solid ingredients are simmered in the liquid for the extraction of their flavour, but the smoothness and gloss of the sauce are much greater if it is "tammied." For this, a tammy cloth is required. There are two methods of tammying a sauce: (*a*) pour it into the middle of the cloth, which should be scalded with boiling water to prevent the sauce from spurting out; fold over the selvedge edges, twist the ends tightly, and squeeze the sauce through by wringing the cloth, as in Fig. 12—two persons can do this more conveniently than one; (*b*)

FIG. 12. TO " TAMMY " A SAUCE BY WRINGING THE CLOTH

rub the sauce through the cloth. The sauce is then reheated, and if cream is to be added this addition is after tammying.

NOTE. Because of lack of help in the domestic kitchen, it is doubtful if two pairs of hands are available to tammy sauces.

EXAMPLES OF ELABORATIONS OF FOUNDATION SAUCES

Béarnaise Sauce.

1 gill white sauce (Béchamel).
½ gill mixed vinegars (tarragon
    and malt).
1 shallot.

6 peppercorns.
yolks of 2 eggs.
½ oz. butter.

1. Chop shallot, crush peppercorns, add to vinegar, boil till reduced to a quarter. 2. Mix in white sauce carefully, add yolks one at a time, with the pan off the fire. 3. Whisk in the butter in small pieces, melting each piece before adding the next; strain or tammy, and use.

Demi-glacé Sauce.

½ pint Espagnole sauce.
1 gill good strong gravy
        or
2 tablespoonfuls liquid meat glaze.

1 dessertspoonful sherry.

1. Strain gravy free from sediment and fat, add to sauce with sherry, simmer for 15 minutes, season. 2. Strain or tammy.

COOKED EGG SAUCES

Success in making this type of sauce, whether a plain custard or one more elaborate, depends upon heating the egg just, and only just, up to the point of thickening (coagulation of egg protein) without curdling. When curdling occurs, the protein hardens, shrinks, and separates from the liquid into flocculent masses. Custard thickens upon cooling, therefore heat a simple custard sauce until it coats the spoon thinly. A whipped egg sauce must be whisked until "frothy"; the whisking entangles air in the egg protein as it coagulates, and this gives the frothy or foam-like appearance. If insufficiently heated to cook the egg, the latter separates quickly from the liquid on standing.

Custard Sauce.

½ pint milk.	1 dessertspoonful sugar (castor).
1 or more eggs.	Flavouring.

For method see CUSTARDS.

A substitute for custard sauce that is easier to make is one made with cornflour to which a yolk of egg is added just before serving (see CORNFLOUR SAUCE).

Whipped Egg Sauce.

1 gill sherry.	2 yolks of eggs.
1 dessertspoonful castor sugar.	Strip of lemon rind.

1. Whisk ingredients in a small white-lined pan until the liquid is thick and frothy. Over-heating will cause it to curdle. 2. Remove lemon rind and serve at once.

Fruit syrup may be substituted for wine.

Hollandaise Sauce.

2 yolks of eggs.	2 tablespoonfuls wine vinegar
2 oz. butter.	or lemon juice.
Pepper, salt.	Cayenne.
2 tablespoonfuls water.	

1. Boil water and lemon juice or wine vinegar until reduced to half, allow the liquid to cool, then add yolks separately. 2. Stir until sauce begins to thicken; whisk in the butter slowly in small pieces, season, and dish. The sauce must not boil after addition of yolks.

COLD SAUCES

Mayonnaise Sauce, the chief ingredients of which are oil and yolk of egg, flavoured and seasoned, is the basis of others of a similar type, which are distinguished by ingredients and flavourings additional to the foundation of mayonnaise. This sauce, the popular dressing for salads, is also largely used in the preparation of many cold dishes, for coating or for serving as an adjunct, or for blending with the ingredients of these dishes.

The *essential to success* is the thorough mixing of the oil with the egg yolk, the texture of a well-made mayonnaise being smooth and glossy and its consistency that of thick cream. In the process of mixing (with a wooden spoon for a small quantity, with a whisk or mayonnaise mixer for larger), the oil is split up into infinitesimally minute globules and, by its gradual addition to the yolk, these ingredients become evenly and thoroughly incorporated one with the other.   As large a quantity as *half a pint* of *oil* can be blended with *one* yolk, but the usual proportion is 1 to 1½ gills.

Proportions.

1 gill best olive oil.	1 teaspoonful good malt or white vinegar.
1 egg yolk.	1 teaspoonful tarragon vinegar.
½ teaspoonful made mustard.	Pepper and salt to taste.

1. Separate yolk carefully from white, add a saltspoonful of salt and half the quantity of pepper.   2. Add oil very gradually, the first tablespoonful drop by drop, stirring constantly, the remainder more rapidly if there is no sign of oil separating from the yolk, lastly the mustard and vinegar and additional seasoning, if necessary.

To keep the oil and egg yolks cool during the mixing process, which is very important, dip a cloth into cold water and wrap it round the basin, this also steadies it.

Mayonnaise sauce must not be too acid in flavour. A crude cheap vinegar should not be used—lemon juice is often substituted for vinegar. If sauce becomes too thick during mixing, add a few drops of cold water from time to time.

Causes of separation of oil from yolk (curdling)—

(*a*) Use of inferior ingredients—oil of poor quality, or egg not perfectly fresh, either of which will also spoil flavour of sauce.

(*b*) Careless separation of yolk from white ; presence of latter conducive to curdling.

(*c*) Omission to mix seasoning with yolk before addition of oil.

(*d*) Too rapid blending of oil with yolk, and allowing ingredients or mixing bowl to become warm.

To counteract curdling, put 2 teaspoonfuls of cold water into a basin, and whisk in curdled mixture gradually ; if this is not effective, add it *drop by drop* to another yolk. The first indication of curdling is the thin appearance of the sauce. The rapid separation of oil from yolk follows.

Varieties of Mayonnaise. By addition of gherkins, capers, herbs, aspic jelly, etc.

Tartare Sauce.

1 gill mayonnaise.
1 dessertspoonful chopped
    gherkins or
    capers.

½ teaspoonful chopped
    parsley.
½ teaspoonful chopped
    tarragon.

Add these ingredients to mayonnaise and mix thoroughly.

Aspic Mayonnaise.

1 gill stiff mayonnaise.   ½ pint aspic jelly.

Dissolve jelly ; when cool, mix in very gradually with mayonnaise, and use before it begins to set.

Mint Sauce.

3 tablespoonfuls chopped mint.
1 tablespoonful castor sugar.

2 tablespoonfuls water.
1 gill vinegar.

Wash and dry mint, remove leaves from stalks and chop very finely. Heat vinegar with water and dissolve sugar in it. Pour hot liquid over mint and let it stand for a couple of hours to extract flavour.

Horse-radish Sauce.

1½ oz. finely grated horse-radish.
1 gill cream.
1 tablespoonful white vinegar.

1 teaspoonful castor sugar.
½ teaspoonful made mustard.
Salt, cayenne.

Whisk cream slightly and stir other ingredients of sauce lightly into cream.

Chaudfroid Sauce.

Used for coating entrées of fish, meat, poultry, and game. A foundation sauce, Béchamel or Velouté (white) or Espagnole (brown) is the basis. To this the addition of aspic jelly, in the proportion of one part of the latter to two parts of the former, with a small quantity of gelatine, enables the sauce to set, and also imparts to it a high gloss, that and great smoothness of texture being characteristics of a well-made sauce of this type.

White Chaudfroid.

½ pt. Béchamel or good
    white sauce.
1 gill stiff aspic jelly.
½ gill cream.

Few drops of tarragon
    vinegar or lemon juice,
    if liked.

1. Warm aspic jelly and the sauce. 2. Allow both to cool slightly ; then mix gradually and carefully together. 3. Strain or tammy, add cream and few drops of lemon juice or tarragon vinegar, and stir

gently until on point of setting, then use at once (see CHAUDFROID OF CHICKEN).

Varieties of Chaudfroid Sauces.

The proportions of ingredients and method same as for white Chaudfroid.

Brown	Foundation	of	Espagnole sauce.
Fawn	„	„	White and brown sauce in equal quantities.
Red	„	„	Tomato sauce.
Green	„	„	White sauce—green herb colouring.

NONDESCRIPT OR UNCLASSIFIED SAUCES

Purée Type.

1. Tomato Sauce.

½ lb. tomatoes (fresh or canned). 1 small carrot.
½ pt. white stock. Small bunch of herbs.
½ oz. butter. 8 peppercorns.
½ oz. lean ham. ¼ to ½ oz. cornflour.
1 small onion or shallot. Pepper, salt.

1. Chop shallot, onion, and ham, slice carrot and tomatoes. 2. Melt butter in white-lined pan, *sauté* ham, tomatoes, carrot and onion, add bunch of herbs, peppercorns, and stock. 3. Simmer for 30 minutes, skim, rub through a nylon sieve. Reheat sauce, mix cornflour with a little water, and add to sauce. 4. Boil for five minutes, season.

2. Apple Sauce.

1 lb. cooking apples. ½ oz. butter.
Sugar to taste (about 2 oz.). ¼ gill water or sufficient
Peel of ¼ lemon or 2 cloves. to cook apples to a pulp.

1. Peel, core, and slice apples, put in pan with water, sugar and lemon rind or cloves, cook to a pulp. 2. Remove flavouring, add butter, rub through a nylon sieve or mash with a spoon until smooth—reheat.

To ensure sauce being a good colour, use apples as soon as peeled, or leave in water until required ; peel with a stainless steel or silver knife, and use wooden spoon and white-lined pan.

3. Bread Sauce.

2 oz. bread-crumbs. 6 peppercorns.
1 small onion. 1 oz. butter or 1 table-
2 cloves. spoonful cream.
½ pint milk. Pepper salt.

1. Rinse a white-lined pan with cold water, put in peppercorns and onion stock with cloves, add milk, bring slowly to boiling point. 2. Simmer for 10 minutes to flavour milk. 3. Remove

onion, cloves, and peppercorns, stir in the bread-crumbs and leave sauce in a cool place on stove for 15 minutes for crumbs to *absorb* milk. 4. Bring just up to boiling point, season, stir in butter or cream, and serve.

Bread sauce must have the consistency of thick cream, neither stiff nor thin.

Syrup Sauce.

2 tablespoonfuls treacle or syrup.   1 gill **water.**
1 dessertspoonful lemon juice.

Boil syrup water and lemon juice for 5 minutes, strain and use.

Jam and Marmalade Sauces.

2 tablespoonfuls jam or marmalade.	Few drops of lemon juice for jam sauces and cochineal
1½ oz. sugar.	to improve colour when red
1 gill water.	jam is used.

Boil water and sugar for 3 or 4 minutes, stir in jam or marmalade, bring to boiling point and boil until light, syrupy consistency; add lemon juice, and strain if jam is used.

Lemon Sauce.

Juice of 1 lemon.	¼ oz. arrowroot.
Rind of ½ lemon.	Water.
1 oz. loaf sugar.	

1. Wipe lemon, rub on to lumps of sugar, strain the juice and make up with cold water to ½ pint liquid. 2. Mix the arrowroot with a little of this and add the rest. 3. Put this in a white-lined pan with the sugar, bring to boiling point and cook for 5 minutes.

Cornflour or Arrowroot Sauce.

½ pint milk.	Strip of lemon rind.
1 dessertspoonful castor sugar.	1 teaspoonful cornflour.

Mix cornflour with some milk, heat remainder with lemon rind. Stir on to cornflour, boil for 5 minutes, remove lemon rind and add sugar.

Melted Butter.

1 oz. butter.	½ pint **water.**
¼ oz. flour.	Salt.

Prepare as for ordinary white sauce. For a sweet sauce omit salt, add 1 teaspoonful castor sugar and any essence or lemon juice to flavour.

Melted Butter (*Beurre Fondu*).

2 oz. fresh butter.	Salt, **pepper.**
1 teaspoonful lemon juice.	

Melt butter, add lemon juice and seasoning ; avoid over-heating or butter will be " oily." Skim and pour, free from sediment at the bottom, into a hot sauce boat. Served with vegetables.

FORCEMEATS

Sage and Onions.

¼ lb. onions.	1 teaspoonful powdered
2 oz. bread-crumbs.	sage.
1 oz. butter.	Pepper and salt.

1. Blanch onions to extract some of the strong flavour, put into cold water, boil until tender. 2. Strain, chop rather finely, add sage, butter, and bread-crumbs, mix and season well.

Too much sage imparts a very bitter flavour to forcemeat.

Veal Forcemeat.

4 oz. fresh bread-crumbs.	½ teaspoonful mixed sweet herbs.
2 tablespoonfuls chopped suet.	grated rind of ¼ lemon.
or 1½ oz. dripping or butter.	Pepper and salt.
1 dessertspoonful chopped parsley.	Egg or milk to bind.

Mix dry ingredients together, add sufficient egg or milk to bind. Stuffing must be crumbly, not over wet, or it will be sodden and heavy when cooked. Too much egg makes stuffing hard and close.

Chestnut Stuffing.

1 lb. chestnuts.	2 oz. butter.
4 oz. bread-crumbs.	Seasoning.
Milk or stock.	Egg.

1. Wash chestnuts, split skin of each on rounded side, put into cold water, boil for 5 minutes and leave in water while preparing. Remove the outer and inner skins. 2. Simmer in milk or stock until quite tender and liquid is absorbed. 3. Mash or rub through a wire sieve, add butter, crumbs and seasoning, and bind with the egg.

FLAVOURING BUTTERS

These are used as accompaniments to grilled fish, meat, poultry, and game, for sandwiches, and in a variety of ways in simple little savouries. Some are also added to sauces just before dishing to impart the flavour of fresh butter and of the ingredient blended with it.

The foundation—fresh butter—is beaten to a cream, more or less highly seasoned, with the addition of various flavourings, herbs, chutney, essences, and pastes.

Maître d'Hôtel or Parsley Butter.

1 oz. fresh butter.	1 teaspoonful lemon juice.
¼ teaspoonful finely chopped parsley.	Salt, pepper, cayenne.

Beat butter to a cream with a wooden spoon, add the rest of the ingredients, set aside to get firm and form into small pats or shapes —different herbs may be substituted for parsley.

Anchovy Butter.

1 oz. fresh butter.	Anchovy essence or
Seasoning.	4 anchovies.
Lemon juice.	

If using anchovies, wash, dry, and remove skin, pound with the butter and rub through a nylon sieve.

Devilled Butter.

2 oz. fresh butter.	Cayenne.
¼ teaspoonful curry paste.	Lemon juice.
½ teaspoonful chutney.	

Pound all the ingredients together and rub through a nylon sieve.

CHAPTER 11

FISH

FISH, as compared with the same weight of butcher's meat, is on the whole less satisfying, and is not as stimulating; nevertheless it is a most valuable food and also affords variety in the diet, which is an important consideration when planning meals. It is apt, however, to occupy too subsidiary a place in the everyday household fare, even when conditions of purchase are easy, as in towns and large centres, where also the *cheaper* but *equally nourishing* varieties are obtainable.

Composition of Fish. The nutritive constituents of fish are the same as those of meat and, as in meat, the chief are also *protein* and *fat*. According to the relative proportions present, which determine its food value and digestibility, fish, excluding shellfish, can be divided into two principal classes.

1. White-fleshed, or lean, such as whiting, sole, cod, plaice, hake, etc.

2. Oily, or fat, which includes salmon, mackerel, herring, pilchard.

The *fibres* of fish are shorter than meat fibres, they are generally finer and are more easily separated, hence one reason for its more easy digestion, but the texture of the fibres varies with the kind of fish : compare the flesh of the whiting or sole with that of cod or of hake and with the coarse meat in the claw of a crab.

Protein. Fish, like meat, is a source of protein, the amount being very similar to that in lean meat. There is less connective tissue in fish and thus less shrinkage in cooking. In boiling and steaming, soluble constituents are squeezed out and fish cooked by these methods is rather tasteless. In contrast, when fish is baked or fried, water is evaporated from it and flavour is concentrated.

Fat. The food value of fish as a source of energy depends upon the amount of fat present, fat or oily fish being in this respect of about the same value as moderately fat meat. The proportion of fat varies greatly from less than 2 per cent in white fish, whiting, the least fat of all fish, containing only 0·3 per cent, while 18 per cent is present in eels, 12 per cent in salmon, and 8 to 15 per cent in herring. In the oily variety the fat is distributed throughout the body, in white or lean fish it is confined to the liver, for which reason white fish is more readily digested and is more suitable for invalids. Fat fish are good sources of the fat-soluble Vitamins A and D, and they also supply vitamins of the B group. White fish do not contain Vitamins A and D, nor are they usually such good sources of the B group.

Water is present in lean or white fish in a larger proportion than in lean meat ; it is more abundant in white than in oily fish. Owing to the large percentage of water present and to the deficiency in fat, white fish, although more digestible, is of much less nutritive value than the oily variety such as the herring, which is an example of a cheap, but very nutritious, food.

COMPARATIVE AVERAGE COMPOSITION OF MEAT AND OF FISH

	Water.	Protein.	Fat.
Meat (lean beef) . . .	75%	15–18	1·5%
Fish	65–85%	16%	0·3%–18%

Economic Value of Fish. The price, which is regulated by the flavour, caprice of fashion, and rarity, is no proof of its actual food value, for the cheaper and more plentiful variety often supplies about the same amount of nutriment as the rarer and more expensive kind. There are, however, exceptions, e.g. if a given weight of salmon and the same amount of haddock are taken, the nutritive value of the expensive salmon is approximately three times that of the cheaper fish—salmon also goes much farther, being more satisfying.

Comparing the white with the oily variety, the *cheaper kinds* of *oily fish* supply the most nutriment for a given sum of money, and those such as the herring are of great use in a diet, especially when the housekeeping budget is small. Fish nevertheless cannot be considered one of the most economical foods; this is on account of the large percentage of waste matter (the inedible parts, skin and bone) and of the greater loss in cooking by some methods, such as boiling, which is partly due to the greater solubility of the constituents of fish. But both waste and loss of nutriment can be considerably minimized by good judgment in the choice and purchase of fish, and by economical preparation and by careful cooking.

Purchase and Choice. Fish is cheapest and best when in season, and is at its best just before spawning ; during that period, it is poor in flavour, the flesh is of a bluish tinge, watery, and lacks firmness, and the curd-like matter (coagulated protein) which is seen between the flakes of boiled, steamed, and lightly baked fish is absent. Some fish, such as cod, are sold all the year round, but for most there is a close season.

Absolute Freshness. If there is the slightest indication of staleness the fish should not be used. The oily and freshwater varieties spoil rapidly, and should be cooked as soon as possible after they are caught. Whitebait, which is not emptied, and mackerel and shellfish decompose rapidly, but some cartilaginous fish, such as turbot and brill, improve if kept for a day or two, if the storage permits.   Fresh fish has no unpleasant odour, the flesh is firm, and the body is stiff, the gills red, the eyes bright and not sunken, and the scales plentiful; a deficiency of scales denotes that the fish is either stale or is bruised, bruising causes rapid decomposition. Red gills and firmness are, however, not always sure indications of freshness, the former may be artificially produced and the latter may be due to storage on ice or in a refrigerator. The flesh of a fish of moderate size is superior in flavour and finer than that of one which is over large. For this reason, and because there is a relatively less waste, a thick slice from a smaller fish is preferable to a thin cut from a large one. When buying a whole fish choose one which is thick and plump and large in girth in proportion to length. The dark skin of flat fish should not look dry and wrinkled; if plaice is fresh the spots are bright red, a brown or tawny colour denotes staleness.

Cod and Salmon.   Both cod and salmon should have the bronzed appearance of silverside of beef when cut. A thick slice from the middle or the head and shoulders are the best cuts for boiling, the tail is apt to become tasteless and overdone by the time the thick part is cooked.

Turbot is distinguished from brill by the large tubercles of uneven size on the dark skin; the dark skin of brill is smooth and reddish brown with yellow or red spots.

Mackerel is highly dangerous unless absolutely fresh—the underside should be white and pearl-like in appearance.

To Clean Fish.   Fish is usually bought ready cleaned, but there are occasions when it may be found necessary to do this at home.

1. Empty the fish, being careful to avoid tearing or disfiguring the skin. For *flat* fish make a small transverse cut just below the gills on the dark side, withdraw the viscera, and remove the gills. For fish which *swim* with the *back uppermost*, such as haddock or mackerel, make a slit from the head halfway to the tail on the underside. Remove the viscera of small fish, such as smelt or mullet, through the gills, make a small incision just below them and with the thumb and finger press the intestines along and remove the gills. Whitebait is not emptied. The *roe* of small fish, such as the herring, is replaced and cooked with it (grilled herring), but that of a large fish requires to be cooked separately, otherwise it will be underdone —the liver is sometimes replaced.

2. After emptying remove any black membrane or blood from the backbone by rubbing with a little salt.

3. If there are scales, scrape them off with a sharp knife, work from the tail towards the head, holding the knife obliquely against the fish. When the scales are difficult to remove, as in some fresh-water fish, plunge it for a minute or two into boiling water until the scales become dull, remove, dip into cold water, and then scale the fish.

4. Remove the fins, except those of gelatinous fish (turbot), also

the eyes ; cut the skin round the eye socket, press the thumb into the head behind the eye, and push it out.

5. Wash thoroughly but quickly in cold water : fish, if left soaking, loses flavour and becomes flabby, but there are exceptions. Salt fish is soaked to remove some of the salt and to soften the fibres, and some freshwater fish must be soaked for some time to remove the muddy flavour. After washing, dry the fish in a clean cloth. Deep-frozen fish should be thawed according to the instructions on the packet.

To Skin and to Fillet Fish. When time is limited, fish filleted by the fishmonger is a convenience, but filleting it at home is an *economy*. Stock can be made from the bones, skin, and trimmings, and used for cooking the fish, and for the accompanying sauce, the flavour of which is superior if made partly with fish stock.

The fillets of a flat fish are detached in four pieces, those of a fish which swims with its back uppermost, in two.

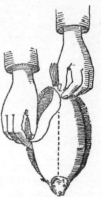

To Skin a Flat Fish (Sole).

1. Cut off the fins, wash and dry the fish, place it on a board with the head away from the worker, and with the dark side uppermost.

2. Cut the skin across just about $\frac{1}{2}$ in. above the tail, raise the skin from the flesh at that point, and with the thumb of the right hand loosen the skin on the right side by running the thumb up from the tail towards the head, as in Fig. 13. Loosen the skin on the left side by using the thumb of the left hand in the same way, or turn the fish round and loosen from head to tail.

FIG. 13. How to
Skin a Sole

3. Hold the tail of the fish firmly down on the board with the left hand, dip the fingers of the right hand in a little salt, this is to prevent slipping, and remove the skin, which has been loosened, by drawing it off sharply from the tail towards the head. The white skin is often left ; to remove it, turn the fish over and proceed as before—if there is any difficulty in drawing off the skin, ease it away with a knife.

To Fillet a Flat Fish (Sole). Use a filleting knife, or a sharp one with a good point, which quite well answers the purpose, the aim being to remove the fillets cleanly from the bones without breaking the flesh.

1. Place the fish on the board with the head away from you, and with the rounded side (from which the black skin has been removed) uppermost, make an incision down the centre of the fish from the head to the tail and close to the backbone.

2. It is easier to remove the left-hand fillet first, which should be done by three quick, clean strokes of the knife from the head to the tail, holding the knife obliquely and close to the bone.

3. Turn the fish round with the tail away from the worker and proceed as before, but working from tail towards head.

4. To remove fillets from underside, turn the fish over with the head away from the worker, and remove the fillets as before directed.

To Fillet Plaice. The skin of plaice is so tough that it is easier to remove the fillets first and then the skin. Remove fillets as directed for sole, then remove the skin from each fillet. Place the fillet with the skin downwards on the board, the tail end next to the worker, and with a sharp knife, held obliquely, remove the flesh without breaking it.

To Skin and to Fillet a Fish which Swims with the Back Uppermost. Wash and dry the fish. Skin *from the head towards the tail.*

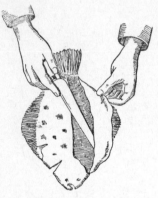

FIG. 14. How to Remove the Fillets of a Plaice

1. Place the fish on the board with its head away from the worker, cut through the skin on either side of the backbone and close to the back fins.

2. Make a cut across just below the head and begin to work off the skin, beginning at the flap, work from head to tail, press the flesh down with the knife, drawing the skin gradually and carefully away. Turn the fish round with the head towards the worker, and remove the skin in the same way from the other side.

3. To fillet remove the flesh cleanly from both sides of the bone and without tearing it, commencing at the head.

Methods of Cooking Fish are the same as for meat : boiling, steaming, stewing, baking, frying, grilling ; fish *must* be *thoroughly cooked*, if underdone it is very unpalatable and also unwholesome.

Suitability of Methods. Those of boiling and frying are the most general English methods and, although so simple, are not always a success. Boiling is the most wasteful of all methods of cooking fish, on account of the very considerable loss of flavouring and nutritive constituents. In frying, if properly carried out, these are retained ; in grilling, on account of the extreme heat applied, and in baking, by reason of some protective covering, bread-crumbs or sauce, there is comparatively very little loss ; in stewing, the extracted matter passes into the sauce in which the fish is stewed, and is not lost ; and in steaming, which is most suitable for small pieces of fillets of fish, it is retained and either served with the fish or used in an accompanying sauce. Therefore steaming and stewing fish are the most nutritive methods of cooking it for invalids. Boiling is the most suitable for a large uncut fish or thick solid piece. Small whole fish can be either grilled or fried.

Garnishes for Fish. The most general for boiled, steamed, baked, stewed, and fried fish are parsley and slices of lemon: for fried fish the parsley is fried. Other simple and suitable garnishes are chopped parsley; chopped egg, the yolk sieved and the white chopped; scraped horse-radish, watercress, and fennel; and lobster coral (see page 89).

Fish Sauces are served separately or are used for coating the fish. The foundation of many is a plain white sauce, its flavour is superior when the liquid used is partly fish stock. To the white sauce anchovy essence, egg, capers, shrimps, oysters, lobster, etc., are added. Hollandaise and sauces of a more elaborate type are most suitable for more expensive fish and for fish entrées.

Boiled potatoes are served with fish.

TO BOIL FISH

A Fish Kettle with a drainer is a convenience, it enables the fish to be easily lowered into the water, to be removed without breaking,

FIG. 15. FISH KETTLE

and the water to drain away from the fish after it is cooked, which is important in dishing it. As a substitute use an ordinary stewpan : for easy removal and to avoid breaking the fish, tie it in a piece of muslin, which should be sufficiently large for the ends to just hang over the sides of the pan; place a plate in the bottom of the saucepan, this prevents the fish from coming into contact with the hot metal and with such violent ebullition of the water.

Preparation. Wash, clean, and remove scales. If whole, cut off the fins, trim the tail, and remove the eyes. The skin of a small piece of fish is removed after it is boiled and the fish coated with sauce. Tie into a neat shape with string.

To Boil.

1. Have sufficient water in the utensil to just well cover the fish. The size of the pan must be suitable to the size of the fish,

too much water and violent ebullition causes loss of nutriment and the skin to break. Put the fish into the water ; pouring very hot water over it or putting it into boiling water breaks the skin of delicate fish.

2. To every gallon of water allow 1 oz. of salt and 2 tablespoonfuls of vinegar or lemon juice; the latter should be used when boiling fish of a delicate flavour ; the acid makes the fish firm and white.

3. When the water is quite hot, but not actually boiling, place the fish gently in (see exceptions to this—mackerel, salmon, salt fish).

4. Allow the water to come up to boiling point, then simmer gently, remove the scum to keep the fish a good colour. The average time required is ten minutes to each pound and ten minutes over ; rapid cooking breaks the skin before the flesh close to the bone is properly cooked.

5. When sufficiently cooked the fish loses its clear appearance and becomes opaque, shows a tendency to come away from the bone and for the skin to crack. If of good quality and not over-boiled there is a curd-like deposit between the flakes. If over-cooked this disappears and the flesh is dry and tasteless.

6. Remove immediately and drain well, place the drainer across the fish kettle, cover with a clean cloth or with the lid.

7. Serve boiled fish on a china fish drainer covered with a folded napkin or paper with the dish beneath.

8. Garnish quickly, send to table very hot and with the accompanying sauce served separately.

Court bouillon is used for cooking fish with an insipid flavour. This is a well-seasoned fish stock : made of fish trimmings with the addition of herbs and vegetables and 1 gill of vinegar (sometimes white wine is used) to 2 quarts of water. This is strained and the fish is boiled in it.

Boiled Salmon. Put into boiling water to preserve the colour, omit vinegar which spoils it.

Boiled Mackerel. Put into the fish kettle, cover gently with *cold* water, hot water breaks the delicate skin : to avoid this, cook, drain, and handle mackerel very gently.

Boiled Salt Fish. Soak for at least 12 hours, place in lukewarm water, or milk and water; milk makes the fish more mellow.

Boiled Turbot. Only trim the fins, do not remove the thick gelatinous parts which are considered a delicacy. Score the dark skin across two or three times, this prevents the white skin from cracking, rub the white side over with a cut lemon, to preserve the whiteness and firmness of the flesh. Cook with white skin uppermost.

TO STEAM FISH

Small fillets or thin slices of fish are suitable.

Method. 1. Prepare the fish as for baking fillets. 2. Place it on a buttered plate, cover with a buttered paper and another plate, or with a saucepan lid. 3. Place the plate over a pan of boiling water, cook for 12 to 20 minutes according to kind of fish and thickness. 4. Dish the fish either with the fish liquor poured over it, or coat it with a sauce, using the fish liquor.

TO FRY FISH

Frying is perhaps the most popular and palatable method of cooking fish ; if well fried it is crisp, dry, free from greasiness and of a golden brown colour ; carelessly cooked it is unattractive in appearance, unappetizing, and indigestible.

Most varieties of fish can be fried either in deep fat or in shallow fat. Deep frying is more suitable for small whole fish (whiting) or fillets, and small pieces of fish ; large fish should be cut into pieces ; shallow fat frying is better adapted to the thicker slices or steaks of fish, which require longer cooking for the heat to penetrate more gradually ; and for oily fish, e.g. herring.

See METHODS OF COOKING (pages 33–5) for principles of frying, temperatures, etc.

Preparation of Fish for Frying. (a) Clean, wash, and *dry thoroughly* in a clean cloth. (b) *Season* with pepper and salt and a few drops of lemon juice, the latter improves the flavour, whitens the flesh, and tends to make it firm. (c) *Coat* with some covering as a protection against the strong heat of the fat and to prevent the fat from soaking in. The coating *must* be even and complete or the fish will have a patchy appearance when fried.

Coatings.

1. The cheapest and easiest coating is that of *seasoned flour* (1 tablespoonful flour, ½ teaspoonful salt, pinch of pepper) which also further dries the fish, and this is often used before coating with egg and crumbs. Fine oatmeal is sometimes used instead of flour for coating.

2. Batter (see BATTERS, pages 191–2).

To give fish additional flavour it is often " marinaded " (see page 39) before it is dipped in batter.

3. Egg and white crumbs. Commercially prepared crumbs are often used instead of white crumbs.

For coating with crumbs plenty are required, and a supply should always be handy : scraps of bread, dried, crushed, and sieved, answer the purpose, but white crumbs give the best result as to evenness in colour.

Preparation of Egg and Crumbs.

1. The *bread-crumbs* must be fine, dry, and smooth. 2. Beat the egg on a plate, but not to a froth ; if eggs are not plentiful a little

4—(E.6149)

water or milk can be added to eke out the quantity. Have in readiness a broad-bladed knife, an egg brush and the crumbs in a large piece of paper.

To Coat Fish with Egg and Bread-crumbs (fillets and small pieces). If the fillets of sole, plaice or haddock are large, cut them across *diagonally* into two or three pieces, this makes them curl up when cooked.

1. Season each and sprinkle with a few drops of lemon juice.

2. Put one piece at a time into the beaten egg, brush over quickly, so that the egg does not penetrate and make the fish soft.

3. Lift the fillet out on the knife, keep it from slipping off with the brush, and let superfluous egg drain away.

4. Drop the fillet into the centre of the crumbs, hold the paper at each end and toss the fish lightly in the crumbs until thoroughly covered.

5. Lift out with the fingers, toss lightly in the hands to remove the crumbs, put the fish on the board and press the crumbs on with a knife on both sides to prevent crumbs from falling off into fat.

6. Place on a tin or plate covered with kitchen paper, and if possible leave for a time so that the coating may set and become firm before frying.

NOTE. Coat a slice of fish or a whole small fish (whiting) as for fillets.

To Fry Fish. Follow the directions given for frying food (METHODS OF COOKING, pages 33–7).

Points Common Both to Deep or Shallow Fat Frying.

(*a*) Use the fat at the correct heat, which is indicated by the blue vapour rising from the centre of the pan, the denser the vapour the greater the heat.

(*b*) Fry a few pieces at one time, too many put into the pan cools the fat, which penetrates the coating.

(*c*) Reheat the fat before frying another quantity.

(*d*) Drain thoroughly and serve very hot.

For Deep Frying use a frying basket except when fish is coated with batter, do not let the pieces in the basket overlap, this tends to disturb the coating.

For Shallow Fat Frying. When frying a fairly thick slice of fish the fat in the pan should reach about half-way up the side of the fish, so that it may be cooked evenly throughout.

To Fry Parsley. Wash the parsley, pick the sprigs from the stalks and dry well in a cloth. After frying the fish, and when the blue vapour has ceased to rise from the fat, put the parsley in a frying basket, immerse and fry until the hissing sound ceases; drain.

Fried Fish Coated with Batter (see BATTERS, pages 191, 192).
Follow directions for making and for using a coating batter.

Fish Fried Whole.   Coat with egg and bread-crumbs.
(a) Flat fish : sole, plaice, slips, and dabs.   Cleanse, skin, wash,
and dry, cut off fins and head, trim tail.   Fry either in deep or
shallow fat.
(b) Whiting.   Skin whiting, leave on head, remove eyes ;   trim
the tail and secure it in the mouth with a tiny skewer made from a
match.   Fry in deep fat.

Fried Whitebait (one pint).   It is very important that whitebait
should be absolutely fresh, as it is not drawn, and it should be kept
as cool as possible before it is prepared, on ice if possible, or covered
in a refrigerator.

Accompaniments : Brown bread and butter.
               Quarters of lemon.

Method.   1. Wash thoroughly in cold water to free from weeds,
handle as little as possible, leave in a basin with a small lump of
ice and place on the ice, or in a refrigerator, until required. 2. Spread
the fish on a cloth to drain, sprinkle another dry cloth with a little
flour, put a small quantity of whitebait into the floured cloth, dredge
lightly with flour and toss in the flour until the fish are evenly coated
and separate. 3. Empty into a frying basket and shake to remove
loose flour. 4. Plunge into very hot fat (400° F.), fry for about
two minutes, shaking the basket gently to keep the fish separate.
5. Remove, let the fat drain off, then turn the whitebait out on to a
paper to drain.   6. Proceed as before until all are fried.   7. Reheat
fat, return the fish to the basket, and fry them a second time for
about two minutes, until crisp and lightly coloured.   8. Drain,
season with fine salt and cayenne, and serve very hot.
NOTE.   If carefully dried and well coated, and the fat is very hot,
the fish will be crisp and separate.

TO BAKE FISH

The savoury method of baking is most suitable for white fish
(small whole fish, slices and fillets), and for insipid freshwater fish.

Three Methods of Cooking Fish in the Oven are—

(a) Simply baking.
(b) Stuffing the fish first with forcemeat : whole fish or slices
are then coated with flour or with egg and brown bread-crumbs
and baked.   Fillets are stuffed, and after baking may be either
rolled in brown crumbs or coated with a sauce.
(c) Baking *au gratin*, that is, the fish is sprinkled with savoury
herbs, etc., and browned crumbs and then baked (sole *au gratin*).

Forcemeat. Veal stuffing for simple dishes ; for more elaborate ones, lobster cutlet mixture and similar forcemeats are used.

Directions for Cooking Baked Fish.

1. Wash, clean and prepare in the ordinary way for cooking.

2. *Dry well*, then coat if desired with some protective covering, seasoned flour, or egg and bread-crumbs. Whole fish (haddock) or fish steaks, should be put into a tin containing sufficient hot fat, about 2 oz. for basting the fish. Put small fillets on a buttered tin and sprinkle lightly with melted butter.

3. Baste whole fish and thick slices occasionally, and let the last time be a few minutes before the fish is removed, so that the surface may be crisp and brown, not greasy and sodden.

4. Cover small fillets, and fish of delicate texture and flavour, with a greased paper.

5. Bake fish in a moderate oven. The time for whole fish and thick slices varies from 20 to 30 or 35 minutes, according to the solidity of the fish ; for fillets allow from 12 to 15 minutes. When sufficiently cooked the coated surface shows a tendency to crack. If fish is not coated, and it is not over-cooked, a soft curd-like deposit should be seen between the flakes.

6. When baking fillets of sole or plaice, fold or roll the fillets from the head to the tail, with the side innermost from which the skin has been removed; this is to prevent the flesh from breaking.

7. Drain baked fish which has been basted.

8. Dish with the sauce poured round fish which has been coated before baking. If fish has not been coated, coat with sauce.

To Stuff a Cod Steak. A middle cut is more suitable as the flap encloses the stuffing ; if from the tail end, remove the bone to make a hole for the stuffing. The steak should be about 1½ to 2 in. in thickness.

To Stuff a Haddock. Prepare as for boiling, trim the tail and dry well. 2. Fill the cavity when the fish has been emptied with veal forcemeat, sew up with a needle and thread, making long stitches, and leave long ends for easy withdrawal. 3. Truss into the shape of S on a large skewer.

To Stuff a Plaice. 1. Clean fish, remove black skin, cut off head and fins and dry. 2. Make a long incision down the centre close to the bone on the side previously covered with black skin. 3. With a knife raise the flesh from the bone on either side to form a pocket. 4. Fill this with the stuffing, raising it in the centre. Coat with egg and bread-crumbs.

To Stuff Fillets of Plaice or Sole. Season well, spread the side from which the skin has been removed with the forcemeat, fold or roll from the head to the tail. Bake on a buttered tin and cover with a greased paper. If rolled in brown crumbs after baking, pour the sauce round, if not, coat with the same.

Stuffed and Baked Haddock.

Ingredients.	*For Coating.*
Fresh haddock.	1 egg.
2 oz. veal forcemeat.	Browned crumbs.
Butter or dripping.	Garnish of lemon and
1 gill anchovy or brown sauce.	parsley.

Method. 1. Prepare and stuff fish and bake in a moderate oven, as before directed, baste occasionally. 2. Serve on a hot dish with sauce poured round, and garnish.

Sole au Gratin.

Ingredients.	*Savoury Mixture.*
1 sole of medium size.	1 teaspoonful chopped parsley.
Brown crumbs.	1 teaspoonful chopped mushrooms.
Melted butter.	¼ teaspoonful chopped onion.
Seasoning.	
Lemon juice.	*Garnish.*
1 gill good brown sauce.	Lemon and parsley.

Method. 1. Clean, wash, and skin the sole, remove head, trim fins and tail. 2. Score each side from the back to the sides

FIG. 16. GRATIN DISH

in oblique lines, so that the flavour of the herbs may penetrate. 3. Mix the parsley, mushrooms and onion together, season the sole with pepper and salt and a few drops of lemon juice. 4. Sprinkle half of the mixture on a buttered " gratin " (fireproof china) dish, lay the fish on it, and spread the remainder of the mixture on top. 5. Sprinkle lightly with brown crumbs and a little melted butter. 6. Cook in a moderate oven for about 20 minutes, when ready add any liquor in the dish to the sauce, strain round the dish and garnish.

NOTE. Plaice can be cooked by the same method.

STEWED FISH (FRICASSEE)

Fish Suitable. Any kind of white fish divided into small pieces or fillets, such as fillets of whiting, plaice, haddock, or small pieces of cod—stewed gently in white sauce made with fish stock and milk.

GRILLED FISH

Follow general directions for grilling meat (see GRILLED CHOP, pages 108–9). Brush the fish over with melted fat, butter or dripping, or oil.

Whole Fish.   Mackerel or herring. Cleanse, remove head and tail, dry well, split open, remove backbone and small bones, and rub away any black membrane with salt.

Slices of Fish should be about 1 in. thick.   Brush over salmon with oil and grill it enclosed in a buttered paper, this tends to preserve the colour and flavour.

SMOKED FISH

Smoked haddocks and kippered herrings, in addition to being a popular breakfast dish, are useful for small savouries, for making fish paste and for giving additional flavour to made dishes of fish such as fish-cakes.

Preparation.   Scald by pouring boiling water over the fish; this loosens the skin of the haddocks and removes some of the fat from " kippers," if desired.

Smoked Haddocks.

Method.   1. Trim off fins and tail and scald : if large, divide into pieces of a suitable size. 2. Put into a pan or tin with milk and cook on a boiling ring or in the oven : place a plate over the pan or tin which prevents evaporation and assists in the cooking.   When the fish is cooked it begins to shrink from the bone. 3. Season with pepper, spread a little butter on the top and serve very hot, with the milk poured round.

Kippered Herrings.

Method.   Either grill or fry in a pan without fat—time 7 to 10 minutes. Grill the cut side first or place the cut side next to the pan for frying.

If cooked in the oven, it is more digestible than either fried or grilled.

SHELLFISH

Shellfish as an appetizing and occasional change are useful; as a class they are generally indigestible and are more or less liable to the development of irritating poisons; some are not clean feeders, while others, such as oysters and mussels, become infected from pollution in their breeding areas.

Raw oysters are considered digestible, but cooking renders them tough and hard, and it has the same effect upon all the molluscs, mussels, cockles, whelks, etc.

In most shellfish there is some inedible part, which is either indigestible or more or less poisonous, e.g. the beard of an oyster, the small black weed in the mussel, the dead men's fingers or gills in the lobster and crab, etc.

Classes of Shellfish. 1. The *crustacea*, of which the most commonly eaten are the crab, lobster, crayfish, (which is similar to the lobster without the large claws, is eaten more abroad and used for the same purposes as lobster) ; the shrimp and prawn, both of which are largely used for garnishing. 2. The *molluscs*, which include the bivalves—oyster, mussel, scallop, and the univalves such as whelks, periwinkles, and limpets.

Uses and Cooking of Shellfish. Shellfish are used for soups (*bisques*), also for a large variety of fish entrées and savouries. Excepting oysters, which are more often eaten raw, all shellfish are boiled; in some cases this is the sole method of preparation, e.g. cockles ; in others boiling is the preliminary step to further elaborations in dressing. Over-boiling makes shellfish tough, and the meat of the claws of lobsters and crabs becomes hard and fibrous.

LOBSTER AND CRAB

Season. Lobsters and crabs are in season during the summer months. Lobster is obtained all the year round, but is at its best from June to September, when oysters are out of season ; crabs are best from April to October.

Choice. Fish of a medium size are best; they should be heavy in proportion to their size, if light they are watery and incrustations upon the shell an indication of age. Lobster less than 9 in. in length must not be offered for sale. If fresh when cooked, the tail of a lobster will spring back sharply if it is pulled out straight, and the joints of a crab are stiff and the shell a good colour. The flesh of the male crab and of the cock lobster is superior to that of the female.

Lobster Spawn consists of a mass of very small greenish blue eggs found beneath the tail of the hen lobster. It is illegal to sell such a lobster.

Lobster Coral. This is the red matter found in the body of the cooked lobster. It is pounded with butter and sieved, and can be used either as a *flavouring butter* for savouries or piped as a decoration to a fish dish. It is also dried, rubbed through a nylon sieve, and used for *garnishing*.

Lobster Simply Dressed.

1 boiled lobster.	Oil and vinegar.
Salad plants.	Brown bread and butter.

Method. 1. Remove the claws by giving them a sharp twist, crack them with a hammer, be careful not to smash them. Split the tail down the centre with a sharp pointed knife. 2. Dish the lobster on a bed of salad sprinkled with oil and vinegar : place the head in the centre, with the split tail and claws arranged round it. 3. Serve with oil and vinegar and thin slices of brown bread and butter.

Lobster Cutlets.

Proportions.	*For Coating.*
8 oz. fresh or tinned lobster.	Beaten egg, bread-crumbs
1 tablespoonful cream.	Cayenne, salt, lemon juice.
¾ oz. butter ⎫	Parsley and lemon.
¾ oz. flour ⎬ panada.	
¾ gill fish stock or milk ⎭	

Method. For making panada, shaping and frying cutlets, follow directions for Fish Cutlets (see RE-HEATED FOOD). 1. Make the panada and let it cool ; chop the meat finely, if the fish is tinned, drain it well before using. 2. Add the lobster meat to the cooled panada, then the cream, seasoning and a few drops of lemon juice, mix well and leave to get cold and firm 3. Form into cutlet-shaped pieces, coat with egg and white crumbs. 4. Fry in deep fat ; after frying insert in the narrow end of each a small claw or piece of the feeler ; dish and garnish with fried parsley and lemon.

Lobster Mayonnaise (see SALADS, page 159).

Dressed Crab.

1 boiled crab (medium size).

Dressing.	*Garnish.*
2 tablespoonfuls salad oil or cream.	Finely chopped parsley.
1 tablespoonful vinegar or lemon juice.	Egg hard boiled.
½ tablespoonful mixed tarragon and chilli	Claws.
vinegar.	
¼ teaspoonful made mustard.	
Salt, cayenne.	
A few white breadcrumbs.	

Method. 1. *To open shell.* Twist off the claws, place the crab on its back, insert the fingers between the body and the shell, and with the thumbs force away the lower part of the shell from the upper. 2. Remove the inedible parts : the poisonous " fingers " (gills) which adhere to the sides of the shell, the small sac (stomach) and the small twisted greenish intestines. Take out the cream-like crab meat from the centre. 3. Wash and dry the shell and rub the outside with a little oil. Make the dressing. 4. Crack the claws, remove the meat and shred it, season well with the dressing. 5. Mix the meat from the centre with dressing and breadcrumbs if used ; season and mix well. 6. Fill the shell, claw meat in the centre, other meat at the side, and decorate with the parsley, chopped white and sieved yolk of egg and the claws. 7. Serve garnished with watercress.

NOTE. As an economy, and when the crab meat is insufficient, fresh white crumbs can be added, using the same proportion as of crab meat. Lobster butter (see LOBSTER CORAL) or parsley butter are often piped in small roses round the shell.

Oysters.

Oysters are at their best during the months spelt with an R, at other times they are not as wholesome. The English oyster is most suitable for eating raw ; for cooking, Dutch, Portuguese, and American answer the purpose. Oysters must be absolutely fresh ; gaping shells denote staleness, and incrustation, age.

To Open an Oyster. Hold the deep shell firmly in the palm of the left hand so as to retain the oyster liquor, insert the knife, an oyster knife if possible, between the two valves and force the shell open.

Cooking. Retain and use the oyster liquor, remove the beard, and be careful not to overheat or to cook oysters sufficiently long to toughen them.

Oyster Patties.

Ingredients.	*Filling.*
½ lb. puff pastry.	1 doz. sauce oysters.
	1 yolk of egg.
	1 tablespoonful cream.
Panada.	Lemon juice.
½ oz. flour.	Salt, pepper, Cayenne.
½ oz. butter.	
½ gill oyster liquor.	*Garnish.*
½ gill milk.	Parsley.

Method. 1. *Prepare pastry cases* (see PUFF PASTRY). 2. *Prepare the filling* : scald the oysters in their own liquor, strain, remove the beards, cut into two or three pieces, and retain liquor. Make the panada, add the cream, egg yolk, lemon juice, and seasoning, reheat to cook egg, add the oysters, and make thoroughly hot. 3. *To fill the patty cases*, which must be hot, pile up the mixture in the centre, put on the small lids, and reheat in oven. 4. Serve on a dish covered with a paper d'oyley, garnish with parsley.

Some Varieties of Fillings for Fish Patties. Shrimp, prawn, lobster, and salmon. Prepare cases and fillings as above directed.

Fish Réchauffés (see DIRECTIONS FOR REHEATING FOOD, page 124).

Fish Soufflés (see WHITING SOUFFLÉ, page 218).

CHAPTER 12

METHODS OF CUTTING UP CARCASES OF ANIMALS

The Choice and Suitability of Joints and Parts of Meat for Different Purposes. The methods of cutting up the carcases of animals vary in England and in Scotland, and in different localities, but there is much similarity in all methods. To the housekeeper, however experienced, the economical purchase of meat, which is the most expensive item in the daily fare, is generally less easy than the selection of most other foods. When choosing a joint or piece of meat, it is well to bear in mind the following: inferior cuts, although inexpensive, are often very wasteful, and are therefore not really cheap, the actual economy in choice being determined by (*a*) comparison with other parts as to relative nutritive value, (*b*) its suitability for the purpose required, (*c*) the proportion of fat and of bone. Select small meat if possible, the flesh of an overgrown or over-fatted animal is coarse in fibre, the bones are large, and there is an undue proportion of fat.

BEEF

Beef is not as digestible as mutton, the fibres being coarser and the connective tissue denser; like mutton, it must also be well hung if to eat tender. The lean should be bright in colour, slightly intergrained with fat, which gives it a " marbled " appearance, the fat a *pale* yellow. If the beef is young, there should be little or no gristle between the fat and the lean : inferior beef is dark in colour, and the fat is a deep yellow : ox beef is superior to the beef of the cow.

NOTE. For roasting and for boiling respectively the sirloin and the silverside are the best, and the ribs and the brisket the next best.

Sirloin. For a large roasting joint, sirloin is the choicest, but it is the most expensive. There are three cuts of sirloin, the *middle* is the *prime* portion, for it has the largest undercut of "fillet." This, being the most tender part, is often sold separately for entrées and for a small roast, but its removal depreciates the value of the joint. When buying sirloin always choose a piece with a good undercut, if possible. The part of the sirloin next to the ribs has very little undercut, and that close to the rump has an extra piece of bone, which makes the joint less easy to carve.

Two sirloins undivided form the " baron of beef " now seldom seen.

Ribs. There are three cuts of ribs; the fore, middle, and chuck ribs. The fore and middle ribs are roasted, the wing rib next to the sirloin is most tender and a favourite joint. The chuck ribs are close to the shoulder, and are more suitable for braising and for stewing.

The ends cut off two or three ribs make an excellent little joint for a small family, the bones can be used afterwards for stock and soup.

Rump. Is one of the most expensive and tender cuts of steak, and

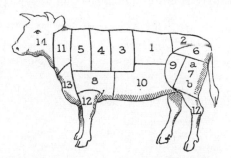

FIG. 17. METHOD OF CUTTING UP BEEF

1. Sirloin.
2. Rump.
3. Fore Ribs.
4. Middle Ribs.
5. Chuck Rib.
6. Aitchbone.
7. Buttock—(a) Topside. (b) Silver-side.
8. Brisket.
9. Thick Flank.
10. Thin Flank.
11. Neck.
12. Shin.
13. Clod.
14. Cheek.

is used for grilling and for superior small entrées (beef fillets). Fillet is usually more expensive and is used similarly.

The Round or Buttock. Consists of very solid meat with little bone and fat, and is therefore an economical part to buy; it is divided into two portions, the upper or topside and the lower or silverside.

(a) *Buttock steak,* which is cut from the round, is much less expensive than rump, but not so tender; the cuts of buttock steak vary in quality, and therefore in price. It is suitable for stewing and for meat pies and puddings.

(b) *The topside* is an economical roast for a fairly large family, but to eat tender it should be well hung; as it has little fat, the butcher is very apt to skewer in a large piece which does not belong to it. It must be well hung, otherwise it is tough.

(c) *The silverside* is not as tender as the topside; it is salted and boiled and served either hot or cold; unless well hung before it is put into pickle it is often hard when cooked. Silverside is dearer than brisket, but is more tender and better in flavour. It can be bought fresh and is usually boiled.

Aitchbone. A cheap cut, but not an economical joint as it has a large awkward piece of bone, and there is a very considerable shrinkage in cooking. The aitchbone is sometimes *roasted*, but more frequently it is boiled, or salted and boiled.

Brisket corresponds to the breast of mutton ; it is a cheap part, but rather fat. If salted or pickled, and boiled and boned and pressed, it makes an excellent cold meat dish.

Flank. (*a*) Thick flank is both cheap and economical, it has no bone and little fat. It is suitable for baking, braising, and stewing, and for pies.

(*b*) Thin flank is rather fat, and is suitable for salting and is used for the same purpose as brisket.

Clod.
Cheek. } These parts are coarse and gelatinous, and are suitable for cheap stews and for soup.
Neck.

Leg.
Shin. } The foreleg is not as coarse in texture as the shin.

Cowheel may be used instead of calves' feet for making jellies; boiled or stewed, it makes a nourishing and savoury dish.

Tongue is expensive ; it is salted and boiled, and may be served hot with a rich sauce, or cold and glazed.

Tail is braised, stewed, and used for soup.

VEAL

Prime veal is the flesh of a calf killed when 8–10 months old.

Veal is obtainable throughout the year, but is at its best from March to the end of July. The flesh of a very young calf is the most esteemed and is of a delicate pink colour, that of an older animal is redder, but more digestible and more nourishing. The lean of young veal in good condition is firm, grain fine, the fat white, and that around the kidneys is hard and fairly plentiful, and the connective tissue is puffy with a blistered appearance : a bluish tinge of the lean and soft moist fat indicates that the veal is not fresh. Veal is less easily digested than some other meats. This may be due partly to the construction of the meat fibres, which seem to elude easy mastication, and partly to its insipid flavour which makes veal less stimulating to the digestive juices. Veal being, like lamb, the flesh of an immature animal, also does not keep well, and should be cooked within two or three days of the date upon which it was slaughtered. To render veal tender and digestible, thorough cooking is very important. When pounded and sieved it is useful in invalid dietaries (veal *soufflé*).

Fillet is the choicest and most tender part, it is also the highest priced, but on account of the very small amount of bone there is practically no waste. The fillet is used as a roast, for cutlets and for various entrées.

Loin is cheaper than fillet, but has a considerable amount of bone ; the best end, which contains the kidney, is superior to the chump end, and is a prime part for roasting ; the loin is often braised, also chops are cut from it.

The Bladebone or Oyster is frequently cut into two and sold for roasting.

Neck (*a*) The best end makes a small roast, but on account of the large proportion of bone it is not economical ; it is also braised and used for chops.

(*b*) The scrag end for stewing.

FIG. 18. METHOD OF CUTTING UP VEAL

1. Fillet.	7. Breast.
2. Loin.	8. Bladebone.
3. Best end of Neck.	9. Fore Knuckle.
4. Chump end of Loin.	10. Hind Knuckle.
5 and 6. Inferior cuts of Neck.	11. Head.

Breast is a cheap cut. It may be stewed, and is often boned, stuffed, and rolled, and either roasted or braised.

" Veal tendons " are the gristly portions, which are cut from the breast and stewed.

Head is boiled and served either hot or cold.

Knuckle fore and hind, both are cheap ; the fore knuckle is more tender, and is used for stews, the hind for stock and for soup-making.

Brains for various light entrées.

Feet for making jelly.

MUTTON

Mutton, like beef, must be well hung. The lean is not as red as that of beef, but it is more easily digested, the fibres being finer and connective tissue less dense ; the fat, which is whiter and harder, is not as digestible as beef fat, particularly when eaten hot. When buying, choose small mutton, which is more tender and less wasteful ; the flesh is plump, the fibre fine, and the bone small. Young Welsh mutton and English Southdown are the best. but chilled New Zealand mutton and lamb, if of superior quality, are scarcely to be distinguished from the home-fed meat.

The Leg is one of the most economical joints for a family, although the price per pound is higher than that of the shoulder, and a large shank bone is not infrequently weighed with it, thus increasing the price per lb. without a corresponding food value, but on the other hand the amount of bone and of fat is much less as compared with other parts. Both leg and shoulder should be short and plump. If a leg is too large, purchase the fillet end (which is

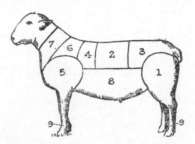

FIG. 19. METHOD OF CUTTING UP MUTTON

1. Leg.
2. Loin, best end.
3. Loin, chump end.
4. Neck, best end.
5. Shoulder.

6. Neck, middle.
7. Neck, scrag.
8. Breast.
9. Trotter.

the most tender) for roasting, or cut a large leg into two, and boil, stew, or braise the knuckle end.

The Haunch consists of the leg with a part of the loin.

The Loin is considered the choicest joint for roasting, but it is expensive on account of the large amount of bone and of fat; the latter should be well trimmed by the butcher. There are two cuts of loin—

(a) The best end with the kidney, which is roasted or baked and used for chops.

(b) The chump end next to the tail has more bone, from this part of the loin large *chump chops* are cut.

The Saddle is the double loin undivided, a joint which is too large for the ordinary household.

The Neck. Where there is a good larder and the family is large, it is considerably cheaper per pound to buy the whole neck, which consists of—

(a) The best end, the most tender and juicy and also the dearest cut; it is suitable for roasting, boiling, braising, and for cutlets, neck cutlets are much smaller than chops cut from the loin. To buy cutlets ready trimmed is extravagant, the price per pound is greater, and there is the loss of the trimmings.

(b) Middle neck is cheaper, has less lean and comparatively more bone—used for stews.

(c) Scrag-end, the cheapest in price, but with a large amount of bone and often very fat—used for cheap stews.

Shoulder is less in price than the leg, but is not a cheap joint, on account of so much fat and of the large blade bone and of the greater shrinkage. It is most suitable as a roast or baked joint : if very large, divide the shoulder into two, roast the blade end and braise the other. The whole shoulder is often boned, stuffed, rolled, and baked or braised.

The Breast is very cheap, but has a large proportion of fat and of skin. If boned and stuffed and rolled it makes an appetizing and economical baked joint.

Trotters or Feet are cheap, they contain a large proportion of gelatinous matter, and make nourishing broths and stews.

Head is cheap, is used for broths and stews—the brains for sauce.

LAMB

Home-fed lamb can be obtained from Christmas to the Autumn, but is dear in the early months of the year ; after March it is more

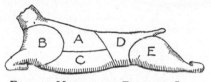

FIG. 20. METHOD OF DIVIDING LAMB INTO THE FORE- AND HIND-QUARTERS

Fore-quarter.   Hind-quarter.
A. Neck, scrag end and best end.   D. Loin.
B. Shoulder.   E. Leg.
C. Breast.

plentiful and cheaper. A large quantity of lamb is imported, the Canterbury lamb of New Zealand being the best. The flesh of the lamb is more delicate in flavour than that of the sheep ; as compared with veal, it is more easily digested ; lamb also should be eaten soon after it is killed.

Lamb, if large, is cut into the same joints as mutton, but when small it is often divided into the hind- and fore-quarters. The fore-quarter consists of the neck, shoulder, and breast, the hind-quarter of the loin and leg ; each of the quarters is usually roasted whole.

PORK

On account of the large amount of fat between the fibres, pork is not as easily digested as either beef or mutton, and should therefore be well cooked. Another and very important reason for thorough cooking is that the pig may be subject to certain parasites—hence the importance of always purchasing pork of from a reliable butcher.

Young pork of good quality is small and therefore not over-fat, the flesh is a pale pink, firm, and fine grained; the fat is softer than that of beef or mutton, is white and free from black specks and kernels; the bone fine; and the rind smooth and thin; that of a mature animal is rough and thick, hence the reason often for the removal of the rind by the butcher before the pork is sold.

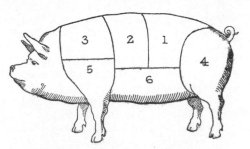

FIG. 21. METHOD OF CUTTING UP THE
CARCASE OF A PIG FOR PORK

1. Loin with kidney.	4. Leg.
2. Fore-loin.	5. Hand.
3. Spare Rib.	6. Spring or Belly.

For roasting joints be sure that the butcher scores the rind.

The Leg is the most economical joint for roasting, it is also salted and boiled.

Loin. The fore-loin is cut with the spare-rib : the hind loin contains the kidney.

Hand. These parts are rather fat and are sometimes salted.

Spring or Belly is salted and boiled, and served either hot or cold, but better cold.

Head is salted and made into brawn.

Pettitoes are the legs below the hock joints; these are generally boiled or stewed.

BACON

Bacon is the flesh of the pig salted and cured ; the hind legs are cured and sold as hams ; the cheeks as " Bath Chaps " ; the fore-legs or shoulders, which have more bone are not so fine in grain, they are frequently trimmed ham shape, and are an economical substitute. Bacon, like pork, should have a smooth, thin rind, the fat should be a pinkish white, firm and free from black specks : the lean of mild cured bacon, which is the best, should be rather pale and free from any yellow streaks, and the bone fine in grain. Fresh bacon of good quality, if properly cured, has no unpleasant smell. To test the freshness of a ham or gammon which may be doubtful, run a skewer or the point of a knife close down to the bone. When withdrawn there should be no unpleasant

smell and no small pieces of lean adhering to the knife or skewer.
When selecting a ham choose one which is thick and short in proportion to its weight.   Yorkshire, Cumberland, and Irish hams are

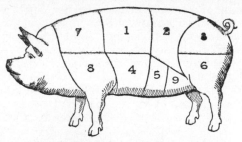

FIG. 22. METHOD OF CUTTING UP THE
CARCASE OF A PIG FOR BACON

1. Back and Ribs.	6. Cushion.
2. Loin and Long Back.	7. Collar.
3. Corner Gammon.	8. Hock.
4. Thick streaky.	9. Flank.
5. Thin streaky.	

the best, but large quantities of Danish, which are of excellent
quality, are sold.

Streaky and Back are best for rashers for frying and grilling, but
are the most expensive cuts.

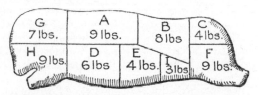

FIG. 23. SIDE OF BACON, WEIGHING 59 LB., CUT INTO
JOINTS WITH APPROXIMATE WEIGHT OF EACH

A. Back and Ribs.	F. Cushion.
B. Loin and Long Back.	G. Collar.
C. Corner of Gammon.	H. Hock.
D. Thick streaky.	I. Flank.
E. Thin streaky.	

Flank is an inferior part and cheaper in price; it is used for boiling.
for " barding," and other purposes.

Hams are expensive and vary in price with the kind.

Gammon is suitable for boiling and for large rashers for frying.

Cushion
Collar   } Suitable for boiling.
Fore-hock

INTERNAL PARTS USED FOR FOOD

These are nutritious, and some are very cheap, for which reasons they should be used where economy is necessary. It is very important that internal parts should be absolutely fresh and free from any suspicion of taint or disease, which is often denoted by discoloration ; as they do not keep well, no length of time should elapse between the time of purchase and of cooking. All internal parts and organs, particularly kidneys and liver, which are connected with the waste products of the body, require scrupulous cleansing by steeping and thorough washing for the removal of blood and of other matter ; blanching also is necessary for some (tripe) ; all fat, membrane, and blood vessels should be cut away. Those of close texture, such as liver, kidney, and heart, require very careful cooking to prevent hardening.

Liver. Calves' liver is the best and also the most expensive. It is usually fried, and is also used for entrées.

Sheep's liver is cheaper, and for some purposes is equally good ; ox liver is the cheapest and is very nutritious, but is coarser and stronger in flavour and requires very *gentle* and *prolonged* cooking.

Kidneys. Unless their freshness is absolutely certain they should not be eaten. Sheep's kidneys are the best and the most delicate in flavour, they should be of a good colour, brown without any greenish tinge and with unbroken skin, plump, firm, dry, and free from any spots or smell; they are generally fried or grilled. Calves' kidneys are usually sold with the loin. Ox kidney is stronger in flavour, should be soaked for a short time before it is used, and cooked slowly; it is suitable for soups, for stews, and for meat pies and puddings.

Lambs' and Pigs' Fry. If dressed with herbs, etc., they make a very savoury dish. Lambs' fry consists of the liver, sweetbread, heart, and some of the inside fat; pigs' fry of the sweetbread, liver, and some inside fat.

Sheep's Pluck is nourishing, it is composed of the heart and liver, sometimes the lungs (lights) are included, but the latter are more often sold separately for animals' food. The pluck is the foundation of "haggis."

Sweetbreads are considered a great delicacy, but are expensive; they are used for entrées and also for invalid dishes, for the latter as they are very light in texture, easily digested, and are less stimulating than other meat. Of the two kinds the belly sweetbread or pancreas and the throat sweetbread, which is the thymus gland of the lamb or calf, the belly sweetbread of the calf is considered the best. It is firm, white, broad, and rather thick, and is most suitable for serving whole. The throat sweetbread is longer, less compact, and darker in colour, it often has a considerable amount of membrane, and is more suitable for dishes in which it can be served in small pieces.

Tripe is the inner lining of the ruminant stomach of the ox; it is very nourishing and easily digested, as the large percentage of connective tissue readily gelatinates on boiling, and the fat, not being distributed throughout the muscle, can be removed. Of the several kinds of tripe, reed, monk's hood book, honeycomb, and blanket, the two last are most often used. As prepared in England, tripe is boiled for 12 hours or longer previous to being sold.

FATS

Suet is the inside fat of the ox and sheep, the best being kidney suet, in which the kidneys are embedded. Beef suet is not as hard as mutton suet, is more digestible, and is suitable for puddings, and suet pastry, mutton suet for frying purposes. Fresh suet should be sweet, firm, and dry, free from kernels, any discoloration or blood streaks.

Lard is the inside fat (flead, flair, or leaf) of the pig; this is melted down and freed from fibrous material.

Meat in Good Condition.

1. No unpleasant odour.

2. Flesh firm, not flabby; moist, not dry, but not over-moist, and when left hanging for a day or two still not over-moist; elastic to the touch, leaving the finger not unduly moist and no mark.

3. Grain fine; in cheaper cuts fibres are longer and coarser.

4. Lean of red meat of good colour, and of a marbled appearance (especially beef), due to the interlining of fat, an indication of a healthy and well-fed animal.

5. Fat, a moderate amount. Firm and free from bloodstains and kernels (small glands), the colour and texture varying with the kind of meat; beef fat is yellowish and less firm than mutton fat, which is white and hard.

Hanging. However good the quality, sufficient time must be allowed for the meat to become tender (see *rigor mortis*, page 27); time varies with weather conditions and with kind of meat. Lamb, veal, and pork do not require as long as beef or mutton. After a certain time, deterioration sets in.

CHAPTER 13

MEAT COOKERY

PRINCIPLES UPON WHICH MEAT COOKERY IS BASED

To cook meat without waste, whatever the method adopted and the ultimate object may be, the aim is the same—to render it tender, appetizing in appearance and flavour, and to retain its nutrient and flavouring constituents, all methods being based upon a few important principles—

1. **Solvent Action of Water** upon the nutrient and flavouring constituents of meat, that of cold water being greater than that of hot, its solvent action decreasing as heat is increased, e.g. steep a small piece of beef, about 1 in. square, for a few minutes in cold water—result, meat colourless, and liquid red.

2. **Coagulation of Protein by Heat.** At a temperature of 140° F., protein begins to coagulate and if temperature remains low, coagulation is slow and protein is more digestible. When temperature increases—160° F. upwards—protein becomes harder and tougher. As temperature rises above 140° F., meat begins to shrink because of the contraction in connective tissue, and juices are squeezed out. The higher the temperature, the greater the shrinkage and consequent loss of juices. In roasting, for example, water is evaporated from the juices and the solids remain, thus flavour is concentrated and nutritive value is not appreciably diminished. When meat is stewed and in direct contact with liquid, the juices pass into it from the meat, but as the liquid is served with the meat as gravy, the loss in nutrients is negligible.

3. **Meat a Bad Conductor of Heat.** The heat applied to the surface penetrates very slowly, thus time must be allowed for the inner or deeper part of a joint to be cooked. To ascertain the interior temperature accurately, a meat thermometer is necessary. Meat, for example, cooked to an interior temperature of 160° F. is medium done; that cooked to a temperature of 176 to 180° F. is well done.

4. **Conversion of Connective Tissue into Gelatine** by heat and moisture.

Boil a small piece of coarse-fibred meat for a short time; notice the fine threads between the fibres. Extreme heat hardens the gelatine.

5. **Development of Flavour and Changes in Extractives** effected by heat; more pronounced under dry than under moist heat.

6. **Boiling and Simmering Points of Water.** Boiling point—212° F.;

simmering point—200° to 210° F.; slow simmering—180° to 190° F. The amount of ebullition varies, being greater on surface of boiling than of simmering water : this is of importance in cooking foods of more delicate texture.

PREPARATION FOR COOKING

1. Weigh, trim, and wipe with a clean, damp cloth. Remove superfluous fat and tie or skewer into shape if necessary. Avoid *washing* meat for roasting, baking, or grilling and small cut pieces. *Wash* (a) salted meats, beef, tongue, ham, bacon, pork, and soak, if necessary, for removal of brine ; (b) all internal parts very thoroughly, such as kidney, tripe, liver, sweetbread, hearts, also heads, feet, tail ; blanching to cleanse being necessary in some cases. Cook all internal parts as soon as possible after purchase.

2. Boning. It is often an economy to bone joints and also to remove superfluous fat, as in sirloin : bones can be used for stock, and fat rendered down for frying or used in place of kidney suet.

3. *Thaw frozen or chilled meat* by placing it in a warm kitchen until defrosted, then cook immediately to prevent escape of juices ; after thawing, meat does not keep so well. To ensure that the frost has been completely removed, place the meat in a moderate oven for the first 10 minutes, and proceed as in cooking English meat.

4. If there is a suspicion of taint, cut away part affected and wash the meat with vinegar and water, or with a very dilute solution of permanganate of potash.

5. Should it be necessary to keep uncooked meat for a day or two in mild weather, where there is no refrigerator, remove any kernel in the fat, as in round or sirloin of beef; it taints before the joint. Hang up in a well-ventilated larder; to protect from flies, cover the joint very loosely with muslin, free circulation of air being most essential, and hang with the cut side uppermost when possible. Dusting lightly with flour, or flour and pepper, assists. Never leave on a dish or plate.

ROAST OR BAKED MEAT

For principles and details of roasting and baking see METHODS OF COOKING (pages 25–7). *Roast meat,* correctly speaking, is that which is cooked in front of a clear open fire, but on account of the construction of the modern kitchen stove and of the general use of gas and electric cookers, "roasting" has been very generally superseded by "baking" or "oven roasting," and the joint so cooked is described as "a roast."

General Directions for Baking a Joint.

1. Wipe the meat, trim if necessary, replace wooden skewers with metal ones, tie or skewer into shape if required.

2. Place the joint on a meat rack in a baking tin, with sufficient

dripping, so that when melted it will well cover the bottom of the tin.

3. Place the joint in a clean, well ventilated and hot oven and cook according to the type of joint. Turn once or twice, if necessary, using two spoons, not forks.

4. Baste if necessary.

5. Serve with gravy, thin gravy with a plain roast or baked joint, thick gravy with one that is stuffed.

Gravy for Roast or Baked Meat. A good gravy is important, a greasy, tasteless liquid being a most unappetizing accompaniment. The quality of the meat (home-fed making the best gravy) has much to do with the flavour; good seasoning and freedom from greasiness are essential.

Thin Gravy. Pour off all the fat from the baking tin, leaving the browned particles of concentrated meat juice behind, add hot stock or boiling water, scrape up the sediment with a metal spoon, boil for 3 or 4 minutes, season, skim or remove any grease from the surface with kitchen paper, strain in to a hot gravy boat.

Thickened Gravy. Pour off most of the fat from the baking tin. If ½ pint of gravy is required, leave 1 dessertspoonful of fat, add 1 dessertspoonful of flour, blending them together with the sediment from the bottom of the tin; place the tin over a boiling ring and brown the flour. Draw the pan aside, add the stock, stir until boiling, and boil for 3 to 5 minutes, season, skim, and strain as directed. Be careful not to burn the flour in browning it, and to thoroughly boil the gravy, otherwise it will taste raw.

ROAST BEEF

Accompaniments.

Thin gravy.
Yorkshire Pudding (see BATTERS).
Horse-radish sauce (see SAUCES) *or* scraped horse-radish.

Preparation of Principal Joints of Beef for Oven.

Sirloin should have a good undercut (choice of meat, page 92). Remove any superfluous fat, trim the flap, turn it under, and secure with a skewer. If the sirloin is too large, the thin end may be cut off, salted, boiled, and pressed like brisket.

Ribs. (*a*) If the joint is a large one, the thin end frequently becomes overdone and dry before the other part is cooked; to avoid this, cut off the thin end, which will make a good small roast for another occasion. (*b*) A joint of one or two large ribs will not stand well, and it is easier to carve and also more economical if boned and skewered into a neat compact round; the bones can then be used for soup.

Round. Skewer or tie into shape. This joint, being solid, requires rather a longer time for cooking than meat with an average amount of bone, also may require basting on account of the small quantity of fat. For cooking times see page 29.

ROAST MUTTON

Accompaniments.

(a) Onion sauce (see Sauces) with shoulder.

(b) Red currant or cranberry jelly with saddle, leg, loin, or neck.

(c) Thin gravy.

Preparation for Oven.

Leg. Remove the shank if it is very long, and place joint in oven with rounded side uppermost.

Shoulder. If large divide and roast the blade end.

Loin and best end of neck. (a) Remove the spinal cord from the chine bone; this, in both the loin and neck, should be well jointed by the butcher or it is difficult to carve; (b) saw across the rib bones of the neck (if not already done by the butcher) about 3 in. from the tips, fold this flap under, and tie into a compact form; (c) if mutton is very mature remove the tough outside skin.

ROAST LAMB

Time for Cooking is longer than for mutton (see page 29), allow 20 minutes to each pound and 20 minutes over.

Accompaniments. Thin gravy and mint sauce.

ROAST VEAL

Time of Cooking. Veal, also the flesh of a young animal, requires 20 minutes to each pound and 20 minutes over. On account of its deficiency in fat, basting is advisable; greased paper or a little fat bacon on the top prevents hardening of the surface.

The Accompaniments supply the deficiencies of veal, viz., the small amount of fat and the insipid flavour.

(a) Grilled or broiled ham or bacon.

(b) Lemon.

(c) Veal forcemeat for stuffing the meat, or made into small balls, fried or baked in the oven and used as garnish.

(d) A good thickened gravy.

Some joints are boned and stuffed (see page 106).

ROAST PORK

Pork requires a longer time for cooking than either beef, mutton, or lamb—allow 30 minutes to each pound and 30 minutes over.

Accompaniments.

(*a*) Sage and onion stuffing (see FORCEMEAT, page 74).
(*b*) Apple sauce (see SAUCES, page 72).
(*c*) Thickened gravy (see GRAVIES, page 104).

Preparation for Oven.

1. Score the rind of loin, spare-rib, and leg rather deeply, at intervals of about ¼ in., and joint the chine bone of the loin and spare-rib unless this has been already done by the butcher.

2. The forcemeat may be cooked with the joint or separately. To stuff the loin make an incision between the bone and the meat on the inner side, put in the stuffing and secure the opening.

BONED AND STUFFED BAKED JOINTS

A boned joint is economical, the addition of forcemeat makes the meat go farther, and also affords variety.   There is greater ease and no waste in carving because of the removal of the bones, which should be utilized for soup or for gravy to accompany the joint.

To Ascertain the Time Required for cooking, weigh the joint *after* it has been boned and stuffed, allowing 25 to 30 minutes to each pound and 25 to 30 minutes over according to the solidity of the joint.

Suitable Joints.   Mutton : leg, shoulder, loin.
Veal : loin, oyster or blade-bone, breast.
Steak : tender beef or rump steak well beaten.

Accompaniments.   (*a*) Forcemeats, the quantity sufficient for size of the joint ;   veal stuffing is very general for boned and stuffed meat, but onion and sausage forcemeats are frequently used, the latter for joints deficient in fat; (*b*) thickened gravy or any suitable sauce such as brown, tomato, piquante.

Method of Boning Joints of Meat.   Use a small, very sharp, pliant and pointed knife ; remove the bones as cleanly as possible from the meat by a scraping and sharp movement of the knife, keeping it close to the bone the whole time.   Take care not to let it slip and to pierce the outer skin or to disfigure the joint.   When the sinews are reached, cut through them and disjoint the bones, removing them as they are freed by the knife, and any pieces of meat adhering to them add to the joint ; remove pieces of gristle and any superfluous fat.   The forcemeat is either put into the cavity made by the removal of the bones, when the joint retains in a more or less degree its original shape (leg of mutton) or it is spread over the surface of the boned meat, which is rolled and tied into shape.

To Bone a Leg of Mutton.   Should the shank be very long, remove part of it; begin to bone from the fillet end by working the flesh back from the bones; disjoint these and remove them as they are freed from the meat; fill the cavity with the stuffing, sew up the ends neatly with a trussing needle and string, so that the joint may look, as far as possible, its original shape.

To Bone a Shoulder of Mutton. Place the joint on the board with the cut surface uppermost; find the position of the bones with the point of the knife, cut through the flesh to their level, and remove them as neatly as possible. Flatten the joint, insert the forcemeat in the aperture made by the removal of the bones or cover the surface with it, roll up tightly into a neat shape and secure with tape or with a trussing needle and string or stout thread.

To Bone a Loin of Mutton. Remove the bones neatly, flatten and trim the joint, cover the cut surface with the forcemeat, roll into shape, and secure as directed above.

To Bone a Breast of Veal. Follow directions for boning a loin of mutton.

Stuffed Breast of Veal.

Veal 3 to 4 lbs.	Rolls of bacon.
2 tablespoonfuls veal forcemeat.	½ pint tomato sauce (see SAUCES).

Method. 1. Remove bones from breast and use for making gravy or stock for sauce. 2. Spread the forcemeat over the meat,

FIG. 24. ROLLS OF BACON ON A SKEWER READY FOR COOKING

roll up tightly, secure with string or skewers, weigh, allowing 25 minutes to each pound and 25 minutes over, cover with a greased paper. 3. Bake in a hot oven and baste occasionally. 4. Remove rust and rind from bacon, roll up, put the rolls on a skewer, and bake in the oven or grill. 5. Serve veal with the sauce poured round, garnish with rolls of bacon.

"POT ROAST" OR "ROASTING IN A STEWPAN"

To heat an oven for the sole purpose of baking one very small joint means waste of fuel; this can be obviated by cooking it in a pan over a boiling ring (pot roast), which is a method suitable only for comparatively small pieces of meat and for small birds. Meat should be relatively thick and compact in proportion to its weight, and preferably of good quality, as for ordinary roasting or baking, e.g. good buttock steak, best end of the neck or loin of mutton: meat

of close texture such as heart, or of inferior quality, requires prolonged and very gentle cooking.

Method for Roasting in a Stewpan. Use an ordinary heavy saucepan with a closely fitting lid. Heat sufficient dripping in it to cover
the bottom to the depth of about 1½ in., and when the fat smokes
as for frying, put in the meat which should, if necessary, be tied
into a neat shape. Cook for a few minutes on either side to evaporate
some water and to concentrate flavour of the meat juices. Cover with
the lid, place the pan over a moderate heat, turning the meat several
times, and cook till tender. For gravy, thick or thin, proceed in the
usual way.

GRILLED MEAT

For principles, etc., see METHODS OF COOKING (page 29).

Meats used for Grilling. Rump and fillet steak, chops, cutlets,
sausages, kidneys.

Accompaniments. *Maître d'hôtel* butter, and fried potatoes in
ribbons, slices or strips. Worcester sauce, grilled tomatoes, and
mushrooms are also frequently served with grilled meats.

Preparation of Griller. The deflector of a *gas or electric griller* must
be glowing and red hot. Use a perfectly clean *grill-pan, heat* it, and
grease the trivet to prevent the meat from adhering to it.

Time of Cooking is determined by the thickness of the piece of
meat grilled, not by weight. If sufficiently cooked, the surface of
the meat has a puffy appearance, is slightly elastic to the touch,
but spongy when raw, and hard and inelastic if overcooked. If
well grilled, the interior should be red and juicy, the meat juices
having been partly sealed in by the great heat applied to the surface
and by rapid cooking and the outside slightly crisp. The flavour is
concentrated by the evaporation of some water from the juices in the
first few minutes of cooking.

Steak : 1 in. in thickness requires 15 to 18 minutes.
Chop : 1 ,,   ,,   ,,   8 to 10   ,,
Cutlet : ½ ,,   ,,   ,,   6 to 8   ,,
Kidneys :   8 to 10   ,,

Kidneys, if overcooked, are very tough and unfit to be eaten.

A Mixed Grill consists of a small piece of steak, a chop or cutlets,
kidneys and sausages, with tomatoes or mushrooms, the amount
varying with the requirements.

Dishing. Grilled meat is not served with gravy. Place the
meat, with tiny pats of *maître d'hôtel* butter on it, in the centre of
the potatoes. Kidneys, if served alone, are dished on croûtes of
toasted or fried bread, with a pat of the butter in the centre of each.

Serve grilled food at once and very hot.

Preparation of Meat.

This should not be fat for grilling.

1. (*a*) Steak. Should not be less than 1 in. thick, beat it slightly to make it tender, and trim, skewer if necessary.

(*b*) Chops and cutlets. Remove superfluous fat and the bone if desired, from a chump chop, tie or skewer it into a neat shape.

(*c*) Kidneys. Wash thoroughly and dry, remove skin, duct, and fat, and split down lengthwise without separating the halves.

(*d*) Sausages and bacon. Prick the former. Remove rind and rust from bacon.

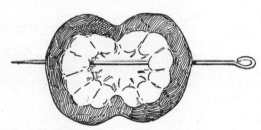

FIG. 25. KIDNEY SPLIT OPEN AND SKEWERED FOR GRILLING

2. Brush over the prepared meat with fat : melted butter, olive oil, or dripping, according to the type of food grilled ; use butter for vegetables, oil or butter for poultry, and dripping as a substitute for butter for most meats.

3. Season with pepper and salt.

Vegetables : *Mushrooms and Tomatoes*. Wipe the vegetables, and trim stalks of the former, cut the latter into halves through the widest part, season and brush over with melted butter. Grill the underside of the mushroom and the cut surfaces of tomatoes first. Time: 4–5 minutes.

Grilled Steak or Chop.

½ lb. rump steak. 2 raw potatoes for potato ribbons.
½ oz. butter or dripping. chips or straws.
½ oz. *maître d'hôtel* butter (see FLAVOURING BUTTERS, pages 74-5).

Method. 1. Prepare *maître d'hôtel* butter. 2. *Prepare potatoes :* wash and peel the potatoes, trim the sides and ends to make them a good shape.

For *straws* cut the potato into slices about ¼ in. in thickness, and these into strips like matches, 2 to 2½ in. long and ¼ in. square.

For *chips,* cut the potatoes into very thin slices. Soak both chips and straws in cold water for about 1 hour, dry thoroughly in a clean towel, fry in deep fat.

3. Wipe the meat, remove outside skin, beat slightly, season with pepper and salt, and brush over with the melted fat. Place

the meat on the heated and greased bars of the grill-pan. Grill under a red-hot griller. Cook quickly to coagulate surface and evaporate some water from the juices. Turn the meat, using two spoons, quickly coagulate surface on the second side. Reduce temperature, and continue to cook for 10 to 15 minutes, turning every 2 minutes.

4. Dish quickly : place pats of the butter on the meat and the potatoes round the dish ; garnish with watercress if available.

5. Serve at once.

BOILED MEAT : FRESH AND SALT
FRESH MEAT

See METHODS OF COOKING (Boiling, page 30).

Suitable Joints. Fresh meat for boiling is wasteful if over-fat. Leg and shoulder of mutton are most suitable.

Preparation for Cooking. Trim away any superfluous fat. To avoid risk of scum settling upon the surface, place the joint in the saucepan of boiling water, with the side downwards which is to be served uppermost.

Accompaniments.

(a) Vegetables : carrot, turnip, and onion cooked with the meat. If young, leave the vegetables whole and cook for 40 to 45 minutes. When old, divide into pieces and allow 1 to 1½ hours. It is important *not* to add vegetables too soon ; most of the mineral matter is thereby extracted and passes into the water, and their value is considerably reduced. Skim meat before adding vegetables.

(b) Parsley or caper cause (see SAUCES).

(c) Mashed turnips, if in season, or any other suitable vegetable.

Dishing. Either coat the joint with the sauce or serve it separately : use the vegetables as a garnish ; if many, serve separately.

SALT MEAT

See METHODS OF COOKING (Boiling, page 30).

Wash the meat first.

If it is over-salt, soak it in cold water for three or four hours and then put it into *cold* water instead of into tepid water, as is usual for salt meat, and bring *slowly* to boiling point ; this tends to extract some of the excess of salt and at the same time softens the meat fibres. Then cook by the usual method.

Time for Cooking. Salt meat requires a longer time and slower cooking than fresh meat : from 25 to 30 minutes or more to each pound and 25 to 30 minutes over, the exact time depending upon the solidity of the joint.

Suitable Joints. Silverside, brisket, and flank of beef.

Accompaniments.

(a) Vegetables : carrot, turnip, and onion are cooked with the meat as for boiled mutton.

(*b*) Small suet dumplings (SUET PASTRY, page 183). These should be about the size of a halfpenny in diameter and are cooked with the meat, being added about 30 minutes before it is dished.

(*c*) Meat liquor : this is served as gravy, a little round the dish with the garnish of vegetables and some in a gravy boat. The remainder, if not too salt, should be used for pea soup, if seasonable.

Boiled Ham or Bacon.

1. **Hams** require to be soaked in lukewarm or cold water, which should be changed once or twice, and frequently if the ham is very salt ; the time required varies with the age, saltness and method of curing : 8 to 12 hours is sufficient for many, 12 to 24 hours or more when the ham has been hanging for a long time and is very hard or very salt.

2. After soaking, scrape the rind and the underside to remove all rusty and discoloured parts.

3. Cover with sufficient lukewarm water (if the ham is very salt use cold water), bring gradually to boiling point, remove scum as it rises, and *simmer* very gently the whole time until the meat is tender, allowing 25 to 30 minutes for each pound.

4. If served cold, let the ham remain in the water until the latter is nearly cold, remove, strip off the rind, and trim the fat.

5. Cover with raspings or, to give a smarter appearance, brush over with liquid meat glaze when the ham is perfectly cold. If served hot, remove from the water as soon as it is cooked, and cover with glaze or raspings. When the latter are used, put the ham in a moderate oven for a short time to crisp and brown the surface, and serve with some suitable sauce.

Bacon. Soak for an hour or so in tepid or cold water, according to degree of saltness, and proceed as for ham.

Hams and bacon, when cooked by the slower method of steaming, are more mellow in flavour ; when steamed, a rather longer time for soaking may often be necessary.

PICKLED MEATS

Meat that is salted or pickled must be of good quality and perfectly fresh. It is necessary to trim it carefully and to remove any kernels or discoloured parts. Silverside or brisket of beef are suitable joints.

Ingredients for Pickling. Either bay salt or common salt or a mixture of both in equal quantities. Bay salt is not so crude as the latter. Saltpetre colours the meat, but tends to harden it ; only a very small quantity is necessary. Sugar and spices are both used, the former having a mellowing effect upon the meat, but these are omitted from the ordinary and simple meat pickle. For pickling, use a vessel with a lid or cover, either an earthenware crock or a wooden trough.

Two Methods of Pickling Meat. (*a*) The wet method is easier, (*b*) the dry method gives a better flavour, but entails more trouble.

Wet Pickle for Beef, Pork, Hams, and Tongues.

1½ lb. of bay or common salt.   ¾ oz. saltpetre.
8 oz. brown sugar.   1½ gallons water.

1. Put all the ingredients into a large clean pan, bring to boiling point, boil for 10 to 15 minutes, skim, strain, and use when cold. Cover the meats to be pickled entirely with the liquid; if insufficient, the meat must be turned each day.
2. After removal from pickle, wash the meat and follow directions for boiling salt meat.

Dry Pickle for Beef, Round or Brisket.

1 lb. bay salt.   ¾ oz. saltpetre.
1 lb. common salt.   ½ teasp. ginger.   ¾ oz. black pepper.
1 lb. brown sugar.   ½ teasp. cloves.   1 dessertsp. allspice.

Method. 1. Before using *dry* pickle, rub the meat over with common salt and leave it for 12 to 24 hours, then drain off brine. 2. Pound all the ingredients together, mix well, and rub mixture into the meat; repeat daily for a week (turning the meat each time) or until the joint is sufficiently spiced. 3. Wash off the pickle before boiling the meat; proceed as for boiling salt meat.

STEAMED MEATS

Both meat and poultry are more tender and also lose less of their flavouring and nutritive substances if steamed rather than boiled, but the process is a slow one, and is therefore more suitable for small joints and for small pieces of meat—chops, cutlets, etc. A quicker method of cooking joints of meat and poultry is in a pressure cooker. For small pieces of meat follow the directions given below.

Steamed Mutton Chop.

Method. 1. Wipe the chop, trim away most of the fat, skewer or tie the chop into a neat shape. 2. Place it on a buttered plate, sprinkle with a little salt, cover with greased paper and another plate or the saucepan lid. 3. Put the plate over boiling water and steam for about 40 minutes. 4. Serve the chop with the meat juice poured over it. *Note.* If for an invalid, remove bone first.

STEWED MEAT

Meat stews include the economical stews made with the coarser and cheaper parts of meat, such as Irish and shin of beef stews, and those which are composed of meats which are more delicate in texture and flavour. Many of these are richer, more highly seasoned and flavoured, also more elaborately prepared and dished, and include *ragoûts*, curries of fresh meats, fricassees and blanquettes, the two latter being made with the white meats, veal, chicken, sweetbread, etc.

The two varieties of stews are : (a) brown, (b) white.

For *white* stews the liquid in which the meat is simmered is thickened with flour at the end, and for *brown* stews with browned flour at the commencement. For cooking white stews and curries use a casserole or white-lined stewpan.

NOTE. If the meat is tough, gelatinous, and coarse, the liquid used for stewing it must be cold when the meat is put into it; also it is unthickened, as a thin liquid will penetrate more quickly and soften the coarse fibres more readily. To soften the fibres of very tough meat before stewing it (shin of beef) dip it for a few minutes into vinegar, or use a meat tenderizer.

BROWN STEW (STEAK, MUTTON, RABBIT)

Characteristics of a Well-made Brown Stew.

(a) A rich brown colour, but not over-dark, and obtained without the aid of " browning " ; to ensure this, careful frying of the vegetables and browning the flour are important.

(b) Freedom from greasiness : this by the removal of fat from the meat and by skimming immediately after the sauce has reached boiling point and before the meat is put in, occasionally during the stewing process, and finally just before dishing.

Causes of Greasiness. Over-heating the roux (butter and flour) in the preparation of the sauce and too prolonged cooking of the stew, which causes the fat to separate from the flour in the sauce.

Addition of Vegetables. These are sliced or cut into dice, and not only add to the flavour, but increase the food value if used, as they should be, in a considerable quantity for the economical and cheaper stews.

The vegetables may be : (a) Fried and slightly browned in the fat when preparing the brown sauce in which the meat is stewed ; having served their purpose of flavouring they are strained out when the stew is dished ; their *removal* makes the sauce smoother, and gives a smarter appearance to the dish. (b) Added to the sauce after the meat has been put in and *not* removed, the sauce having been prepared with the brown roux of fat and flour only or with the addition of a little onion fried in the fat before the flour is added. (c) As a *garnish* and cooked separately, the vegetables being cut into various shapes and boiled till tender in salted water or stock ; the trimmings should be used for flavouring the sauce.

Garnish. A neat and suitable garnish adds considerably to the appearance and flavour of a dish of stewed meat, and, if abundant, to its food value. Vegetables in dice or fancy shapes, grilled tomatoes and mushrooms, peas, French beans, fried or toasted croûtes of bread, slices of lemon, parsley, cooked pulse, macaroni, vermicelli, savoury suet pastry balls, etc.

Average Proportions for a Brown Stew.

1 lb. meat.	Vegetables to flavour
1 oz. flour.	(carrot, turnip, onion).
1 oz. fat.	Seasoning.
¾ pint liquid, water or stock.	Suitable garnish

General Method of Preparation.   (Details on STEWING, see page 31.)

1. Wipe the meat, trim off superfluous fat, and cut into neat pieces.

2. Heat the fat in the stewpan ; when smoking, fry the meat lightly on both sides, browning it slightly, then remove.

3. Reheat the fat, add the sliced onion and colour slightly; if necessary, pour away any superfluous fat.

4. Add the flour, blend with the fat, and fry slowly until the roux is a rich brown colour, but not burnt.

5. Add the stock or water, season with salt, bring to boiling point and skim.

6. Put in the meat, add the carrot and turnip, cut into slices or small pieces ; if these vegetables are to be retained when the stew is dished add them later, allowing just sufficient time for them to become quite tender, not " mushy."

7. Cover the pan tightly and simmer gently for 2 to 2½ hours (according to quality of meat) till the meat is quite tender, but not in rags and with little flavour, most of it having passed into the liquid. Skim occasionally while cooking.

8. Arrange the meat in the centre of the dish, skim the sauce well, season it, and strain it over the meat.   Garnish neatly, either with the vegetables cooked in the stew, or separately, or with any other suitable garnish, which should be cooked in readiness and hot.

WHITE STEW

Fricassee (Veal, Chicken, Rabbit).

Ingredients.	*For Sauce.*	*Garnish.*
1 lb. fillet of veal.	1 oz. flour.	Rolls of bacon grilled or
1 onion.	1 oz. butter.	baked.
6 button mushrooms.	1 gill liquid from	Lemon.
Small bunch of herbs.	veal.	Parsley.
2 or 3 peppercorns.	1 gill milk.	Crescents of fried bread.
Seasoning.	¼ teaspoonful lemon juice.	
Water or white stock.		

Method.   Cut veal into pieces about 1 in. square, put into a white-lined pan or casserole, and barely cover with water; bring to boiling point and skim ;   add the herbs, mushrooms, peppercorns, and salt, and simmer for about 1 hour ;   when the meat is tender, strain off the stock.   2. Make a white sauce with the butter, flour, stock and milk, add seasoning and lemon juice, and reheat the meat in the sauce.   3. Arrange the fricassee on a hot dish and garnish smartly with the lemon, parsley, rolls of grilled bacon, and fried bread.

NOTE. (a) The sauce may be enriched by the addition of 1 to 2 tablespoonfuls of cream at the last.

(b) When using rabbit, steep and cleanse it and joint, cut hind legs into two : cut a chicken into small joints and stew in stock.

Blanquette. Is prepared like a fricassee, one or two yolks of eggs being added at the last to the sauce, which must not be allowed to boil again.

CURRY OF FRESH MEAT

Beef, mutton, veal, tripe, poultry, game, rabbit.

Veal Curry.

1 lb. fillet of veal.	½ oz. shredded coco-nut or a few
1 small apple finely chopped.	almonds blanched and chopped.
1 small onion ,, ,,	½ gill boiling water.
1 oz. flour.	2 gills white stock.
1 oz. butter.	½ teaspoonful lemon juice.
½ oz. curry powder.	*Garnish.*
½ teaspoonful curry paste.	4 oz. Patna rice.
Salt.	Slices of lemon, chilli skins.

Essentials to Success. 1. To preserve the colour and flavour, use a white-lined pan or casserole. 2. A curry sauce must be well skimmed to avoid greasiness, and well cooked to develop the full flavours of the ingredients of curry powder and paste ; if insufficiently cooked, it is crude and rough in flavour. 3. The rice served with curry must be white, tender, and dry, but not hard, each grain being separate. Rice should be served very hot.

To Prepare Curry. Remove skin and fat from meat and cut into neat pieces, not less than 1 in. square, poultry and rabbits into small joints ; soak the coco-nut or almonds (these give a nutty flavour) in boiling water for 20 to 30 minutes and strain. 2. Heat the butter, fry the meat *slightly* in it, on both sides, and remove. 3. Fry the onion slightly, add the curry powder, and cook very slowly for 30 to 45 minutes, until it looks oily, then add flour, apple, water strained from coco-nut or almonds, stock, curry paste, lemon juice and salt, bring to boiling point and skim. 3. Add the meat and simmer for 1½ hours till tender, skimming when necessary and just before dishing.

To Boil Rice for Curry. Patna rice is more suitable than Carolina, the grains are pointed and separate more easily when dried. Wash the rice in several waters until it runs clear. 1. Cook in a white-lined pan, three parts full of rapidly boiling water, add 1 dessert-spoonful salt to every quart, and a few drops of lemon juice to whiten the rice. 2. Boil quickly, with the lid off, remove scum as it rises, and stir occasionally ; this and the rapid ebullition of the water keep the rice in suspension and ensure uniform cooking. Cook till tender, about 10 to 12 minutes, the time depending much upon the quality of the rice.   3. Strain in a colander, rinse well with hot water to separate grains, spread on a hot plate and dry for about 30 minutes in a cool oven, stir lightly with a fork to separate grains and keep hot.

If the curry is cooked in a casserole and sent to table in it, the rice is served separately.

To Dish a Curry.   Arrange the dried rice, which must be very hot, in a border round the dish, place the curried meat in the centre, garnish with parsley, slices of lemon, and shredded chilli skins, or serve the rice separately.

To Curry Cooked Meat and other Cooked Foods, fish, vegetables, pulse, the curry sauce is prepared as by method given, but before the food is added, the sauce must simmer for at least 45 to 60 minutes to develop the flavour of its different curry ingredients.   The food to be curried must be allowed to steep in the hot sauce for some time, so that it may absorb the full curry flavour.   If the sauce is allowed to boil, this would harden meat and break up fish, eggs, vegetables.

STEWED SWEETBREAD

Sweetbreads taint quickly; they must be very fresh, and used quickly after purchase (see INTERNAL PARTS USED FOR FOOD, page 100).   Whatever the method of cooking may be, *blanching* is necessary to make them white and firm.

To Prepare for Cooking.   Wash and soak in cold water, with a little pinch of salt, for an hour at least, to remove blood; drain and rinse; put the sweetbread into a pan, cover with cold water, add a few drops of lemon juice, bring slowly to boiling point, simmer gently for 3 to 4 minutes.   Put into cold water, remove fat and membranous parts, being careful not to break the sweetbread, wash and use.   If not required immediately, press until cold between two plates, with a small weight on top, not sufficiently to crush them.

1 pair calf's sweetbreads.	1 oz. cornflour.
½ pint white stock or milk.	1 tablespoonful cream.
1 small onion.	Lemon juice.
1 small bunch herbs.	Seasoning.

Method of Cooking.   1. Put sweetbreads into a stewpan or casserole, cover with hot white stock, or milk, or stock and milk, add the onion and herbs and simmer gently for 40 to 60 minutes.   2. Remove from the pan, strain off the stock, and make a sauce with it, the flour and butter, season, return sweetbread to it, reheat, add cream and lemon juice just before dishing.

Other Methods of Cooking Sweetbreads.

(a) Cut into slices, coat with egg and crumbs and fry.

(b) Braise (see BRAISING) and serve on spinach.

(c) Stew with mushrooms.

For an invalid's dish, stew simply without onion and herbs.

FRIED MEAT

Fried Liver and Bacon.

A simple and nourishing dish, but one that must have *constant attention* while it is cooking, lack of which often renders it unappetizing and indigestible.

½ lb. calf's liver.	Seasoning.
¼ lb. thin slices of bacon.	¼ pint stock.
½ tablespoonful flour.	Parsley.

Method. 1. *Cleanse thoroughly,* wash in slightly salted tepid water, drain and *dry* well. 2. Cut into slices about ¼ in. thick; if over-thin, the liver when cooked is hard and dry. 3. *Coat* with seasoned flour (1 tablespoonful flour, ½ teaspoonful salt, ¼ level teaspoonful pepper) *just before frying*; if coated long before, the liver becomes moist and sodden and does not fry well. 4. Heat the pan slightly, remove rust and rind from bacon, fry, and remove on to a hot dish and keep hot. 5. Fry the liver in the bacon fat, not too rapidly, on both sides; the surface should be slightly crisp and brown, and the liver thoroughly cooked; before removing, test one piece. When cut through, the liver should not be red in the centre. A little extra fat may be required for frying.

To Make the Gravy. Leave about 1 teaspoonful of fat in the pan, blend with it a teaspoonful of flour, brown, add the stock, bring to boiling point, boil for 3 or 4 minutes, skim well, and season.

To Dish. Place the liver in centre of dish with the bacon on the top, strain the thickened gravy round.

Fried Mutton Cutlets (Coated).

Dishes of fried mutton cutlets are designated by different names, which are frequently derived from the particular sauce or garnish accompanying them, but the methods of preparing and frying the cutlets are the same for all.

1¼ lbs. best end neck of mutton (5 or 6 cutlets).	Fat for frying 2 or 3 oz.
Dried white crumbs.	Suitable sauce (tomato, brown, piquante, see SAUCES).
Egg.	Garnish of vegetables in dice or small fancy shapes or other suitable garnish.
Seasoning.	
Duchess potatoes (optional).	

Choose well-hung small mutton, preferably without an interlining of fat and of lean, which is wasteful; it is extravagant to buy cutlets ready trimmed; the fat can be clarified and the trimmings of lean used for stock.

To Trim and to Prepare Cutlets for Frying. 1. If the chine bone has not been removed, stand the piece of meat with the chine end resting on the board and the end of the ribs standing up, saw the chine bone away cleanly, being careful not to cut into the meat, then saw across the rib bones, leaving them equal in length and about 3½ in. long, the actual length depending upon the size of the " fillet." 2. Wipe the meat and cut through the flesh exactly midway between each bone, so that each cutlet is of even thickness. If large mutton, a " false cutlet," that is one without bone, can be obtained by cutting close to the bones rather than midway between each when dividing the cutlets.

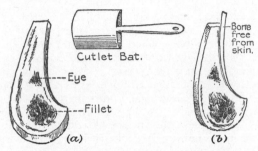

Cutlet Bat.

---Eye

---Fillet

(a)

Bone free from skin.

(b)

FIG. 26. (a) CUTLET BEFORE TRIMMING
(b) CUTLET TRIMMED

Flatten the cutlets slightly with a wetted cutlet bat or rolling pin, trim away superfluous fat, leaving only a narrow rim to hold the " eye " and " fillet " together; if this is broken, the smart and compact appearance of the cutlet is spoiled. 4. Scrape the skin away from the whole length of the underside of the bone and the fat and skin entirely from the tip, leaving ¾ in. quite clean for the cutlet frill. 5. Coat with egg and bread-crumbs, press on the crumbs well and scrape them away from the back and tip of the bone.

Duchess Potatoes.

Ingredients.

½ lb. cooked and sieved potato.	1 yolk of egg and a little
½ oz. butter.	cream or milk.
	Seasoning.

Boil, *dry well*, and sieve potatoes, melt the butter, add the potato, the egg, seasoning, cream or milk, mix thoroughly, and beat well to bind the mixture. To use, there are two methods—

(a) Turn the potato on to a slightly floured board and with a knife form a roll; cut roll into 1½–2 in. lengths, place on a greased tin, and mash lattice-fashion with a knife.

(b) Force potato on to a greased tin. Use a fairly large bag and a vegetable pipe-rose design. Brush over potatoes with yolk or white of egg diluted with milk; reheat and brown in oven.

A forcing bag and pipe of this size are suitable for piping vegetable *purées* (pea *purée*) when decorating meat entrées and for laying out éclairs and meringues and soft cake mixtures in fancy designs.

 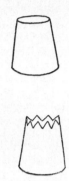

FIG. 27. FORCING BAG   LARGE FORCING PIPES

To Use Bag and Pipe. Drop the pipe into the bag, half fill it with hot potato mixture, close the mouth of the bag by twisting it from right to left until the potato within is a firm and compact mass and just appearing at the nozzle of the pipe; then use as directed above.

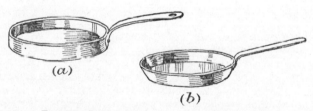

FIG. 28. SAUTÉ PAN   FRYING PAN

Sauce and Garnish. Prepare these before frying the cutlets and keep hot. For a plain dish of mutton cutlets, a simple sauce and garnish, such as a macedoine of vegetables, peas, shredded beans, etc., are suitable, but, with the more elaborate dishes, the richer sauces and more elaborate garnishes are used.

To Fry Cutlets. 1. Use a frying or sauté pan with sufficient fat to cover the bottom to the depth of about $\frac{1}{4}$ in.; when the fat is smoking, arrange the cutlets in the pan, a little distance apart and with the side which is to be served uppermost next to the pan, the first side fried being the best. 2. Fry first on one side, then on the other, until crisp and a golden brown colour, turn again if necessary; time, 7 to 10 minutes, according to the thickness of the cutlets, which must be juicy when cut, but not underdone.

To Dish Cutlets. As with all hot dishes, and particularly in relation to hot meat entrées, it is important to dish *smartly*, but *quickly*, so that the dish may be quite hot when sent to table. For this reason, all adjuncts to the dish-garnish, sauce and vegetables, must be in readiness and very hot. Except as a dish served in plain household fare, it has become the vogue to serve cutlets and fillets, and other meat entrées, on the dish with the garnish *only*, sauce, and vegetables separately. The cutlet frills are also more or less optional. With everything in readiness, arrange the cutlets neatly down the centre of the dish in a slightly sloping position or in a semicircle with the bones on the inside.

Garnish with the macedoine (various vegetables cut into fancy shapes) previously heated in a little stock or water and seasoned. Serve the sauce in a hot sauce-boat and the potatoes in a hot vegetable dish.

NOTE. Mutton cutlets, egged and crumbed, are frequently fried in deep fat, but it is advisable to par-roast the best end of neck before preparing the cutlets.

Fried Fillets of Beef.

This is not a cheap dish, and it can be very extravagant if the fillets are wastefully cut and trimmed.

1 lb. fillet of beef or tender rump steak.	Seasoning. Clarified fat or butter for frying.
1 or 2 tomatoes (small).	½ pint sauce (brown, tomato or other suitable sauce).
¼ oz. *maître d'hôtel* butter (see FLAVOURING BUTTERS).	

To Prepare Fillets. 1. Wipe the meat, remove any skin or tendon, cut into slices about ¾ in. thick, flatten slightly, and cut neatly into small rounds about 2½ to 3 in. in diameter. Beef shrinks considerably in frying. 2. Slice tomatoes, season, and put a tiny piece of butter on each slice; cook for a few minutes in moderate oven just before required. Prepare *maître d'hôtel* butter, put aside, and cut into small rounds when firm. 3. Season fillets lightly, and fry quickly in hot fat, turn when one side is cooked; the time required is about 7 to 8 minutes; when cut, the inside of the fillets should be red, not raw, and juicy, if properly fried.

To Dish. Lift the fillets from the pan with a knife, allowing the fat to drain off, and arrange in a line or in a circle. 2. Place on each fillet a round of tomato and a tiny pat of the butter. 3. Strain the sauce round.

Other Garnishes. Button onions fried in butter, mushrooms, etc.

BRAISING

Braising is a combination of stewing and of baking or roasting whereby a particularly fine flavour and aroma are developed, because the loss by evaporation is so slight and the braise is cooked on a foundation or bed of vegetables and other savoury ingredients called the "mirepoix." The "braisoire," or braiser proper, can be used, but an ordinary strong stewpan (not enamel-lined) or a casserole with lid answers the purpose quite well, its capacity being proportionate to the bulk of the food braised; there should be a space all round between the "braise" and the sides of the pan to prevent the joint from being scorched by immediate contact with the hot sides. The first part (the longer) of the process of braising is carried out on a boiling ring, and the second part in the oven.

Barding and Larding. The meats suitable for braising are generally lean and deficient in fat; this deficiency is supplied by bacon, which is either used to cover the breast of poultry or game or the surface of small joints, and is termed " barding," or it is inserted in small strips or " lardoons," and this is called " larding."

Larding Bacon. Any firm fat bacon will answer the purpose. A larding needle is necessary for larding. This is made in various sizes to suit the size of the lardoons used, it is a thin metal tube, sharply pointed at one end, and at the broad end split into four divisions to take and to grip the lardoons.

The Mirepoix and How to Prepare It. Much of the success of a braise depends upon the mirepoix, which imparts the aroma and flavour peculiar to braised foods. The mirepoix consists generally of an equal quantity of onion and carrot and half that of turnip, bacon, a bunch of herbs, a little butter or good dripping, stock, and for a rich braise a little wine. *To prepare* the mirepoix. 1. Slice the vegetables thickly, cut the bacon into small pieces, melt the butter, add the bacon and vegetables, and fry slightly. 2. Add the bunch of herbs, a little salt, and sufficient stock to just cover the vegetables. 3. Bring to boiling point and use as directed. The liquid from the mirepoix is very rich in flavour; this is utilized when the meat is removed.

Meat Suitable for Braising. Small boned and stuffed joints, poultry, game, fillets and cutlets of meat, sweetbreads, hare, rabbit, etc.

Method of Cooking a Braise. 1. Place the larded joint or piece of meat on the mirepoix, cover with a greased paper, and tightly fitting lid of the stewpan or casserole. 2. Cook on a boiling ring for two-thirds of the time, baste frequently. 3. Remove the stewpan to a moderate oven, baste, and during the last 20 or 30 minutes remove lid and paper to crisp the lardoons; care must be taken that the liquid does not reduce too much while the pan is in the oven. 4. Place the braised meat on a hot dish, strain the liquid from the mirepoix, reduce it in a small pan to the consistency of syrup, skim well, brush over the meat with the glaze, and dish the meat with accompaniments as directed.

To Cut Lardoons. Place the bacon with the rind downwards on the board and cut off slices ⅛ to ¼ of an inch in thickness. The bacon should be sliced parallel with the vein in it, not across it, or the lardoons will break when used. Cut the slices into strips about 1½ to 2 in. in length with even and square ends. The size of the

A FOWL "BARDED"
WITH FAT BACON

ARRANGEMENT OF
"LARDOONS" SHOWING
ALTERNATE STITCHES

FIG. 29

lardoons varies slightly with the size of the piece of meat to be larded, whether a joint or a fillet or cutlet : let the lardoons get quite cool and firm before use.

To Insert Lardoons. Place one in the split end of the needle, the pressure as it is drawn through the meat keeps it firm, and insert the point in and *across* the grain of the meat ; take a stitch about

FIG. 30. LARDING NEEDLE

⅓ in. deep and ¾ in. wide, draw it sharply through, leaving the projecting ends equal in length. Arrange the lardoons in parallel lines about 1 in. apart, the stitches in one row being directly beneath those in the alternate. When larding the breasts of birds, insert the lardoons on either side of and at right-angles to the breastbone. If the lardoon is too large it is pressed out of the needle as it passes through the meat, if too small the needle cannot grip it.

Braised Veal.

Ingredients.

1½ to 2 lbs. fillet of veal.
Larding bacon.
¼ pint tomato sauce.
3 to 4 tablespoonfuls veal forcemeat.

Garnish.

Cooked green peas or any suitable garnish.

Mirepoix.

Onion, carrot, turnip.
½ oz. butter.
1 oz. fat bacon.
Bunch of herbs.
Salt.
Stock.

Method. Follow the directions given for cooking a braise. 1. Prepare mirepoix and forcemeat, spread the latter on the veal, roll it up into a neat shape, secure with small skewers, lard the surface, and proceed as directed. 2. Allow about 1½ hours for cooking. 3. Remove the meat to a hot dish, pour off the liquid from the mirepoix, reduce, and brush over the meat with it. 4. Pour the sauce round and garnish.

Variation. A piece of tender rump steak stuffed and larded.

IMPORTED MEAT: (a) FROZEN, (b) CHILLED

Of these two varieties, there are several grades or qualities, but the flavour of the best quality of *chilled*, when thoroughly thawed and well-hung, compares by no means unfavourably with the home-fed beef and mutton. Imported meat is obtainable all the year; the best quality of beef comes from the Argentine, and mutton and lamb (Canterbury) of the best grade from New Zealand; lamb is in the best condition from March to September. The price of English meat is generally higher than chilled meat; frozen meat is cheaper than the chilled. On account of a limited purse, the housewife often has to purchase imported meat, and she should be able to distinguish between the two kinds.

Frozen meat is kept in a refrigerating chamber at a temperature just below freezing point, and the meat becomes solid, spicules of ice being visible throughout. When required, it must be de-frosted, which must be gradual. When frozen meat is not sufficiently thawed, liquid exudes from it as it stands; this, the flabby condition, and the very white colour of fat, indicate that the meat is *frozen, not chilled.*

Chilled meat is stored at a temperature just sufficiently low to prevent decomposition; the meat juices do not exude when it is thawed and allowed to stand, and the full flavour is retained. When meat is frozen, the juices contained in the muscle fibres expand and cause the latter to rupture, so when the meat is defrosted, the juices escape. Should frozen meat not be sufficiently thawed when purchased, place the joint in a cool place to continue the process, otherwise, when cooked, the surface will be done before the heat has penetrated to the deeper parts, which will be underdone and unpalatable in appearance and flavour.

CHAPTER 14

REHEATED FOOD

RÉCHAUFFÉS OF MEAT AND OF FISH

FROM an economical standpoint, that is, the utilization of the "left-overs" and scraps of food in the larder or refrigerator, the reheating and redressing of already cooked food, which is a test of good management in relation to the food of the household, is an important branch of cookery, but not on this account only. Cooked food, particularly meats and fish, lack flavour, and are indigestible if *recooked*. Recooking toughens the fibres and still further hardens the protein and makes such réchauffés difficult of digestion. Therefore both meat and fish which have been already cooked *require* to be and *must* be reheated only, neither recooked nor over-heated. Also both meat and fish lose some of their nourishing properties in cooking, and this loss should be supplemented or the food value is lessened, which is a point to be considered when planning a meal, particularly for a family of growing children. In addition to these points, the minor but still important ones of judicious and suitable seasonings and flavourings and of suitable accompaniments, which will supplement any deficiency in food value if necessary, are all factors in determining the success and value of a réchauffé. Again, variety as to additional ingredients and methods of reheating is important, a frequent repetition of hash or mince, however well made, soon becomes monotonous. Also some réchauffés can be made more attractive if prepared and served in small individual dishes or cases, e.g. mince in small cases of pastry—fish in small scallop shells, etc. (see FISH SCALLOPS).

General Directions for Reheating Meat and Fish.

1. Utilize all scraps of food, gravies, sauces, vegetables, but use nothing that is not absolutely fresh.

2. *Meats.* Trim from the bone, remove fat and gristle and any inedible part, the retention of the cooked fat, particularly in hash or mince, makes a réchauffé greasy ; fat is supplied in the sauces and panada, and by the addition of butter. Use the bones and trimmings for stock for the sauce or gravy.

Fish. Free from skin and bone. Use bones and trimmings for stock.

3. Finely divide meats and fish, this allows the flavourings and seasonings to permeate and the heat to penetrate quickly to all

parts, which reduces the time for reheating and the risk of making the food tough.

Chop or pass meat through the mincer or slice finely ; flake fish coarsely or finely according to purpose for which it is required.

4. Any added ingredient must be cooked first : the short time necessary for reheating does not allow time for raw food to be thoroughly cooked, e.g. onion in rissole or *croquette* mixture, potatoes in fish cakes, rice in cutlet mixtures.

5. Additional moisture in the form of a sauce or gravy is necessary. Both meat and fish lose moisture in cooking, particularly meat, for which reason meat a little underdone is preferable for réchauffés, e.g. a shepherd's pie may be dry and unpalatable if the meat is not sufficiently moistened.

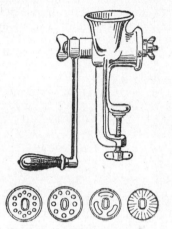

To reheat meat in a sauce, a white or light coloured sauce is suitable for white meats (veal, poultry, rabbit), a brown sauce for meat or game (hash or mince), and a white sauce for fish.

FIG. 31. MINCING MACHINE

6. A panada or thick binding sauce, is necessary for binding together the minced ingredients for *croquette* and similar (*kromeski*) mixtures, the consistency of the mixture, which should be soft and creamy, depending upon the panada. This *must* be well cooked, otherwise the mixture has a raw flavour, for if the reheating is properly carried out, the heat penetrating to it is not sufficient to cook the raw flour.

Proportions for Panada.

(a) ½ oz. flour, ½ oz. butter, 1 gill liquid (stock or milk) for ½ lb. *meat*.
(b) ½ oz. flour, ½ oz. butter, ½ gill liquid (stock or milk) for ½ lb. *fish*.

Less liquid is used for a panada for fish, as the latter is generally moister than meat. If meat is very dry, the gill of panada may be insufficient; then add gravy or stock to give the necessary moisture and consistency.

7. *Seasonings and Flavourings.* Cooked meat and fish, being rather insipid, require to be well seasoned and nicely flavoured, which must be left to individual taste and to discretion in their use.

For *croquette* mixtures, etc., a mixture of meats and a little salt meat, such as boiled beef, ham, or tongue, with fresh meat, are an improvement. Cold meat, too, is often steeped in a little oil and vinegar seasoned and flavoured with herbs (a *marinade*) before it is redressed ; this moistens it and gives additional flavour. For white meats, lemon rind and juice, parsley, herbs, nutmeg, and tomato are suitable seasonings ; for others onion, tomato, mushroom, curry paste and powder, and bought sauces are all used, but a flavouring of fresh vegetables is preferable to that of bought sauces, which, when used, should be added sparingly.

8. The protection of food during reheating from the direct heat of the oven or of hot fat is very necessary. In the oven, by enclosing in pastry or in batter (toad-in-the-hole), or by a covering of potato (shepherd's pie) ; in hot fat, by a coating of batter (*kromeskies*), of egg and crumbs (croquettes), or by enclosing in pastry (rissoles).

9. Dish neatly and garnish suitably—fry parsley for fried mixtures.

10. It is often an improvement to some réchauffés if a little good sauce or gravy is served separately.

Hash or Mince

1. To reheat meat in the form of a hash or mince, put it into a hot sauce and let it steep in the sauce for 30 minutes to become quite hot and to absorb the flavour of the sauce, which must on no account be at boiling point when the meat is added, and must be kept below simmering point the whole time, otherwise the meat will be tough and indigestible.

2. The success of a hash or mince greatly depends upon the sauce. Use the bones and trimmings of the joint for stock in the preparation of the sauce. Make a good brown sauce in the ordinary way, using vegetables for flavouring, cook for 30 minutes, season, skim, strain, and use.

INGREDIENTS AND PROPORTIONS

Meat.	Sauce.	Flavourings.	Accompaniments.
1 lb.	¾ pint brown sauce.	Any suitable to meat used.	Sippets of toast for *hash*. A border of cooked macaroni or rice (3 to 4 oz.) or mashed potato for *mince*.

Method.

1. **Hash.** (a) Cut the meat into neat slices, remove skin, gristle, and fat; if too thin the meat is inclined to be hard. (b) Follow directions given for reheating—garnish dish with the sippets.

2. **Mince.** (a) Chop the meat finely or put through the mincer. Add it to the sauce : a mince must be neither " sloppy " nor " stodgy," (b) reheat as directed, (c) arrange macaroni, rice, or potato round dish with the mince in the centre.

NOTE. To supply additional nutriment two or three poached eggs are sometimes served on the top.

Mixture for Meat Croquettes, Cutlets, and Rissoles.

Any meat or mixture of meats—white or red—poultry, game or rabbit can be used with suitable flavourings and seasonings.

Proportions.	*Seasoning and Flavouring.*
½ lb. cooked meat.	1 teaspoonful chopped parsley.
1 gill stock ⎫	Pepper, salt.
½ oz. flour ⎬ Panada.	Chopped, cooked onion for flavouring.
½ oz. butter ⎭	

Method. Make the panada; chop meat finely, otherwise the mixture is not smooth. Add seasonings and flavourings, add to the panada and mix well. Turn the mixture on to a plate to get cold and firm, then use as directed.

1. *For Croquettes.* 1. Form into 6 or 8 cork shaped pieces even in size. 2. Coat with egg and bread-crumbs, press the coating on well and coat a second time, this improves their appearance. 3. Fry in hot, deep fat, until crisp and firm, drain well. 4. Dish piled on a paper d'oyley and garnish with fried parsley.

2. *For Cutlets.* 1. Form into 6 or 8 cutlet shaped pieces, egg and crumb twice, put a piece of macaroni in the end of each, and fry in deep fat. 2. Dish as for croquettes.

3. *For Rissoles.* About 2 tablespoonfuls of the mixture and 2 oz. of short crust. 1. Roll out the pastry very thinly and cut into rounds about 4 to 4½ in. in diameter. 2. Place a little of the mixture on each, wet the edges of pastry, fold in two, and seal. 3. Coat with egg and crumbs, fry in deep fat.

A Variation.

To economize meat, if necessary, use cooked mashed potato as for fish cakes—the proportion ⅓ to ½ of potato to meat.

Kromeskies (Veal, Chicken, Rabbit).

These make a dainty small entrée; just the scraps and trimmings of white meats and of ham or tongue can be utilized.

PROPORTIONS

Mixture.	*Coating Batter.*	*Panada.*
3 oz. cooked white meat.	2 oz. flour.	¼ gill milk.
1 oz. cooked ham or tongue.	Pinch of salt.	½ oz. flour.
Seasoning and lemon rind.	1 dessertspoonful salad oil.	½ oz. butter.
3 button mushrooms.	¼ gill tepid water.	*Garnish* of lemon and parsley.
Thin slices of fat bacon.	1 white of egg.	

Method. 1. Prepare coating batter (see BATTERS, MAKING AND FRYING, page, 194). 2. Mince the meats and mushrooms finely, add the seasoning, grated lemon rind, and mix well with sufficient panada to bind the mixture to a soft consistency. 3. Form into small cork-shaped pieces of an even size, and wrap each in a small and *very* thin slice of bacon—if thick, the bacon will be under-cooked. 4. Dip the rolls in the batter, fry in moderately hot fat till crisp and a golden brown colour ; drain well. 5. Serve garnished with the lemon and parsley.

RÉCHAUFFÉS OF FISH

1. For these dishes any kind of cooked white fish is suitable, to some the addition of a little smoked haddock is an improvement, and also affords variety in flavour.

2. The sauce left over with boiled fish should be used, and it is often sufficient for binding and moistening a fish mixture.

3. Cooked fish is more insipid than meat, and requires to be very well seasoned and nicely flavoured ; lemon juice which is used for most dishes, parsley, and anchovy essence are the most general flavourings.

4. Lemon and parsley, fried or not, are used for garnishing.

Fish Cakes.

Proportions.

Double the quantity of fish to potato or ⅔ fish and ⅓ potato.
½ lb. cooked white fish.
¼ lb. cooked mashed potato.

½ oz. melted butter.
1 teaspoonful chopped parsley
Seasoning and lemon juice.
White sauce or egg to bind.
Garnish, lemon and parsley.

Method. 1. Free fish from skin and bone and divide very finely, add the potato, chopped parsley, lemon juice, and seasoning. 2. Add to it the melted butter and sufficient sauce or egg to bind the ingredients, mix thoroughly. 3. Turn on to a plate in a round cake. 4. When cold, divide into eight pieces and shape into neat flat round cakes equal in size. 5. Coat *twice* with egg and bread-crumbs. 6. Fry in the ordinary way in deep fat. 7. Garnish with lemon and fried parsley.

Mixture for Fish Croquettes and Cutlets.

Proportions.

½ lb. cooked fish.
½ oz. butter ⎫
½ oz. flour ⎬ Panada.
½ gill milk ⎭

Seasonings and flavouring and garnish as for fish cakes.

Method. 1. Free fish from skin and bone and flake very finely, add the seasonings and flavourings and sufficient panada to bind the ingredients together into a soft, smooth mixture. 2. Follow directions for shaping, coating, and frying meat croquettes and cutlets. If there is any white sauce, use it instead of panada.

Fish Scallops.

Proportions.

¼ lb. cooked white fish.	⅓ lb. cooked sieved potato.
⅛ pint thick white sauce.	Pepper, salt, lemon juice.
Fresh white crumbs.	Melted butter.

Method. 1. Butter some china scallop shells, sprinkle lightly with fresh white crumbs and put a little sauce in the bottom of each. 2. Divide the fish into large flakes, put some in each shell, season with pepper, salt, and lemon juice, cover with sauce, then with a thin coating of crumbs and sprinkle a little melted butter over the surface. 3. Pipe the potato round each shell. 4. Reheat in a quick oven—the surface should be nicely browned.

Some Hints on Using Up Larder Scraps.

A good housekeeper wastes nothing that is fit for food, only rejects food tainted or too stale: there is always a certain amount of scraps, but every particle of food, liquid or solid, can be utilized in some way.

1. Bones and scraps of meat, fresh and cooked, for the stock-pot or to be used for soups, sauces, and gravies.

2. Sauces and gravies in the reheating of food.

3. Remains of joints, poultry, game; tongue, ham, bacon for réchauffés.

4. Scraps of fat, raw and cooked, for clarifying and used for frying.

5. Cooked fish for réchauffés.

6. Trimmings and pieces of raw and cooked vegetables; raw for stock, soups and stews; cooked, for salads and also reheated.

7. Dry cheese, grated and used for cheese dishes and those au gratin.

8. Scraps of bread, as crumbs with flour for suet puddings, etc.; dried and browned in oven, used as raspings; dried, not browned, for coating fried fish.

9. Stale cakes for sweet dishes and steamed puddings of custard type.

10. Remains of cold or hot sweets, redished with or without additions in one *dish* or in individual portions. Hot sweets reheated.

CHAPTER 15
POULTRY AND RABBITS
POULTRY

POULTRY includes all the domestic birds suitable for food : fowl, turkey, goose, duck, and pigeon. The composition is similar to that of meat, but poultry of good quality is a high-priced food, for it costs more per lb. than meat, on account of the large proportion of waste—the carcase, bones, and inedible parts.

The flesh of chicken, fowl, and turkey is more easily digested than butchers' meat, because the fibres are shorter and the flesh is not so interlined with fat, which, in poultry, is found beneath the skin and surrounding the intestines. The white meat (breast and wing) of poultry is more digestible than that of the legs, which is coarser fibred and darker in colour on account of the greater muscular activity in those parts.

Choice of Poultry. In young poultry, the legs are smooth and pliant, the scales are not coarse, and are only slightly overlapping, and in the male bird the spurs are small scaly knobs. The feet are supple, the beak and breastbone pliable, the tip of the latter being merely cartilage. The skin is white and unwrinkled, the breast plump and white. The quills in the wings are not difficult to remove, there is an abundance of pin feathers, an absence of long hairs, especially upon the thighs, and plenty of down under the wings and over the body generally. The comb and wattles of young fowls are small. If *fresh* there is no unpleasant odour, and the flesh is firm and shows no trace of a bluish or greenish tinge. The eyes of freshly killed poultry are clear and not sunken, the feet soft and limp, and the feathers soft and full. Poultry which has been kept in " cold storage " can be distinguished by the skin, which is not such a good colour, and is sometimes broken and the flesh is shrunken —such poultry is also cheaper in price.

Hanging. As with meat, poultry to be tender must be hung until the period of *rigor mortis* has passed. It should be suspended by the feet in a cool, dry, well-ventilated larder ; the time for hanging varies with the kind of bird and with weather conditions. A fowl or chicken should hang for at least 24 hours, geese or ducks for a day or two, turkeys for 3 to 5 days.

Poultry must never be overhung, the slightest greenish tinge of the skin denotes the bird is not fresh.

Fowls. Surrey fowls and chicken are considered the best. The colour of the skin and legs varies with the breed : birds with a white skin are considered best for boiling, game birds and those with yellow skins and black legs for roasting. A bird for roasting, grilling, or frying, should be young and tender, but for the longer and slower process of boiling, stewing, or braising, an older and, therefore, cheaper, bird answers the purpose. If an old fowl or turkey is to be roasted, steam it first for half of the time, then it will roast quite well, provided it is well basted. A bird is considered a chicken until it is 9 months old : a capon is a fowl hormone-treated to grow to a very large size, its flesh and that of the female (*poularde*) is much finer in flavour than that of the ordinary fowl.

Broilers. This term is applied to chickens that are reared under controlled conditions in special houses. They are considered ready for killing from 10 to 12 weeks old, and are sold trussed ready for cooking.

Turkeys. Those bred in Norfolk are considered of the finest flavour. The flesh of a turkey of medium size is much more tender and delicate in flavour than that of a very large bird ; the cock bird is suitable for roasting, the hen bird is better boiled. When young, the legs of the cock bird are smooth with short spurs ; pale or reddish and rough legs and the flesh purplish in colour, with long hairs, indicate age.

Turkeys should be hung for at least 3 days before they are cooked.

Geese and Ducks, when young, have yellow, pliable feet and bills which become darker as they mature ; the webbing of the feet should be soft and easily torn, and the underside of the bill soft and pliable, and easily broken if bent. The breast of a young bird should be plump, but not over-fat, the skin white and smooth, and the breastbone pliable. Old birds have stiff quills, blunt at the tips, and the feathers are not so soft. A goose, if over a year old, is not suitable for the table ; green geese are from 2 to 3 months old ; Aylesbury ducks and ducklings are considered the best. Ducklings are in season from March to August, ducks from August to March.

Pigeons. The legs of young birds are slender and pinkish in colour, and the breast is plump ; the flesh of a pale coloured bird is considered more delicate than that of the darker kind. The tame pigeon is smaller than the wood pigeon and, as the flesh quickly loses flavour, it should be cooked soon after it is killed. A wood pigeon is better if hung for 2 or 3 days.

PREPARATION OF POULTRY FOR COOKING

To Pluck and Singe Poultry. To prevent the feathers from flying about, avoid a draught when plucking birds. The feathers come out more easily if the bird is still warm when it is plucked. Remove the feathers first from the legs and wings ; the flesh of the breast being very tender, leave this until the last. Begin to pluck from the tail towards the head, drawing the feathers out with a backward pull and against the direction in which they lie ; if the bird is very young and the flesh tender, pluck from the head towards the tail, to avoid tearing the skin. For the wing feathers it is necessary to use a small knife, be careful to remove all stumps of feathers : should the wing feathers be very difficult to remove, dipping the tips of the wings in boiling water makes their removal easier. To dip the bird in boiling water before plucking it is not advisable; it makes plucking easier, but the skin soft and likely to tear. After all the feathers are removed, singe the bird to remove the long hairs on old birds and the down on young ones. Use a taper, or hold the bird over a gas jet, but be careful neither to blacken nor to scorch the skin.

To Draw a Fowl. Be very careful not to break the intestines or gall bladder; the latter is a greenish looking sac attached to the liver, and if broken a very bitter flavour is imparted to any part the gall may touch.

1. Place the bird on the board with the back uppermost and the head towards you. Slit the skin down from the head for 3 or 4 in., detach the neck from the skin and cut it off close to the body, cut off the head and some of the skin, leaving about 3 or 4 in. Draw out the windpipe and gullet and remove the crop. This is a membranous bag, which adheres closely to the skin of the neck. Put the neck into cold water with a little salt.

2. Turn the bird on its back with the head towards you. Insert the first finger at the neck aperture and loosen the internal parts by breaking the small ligaments, but do not draw from this end.

3. Turn the bird round ; make a small slit with a sharp knife between the tail and the vent, cut away the latter. Insert two fingers, taking care not to further enlarge the aperture and to tear the skin ; grip the gizzard firmly with the crooked fingers, and with it draw out the rest of the organs. Be careful to remove all ; the kidneys lie in the hollow near the backbone, and the lungs, a pinkish, spongy mass, are embedded on either side of the backbone in the ribs. Remove the soft fat near the neck and vent, and cut away the oil bag near to the tail or parson's nose.

4. Wipe the surface with a clean, damp cloth, then the inside thoroughly. If there should be any disagreeable odour, rinse the inside with cold water, to which a very few crystals of permanganate of potash should be added, then dry with a clean cloth.

To Truss a Fowl for Roasting.

1. For the legs of a roasting fowl to be tender, it is necessary to *remove the sinews*, particularly if the bird is not young. To draw the sinews, cut through the skin about $1\frac{1}{2}$ in. below the hock joint, being careful not to sever the tendons. Place the leg, at the point where the skin has been cut, over the edge of the board, press it down, and snap the bone. Then hold the bird firmly on the table with the left hand, give the foot a sharp twist and a pull, and the foot will come away with the sinews. If the bird is old the sinews,

seven in all, must be taken out one by one; insert a skewer beneath each and with a twist draw the sinew away. Scald the piece of each leg in boiling water and peel off the outer skin.

2. Put the bird *breast downwards* on the board, draw the skin at the neck over the back to close the aperture, and fold the wings backwards and inwards over the flap of skin.

3. (*a*) Turn the bird over with the breast uppermost and push the tail through the slit in the skin; this closes the aperture.

(*b*) Push the legs backwards towards the wings, the latter being a little lower than the level of the legs, press the legs well into the sides and downwards, which gives the breast a plump appearance.

(*c*) Thread a trussing needle with a long piece of fine string and

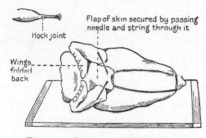

Flap of skin secured by passing needle and string through it

Hock joint

Wings folded back

FIG. 32. SHOWING METHOD OF FOLDING WINGS OF FOWL AND SECURING FLAP OF SKIN

FIG. 33. FOWL TRUSSED FOR ROASTING

pass the needle through the wing and leg on one side, through the body, and through the leg and wing on the other side.

(*d*) Turn the fowl over, pass the needle through the tips of the wings and through the flap of skin, and tie the two ends of string, but not too tightly, or the bird when cooked will not stand evenly upon the dish. Remove the needle.

(*e*) Bring the ends of string together down to the tail end, tie round the tail, then press the two legs together with the shanks standing upright and tie the string securely round them.

To Truss a Fowl for Boiling. A boiled fowl is trussed similarly to one that is roasted, except that the legs are secured *within* the body cavity and not outside. This is to give a smooth surface for coating evenly with sauce.

1. Pluck, singe, and draw the bird as for roasting, wipe it outside and inside with a clean, damp cloth.

2. Cut the skin round the hock joints, twist the shank sharply and remove it with the foot, drawing out with it the sinews from the leg.

3. Insert a finger in the aperture made for drawing and pass it between the skin and the flesh of the thigh and drumstick until the leg is quite free from the skin. Place the thumb against the

hock joint and force the leg upwards and backwards into the interior of the bird; this is called " pocketing " the legs; push the skin which covered the drumstick inside. Proceed in the same manner with the other leg. Then draw the skin smoothly over, enclosing the tail and closing the aperture.

4. Truss as for roast fowl, bring the ends of string forward, twist it twice tightly round the tail end, and over the hock joints to prevent the legs from slipping backwards and upwards and from breaking through the skin. Tie the ends of the string securely.

To Truss Ducks and Geese.

(a) The wings are *not* folded back. The ends are cut off and the

FIG. 34. FOWL TRUSSED   FIG. 35. DUCK TRUSSED
FOR BOILING   FOR ROASTING

wings are secured with the legs to the sides of the bird as in trussing a fowl.

(b) The feet of a goose or duck are cut off at the first joint, but those of ducklings are left on; they are dislocated at the hock joint by a sharp twist, then folded back and crossed on the back of the bird just above the tail, which is drawn through the vent.

(c) Flatten the breastbone with a rolling pin by pressing gently.

The Giblets consist of the gizzard, liver, and heart. These, with the neck and feet, should be used for stock for making the accompanying gravy.

1. (a) Remove the gall bladder carefully from the liver and any parts that have a greenish tinge, otherwise the flavour is very bitter.

(b) Remove the fat from the gizzard, make a cut through the thickest part to the inner lining, taking care not to pierce it or the sac of stones will be broken, remove the latter and the tough outer and inner skin of the gizzard.

(c) Remove membrane and blood vessels and clotted blood from the heart.

2. Soak the giblets and the neck in tepid water with a little salt for about 20 minutes.

3. Remove the tips of the toes, scald the feet, and peel off the skin.

To Stuff Poultry. A fowl is sometimes stuffed, as this makes it go farther. Then use veal forcemeat or seasoned sausage meat.

To Stuff a Fowl. Put the forcemeat in at the neck end, between the skin and the breast, there should be sufficient to well fill the skin and to make the bird look plump : draw the skin over and secure with a needle and stout thread. If much stuffing is desired, then put the rest into the body cavity. If the flesh of a fowl is dry, it is an improvement to put a lump of butter inside the bird before it is trussed.

To Stuff a Turkey. If using two kinds of forcemeat, put the veal forcemeat in the neck end and stuff the body cavity with chestnut forcemeat or with sausage meat.

Roast Fowl.

Accompaniments.

A tender fowl or chicken.
Fat, butter or dripping for basting.
Fat bacon for covering breast.
8 to 10 small thin rolls of bacon.

½ pint bread sauce (see SAUCES).
Thin good gravy (½ to ¾ pint).
French salad.

Method. 1. Pluck, singe, draw, and truss bird for roasting (see directions, pages 131–3). Use giblets, neck, and feet for making stock for gravy.

2. Cover the breast with greased paper or, better, with two thin slices of fat bacon, which should be slit in two or three places to prevent it from curling up, tie it on with fine string or coarse thread and cover with greased paper. " Barding " with fat bacon imparts flavour to the flesh and keeps it moist and tender.

3 Place the bird on a rack in a baking tin in a hot oven and baste occasionally. The time varies with the age and size of the bird ; allow about 45 minutes for a small "spring" chicken, and 1¼ to 1½ hours for a larger and older bird.

4. Prepare bread sauce and, a short time before the bird is ready, put the rolls of bacon on a skewer and cook in the oven until transparent and slightly crisp.

5. About 10 minutes before the bird is ready, remove the paper and bacon and baste well, this is to brown the breast delicately.

6. Place the fowl on a hot dish, pour off the fat in the tin, and with the stock make a thin brown gravy as for roast meat.

7. Garnish the dish with rolls of bacon and a little parsley. Serve the gravy, bread sauce, and French salad separately.

Boiled Fowl.

A white skinned fowl.
1 pint white coating sauce.
Carrot, turnip, onion.

1 hard boiled egg.
Chopped parsley.
Slices of lemon and parsley.

Method. 1. Pluck, singe, draw, and truss fowl (see directions, pages 133–4).

2. Rub the breast with lemon juice to whiten it and wrap it in a greased paper.

3. Place the bird with breast downwards in a pan of boiling white

stock or of fresh meat boilings with the prepared giblets. If boiling water only is used, add a small onion, a small piece of carrot and turnip and a little salt.

4. Simmer slowly until tender; the time depends upon the age and size of the bird. Allow 1 hour for a tender young fowl, and a longer time for an older bird. If cooked rapidly, the flesh is hard and tasteless.

5. Make the sauce, boil the egg, cut in half, and sieve yolk.

6. Allow the water to drain from the fowl, remove the string, and wipe the bird with a clean dry cloth (it will coat better) and place on a hot dish.

7. Coat it smoothly with the sauce, allowing it to cover the bottom of the dish evenly. Decorate the breast with sieved yolk of egg and chopped parsley : fill the halves of the egg with the remainder of yolk and use these with the lemon as garnish.

Other Sauces suitable are : parsley, Béchamel, and egg.

Steamed Fowl. Prepare as for boiling; a longer time is required for cooking. Steam in an ordinary steamer or, better, in a double pan. A fowl may also be cooked in a pressure cooker, whereby the time required is reduced.

Chaudfroid of Chicken.

A boiled chicken.	Salad and crimped cucumber.
¾ pint white Chaudfroid sauce (see CHAUDFROID SAUCE, page, 71).	1½ gills aspic jelly (see JELLIES, page 226).
Chervil and tarragon or chilli skin.	French salad dressing (see SALAD DRESSINGS).

Method. 1. Cut the chicken into neat joints, remove the skin, trim neatly, and chop off the ends of leg bones. Place the joints on a rack with a dish beneath.

2. Have ready the Chaudfroid sauce, stir gently until it begins to thicken, and coats the back of a wooden spoon.

3. Mask each joint smoothly with the sauce. When the coating has set, decorate with the chervil or tarragon or neatly cut pieces of chilli skin, first dipping each decoration into liquid aspic jelly.

4. When the decorations are set, pour the liquid aspic jelly, which must have no sensible warmth in it, over the pieces of chicken, and leave to set.

5. Arrange a bed of salad on a dish, sprinkle lightly with French salad dressing, and pile the pieces of chicken neatly on this.

6. Garnish with salad, chopped aspic jelly, and crimped cucumber.

NOTE.—The correct consistency of the sauce is important : if too thin the surface of the meat will show through ; if too thick, the surface of the sauce is not smooth. In cold weather, should the sauce become too thick and begin to set while it is being used, place the basin containing it over warm water until the sauce is of the right consistency again for coating.

TO BONE POULTRY AND GAME

Large birds, such as the fowl or turkey, or small ones, such as the pigeon or quail, are boned. The bird may be either prepared for a galantine and braised or boiled ; or stuffed and reshaped. It is easier to bone a bird which has not been drawn.

Essentials to Success.   1. A small, very sharp knife, the point of which must be kept close to the bone.   2. To remove the flesh completely without tearing it, and leaving the carcase and bones clean.   3. Not to break the skin.   4. Not to pierce the carcase and to break the viscera inside.

To Bone a Turkey or Fowl for a Galantine.   1. Pluck and singe the bird, cut off the head, remove the neck, windpipe, gullet, and crop.   2. Draw out the sinews of the legs, cut off the legs at the hock joints and the wings at the second joint distant from the body ; dislocate the wing and leg joints connecting them with the carcase by giving each a sharp twist.   3. Place the bird on the board with the back uppermost, cut through the skin from the neck to the tail and with the point of the knife, keeping it close to the carcase, work the flesh very carefully away from the ribs, breastbone, and abdomen ; bone the other side in the same way and take out the carcase. Cut away the tail and the end of the intestines, and place the bird flat on the table, with the skin downwards.   4. To bone the legs, cut through the ligaments attaching the thigh to the body, push the leg inwards from the hock joint, and from the point where the leg was dislocated work away the flesh downwards to the next joint ; sever the joint, remove the thigh bone and work the flesh away from the drumstick, then turn the leg inside out. Proceed in the same way with the other leg.   5. Remove the wing bones, working the flesh away in a similar manner.   6. Push the skin of the legs and wings inside.   7. Spread the bird on the board, remove any sinew, gristle, or discoloured parts at the neck and tail.   8. Use for a galantine as directed.

Galantine of Fowl.

A boiling fowl.	2 truffles, if liked.
1 lb. sausage meat.	Pepper and salt.
4 oz. cooked ham or tongue.	Aromatic seasoning.
¼ oz. blanched pistachio nuts.	Meat glaze.
2 hard boiled eggs.	¼ pint aspic jelly (see JELLIES, page 226).
Finely grated rind of ¼ of a lemon.	Crimped cucumber, endive or small cress.

Method.   1. Bone fowl as directed for galantine, place the bird with skin downwards upon the board, distribute the flesh evenly, and flatten slightly with a rolling pin.   2. Split the nuts, cut the truffle into small pieces, and the egg and ham into strips.   3. Season the flesh of the bird and sprinkle lightly with aromatic seasoning, spread over it half of the sausage meat, arrange truffle, egg, nuts, and ham in lines from the tail to the neck, season and cover with remainder of sausage meat; if the knife is dipped into warm water it is easier to spread.   4. Roll up and secure the ends by drawing the skin well over.   5. Wrap in a clean pudding cloth, avoid letting the hem come on the breast of the fowl and marking it, tie the ends tightly, and put a safety pin in the centre to avoid a " waist."   6. Put into boiling stock or water and cook gently for 1½ to 2½ hours, the time depending upon the age of the bird.   Empty the carcase, wash it and the bones, and add to the stock ; if using water only, add a little vegetable.   7. When cooked put the galantine into a clean cloth, secure tightly, and place between two dishes with a 2 lb. weight on top.   8. When quite cold, brush over with liquid meat glaze, cut off the ends, and serve decorated with chopped aspic jelly, cucumber, and small salad plants.

NOTE.   The galantine may be coated with white Chaudfroid sauce, instead of with glaze, decorated smartly and masked with aspic jelly (see CHAUDFROID OF CHICKEN).

RABBITS

When Seasonable.   Rabbits and hares are in season from September to March.

Choice.   In young rabbits and hares the claws are smooth, sharp, and pointed, and the small nut or knob under the paws should be well developed ; the ears are soft and thin and tear easily ; the cleft in the jaws is narrow, and the teeth are small and white. A thick haunch, dry ears and rough blunt claws denote age. When freshly killed the flesh is moist and of a slightly bluish tint.

Rabbits must be perfectly fresh. The flesh should be firm and plump, and free from discoloration. The wild rabbit is smaller in size and less fat than the tame rabbit, the flavour of its flesh is stronger, but is considered better than that of the tame variety, the flesh of which is whiter and more delicate. For roasting, young rabbits and leverets (hares in the first year) should be chosen. Older rabbits are suitable for boiling, stewing, and broths; older hares for jugging, for soups, and for made dishes.

Hanging.   Rabbits, like fowls, should be cooked while very fresh, hanging for one day is sufficient.

Hang rabbits in a current of air in a cool, dry place. If a rabbit is to be kept for a day or two, paunch it as soon as possible after it has been killed; leave the skin on, this prevents the flesh from becoming dry, hang it up by the hind legs.

To Paunch, Skin, and Clean a Rabbit.   To Paunch.   Split the skin of the abdomen right down to the tail, take out the stomach and intestines, be very careful to remove entirely the small piece of intestine close to the tail and any discoloured pieces, and to thoroughly cleanse this part.

To Remove the Skin.   1. Cut off the ears close to the head, the tail, and the fore and hind legs at the first joint. 2. Loosen the skin from the sides of the body, working it away towards the tail, turn the hind legs inside out and pull the skin off. 3. Then draw the skin off, working towards the shoulders, and remove it from the fore-legs in the same way. 4. Draw the skin off the head, easing it away with a sharp pointed knife and remove the eyes.

To Clean. 1. Remove the kidneys and the fat in which they are embedded, break the skin (the diaphragm) between the chest and the lower part of the body, and remove heart and lungs. Remove the gall bladder from the liver and use the liver and the heart and kidneys for making stock or gravy. 2. Wash the rabbit very thoroughly in salted water, changing it two or three times, and leave to soak for 30 minutes. Wild rabbits, on account of the strong flavour, may be left to steep for an hour or more, changing the water once or twice. To remove the strong flavour, *blanch* a rabbit before cooking.

For **Fricassee of Rabbit** (see page 114).

To Truss for Roasting. 1. If to be stuffed, put forcemeat into the body cavity, and sew it up, using coarse cotton or thread, leave long ends free for easy withdrawal after the rabbit is cooked. 2. Make a small cut on the under surface in the fleshy part of the thighs; this enables the back to be kept straight and not arched. Bring the hind legs forwards and the front ones backwards, with the former outside and just overlapping the latter. Fix the legs by passing a skewer through the fore and hind legs from one side to the other and secure with string. 3. To keep the head in position, raise it and run a skewer down the mouth and neck to fix the head back between the shoulders.

Brown Stew of Rabbit.

1 rabbit.	¾ pint water or stock.
2 oz. dripping.	1 tablespoonful flour.
1 onion.	salt, pepper.
2 cloves.	¼ lb. fried or grilled bacon.

Method. 1. Cut rabbit into neat joints; roll joints in flour. 2. Slice onion, fry joints and onion in the hot dripping. 3. Add stock, seasonings and cloves; simmer till tender. 4. Remove joints and keep hot on serving dish; thicken gravy and strain over the joints. 5. Arrange bacon neatly on the dish.

CHAPTER 16
GAME

THE wild animals that are protected by law during certain months of the year are termed " game," which includes (*a*) *four-footed* game —hares, and venison, the flesh of deer ; (*b*) *feathered* game, such as pheasant, partridge, and grouse, which are preserved. In addition to these a number of *wild birds* are also used for food—the woodcock, plover, ptarmigan, etc. ; *water-fowl*—the moor-hen, teal, widgeon, wild duck ; and *small birds*, such as the quail, ortolan, wheatear, etc., all of which are roasted and served in a similar way.

Season for Game. Game is not in season between March and August, but a good deal of foreign game is sold during that period.

Hares	are in season from			September to March.
Venison (buck) is	,,	,,	,,	June to September.
Venison (doe)	,, ,,	,,	,,	October to end of December.
Grouse	,, ,,	,,	,,	12th August to 9th December.
Partridge	,, ,,	,,	,,	1st September to end of January.
Pheasant	,, ,,	,,	,,	1st October ,, ,, ,,
All other wild birds	,,	,,		1st August to end of February.

Nutritive Value and Digestibility. Game is less fat than either butchers' meat or poultry, the fibres are short and fine and, as it is easily digested, and the flesh is nourishing, game is often given to convalescents. The exception is water-fowl, the flesh of which is oily and close in texture. The legs of game (unlike those of poultry) are more tender than the wings, the latter having more muscular action.

Choice of Feathered Game. As it is very frequently sold unplucked, it is more difficult to judge of the age and condition of game than of poultry. A young bird has smooth and pliant legs, with round or short spurs in the male, the feet are supple and moist, especially in water-fowl, and the beak is pliable. When the feathers of a young unplucked bird are turned back, the breast should look plump and the flesh feel firm ; the long quill feathers are pointed, not blunt, the plumage is soft, and the colour not as bright as that of an older bird. The eyes so sunken as to be scarcely visible, the very easy removal of the feathers from the abdomen, and a greenish tinge of the skin on that part, are indications that some time has elapsed since the bird was killed. Do not purchase a bird that has been badly shot; before some parts are tender others will have become unfit to be eaten. Young grouse are distinguished by the short spur, dull plumage and V-shaped quills, young partridges by the yellow legs and dark bill and by the whiteness of the breast when the feathers are lifted. The flesh of the hen pheasant is more delicate than that of the cock-bird.

How to Distinguish Foreign from English Game. It can be procured when English game is out of season, the plumage is often very much crushed, on account of close packing and length of time in transit. It is often cheaper than English game, the flesh is hard, the result of cold storage, and when cooked the flavour is inferior to or different from that of fresh English game.

Hanging of Game. For the flesh to become tender and to acquire the desired flavour, game (with few exceptions) requires to hang longer than poultry.

1. Birds should not be plucked or drawn before hanging : they should hang in a current of air in a well-ventilated larder or pantry, with a free circulation of air round each. If flies are troublesome, dredge the birds with pepper or enclose in very loose muslin bags. Tie the neck of the bird tightly with string to prevent the entrance of air by the throat and hang up the bird feet downwards; it will keep longer if a small piece of charcoal is inserted in the vent.

2. The time allowed for hanging is determined by the kind, age, and condition of the game ; upon the weather—it will keep well in cold, dry, windy weather, but spoils quickly when it is close and damp ; upon storage accommodation, and upon individual taste. Old birds require longer hanging than young ones, and those which are badly mangled with shot or bruised do not keep well. Unless it is to be eaten " high," game is ready for cooking if the tail feathers come out easily when pulled. Should a bird be unpleasantly tainted, wash the parts with salted water to which a little vinegar has been added, rinse and dry well.

Water-fowl, on account of the oiliness of the flesh, which quickly becomes rancid, and *small birds*, which are *not drawn*, should not be kept for more than one day. Pheasants require 5 to 6 days, otherwise the flavour is not developed. Grouse 3 or 4 days, and ptarmigan must be well hung; if not, the flesh is hard and tough.

Venison must be well hung, in cold weather for a fortnight. Before hanging, dredge well with a mixture of black pepper and ground ginger, examine and wipe it with a clean cloth daily. Should it show any signs of taint, wash well, dry thoroughly, and sprinkle with pepper and ginger, but wash this off before roasting. In a haunch, which is the choicest joint for roasting, the flesh round the bone is the part which first becomes tainted. To test its condition, run a small sharp knife down into the joint ; this, when withdrawn, should have no unpleasant odour if the venison is fresh.

To Pluck, Draw, and Truss Game.

1. *Pluck* game carefully, as the skin is very tender, particularly if the bird is well hung. Cut off the toes, scald and skin the feet.

2. *Draw* as for poultry.

Birds which are not drawn are the woodcock, snipe, and plover, and a few small birds, but for hygienic purposes the custom is often not observed.

Never wash game, unless the flesh is tainted, wipe the birds inside and outside with a damp cloth.

3. *Truss* as for roast fowl, except that the wings are not folded across the back, but are cut off at the first joint and secured with the legs to the sides of the body.   The heads of woodcock and snipe are not removed, but the skin is stripped off and the long beak is passed through the wings and legs from one side of the body to the other as a skewer.

To Roast Game. The flavour of young, tender and well-roasted game is superior to that which is cooked by the more elaborate methods, for which older and tougher birds can be used.   Only young birds should be roasted, old grouse and partridges should never be cooked by this method, braising or stewing being suitable.

1. On account of the deficiency of fat, cover (bard) the breast with fat bacon.

2. If the bird is not very young and the flesh is dry, it is an improvement to put a lump of butter, seasoned with pepper and salt, or a few small pieces of juicy steak, inside the body cavity.

3. Cook in a moderately quick oven (see table) ; old birds require longer cooking.

4. A short time before the bird is cooked, remove the bacon, baste well with butter, dredge lightly with flour, baste again, and return to the oven.   This browns the breast and gives the frothy appearance characteristic of roast game.

5. Dish small birds such as woodcock or snipe upon a thick slice of buttered toast or upon a croûte of fried bread.

The Usual Accompaniments to Roast Game are—

1. A thin but good and well seasoned gravy ; for this the giblets should be used.   The gravy is served separately.

2. (*a*) Bread sauce; (*b*) fried crumbs; (*c*) chip potatoes; (*d*) a simple green salad of lettuce sprinkled with oil and vinegar.

3. Garnish of watercress.

NOTE. With particular kinds of game special accompaniments are served, e.g. with wild duck, a sauce flavoured with orange and orange salad.

Roast Pheasant.

Accompaniments.

Pheasant.	Thin gravy.
Fat bacon for barding.	Potato chips or straws.
Butter for basting.	Bread sauce.
Vinegar, pepper, salt.	Fried crumbs.
Watercress for garnish.	

Method. 1. Pluck the bird, reserving two or three of the best tail feathers for decoration ; draw, singe, cut off the toes, scald, and skin feet, wipe the outside and inside with a damp cloth. 2. Put a small piece of well seasoned butter or a few pieces of juicy steak inside if the flesh is dry. Truss as directed and cover the breast with fat bacon and greased paper. 3. Roast in a hot oven for 40 to 50 minutes, according to size and age of bird ; just before the pheasant is ready to be taken from the oven, baste the breast, dredge with flour, and baste again, return to the oven for a few minutes to brown the surface and to give it the frothy appearance. 4. Place bird on a hot dish, remove skewers or string. With the giblet stock make a good thin gravy as for roast meat. 5. Fix the tail feathers in position, garnish with watercress sprinkled lightly with vinegar and seasoned. 6. Serve the gravy, potatoes, bread sauce, and fried crumbs separately.

NOTE. The general method for roasting is practically the same for all kinds of game, the differences being in some details of preparation, in mode of dishing and accompaniments, such as sauces, garnish, etc., suitable to the particular kind of game.

A salad is often served with game, it should be a simple one either of lettuce only or of a few green salad plants sprinkled with French dressing.

AVERAGE TIME FOR ROASTING : POULTRY, GAME

Chicken.	¾ to 1 hour
Capon or Poularde .	1¾ to 2 hours.
Fowl .	1½ hours.
Pigeon .	20 to 25 minutes.
Turkey (large 10 to 12 lbs.)	2½ to 3 hours.
Grouse .	35 to 45 minutes
Partridge	25 to 30 minutes.
Pheasant	40 to 50 minutes.
Plover .	20 to 25 minutes.
Woodcock	30 minutes.
Snipe, Quail, Ortolan	15 to 20 minutes.

HARE

Choice. (See RABBIT, page 138.)

Hanging. Hares must be well hung to become tender and to be well flavoured ; hang in a current of air in a cool place.

A *hare* should *not* be *paunched* until it is skinned, and if fresh and the weather is dry and cold, it may hang for 6 to 7 days, but it does not keep well in close, wet weather. Hang a hare by the hind legs, tie a cup over the mouth to catch the blood, which should be kept if the hare is to be jugged or used for soup.

To Paunch and Remove the Skin. See RABBIT, page 138, but with the following difference—when breaking the diaphragm, hold a basin to catch the blood, which should be mixed at once with flour to prevent coagulation.

After cleaning, wipe the hare inside and outside or wash quickly in cold water and dry.

Jugged Hare.

1 small hare.
2 oz. fat.
1 pint stock.
1 onion stuck with cloves.
1 bouquet garni.
Salt, 10 peppercorns.

1 oz. flour for thickening.
1 oz. fat.
¼ pint port wine.
1 small teaspoonful red currant jelly.

Forcemeat.

2 oz. breadcrumbs.
1 oz. chopped suet.
2 teaspoonfuls chopped parsley.
A good pinch dried thyme.

¼ teaspoonful salt.
Good pinch pepper.
1 egg.

Method. 1. Cut hare into neat joints, and fry them in fat. 2. Place hare in fireproof dish with the onion and seasonings; add the stock. 3. Cover dish tightly. 4. Cook in moderately hot oven till tender— about 3 hours. 5. While hare is cooking, make up the forcemeat into neat balls, egg and crumb them and fry in deep fat. Add to hare 20 minutes before it is ready. 6. When hare is tender, remove the joints and balls, and keep hot. 7. Add blended flour to the gravy; boil well, correct seasoning and add jelly. 8. Add blood, reheat and add wine. 9. Arrange joints of hare on a hot dish and strain the gravy over. 10. Garnish with the forcemeat balls and, if desired, *glacé* cherries.

Roast Hare.

A young hare.
Veal forcemeat.
½ pint milk } for basting.
Dripping
Fat bacon for back.

1 pint of good brown thick gravy or sauce.
1 glass port wine.
Red currant jelly.
Rolls of bacon } Garnish.
Fried forcemeat balls

Method. 1. Paunch, wipe, stuff, and truss hare, and in preparation for cooking follow the method for rabbit. 2. Roast in a hot oven; allow about 1 hour for a leveret, 1¼ to 1½ hours for a hare; baste frequently with dripping and milk, the mixture makes the flesh mellow and moist. 3. When nearly done, remove paper and bacon, dredge with flour, and leave until the back is brown. 4. Make a good brown gravy, thickened in the pan (see GRAVIES, page 104), skim well, and add the port wine. 5. Strain a little round the hare, arrange the garnish, and serve with red currant jelly.

CHAPTER 17

VEGETABLE COOKERY AND SALADS

VEGETABLES

UNTIL more recent years, the use of vegetables in the diet has been much neglected, their dietetic importance insufficiently appreciated, and the method of cooking not only wasteful, but much inferior to the Continental. The greater attention and encouragement given now to the production of home-grown vegetables, with facilities to the growers for better marketing of them and the increase of imported produce, offers much greater variety of vegetable foods, and greater attention is being given to this branch of cookery. Lack of variety in the food itself, waste before cooking, and of "left over" vegetables, monotony of method generally used, viz. cooking in a large quantity of boiling water, sloppiness, and slovenly dishing, are all faults to be found in vegetable cookery. Vegetables, in addition to being accompaniments to meat dishes, are served as the "dressed vegetable" or "vegetable *entremets*," a separate course in the menu, and they are also used as substitutes for meat.

Plants and Parts of Plants Used as Vegetables.

Roots. Carrot, parsnip, horse-radish, beetroot, salsify, celeriac, turnip.

Bulbous Roots. Onion, shallot, leek (elongated bulb).

Tubers. Potatoes, Jerusalem artichokes.

Flowers or Head. Cauliflowers, broccoli.

Leaves. Cabbage, spinach, lettuce, curly kale, turnip tops, brussels sprouts.

Fruit. Cucumber, tomato, bean (the pod), pulse (seeds).

Blanched Stems. Celery, seakale, chicory; by banking or earthing up the stems of these, plants are whitened and bleached, and have a sweeter and milder taste.

Classification of Vegetables.

1. Roots and tubers.
2. Green vegetables.
3. Blanched stems of vegetables.

Composition of Vegetables.

1. *Protein.* With the exception of pulse (peas, beans, lentils), which are rich in protein, vegetables contain little body-building material.

2. *Carbohydrates,* in the form of starch, sugar, and cellulose.

(*a*) *Starch* is the chief nutrient of roots and tubers; percentage is highest in the potato, less in other tubers and in root vegetables; in green leaf vegetables there is practically none.

(b) *Sugar*, source of energy. The proportion is highest in beetroot, carrot, and turnip. The carrot is rich in sugar, and on account of the mineral salts and vitamins present is of considerable value in children's diet; it is much more nutritive than turnip.

(c) *Cellulose*, the fibrous framework or roughage becomes coarser and tougher as the vegetable matures. In some, it is too tough for them to be eaten raw; compare the succulent leaf of a young lettuce and that of a cabbage.

3. *Fat*. No appreciable amount present, the deficiency is supplied by the addition of butter and by accompanying sauces.

4. *Mineral Matter*. Principally potash salts, for which vegetables are chiefly valuable, they are present in green vegetables in a relatively large percentage, and on account of their solubility are often to a great extent lost by the method of and by careless cooking.

5. *Extractives*, e.g. asparagin in potatoes.

6. *Vitamins*. A, B, and C are all represented, the class and quantity varying with the particular vegetable. Vitamin C, is present in tomatoes, some roots and green-leaved vegetables—lettuce, cabbage, etc.; but prolonged cooking and the addition of an alkali such as bicarbonate of soda, destroy it. Vitamin B resists the ordinary temperature of boiling water for some time, but is also destroyed by alkali. Vitamin A is almost insoluble in water, therefore there is little or no loss during the boiling of vegetables. It can be destroyed by oxidation at high temperatures.

7. *Water*. A large percentage is present in all vegetables and makes them a bulky food.

TABLE OF APPROXIMATE PERCENTAGES OF THE CHIEF CONSTITUENTS
OF VEGETABLES

Vegetables.	Nitrogenous Matter	Carbohydrates.	Mineral Matter.	Water.
Artichokes, Jerusalem .	2·5	16·5	1·0	79·5
Beetroot	1·5	9·5	1·1	87·5
Cabbage	1·1	5·8	1·3	89·6
Carrots	0·5	11·6	0·9	86·5
Cucumber . . .	0·6	2·5	0·5	96·0
Peas (green) . . .	4·5	16·0	0·9	78·0
Potatoes	2·2	18·0	1·0	78·3
Spinach	2·1	3·0	1·8	92·0
Turnip	0·9	5·0	0·8	89·0
Vegetable marrow . .	0·06	3·6	0·5	94·8

Value in the Diet. The actual food value of vegetables is not high, but on account of the presence of mineral salts and of vitamins, *fresh* vegetables are of great importance in the daily diet, particularly in that of young and growing children. The cellulose or fibrous framework (roughage) gives bulk to the food, assists digestion indirectly by inciting the peristaltic or churning movement of the digestive tract, and by the elimination of waste matter from the system prevents constipation. In old vegetables the cellulose is coarse and very woody and indigestible.

Digestibility. On account of the presence of the roughage, of sulphur and of so much water, vegetables as a class of foods are not as digestible as others, and the roughage and high percentage of water make them a bulky food.

Roots and Tubers. The chief nutrient is starch, its percentage varying with the vegetable, being highest in the potato and less in other tubers and roots. Sugar percentage highest in the beetroot, least in the turnip. Being high in the carrot, this and the mineral salts and vitamins present make the carrot of considerable value in children's food.

Green Vegetables in relation to the maintenance of the health of the body rank first in the importance in the diet, because of the presence of mineral salts and of Vitamin C. The latter is reduced in value as the vegetable matures or is stored, therefore the greater the dietetic value of young and freshly gathered green vegetables.

Blanched Stems contain no appreciable amount of protein or of fat, a high percentage of water, roughage, and extractives of flavouring matter.

Changes which take place in cooking vegetables—

1. Extraction of the very soluble mineral salts and extractives.
2. Softening of fibre.
3. Rupture of starch cells and gelatination of starch.
4. Lowering of vitamin value of green vegetables. Over-cooking in boiling water is destructive to Vitamin C, and the still not infrequent custom of adding bicarbonate of soda to the water for green vegetables is also destructive to vitamins.
5. Absorption of water, which further increases their bulkiness: this is important in relation to the method of cooking used.

GAIN OF WATER ON COOKING VEGETABLES

	Percentage of Water in Raw State.	Percentage of Water After Cooking.	Increase.
Parsnip . . .	82·0	97·2	15·2
Cabbage . . .	80·0	91·6	11·6
Spinach . . .	90·0	98·0	8·0
Cauliflower . .	90·8	96·4	5·6
Seakale . . .	93·3	97·9	4·6
Vegetable Marrow .	94·8	99·1	4·3

Aim in Cooking.

1. To minimize the destruction of vitamins and loss of mineral salts and extractives.

2. To cook sufficiently to soften the fibre and to make starch digestible.

3. To preserve colour, flavour, and shape.

4. To prevent unnecessary absorption of water.

Purchase and Choice. Freshness is very important; stale vegetables are most unwholesome: they quickly ferment, particularly the green variety. The flavour of all vegetables is best when they are young and plentiful, and if cooked very soon after removal from the ground, or freshly cut. Old vegetables are only suitable for flavouring.

Roots and Tubers should be fairly free from soil; much earth adhering to them increases the weight and consequently the price per pound of actual vegetable. They should be firm and crisp, free from spade-marks and from any signs of decay or discoloration.

Green Vegetables. All leaf vegetables should be bright in colour, crisp, and not wilted; the ribs of large leaves should snap sharply when broken across. Choose cabbages with closely-growing leaves, brussels sprouts compact and round, cauliflowers with a firm white head and the flower closely grown. Beans and peas should be bright in colour, and the pods crisp and of a medium size; beans firm; and pods of peas well-filled but not over-full.

Blanched Stems of vegetables, such as celery, chicory, and seakale should be firm, white, and crisp. Celery to be eaten raw should be bought after the first touch of frost, which makes it crisp; use the outer stalks for boiling and stewing, and the green tops and coarse stalks for flavouring purposes.

Methods of Cooking.

1. Boiling.	3. Stewing.	5. Braising.
2. Steaming.	4. Frying.	6. Baking.

All methods are used, but since the mineral salts are of so much value in the diet, the object is to conserve these as far as possible, therefore the methods used vary in value as they retain or part with these constituents. Because of the still common method of cooking vegetables in a large quantity of boiling water, the greater part of the soluble mineral matter passes into the water and is lost. When cooked in a steamer over boiling water, the loss is not so great, but the mineral salts and extractives are best retained by stewing, the conservative method being ideal for cooking vegetables.

General Rules for Cooking and Serving Vegetables.

1. Careful preparation: peel or scrape well, wash and steep if necessary.

2. Scrupulously clean utensils to avoid spoiling colour and flavour.

3. Thorough steady cooking. Avoid over-cooking vegetables.
4. Remove any surface scum while boiling, if necessary.
5. Season with salt; insipid vegetables are unpalatable.
6. Drain well; take care to preserve shape, e.g. artichokes.
7. Service. As soon as cooked, dish quickly; serve "piping hot";
tepid vegetables spoil any meal. Have both vegetable dish and
sauce, if used, ready and very hot.
8. Supply deficiency of fat with butter or by the accompanying
sauce. Sprinkle with the oiled butter; toss in butter.

Preparation for Cooking.

1. Trim or peel economically; remove coarse stalks and leaves,
damaged or decayed parts.
2. Wash and rinse thoroughly, particularly vegetables growing
close to the ground, e.g. spinach, to ensure preservation of colour
and flavour.
3. Leave in cold water for a short time, add a little salt for removal of slugs and small insects; prolonged steeping extracts some
of the soluble matter.
4. Drain after removal from water.

Roots and Tubers. Scrub well to remove loose earth. Scrape those
with thin skins (carrots) and peel those with thick skins (turnips)
to the dark ring. Cut large vegetables into halves and quarters.
Artichokes: while scraping or peeling, dip constantly into a basin
of cold water to prevent staining and leave them in cold water,
adding a few drops of lemon juice or vinegar to prevent discoloration. Beetroot: wash carefully; if the thin skin is pierced or the
fine roots cut, the beetroot loses its colour.

Green Vegetables.

1. Cabbage variety. Remove outside and coarse leaves; cut
into quarters and remove as much of stalk as is necessary. Cut off
coarse ribs from leaves of curly kale and of small greens.
2. Brussels sprouts. Trim and cut each sprout across the small
stalk twice transversely; this assists in cooking.
3. Cauliflower. Trim away most of the leaves and stalk, leaving
sufficient to hold it together; scoop out centre of stalk.
4. Spinach is very gritty; remove every trace; wash spinach
several times, six or seven, in cold water, each time removing from
basin into colander, so that basin is free from grit; finally allow the cold
water from the tap to flow freely through spinach in the colander.
5. Peas and beans. Shell green peas and broad beans, and slice
runner beans only a short time before cooking, as they quickly
become dry; leave in water until required.

Blanched Stems. Wash and brush carefully to remove soil and
grit; cut into lengths, tie in small bundles, leave in water to prevent discoloration, adding a few drops of lemon juice.
Asparagus: cut stems into even lengths, lightly scrape them,

removing small leaves; tie into bundles and leave in water until required.

Vegetable marrow: cut down centre, remove seeds, peel; cut transversely into moderate-sized pieces. Put into a basin, sprinkle lightly with a little salt; this withdraws some of the moisture, and the marrow is firmer when boiled.

NOTE. Some vegetables with a strong flavour, such as onions or celery, may be blanched before they are cooked.

Boiling Vegetables. Use a pan suitable in size for the bulk of vegetables, with the quantity of water necessary for the vegetables to be cooked. When boiling, add salt and vegetables; cover with the lid and keep covered; and boil steadily. Vegetables absorb water, become watery and sodden, and lose colour and flavour if water boils intermittently or is allowed to simmer. Should scum appear, remove it.

1. *Roots and Tubers.* Boil quickly, but steadily, those with close, dense fibre, such as carrots and parsnips; less quickly those with tender fibre, such as turnips and Jerusalem artichokes; rapid ebullition breaks them.

2. *Green Vegetables.* Boil quickly in small amount of water (approximately ¼ pint to 1 lb. vegetables). Maintain temperature when adding the vegetables —if a large quantity is being cooked, add by degrees, so that the temperature is not reduced too much.

(*a*) Spinach. If young, no water is required for cooking beyond what clings to the leaves after washing; if old, a few tablespoonfuls are required. Put spinach into pan in layers, sprinkling each very lightly with a little salt; stir occasionally to ensure uniform cooking. Drain well in colander, using a vegetable presser. Either chop finely or sieve, season, add a little butter, and reheat.

(*b*) Green peas. Add to the boiling water, mint and one teaspoonful of sugar to 1 pint of shelled peas; this improves colour and flavour, and develops the natural sweetness. Drain well and toss in hot melted butter.

Runner beans. Boil as directed, drain; toss in pan in a little hot butter.

Blanched Stems of Vegetables. Add one tablespoonful of lemon juice or vinegar to 1 gallon of water. Boil steadily, drain well, and dish, if liked, on a slice of toast; coat with white sauce.

Asparagus. Use pan sufficiently large and deep, preferably one with a strainer; failing this, place bundles with tips all in one direction in a piece of muslin, with ends lying just over the edge of pan for ease in removal. Avoid breaking tips, but gently drain; serve with "oiled butter."

Oiled Butter. Heat butter, remove scum as it rises, add a few drops of lemon juice, and serve hot in a sauce-boat.

Vegetable Marrow. Boil gently or steam, drain well, serve on a piece of toast to absorb moisture, and coat with white sauce.

The time is determined by the age, texture, and size; for young vegetables with tender fibre, allow about 20 minutes; and about double that time or longer for those which are coarse and dense in fibre.

Artichokes, Jerusalem, about 30 to 35 minutes.			
Asparagus	,,	20 ,, 30	,,
Beans (broad)	,,	20 ,, 40	,,
Beans (French)	,,	15 ,, 20	,,
Brussels sprouts	,,	12 ,, 15	,,
Cabbage	,,	15 ,, 20	,,
Cauliflower	,,	15 ,, 20	,,
Carrots (young)	,,	30	,,
Carrots (old)	,,	1 hour	
Green peas	,,	20 to 30	,,
Potatoes (young)	,,	15 ,, 20	,,
Potatoes (old)	,,	25 ,, 30	,,
Seakale	,,	30 ,, 40	,,
Spinach	,,	15 ,, 20	,,
Vegetable marrow	,,	15 ,, 20	,,
Beetroot	,,	1½ to 2 hours.	
Onions	,,	1 hour.	

Steaming Vegetables. Some vegetables, like potatoes, may be steamed but the longer time required for cooking increases the loss of mineral salts and vitamin content; this method is not advisable for green vegetables.

Stewing is most suitable for the blanched stems of plants, such as seakale, celery, etc., and is economical as regards the food value of the vegetable. It can be stewed in a little stock or water, which should be used for the sauce with which the vegetable is coated after cooking, or it may be stewed in a white sauce.

Braising is a popular method of cooking a dressed vegetable, but is more elaborate (see BRAISING).

Frying. All vegetables, except potatoes (also fried in the raw state), are cooked first, covered with a protective coating, batter or egg and crumbs, and fried in deep fat.

Baking. Some vegetables, such as marrow or tomatoes, are stuffed, then baked; others are served *au gratin*, being covered with a sauce and bread-crumbs, and generally with the addition of grated cheese and browned in the oven, e.g. cauliflower *au gratin*.

Purées of Vegetables. Some vegetables are more digestible if sieved or mashed with a fork or spoon, e.g. potato, turnip, etc.

Economies in Use of Vegetables.

1. Add parings and trimmings of suitable vegetables to the stock-pot for making vegetable stock and sauces.

2. Use the older and less expensive for flavouring.

3. Use water in which vegetables have been cooked for sauces and stock.

4. Never waste cooked vegetables; they are useful additions in a salad and in soups; they can be reheated in numerous ways as additions in making small appetizing dishes. Be careful in hot weather, vegetables quickly ferment and turn sour.

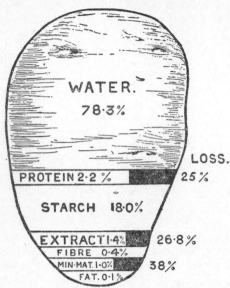

WATER. 78·3%

LOSS. 25%

PROTEIN 2·2 %

STARCH 18·0%

EXTRACT 1·4% 26·8%
FIBRE 0·4%
MIN·MAT. 1·0% 38%
FAT. 0·1%

Fig. 36. Percentage Composition of a Potato and Loss of each Constituent on Boiling
(*By courtesy of Messrs. Edward Arnold & Company*)

POTATOES

The ways of serving potatoes are innumerable, but the real test of efficiency in potato cookery is to be able to cook this simple vegetable to perfection by the most simple methods, viz., those of boiling, steaming, and baking. For boiling, steaming, and baking, old and mealy potatoes are best, waxy and young potatoes being more suitable for frying and for salads. When boiled, steamed, or baked, potatoes should be dry and floury, and crisp and dry when fried.

The young potato is richer in protein than the old, is juicier and waxy, and solid in texture when cooked, the starch cells being immature in the young plant. New potatoes are less easily digested, and are not suitable for young children nor for invalids. Towards the commencement of spring the potato is not so floury when cooked; this is due to a partial change of some of the starch into dextrin (sugar), which gives to it a sweetish taste and a waxy texture.

For the retention of nutrients and as a means of saving labour, the most economical way of cooking old potatoes is to boil, steam, or bake them in their jackets; but they *must* be perfectly sound. For boiling, steaming, and baking, choose potatoes equal in size, so that they may cook evenly.

Boiled Potatoes. Brush well, wash and peel thinly for economy and because there is considerable nutriment in the potato just below the surface; remove eyes and any discoloured parts, rinse, and leave in water.

1. Boil in a pan just large enough to hold the vegetables, and

with sufficient water to just cover them. Add 1 tablespoonful of salt to 1 gallon.

2. Boil steadily and moderately quickly; violent oscillation in fast boiling water breaks them and makes them watery.

3. Cook until just tender; test by piercing with a skewer; drain off *all* the water.

4. Dry thoroughly, put the lid half on and leave the pan on the stove, where it will keep hot for 5 to 10 minutes; shake the saucepan occasionally to give the potatoes a floury appearance.

Steamed Potatoes.

1. Prepare as for boiling. Cut large ones into halves or into pieces even in size.

2. Place in an ordinary steamer, sprinkle with salt, cover with lid.

3. Cook over quickly boiling water until tender; steaming will take half as long again as boiling.

4. When just tender, remove the steamer; cover the potatoes with a cloth, put the lid half on; leave the potatoes in a warm place for a few minutes; shake occasionally.

Potatoes Boiled in their Jackets.

1. Choose potatoes equal in size and perfectly sound, prepare in the usual way.

2. Cook in boiling salted water, adding double the usual proportion of salt.

3. Boil at a moderate rate until they feel tender when pierced with a skewer—about 30 minutes.

4. Drain off water, cover with a cloth, leave for a few minutes in warm stove, shaking the pan occasionally.

5. Either serve the potatoes in their jackets or peel very quickly, and serve in a hot vegetable dish.

Baked Potatoes.

1. Prepare as for boiling, dry well, *prick* the skin, or cut it through the long axis down centre, to prevent it from cracking and to allow of evaporation of moisture.

2. Bake in a *moderate* oven. When tender, the potato should feel soft if pressed between finger and thumb. If the oven is too hot, the skins are hard and charred; this prevents moisture from escaping, and the deep parts are heavy and wet.

Roast Potatoes.

Dripping and salt are required.

1. Wash and peel potatoes.

2. Put them into boiling salted water and cook for 10 minutes (par-boiling); drain and dry in a cloth and divide, if large.

3. Melt some dripping in a baking tin, add the potatoes and cook

in a moderate oven for about 30 to 40 minutes until evenly browned all over and tender ; baste and turn occasionally.

4. Drain from the fat, sprinkle with salt, and serve.

NOTE. If roasted with the meat, put them into the meat-tin sufficiently soon for them to be ready when the meat is cooked.

Potato Croquettes.

¼ lb. cooked sieved potatoes.	¼ teaspoonful chopped parsley.
½ oz. butter.	Seasoning.
1 yolk of egg.	Egg and bread-crumbs.

Method. 1. Melt the butter, add the potatoes, parsley, seasoning, and yolk of egg ; mix over heat until smooth, and to bind the mixture by cooking the egg.

2. Turn on to a plate and leave to get cold.

3. Divide into pieces of an equal size, flour the hands slightly, and form into balls, rolls, or flat cakes.

4. Coat the croquettes twice with egg and bread-crumbs. A double coating is a preventive against " bursting " in frying.

5. Fry in deep fat ; have sufficient fat to cover the croquettes, and do not raise the frying basket from the fat until the coating has set, otherwise the croquettes will burst.

6. Drain well on paper and garnish with fried parsley.

For **Potato Ribbons, Chips, and Straws** (see GRILLED STEAK OR CHOP, page 109).

PULSE VEGETABLES

The principal pulses are lentils, the red or Egyptian lentil and the purplish-green lentil, haricot beans, butter beans, split peas, and dried green peas.

Food Value. Pulse is a cheap and valuable source of protein, which is termed *legumin*. On account of the high percentage of protein present, and because for a given sum pulse will yield more protein than any other food, it is an excellent and cheap substitute for meat, and is therefore valuable not only in a purely vegetarian diet, but also in the ordinary household fare (see MEATLESS COOKERY). Lentils are richest in protein and peas contain the least. Pulse is comparatively rich in carbohydrates, but it is deficient in fat; hence its use with fat foods, e.g. pork and pease-pudding. Of mineral matter in pulse, lime salts are present and of sulphur there is less in lentils than in either peas or beans.

COMPARATIVE AVERAGE PERCENTAGE OF CONSTITUENTS OF PULSE AND MEAT

Food.	Water.	Protein.	Fat.	Mineral Matter.	Carbo-hydrates.
(*a*) Lentils . . .	11·7	23·2	2·0	2·8	58
(*b*) Meat of medium fatness.	73·1	20·5	5·4	1·0	None

Digestibility. Unless well cooked, pulse is not readily digested. This is partly due to the tough outer skin, to the bulkiness, as pulse takes up a large amount of water in cooking, and to the presence of sulphur, which tends to produce flatulence. Of all pulse, lentils are most easily digested ; the outer skins are less tough, and they contain less sulphur than either beans or peas.

Important Points in the Preparation and Cooking of Pulse.

1. Use fresh pulse ; if old or stale, even long steeping and prolonged cooking fail to completely soften them ; for this reason store in a large quantity only when the use is frequent and extensive.

2. Wash thoroughly first and then *steep* ; steeping is most essential. Use *cold soft* water ; the legumin (protein) is apt to unite with the lime salts, hence pulse does not soften so readily in hard water. For this reason either soften the water by the addition of a little bicarbonate of soda (1 teaspoonful to 1 lb. of pulse) or use cold " boiled water " for steeping. The time required varies with the kind of pulse and with the toughness of the outer coat. Steep lentils for 2 or 3 hours, beans for 12 and split peas for 24 hours.

3. Unless soda has been added to the steeping water, use it for cooking, as in soaking some of the mineral matter and protein of the pulse have been extracted. Salt hardens pulse; add *salt* to pulse *after cooking*.

4. *Slow* and *thorough* cooking. A double saucepan ensures this. The time varies with the kind and freshness of the pulse. Allow 1½ to 2 hours for haricot beans, more for split peas, and about 1 hour for lentils.

5. " Sieving " : this reduces the pulse to a *purée*, increasing its digestibility, and removes the indigestible outer coat.

6. Addition of fat, or combination with fat foods to supply the deficiency of fat, a little added, softens the pulse during the process of cooking, as in sautéing lentils for lentil soup.

General Uses of Pulse Foods.

(a) Soups largely.

(b) Curries : haricot beans, butter beans, and lentils are used. Cook the pulse thoroughly, but not to a pulp. Prepare a curry sauce and follow directions for currying cooked food (see page 115).

(c) Croquettes, rissoles, and cutlets. Stew haricot beans or lentils, with flavourings, to a stiff pulp ; sieve; season and flavour, bind with egg ; shape, and fry as for meat croquettes.

(d) As a vegetable and an accompaniment to meat, or in salads (haricot and butter beans).

PRESERVED VEGETABLES

The freshness of vegetables—therefore they should be eaten as soon as possible after they have been removed from the ground or picked—is important, as affecting their value in the diet. During preservation by canning or freezing, usually only a short time elapses between the picking of the vegetables and processing; thus loss of nutrients is reduced to a minimum. Because of the heat necessary to sterilize the vegetables in canning them, there is some loss of vitamin content; but the nutritional value of canned or frozen vegetables is considered to be as good as that of corresponding fresh vegetables.

SALADS

Salads, particularly those made with raw green-leaved vegetables, are of considerable dietetic value, as the saline matter, chiefly potash salts, which is partly extracted by cooking, is preserved in the raw vegetable. Salads are the means of supplying some of the water required daily by the system, and they are refreshing and cooling in hot weather. They also indirectly assist in digestion by giving bulk to the diet. Some plants contain an essential oil ; this imparts the characteristic odour and flavour to the salad plant, which stimulates the activity of the digestive organs. Nutriment also is supplied by the oil in the dressing. In the daily inspection of the larder, a thrifty housewife can often utilize " left-overs " of cold vegetables and remnants of other dishes and foods, and make them into a dainty and attractive salad with very little further expense.

Place of Salads in the Menu. Salads are served as adjuncts to both hot and cold meat, or as a separate dish ; for the former purpose they are usually plain, with a simple dressing, but for the latter a combination of ingredients is used, and the garnish and dressing is more elaborate.

Foundation Ingredients. For a vegetable salad almost every kind of vegetable, both raw and cooked, can be used ; the salad may consist of one vegetable only, such as lettuce, or potatoes, or of two or more. Then the vegetables may be combined with meat, poultry, game, fish, sausage, tongue, ham, eggs, cheese, pulse, nuts, and fresh fruits, such as apples, bananas, orange ; thus there is great scope for much novelty and variety in salad-making.

Vegetables. Green vegetables : lettuce, endive, white cabbage, small cress, watercress, lamb's lettuce ; beetroot, celery, beans, peas, radishes, artichokes, carrots, potatoes, haricot beans, are all used.

Meats for a salad should be well flavoured ; braised, smoked, or salt boiled meats are most suitable ; also roast poultry and game. Meat should be cut into neat pieces of moderate size. To afford additional flavour, meats, and also fish, are steeped in a *marinade* (see GLOSSARY) before they are added to the salad.

Fish with firm flesh and a pronounced flavour is most suitable ; such as salmon, halibut, turbot ; also shellfish ; lobster, crab, shrimp, and prawn. Anchovies and herrings are also used for garnish. Flake or cut fish into cubes.

Preparation of Vegetables for Salad.

1. Remove discoloured leaves, separate the leaves of lettuce and endive ; wash thoroughly in cold water to remove grit and small insects, then again in fresh water. Give particular attention to watercress, which may be dangerous unless very thoroughly cleansed ; remove the black seed capsules from small cress and scrub and wash celery.

2. If green salad plants are very limp, steep them in cold water, but for a short time only ; if they are allowed to lie in salted water the leaves become slimy.

3. Drain very thoroughly. Shake the plants as dry as possible in a salad basket, if available ; if not, in a colander, or in a sieve, and then toss lightly in a clean cloth, being careful not to bruise delicate leaves.

Fig. 37. Salad Basket

4. Divide green vegetables with a silver or stainless steel knife, or break with the fingers, handling lightly and as little as possible.

5. Cooked vegetables, when used, should be firm ; if soft and pulpy they become " mushy " in the salad.

SALAD DRESSINGS

These consist of oil, vinegar, and seasonings and flavourings, and they may be quite simple and inexpensive, or rich. The two chief classes of dressings are : (*a*) the French dressing— this is a simple one, consisting of oil and vinegar, seasoned and flavoured, and is suitable for light green salads and for those accompanying roast meats; (*b*) mayonnaise—this is used for the more elaborate salads, and for those which are served as a distinct dish, such as lobster mayonnaise, etc. In addition to these, there are many inexpensive and quickly- and easily-made dressings ; also the proprietary salad sauces.

When making a salad dressing, whether simple or plain, its *success depends upon judicious seasoning and flavouring,* and upon the *careful blending of the oil and vinegar.* In all dressings add the vinegar last and very gradually ; they should not be over-acid in flavour. The usual proportions are two tablespoonfuls of oil to one of vinegar ; more or less oil is used according to individual taste. The best and purest ingredients are necessary for a salad dressing ; inferior oil and vinegar impart a rancid and crude flavour.

Oil. The best olive oil, or other suitable oil should be used; inferior oil is acrid in flavour, dark in colour, and congeals readily in cold weather. Keep oil in a cool, dark place in the storeroom or cupboard, and purchase only in a small quantity, as it quickly turns rancid. Cream, and sour cream, also condensed milk, are used in some dressings in place of the oil.

Vinegar. White vinegar is the best to use : lemon juice is often substituted for vinegar, it is more delicate in flavour and its acidity is less crude than that of vinegar.

Seasonings and Flavourings. Pepper, salt, cayenne, herbs (tarragon, chervil, parsley), aromatized vinegars, pickles are used. If the flavour of onion is desired, add a soupçon of finely-chopped garlic, shallot or onion to the salad, or sprinkle with a few drops of onion juice ; rub the salad bowl over with an onion or shallot, or rub it on to the inside of a crust and put the latter at the bottom of the salad bowl. Avoid any over-seasoning or over-flavouring, which would overpower the distinctive flavour of the chief ingredients.

1. **Mayonnaise Dressing** (see MAYONNAISE SAUCE, pages 69-70).

2. **French Dressing.**

2 tablespoonfuls oil.   ½ teaspoonful salt.
1   „   vinegar.   ¼   „   pepper.
¼ teaspoonful made mustard.

Method. Mix the seasonings and oil; lastly the vinegar, drop by drop. This dressing is varied by the addition of a little finely-chopped tarragon, chervil, or parsley, and sometimes a little sugar is added. When a plain lettuce salad is used to accompany game or poultry, sprinkle it first with oil, then with the vinegar ; the leaves become flabby if vinegar is added first.

Points in the Preparation and Dressing of a Salad.

1. Young, fresh, crisp vegetables and thorough cleansing in cold water.

2. Careful drying: the dressing does not blend with the other ingredients if they are wet, and it becomes thinned down and impoverished in flavour.

3. A well-made dressing, sufficient only for well mixing the salad ; too much makes green-leaved salad plants flaccid, and the salad over-rich.

4. Mix the ingredients of the salad thoroughly but lightly with the dressing ; avoid crushing delicate leaves of the salad plants.

5. Dress a salad only a short time before it is required ; green salad plants quickly lose their crispness.

6. Dress a salad high in the bowl and garnish attractively. In a mixed salad reserve ¼ to ⅛ for the top layer and for garnishing. The chief ingredients of the salad should be represented in the garnish. The heart of a lettuce, a little endive or cress, and the yolk of an egg sieved and the white chopped, make a simple but pretty garnish.

Green Salad.

1 lettuce.	½ small endive.
Watercress.	2 tomatoes or beetroot or radishes.
Mustard and cress.	1 hard-boiled egg.
French dressing or mayonnaise.	

Method. 1. Prepare salad plants as directed ; scald tomatoes and remove skin ; cut tomatoes or beetroot and egg into neat pieces, reserving some of each and the best pieces of the salad plants for garnish.

2. Mix the vegetables, etc., lightly with a little dressing ; pile in the centre of dish and garnish.

Mixed Salad (Winter or Summer).

For this, use a variety of cooked vegetables, according to the season of the year.

In winter ; haricot beans, beetroot, cauliflower, carrot, celery, potatoes, Jerusalem artichokes, etc. ; in summer, new potatoes, peas, French beans, radishes, cucumber, with some green-leaved salad plants. Prepare the vegetables, season well with pepper and salt, mix lightly with a dressing, arrange on a dish, and garnish.

Lobster Mayonnaise.

1 cooked lobster.	French or curly lettuce.
Mayonnaise sauce (See SAUCES,	Cucumber and small cress.
page 69).	Hard-boiled egg.

Method. 1. Remove the meat from the lobster, reserve the meat from the tips of the claws, the feelers and the coral for garnishing, dry the coral (see LOBSTER CORAL, page 89).

2. Cut the lobster meat into small pieces or shred coarsely, season with cayenne, salt, and lemon juice.

3. Prepare the salad vegetables and drain.

4. Put a few lettuce leaves at the bottom of the salad bowl, and the lobster meat in layers, pile up high, sprinkle lightly with the dressing and coat the top layer rather thickly with mayonnaise : decorate the top with the head or claws or feelers and garnish smartly, use the dried coral.

NOTE. Tinned lobster can be used. Fresh or tinned salmon also make a variety for a fish mayonnaise.

CHAPTER 18

FRUIT

Composition and Importance of Fruit in the Diet. Fruits are chiefly valuable for their fruit acids, some containing two or more, and for their mineral matter, vitamins, and sugar: they are similar in composition to vegetables. All contain a high percentage of water; fat and protein in very small and varying amounts; a fair proportion of carbohydrates, which are present as cellulose (the fibrous framework of the fruit), also as starch in a small quantity, and as sugar, fruit sugar being easily digested. Pectin (see JAM-MAKING) is present, also mineral matter and fruit acids (malic, citric, oxalic, and others). On account of the vitamins in fruits, they are of greater value if eaten raw, since heat destroys them or reduces their content. The most nutritive fruits contain the most sugar, and these are excellent for children, e.g. bananas, apples, grapes; and the dried fruits, figs, dates, and prunes. For those who should avoid sugar, plums, peaches, apricots, and raspberries are suitable, as they contain less sugar.

The general composition of fresh fruit is—

Water	.	. 85 to 90 per cent.	Carbohydrates	. 5½ to 10½ per cent.
Protein	.	. 0·5 ,, ,,	Cellulose .	. 2½ ,, ,,
Fat	.	. 0·5 ,, ,,	Mineral matter .	0·5 ,, ,,

Fresh " ripe " fruits are useful and important in the daily diet, and are very essential to the health of the growing child. Fruit is not only cooling and refreshing, but it can supply in a very palatable form some of the water required daily by the body, and this is a matter to be taken into account in feeding young children, who are very inclined to be thirsty. Fruit acids and cellulose have a laxative effect; but in unripe fruit, the acids and the cellulose are relatively in excess, and then it proves irritating to the digestion, and is conducive to colic and to other similar disorders.

AVERAGE PERCENTAGE OF CHIEF CONSTITUENTS OF SOME FRUITS

Fruit.	Water.	Protein.	Mineral Matter.	Carbo-hydrates.
Strawberry . . .	90·3	1·0	0·6	5·3
Banana	75·0	1·3	0·8	22·0
Dried figs	18·7	4·2	2·4	74·0

Cooking increases the digestibility of fruit for some people by softening the fibre ; it also destroys any bacteria which may be present. The seeds in berries often cause irritation : this can be prevented by cooking the fruit to a pulp or *purée*, and by sieving it, as in making " Fruit Fool." Or the juice can be squeezed from the fruit after it has been cooked, and then either used as a beverage or for making jelly, both of which are useful for children and invalids.

The most usual method of cooking both fresh and dried fruit is to stew it in a thin syrup (sugar and water) ; by so doing none of its properties are lost. Stewed fruit forms the foundation of many sweet dishes.

Points in Stewing Fruit.

1. Use a fireproof dish or white-lined pan with a lid.

2. White or brown sugar may be used for the syrup according to the fruit to be stewed.

3. Avoid a watery syrup ; the actual quantities of sugar and water must partly depend upon the juiciness and the acidity of the fruit. Less water is required when the fruit is to be stewed to a pulp.

4. Cook fruit very gently, either over a low heat or in a slow oven : rapid cooking breaks it or reduces it to a pulp. Whole large fruit, such as apples and pears, and pieces, such as rhubarb, quarters of apples and pears, should be unbroken. Stone fruit and berries should be kept as whole as possible. If an oven should be in use for another purpose and the temperature is suitable, utilize any available space.

Stewed Fresh Fruit (Apples).

Proportions.

1 lb. firm, unbruised apples; ½ pint water; 4 ozs. sugar.

Method. 1. Dissolve the sugar in the water very slowly, boil for 7 to 10 minutes without stirring.

2. Peel, quarter, and core the apples.

3. Place in the syrup and simmer till tender.

4. Dish the apples with the syrup poured over.

NOTE. All fresh fruit is similarly stewed.

Stewed Dried Fruit.

Figs, apple-rings, pears, prunes, apricots.

Proportions.

½ fruit soaked in 1 pint water, except for apple-rings, which require 1½ pints.

2–4 oz. sugar to each pint of water.
Lemon rind or any other suitable flavouring ; cloves, cinnamon, etc.

Method.   1. Wash the fruit well, steep in cold water for 12 hours.
2. Simmer the fruit in the water until tender.
3. Add the sugar, dissolve it and simmer for about 5 minutes.

Fruit Fool (Gooseberry).

Fool may be made with any suitable fruit, such as rhubarb, gooseberries, raspberries.

Proportions.

1 lb. green gooseberries.	*Custard.*
3 to 4 oz. sugar.	1 gill milk.
1 gill water.	1 egg.

Method.   1. Prepare gooseberries and stew them with the sugar and water, rub through a nylon sieve.
2. Make a boiled custard with the egg and milk.
3. Add this to the *purée*, and more sugar if required, and mix well.
Instead of the custard, 1 gill of cream or milk and cream can be used. Less water is used than for stewing fruit in syrup.

CHAPTER 19

PASTRY

As *flour* is the foundation of pastry, also of bread and cake, and is the most common ingredient in daily use, some knowledge of its constituents and their properties is useful, as these determine not only the relative food value, but also the suitability for special purposes in cookery, of the different varieties of flour.

A longitudinal section of a grain of wheat under the microscope shows the following parts.

The " germ," which is to form the young plant, is characterized by its richness in protein, and in *fat*; the "endosperm" or central portion by the large proportion of *starch*, and the "outer coating of bran" by the preponderance of *mineral matter* and of *cellulose* present. Vitamins of the B group are present both in the germ and in the bran.

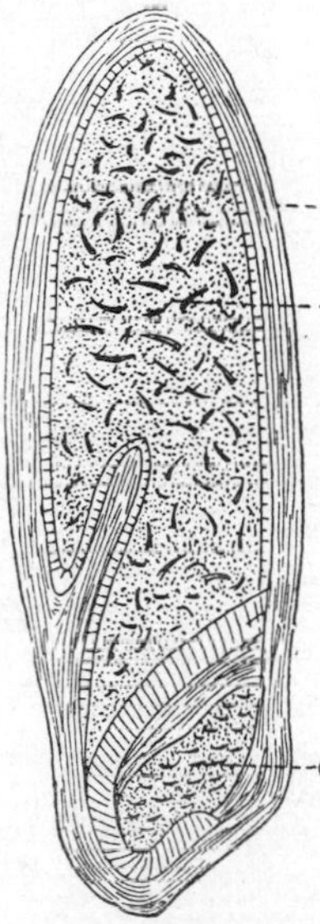

The flour of wheat, when mixed with water, is converted into a tenacious dough or paste, which characteristic is due to the peculiar property of its constituent *gluten*. This becomes viscid or sticky when moistened. Hence the reason why other cereals, barley, rice, oats, and maize, which contain protein in other forms, but not as gluten, require to be mixed with a certain proportion of wheaten flour to form

FIG. 38. LONGITUDINAL SECTION THROUGH A GRAIN OF WHEAT (LOW POWER VIEW)

(*By courtesy of Messrs. Edward Arnold & Company*)

a dough or paste, for starch alone when mixed with water has no cohesion.

The relative proportions of gluten and of starch vary in different wheats, for which reason different blends are used. In milling the whole grain is broken up, and the parts are separated, and by the mechanical process of sifting they are blended in varying proportions to produce varieties and different grades of flour. In wholemeal the three parts of the grain are retained; the white flour from which the bran and certain portions of the germ are eliminated is sifted and graded to produce the two chief classes of flour—ordinary households and patents. Household flour contains more gluten than the latter, it is darker in colour, and is used for all general purposes, for bread, simple pastries, and cakes. The fine pastry flours are richer in starch and poorer in gluten. They are whiter than household flour and more suitable for fancy breads and for the richer and lighter pastries and cakes.

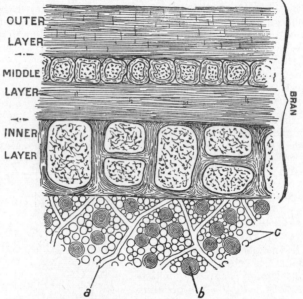

FIG. 39. SECTION THROUGH PART OF A WHEAT GRAIN
(MORE HIGHLY MAGNIFIED)

(*a*) Honeycomb of cellulose; (*b*) starch grains; (*c*) particles of gluten.

(*By courtesy of Messrs. Edward Arnold & Company*)

NOTE. Government Orders and Regulations (1956) are in force, which state that all flours, with the exception of flour containing all the products from milling wheat, must be enriched by the addition of calcium (*creta praeparata*)—14 oz. per 280 lb. sack, and all flours must contain not less than—

1·65 mg. iron per 100 g. flour.
0·24 mg. thiamine (B_1) per 100 g. flour.
1·60 mg. nicotinic acid per 100 g. flour.

Varieties of Pastry. Short crust, flaky, rough puff, suet, puff, and hot water crust. Other preparations, Genoese and Choux pastries (see Chap. 29), which are largely used in the preparation of sweet dishes, and confectionery and cheese pastry, which is merely a variation of very short crust or pastry, are included.

Ingredients of Pastry. (*a*) Flour must be of good quality, fresh, very dry, and free from lumps ; good flour is white with a slightly yellow tinge and adherent, retaining its shape when pressed in the hand. Damp flour makes heavy pastry ; if it is damp, dry it in a warm place, but it must be quite cold before using it. Sieving flour is necessary to free it from lumps and to aerate it.

(*b*) *Fats* used are butter, lard, good dripping, clarified fat, margarine, suet, and vegetable fats. The richness and flavour of the pastry are determined by the kind of fat and by the proportion used. Any rancidity of flavour becomes more pronounced after the fat is cooked, therefore it must be fresh and sweet and good in quality ; it also should be kept in a cool place before use. *Butter* is best for the richer pastries, and fresh butter for puff pastry; saltness and much moisture in the fat used for pastry makes it heavy. To remove the salt and also the buttermilk, wash the butter in cold water, squeeze it well in a floured cloth to dry it, and leave it for a time to get firm and cool again ; in very hot weather put it into very cold water and dry as before, or put it into a refrigerator.

A *mixture of fats*, such as lard and margarine, is economical, and makes excellent pastry. The use of good margarine is preferable to inferior butter. *Lard* makes light pastry, as it tends to lessen the cohesion of the flour, but it is more often used with other fats; it lacks the fine flavour of butter, and if inferior and used alone, it often imparts an unpleasant taste to pastry. Certain proprietary hydrogenated fats make good pastry.

Methods of Addition of Fat in Pastry.

i. Rubbing into the flour (short crust).

ii. Shredding finely or chopping and mixing with the flour (suet crust).

iii. Spreading over the surface of the paste and rolling it in (flaky).

iv. Mixing it in small pieces with the flour and water and rolling it in (rough puff).

v. Enclosing it in the paste and rolling it in (puff pastry).

vi. Melting it with milk or water and mixing with the flour (raised pie crust).

For methods iii, iv, and v, the fat should, if possible, be of the same consistency as the pastry ; if too soft, it melts and is rolled out; if too hard, it breaks through the paste ; when hard, work it with a knife or spoon upon a plate before using it.

(*c*) *Baking Powder* is only necessary when the proportion of fat is less than half that of the flour, as in very plain, short, and suet crusts. Pastry made with too much baking powder is dry, and very quickly becomes stale. When baking powder is used, the pastry should be quickly mixed and baked immediately.

(For composition, etc., of baking powder, see CAKES, page 249.)

(d) *Water*. The average proportion is ½ pint to 1 lb. flour, but the amount varies slightly with the kind of flour and other conditions. Some flour is more absorbent of moisture than the household. Less water is required, (a) as the proportion of butter is increased, (b) when eggs are used, (c) when the fat is melted, as in hot-water crust, (d) when the fat has been reduced to a half-melted condition, due to prolonged contact with hot hands, and to weather conditions.

Principles Underlying Methods of Pastry-making.

1. Air and other gases expand upon a rise of temperature. Water, when heated, gives off steam.

2. Starch cells of flour, when exposed to heat and moisture, swell and absorb the fat.

3. Gluten of flour, being absorbent of water, swells and forms a cohesive mass, in which air is entangled. The latter expands when heated, and thus with steam raises the pastry, and makes it light. The heat affecting the gluten, makes the pastry set and retain its shape.

Characteristics of well-made Short and Flaky Pastries.

(a) Lightness, and (b) shortness or flakiness. The lightness is determined by the amount of air or gas entrapped or enclosed, by the volume of steam given off, and by expansion in baking; the shortness or flakiness upon the kind and amount of fat or shortening used and dexterity in its method of addition to the flour or paste. The term short is applied to pastry which crumbles easily, and this is irrespective of lightness, e.g. shortbread is short and crisp, but not light, whereas short pastry is short and also light.

General Directions for Making Pastry, Mixing, and Rolling it Out. The *aim* in making pastry is to introduce as much *cold air* as possible during the processes of mixing and rolling The cooler the air entangled, the greater is its expansion in the oven, and the lighter the pastry. Working in a cool room, cool hands, and a marble or slate slab, if available, are aids to this end. Cool utensils and ingredients (except for hot water crust) before using them, and handle the pastry quickly and lightly, and as little as is possible. If the hands are warm, wash them a short time before in hot water.

Mixing of Pastry. This is an important factor in obtaining good results.

(a) Sieve together the dry ingredients, flour and salt, and baking powder, when used ; if the latter is not equally distributed, the pastry does not rise uniformly (b) Use a knife with a broad blade for mixing, a knife being cooler than the hands. (c) For mixing, use water freshly drawn from the tap, it is cooler and more aerated than that which has been standing ; add the water gradually to avoid the risk of making the pastry over-moist. Mix briskly with the knife to avoid scrappiness, and to keep it of a uniform consistency throughout, adding water as long as the pastry is very " crumbly." If it has been properly mixed and of the right consistency, it should be soft and elastic, it should not adhere either to the fingers or to the basin, and should leave the basin quite clean. Be careful that pieces clinging to the fingers are not rubbed off into the pastry; this makes it rough when rolled out. (*d*) The uniform distribution of the fat is most essential, whatever the method by which it is added. If not evenly distributed and thoroughly incorporated, the pastry has a streaky appearance, and when baked some of the fat must of necessity melt out before it is absorbed, leaving the pastry tough and hard. (*e*) It is a good plan to leave pastry in a cool place for a time before rolling out. This is really necessary in hot weather.

Rolling Out Pastry. Light manipulation and deft handling are essential to the lightness of pastry ; and in rolling it out to prevent it from sticking and not to stretch it; if stretched, pastry shrinks when cooked.

(*a*) Dredge the board and rolling pin lightly with flour, the pastry itself only when it is absolutely necessary. Flour rolled into it makes it heavy, and often in this way, when making a small quantity of pastry, flour is used much in excess of the amount proportionate to that of the fat used.

(*b*) Turn the pastry on to the floured board, form it into a neat, flat, slightly oblong shape, press it lightly in two or three places.

(*c*) To roll out the paste press the rolling pin lightly but sharply upon it ; press it out before you with short, quick, light, and forward strokes ; take care there is no unnecessary friction, and exert pressure with both hands, otherwise one side will be curved instead of straight. Lift the pin between the strokes, always roll in one direction—forward—and begin to roll, and stop rolling just short of the edges to ensure uniform thickness. To ascertain if pastry is sticking, lift it lightly at the edges, and to avoid unnecessary handling and stretching it, turn it over the floured pin and unroll it, as you would a blind, on to the freshly dredged board.

(*d*) If the pastry is not broad enough, never stretch it or roll it across the width from right to left, but turn it at right-angles to its original position on the board, and roll to the required width. The rolled side of pastry is the smoothest, and should be used uppermost.

(*e*) Pastry (except when baking powder is used in it) is lighter if it is put aside in a cool place for a short time before it is baked ; it is also less likely to shrink as much when cooked. Place it on a floured plate or tin and cover with a floured paper ; never put it direct upon the ice, which makes it damp, and if left for a length of time it becomes hard on the surface.

Temperature and Management of Oven. This is very necessary, for the baking of pastry is equally as important as the making;

however well made it may be, if badly or indifferently baked, the pastry is a failure.

The management of the oven of a coal range, which is not often to be found in the town household now, and of the earlier types of gas cookers, was not always easy; but with the modern and efficient gas, electric and solid fuel cookers constructed upon the principles for the conservation and distribution of heat, and which are supplied with means of regulating and gauging the heat to a nicety, the risk of failure is reduced almost to a minimum. Nevertheless, the intelligent housewife finds she must still rely upon her own experience and judgment as to the heat required and the position in the oven

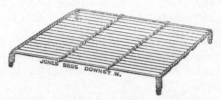

FIG. 40. PASTRY OR CAKE RACK

suitable to the food being cooked. Scrupulous cleanliness is always necessary. It must be ready and at the temperature required.

1. A hot oven is important for the expansion of the air or gas in the pastry, for the formation of steam and to swell the starch cells in the flour, the degree of heat varying slightly with the kind of pastry, the hottest oven being required for puff pastry. Putting pastry in a cool oven causes the fat to melt and to run out before it can be absorbed by the flour, the heat of the oven being insufficient to swell the starch cells; such pastry is greasy, tough, heavy, and most unpalatable. Put into too hot an oven, the pastry does not rise well; the surface quickly sets and forms a thin crust, which colours and browns before the entrapped air and steam have had sufficient time for full expansion; such pastry is not crisp and light, but hard. In a gas or electric oven, pastry is best cooked upon the top shelf for the pastry to set and rise and colour; then if a pie, remove to a lower shelf, to cook the contents by the bottom heat. When a coal range or a gas cooker of the old type may still be in use, the homely test for the heat of oven with a small piece of pastry or thin white paper is useful when in doubt as to the heat of oven. A thermometer can be used, but is not practical in the ordinary household.

2. When baking very light pastry such as puff pastry, the oven must *not* be used for any other purpose.

3. Open and close the oven door gently, avoid opening it before the pastry has set, and afterwards only when absolutely necessary. A current of inrushing cold air will check the rising, particularly of very light pastry, and often cause it to drop or to rise unevenly.

4. If pastry is colouring too quickly, protect it with a double sheet of thin paper. Covering pastry too soon prevents it from rising.

5. To allow steam to escape from any food enclosed in pastry is important as affecting its lightness, hence the reason for a hole in the centre of a meat pie, cuts across sausage rolls, and small holes in a fruit pie.

Cooling Pastry. If pastry is to be eaten cold, let it cool slowly in the warm kitchen. Rapid cooling in a draught or in a cold larder makes it heavy. If pastry is cooked in tins, remove it and place it slightly tilted on a pastry rack or sieve to allow evaporation of moisture.

APPROXIMATE TEMPERATURES OF OVEN

Puff pastry	450° Fahrenheit.
Short pastry	400°–425° ,,
Meat pies	450° ,,

for about 20 minutes, then reduce to 325°–300° F.

To Glaze Pastry. Glazing gives a smart finish—the pastry is generally glazed before it is baked.

Meat Pies, Patties, Sausage Rolls, etc. Brush over with well beaten egg, which can be diluted with water or milk for economy : if a richer colour is required, use the yolk mixed with a little water, and for quite plain pastry milk answers the purpose. Pastry which is baked for a long time should be glazed just before or immediately after removal from oven, e.g. game or raised pie.

Fruit Tarts, Puffs, etc. Brush plain pastry lightly over with cold water or milk and dredge with castor sugar, or when nearly baked brush better pastry over with slightly beaten white of egg and dredge with the sugar and return to the oven for a few minutes to set the egg. This is a " meringue " glaze or coating.

AVERAGE PROPORTIONS OF FLOUR AND FAT

Suet.	Short.	Rough Puff, Flaky.	Puff.	Raised Pie Crust.
½ lb. flour 3 to 4 oz. suet	½ lb. flour 3 to 5 oz. fat.	½ lb. flour 5 to 6 oz. fat	½ lb. flour ½ lb. fat	½ lb. flour 2 to 2½ oz. fat
2 level teaspoonfuls baking powder	(1 level teaspoonful baking powder when 3 oz. used)			

Water. Approximately ½–1 gill to ½ lb. household flour for simple suet and short crust.

Salt. To develop flavour of flour, about ¼ teaspoonful to ½ lb. flour.

Lemon Juice used for flaky, rough puff and puff pastries tends to counteract the richness and to make the pastry light.

Yolk of Egg mixed with water makes pastry short and light—the whole egg with water slightly increases the tenacity of the paste.

Castor Sugar in a small quantity for short pastry tends to make it short, but too much renders it heavy.

SHORT PASTRY OR CRUST

This is one of the most wholesome; and, because the fat is so thoroughly and evenly mixed with the flour by rubbing it in, it is more digestible than the richer flaky and puff pastries. It is mostly used for sweet dishes and for economical savoury pastry.

Fats. For a rich crust butter may be used, but lard, clarified fat, margarine, and vegetable fats are used, generally a combination of two; this is often an economy as regards the fat, and makes excellent short crust.

Method. Follow general directions for mixing and rolling out pastry.

1. Sieve flour, salt, and baking powder, if used, into a clean basin, add the fat, cover with the flour, and cut into small pieces; shred hard fats such as vegetable fat or clarified fat, first before rubbing into flour, which is necessary in cold weather.

2. Rub the fat lightly into the flour with the tips of the fingers until the mixture is as fine as bread-crumbs, lifting the flour up to entangle cool air and to prevent the fat from becoming too soft.

3. Form a well in the centre, mix with cold water, using only just sufficient to make a soft paste, but it must not be sticky : too much water makes short pastry heavy, and not short.

4. Turn on to a floured board, form into a neat, flat and slightly oblong shape with the tips of the fingers, and roll out *once* only to the required thickness and use. Repeated rolling makes short pastry heavy.

Varieties of Short Crust.

(a) *Biscuit Crust* for fruit pies and other dishes.

To ½ lb. flour allow 5 oz. fat, ½ oz. castor sugar, and 1 yolk of egg. Add the sugar after the butter has been rubbed in, and to the water for mixing add the yolk of egg.

(b) *Pastry for Covering Rissoles.* Add part of a whole egg to the water for mixing, this makes the paste short and light, and also rather more tenacious, an advantage, as pastry used for covering fried food should be very thin.

(c) *Cheese Pastry.* An elaboration of good short crust, with the addition of cheese, and mixed with egg (see CHEESE COOKERY).

FRUIT PIE

The pastry for a fruit pie should be thin, a good short crust is the most suitable, but biscuit crust and flaky and rough puff are also used.

Short Pastry.

4 oz. flour.	1 lb. fruit, fresh or bottled.
Pinch of salt.	2 to 3 oz. sugar.
Fat in proportion to richness	Water.
required.	White of egg and castor sugar
¼ gill water (about).	for glazing (optional).

Method. 1. Make pastry (see SHORT PASTRY) and leave to cool while preparing fruit; prepare fresh fruit in the ordinary way for cooking. 2. *To fill* dish. Use a deep one, on account of the juice, half fill it with the prepared fruit, then add the sugar and the rest of the fruit; if sugar comes into contact with the pastry it makes it sodden ; pile the fruit up high in the centre, using a pie-cup if there is not sufficient ; press the fruit down well, it shrinks more than meat. Add a little water; stone fruits require more than the juicy variety. 3. *To cover* the pie-dish. Roll out the pastry rather less than ¼ inch in thickness, and proceed as for meat pie, except (*a*) decorate the edge with very small scallops, about ⅛ in. apart ; and for the escape of steam, with a skewer pierce 4 small holes in the sides of the cover—a fruit pie is not decorated with leaves. 4. *To bake.* Place the pie on a baking tin, this for easy removal and to avoid risk of the juice boiling over on to oven shelf, and put it into a hot oven at first (it should not be as hot as for a meat pie) to set the crust quickly before there is much shrinkage of fruit. By so doing the pastry keeps its raised shape. Move the pie to a lower shelf or lower the temperature to complete the cooking of pastry and fruit.

5. When the pastry close to the rim is firm, it is sufficiently baked ; test the fruit with a skewer. Should the pie be colouring too quickly cover with paper sprinkled very lightly with water. The time allowed for baking is usually about 35 to 40 minutes, but varies with the thickness of the pastry and the kind of fruit. 6. Glaze with the white of egg and castor sugar as directed (optional).

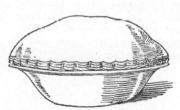

FIG. 41. FRUIT PIE READY FOR BAKING

How to Use Pastry for Open Tarts and Tartlets (Jam and Other Fillings), Flans and Patties. Both good short crust and puff pastry are suitable for all of these except flans, for which short pastry is used.

Fillings for Open Tarts and Tartlets.

(*a*) Jam.

(*b*) Fresh fruit ; if it requires longer cooking than the pastry, partially cook it first.

(*c*) Custard (eggs and milk).

(*d*) Syrup and bread-crumbs: 1 gill syrup, ½ gill bread-crumbs, grated rind and juice of half lemon.

(*e*) Cake and pudding mixtures, e.g. Castle and Bakewell mixtures. Open tarts and tartlets are made by two methods—

1. The pastry is baked first and the jam is added after baking.

2. The jam, or any filling, is baked with the pastry.

(*a*) **Open Tarts with Jam or Other Fillings.**

1. (*a*) Grease a plate or shallow tin, roll the pastry out rather less than ¼ in. in thickness and a little larger than the plate or tin, cover it with pastry without stretching it, press the pastry on well and trim the edges. (*b*) Roll out the trimmings, cut a strip of pastry sufficiently long and broad to cover the rim of the plate, wet the rim of pastry lining the plate and lay the strip on it, join the ends neatly, press the edges together, decorate by scalloping the edge (see MEAT PIE) or by marking the rim with a fork or back of a knife or spoon. (*c*) Prick the bottom of the pastry, lay over it a piece of greased paper, put on the paper some cubes of crusty bread or a little raw rice, this prevents the pastry from blistering and losing its shape in baking. (*d*) Bake in a quick oven till set and cook about 30 minutes, remove paper, etc., and return to the oven to dry the bottom of the pastry. (*e*) If the tart is to be served at once, spread the jam over the centre and return to the oven for a few minutes to make perfectly hot.

2. If the jam is to be cooked in the tart, line the plate as directed above, prick the bottom and before laying the strip of pastry on the rim of pastry lining the plate, put jam in the centre, being careful not to touch the rim with it. From the rolled out trimmings cut narrow strips of pastry, twist these and arrange them lattice fashion across the tart. Wet the ends to secure them, put on the rim of pastry, press the edges together, and finish as before.

When the fillings are custard, fresh fruit, cake, and pudding-like mixtures, bake them with the pastry.

(*b*) **Tartlets.** 1. Roll out the pastry to about ⅛ in. *in thickness*, and with a plain or fluted cutter mark out rounds of pastry, which should be rather larger than the patty pans, to allow for depth of patty pan and shrinkage of pastry. 2. Grease the patty pans when using short crust ; line with the rounds of pastry, prick the bottom. Add filling, if it is to be baked in pastry cases; if not, put a small piece of paper with a little uncooked rice in it in each.

(*c*) **Patties, Pasties, etc.** These are made in different ways.

1. In small patty pans or in plates or larger tins, which are lined

with pastry and the filling, meat, fruit, mincemeat, etc., is covered with pastry.

2. The filling is simply enclosed in a piece of pastry, e.g. sausage rolls, Cornish pasties, jam turnovers.

3. Cases of rich pastry are made and baked and then filled. (See PUFF PASTRY PATTIES and *Vol-au-vent*, pages 181, 182.)

NOTE. All these may be used both for savoury and for sweet fillings.

To Cut Out Linings and Covers for Patties and Pasties. If using rich flaky or rough puff pastry, it is not necessary to grease the tins.

FIG. 42. FLAN RINGS

Roll out the pastry less than ¼ in. in thickness, and with a plain round cutter cut out rounds, the cutter being large enough to fit loosely over the patty pan to allow for depth of tin and not to stretch pastry. Cut out the covers first, then roll out the trimmings, and use for lining the patty tins and for decorations. The linings should be thinner than the covers, otherwise the pastry is apt to be under-cooked. For large pasties follow the same directions. When the filling is meat or some savoury mixture, make a hole in the centre, decorate with leaves, and glaze with egg ; if a sweet filling, such as mincemeat or fruit, glaze with white of egg or water and castor sugar.

For plain household fare, a light short crust for meat patties and pasties answers the purpose, and requires less time to prepare.

Jam Puffs or Turnovers. Short crust can be used, but flaky or rough puff pastries are more suitable.

Cut out rounds of pastry about 4 or 5 in. in diameter, damp the edges half-way round with cold water, place a little jam in the centre of each, fold over, press the edges well together, and scallop or leave plain, glaze with beaten white of egg or water and castor sugar. Another method of shaping is to bring the edges together to form a triangular shape, the joins being beneath.

Pastry Flans. A flan is really an open tart, the pastry case being shaped inside a pastry or " flan " ring, which may be oval or round or plain or fluted; it is about 1 in. in depth. The case is filled with some sweet mixture, which is either baked with the pastry or the case is filled after baking, the latter being the more general method.

To Make and Bake a Flan. 1. Use short crust, the pastry must *not* be *too rich* or the case will break when lifted. 2. Grease the ring inside and place on a baking tin. 3. Roll out the pastry to less than ¼ in. in thickness and in the shape of the flan ring, but larger in all directions by about 2 in.   4. Drop the pastry into the centre of the ring, press it well into the ring, so that it may take the shape of the ring, press it well down at the bottom, that the lower edge may be sharp when the flan is baked. Trim off the edges evenly. 5. Prick the pastry at the bottom, and, if the flan is to be baked before it is filled, line it with greased paper as for an open tart. 6. When baked remove paper and rice, and return to the oven to dry for a few minutes. Serve either hot or cold.

Fillings. Various sweet preparations.

A macedoine of fruit, stewed fruit, tinned fruit, fruit *purée* with cream, custard, etc.

ROUGH PUFF PASTRY

The lightness of rough puff and flaky pastries is mostly due to steam and to the amount of cold air which is entrapped by folding the pastry, therefore it is most important not to expel air by careless

FIG. 43   FIG. 44
METHOD OF FOLDING ROUGH PUFF PASTRY

rolling out; the fat is thoroughly incorporated with the flour by rolling the pastry out several times.

Proportions.

8 oz. flour.	½ teaspoonful salt.
4 to 6 oz. fat.	½ teaspoonful lemon juice.
Cold water to mix (about 1 gill).	

Method. (See GENERAL DIRECTIONS FOR MAKING PASTRY—MIXING AND ROLLING.) 1. Sieve the flour and salt into a basin, add the fat, cover with the flour, and cut the fat into pieces the size of a walnut. 2. Add the lemon juice and cold water, and mix very lightly to an elastic paste, but be careful not to break down the fat; if this is done the pastry tends to be short rather than flaky. 3. Turn on to a floured board, press the pastry lightly together, but do not knead it. 4. Roll it out lightly and evenly into a strip about three times as long as it is broad and about ¼ in. thick. 5. Fold it in three, as in Fig. 43, seal the edges by pressing them sharply together with the rolling pin to enclose some air, as in Fig. 44. 6. Turn the pastry half round with the fold to the right, then press it in two or three places with the rolling pin to make small ridges, as in Fig. 44. This distributes the entrapped air and prevents it from collecting in a large bubble, which is very difficult not to break when rolling. 7. Roll out as before, being careful not to roll over the top and bottom edges ; this would expel the air and make pastry uneven in thickness, and it would rise unevenly. 8. Fold again in three, half turn, press in two or three places as before, and roll out again. 9. Repeat until the pastry has been rolled and folded four times, then roll out to the required size and thickness.

Rough Puff Pastry used to Cover a Meat Pie.

NOTE. In handling and using the pastry, avoid stretching it ; this results in undue shrinkage from the edge of the dish when it is baked.

FIG. 45. FLAKING OR OPENING UP THE EDGES OF PASTRY

1. Roll out pastry into a strip rather less than $\frac{1}{8}$ in. thick and about $1\frac{1}{2}$ in. larger in all directions than the pie-dish.

2. Cut from this a narrow strip of pastry long enough to encircle the rim of the dish and about $\frac{3}{4}$ in. wide ; it should be rather wider than the rim of the dish, so that it may overlap very slightly both the inner and outer edges.

3. Wet the rim of the dish, press the strip of pastry on well, join the ends without overlapping; if stretched, the rim will shrink away from the outer edge of dish when cooked, drawing the cover with it.

4. Wet this strip of pastry, using a pastry brush for the purpose, and lay on the piece to cover the top, press the edges well together, ease it slightly towards the centre of dish, avoid dragging it over the edge.

5. Hold the dish up in the left hand, and with a sharp knife, holding it in an oblique position, so that the edges of the pastry may slope outwards (this is to allow for shrinkage in cooking), trim the edges neatly with short quick strokes, cutting away from you.

6. To *flake* the edges. Flour the first finger of the left hand, press it lightly down on the rim of pastry, and with the back of a floured knife, sharply tap with a slightly lifting movement the

edges all round. This gives the edges the appearance of leaves or flakes, and it also assists in the rising of the pastry by opening up the edges.

7. To *scallop* or flute the edges, draw the back of the floured knife sharply upwards and slightly inwards across the edges of the rim, the space between each scallop being about ¾ in. ; at the

FIG. 46. SCALLOPING THE EDGE OF PASTRY

same time press the pastry in front of the knife downwards and outwards with the thumb of the left hand in order to form the scallop.

8. Make a hole in the centre of the pie to allow steam to escape; this is most essential as affecting the lightness of the pastry.

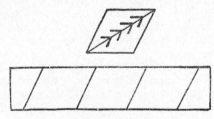

FIG. 47. HOW TO CUT OUT LEAVES
OF PASTRY

9. Brush over with beaten egg; be careful, however, not to coat the edges, because this would seal them and prevent the pastry from rising.

To Cut Out Leaves. Roll out the trimmings, divide the pastry into strips about 1½ in. wide, cut these across obliquely into diamond-shaped pieces, mark with the back of the knife in imitation of the veins, brush over with egg, and arrange these *round* the hole in the centre, keeping it open for the escape of steam.

Meat Pies.

Rough puff and flaky pastries are generally used to cover a pie;
flaky pastry when cold is shorter than rough puff, and is preferable
for a pie to be served cold. The success of a meat pie depends not
only upon the pastry, but upon the contents, seasoning, and gravy.

Proportion of Crust and of Meat.

1 to 1¼ lb. meat.
½ lb. flour for pastry.

Meat. A large variety, beef, veal, rabbit, poultry, game, which
may be used separately or two or more kinds together. Meat for
pies should be tender; if the coarser and tougher parts are used it

Fig. 48. Meat Pie Ready for Baking

is advisable to partially cook the meat first, but it must be quite
cold when covered with the pastry, otherwise the latter is heavy.
Cut meat into small pieces, or thin small slices, and roll it ; joint
rabbits, poultry, and game, remove large bones and divide into
neat pieces ; cut small birds into four. A little tender steak is
often added to a game pie to enrich the gravy and the flavour.

Seasonings and Flavourings. The seasoning of a meat pie should
be sufficient to require none or very little when eaten. Allow
about 1 teaspoonful salt, rather less than ⅛ teaspoonful pepper to
each pound of meat, mix this with 1 dessertspoonful flour and dip
the meat into the seasoned flour, which thickens the gravy. Those
pies which are eaten cold require more seasoning.

To give additional flavouring, ham, bacon, hard-boiled egg,
forcemeat, herbs, etc., are used ; for white meats the grated rind
and the juice of a lemon.

Good Stock or Gravy, well seasoned, is important. Allow
about 1 gill to 1 lb. meat, add half of it cold, before the pie is baked;
after it is cooked, add the remainder hot. When the pie is to be
served cold the stock or gravy used should be in a jelly; if not,
dissolve a little gelatine in it, using ¼ oz. to ½ pint liquid.

To Fill the Dish. Distribute the well seasoned meat and the
additions evenly, pack the meat rather loosely; if too tightly pressed
down the meat does not cook so well, and is not so tender ; pile it

up in the centre to support the pastry, if there is not sufficient meat use an egg-cup or pie funnel. Add water, stock, or gravy.

Baking a Meat Pie.

1. Put pie on a baking tin and bake for about 1½ hours. Place the pie in a hot oven for the first half hour to set the pastry; when well risen and beginning to colour, reduce the heat to cook the meat more slowly. As soon as the pastry is dark enough, cover it with a double piece of paper; run a skewer through the hole in the top to test if the meat is cooked.

2. Add good hot stock through the hole in the centre.

3. Wipe the dish with a wet cloth and garnish with parsley.

NOTE. The edges of a large pie baked in a small oven often get too dark; to prevent this, tie a band of well greased paper round the rim of the dish and cover with kitchen paper, but the pastry must be well risen before the pie is covered or the pastry will not be so light.

Beefsteak and Kidney Pie.

Pastry.

1 lb. tender steak.
1 sheep's kidney or 2 oz. ox kidney.
Salt, pepper.
1 dessertspoonful flour.
1 gill good stock or gravy.

½ lb. rough puff.
(4 to 6 oz. fat to 8 oz. flour.)

Method. 1. Prepare rough puff pastry. 2. Wipe the meat, remove skin and superfluous fat, beat it slightly, and cut into 1-in. cubes or into small thin slices. 3. Steep kidney in cold water, wash, remove skin, fat, and core, and cut into small dice or thin slices. 4. Mix flour, pepper, and salt together, dip meat and kidney in it, roll a piece of kidney and a small piece of fat in a slice of steak. 5. Place the meat in a pie-dish, pile up in the centre, and add ½ gill of good stock. 6. Follow directions already given for covering a meat pie with pastry and for baking and serving it.

NOTE. A few potatoes, a parboiled onion sliced, a few cooked haricots or a little carrot may be added to a plain pie when the quantity of meat is small.

Veal and Ham Pie.

1 lb. tender veal (fillet).
4 oz. bacon or ham.
1 hard-boiled egg.
1 teaspoonful chopped parsley.
Pinch of sweet herbs.

Grated rind and juice of ¼ lemon.
1 teaspoonful salt.
⅛ teaspoonful pepper.
1 gill white stock.
½ lb. rough puff pastry.

Method. 1. Make pastry and use for pie as directed. 2. Prepare meat; wipe veal, remove skin and fat, cut into 1-in. cubes and the bacon or ham into dice or small thin slices. 3. Mix pepper, salt, parsley, lemon rind, and sprinkle over the meats. 4. Put a layer of meat in the pie-dish, then slices of egg and the rest of the meat, add ½ gill white stock. 5. Proceed as for beefsteak pie. 6. If the pie is to be eaten cold, and the stock used is weak, it may be necessary, to ensure it setting in a jelly, to add a little gelatine to that which is added to the pie *after* it is baked (see page 177).

Fresh Meat Patties (Veal and Ham).

¼ lb. rough puff pastry.	Seasoning.
4 oz. uncooked veal.	Grated lemon rind.
1 oz. bacon or ham.	Stock.
¼ teaspoonful chopped parsley.	

Method. 1. Prepare pastry, cut veal and ham into small dice, mix with the seasonings and moisten with a few drops of well seasoned stock. 2. Follow directions given (page 173) for lining and covering patty pans for patties. Line the patty pans with the pastry, fill with the meat, piling it up rather high in the centre, wet the edges, cover with the rounds of pastry, seal, make a hole in the centre, flake the edges and brush over with beaten egg or milk. Decorate round the top with small leaves of pastry. 3. Bake in a hot oven for 40 to 45 minutes, pour in a little hot stock through a small funnel and serve hot or cold.

Variations. (*a*) Beef patties, substitute good tender steak for veal and ham. (*b*) Chicken and ham or tongue with same seasonings as for veal and ham. (*c*) With cooked meat, scraps of meat, game, and poultry mixed with a sauce and well seasoned.

Any of the fillings suitable for patties may be used for small meat turnovers or puffs.

FLAKY PASTRY

Proportions.

8 oz. flour.	¼ teaspoonful salt
6 oz. butter or margarine and lard in equal quantities.	¼ teaspoonful lemon juice. Cold water to mix (about 1 gill).

Method. 1. Sieve salt with flour into a basin and divide the fat into four equal portions, rub one portion lightly into the flour as for short crust. 2. Add the lemon juice and sufficient water to mix to an elastic paste, knead very lightly on a floured board till the pastry is free from cracks. 3. Roll out into a strip about three times as long as it is broad, and rather less than ¼ in. thick. 4. With the point of a knife spread one of the three remaining portions of fat in small flakes over two-thirds of the surface of the paste, and in even rows to within about 1 in. of the edge all round. If the fat is too close to the edge, it is pressed out of the pastry when it is rolled. Dredge the fat very lightly with flour. 5. Fold the pastry in three with the plain part in the centre, so that there is an alternate layer of fat and of paste. 6. Turn the pastry half round with the folded edge to the right of the worker. 7. Press the edges sharply together to enclose air and press the pastry in two or three places to form ridges as in making rough puff pastry and for the same reasons. 8. Roll out again into a narrow strip, being careful *not to roll over* the *edges*, and proceed as before until the remaining portions of fat have been used. Lastly, roll out to the thickness required.

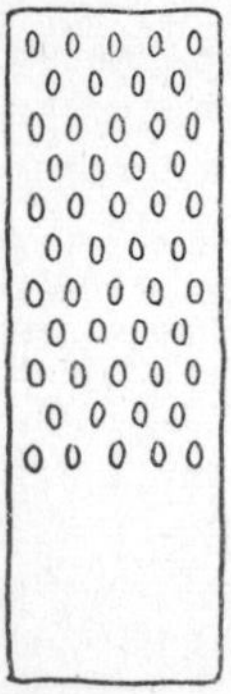

Sausage Rolls.

Proportions.

½ lb. flaky or rough puff pastry.   Egg for coating.
¼ lb. sausages.

Method. 1. Parboil sausages, remove skin, cut each into two or four pieces according to size of roll and leave to get cold. 2. *Prepare the pastry.* Roll into a long strip about ⅛ in. thick ; divide the strip down the centre and cut each half into three or four oblong pieces. 3. Turn them with the rolled side downwards, wet the edges of pastry, place a piece of sausage in the centre of each piece, fold in two ; press the edges together, seal, trim, and flake the edges. 4. Brush with beaten egg and make two or three cuts across the top for escape of steam. 5. Bake in a quick oven for about 35 minutes.

Fig. 49. But-
ter Spread
in Flakes on
Pastry

Variations. Mixtures such as are used for rissoles—minced chicken, and ham, etc.—can be used.

PUFF PASTRY

Proportions.

Equal quantities of flour and of *fresh* butter, or other suitable fat.
½ teaspoonful lemon juice to ½ lb. flour.
Sufficient cold water to mix.

Uses. For patties, *vol-au-vents*, and many sweet dishes.

Essentials to Lightness of Pastry.

(*a*) Coolness of ingredients before and during preparation of pastry.

(*b*) Butter free from salt and moisture and as nearly as possible of the same consistency as the paste.

(*c*) Enclosure and retention of air in the pastry and allowing it to cool at intervals during rolling.

(*d*) Careful avoidance of draughts while in the oven.

Method. 1. Shape fat into a flat square pat and leave to get cool and firm. 2. Sieve flour and mix with water and lemon juice to an elastic dough. 3. Turn on to a floured board or on to marble or slate slab if available, and knead lightly for 10 to 15 minutes until the paste is perfectly smooth and elastic, and no longer sticks to the fingers. 4. Roll out into a strip sufficiently long and wide to enclose the butter. 5. Place fat on it and fold the pastry in two over it, flatten it in two or three places with the rolling pin and roll out lightly and evenly into a long strip, being careful the fat does not break through and not to roll over the top and bottom edges. 6. Fold the strip in three, press down the folds, and put the pastry aside to cool for 15 minutes. Do not seal the edges of pastry, as in making rough puff and flaky pastries; this is to prevent the collection of large air bubbles, which tend to make this very light pastry rise unevenly. 7. To roll out the pastry the next time, place it on the board with the folded edge to the right, roll and fold twice then put aside again to get cool; each roll and fold is termed a "turn," and puff pastry requires seven turns. The repeated rolling is necessary to incorporate the large proportions of fat thoroughly with the flour, and the repeated folding makes puff pastry very light. 8. Repeat this until the pastry has had seven rolls and folds. 9. Roll out to size and thickness required and use as directed. Before baking, leave the pastry in a cool place for 10 to 15 minutes. 10. Bake in a very hot oven, being careful that the door is not opened until the pastry is set and that no draught enters.

Patty and " Vol-au-vent " Cases (Puff Pastry).

The fillings for these cases are either savoury or sweet.

To Make Patty Cases. ½ lb. of puff pastry will be sufficient for about eight cases.

1. The pastry having had seven rolls and folds must be perfectly cool, roll it out to ½ in. in thickness, and leave for 5 to 10 minutes to allow for shrinkage in cooling before cutting out.

2. Use a plain cutter 2 to 2½ in. in diameter for cutting out the patties. Dip it into hot water, this gives a cleaner cut than when floured, use it wet and stamp out the rounds sharply without pressing heavily on the pastry. Be careful not to cut too near the edges of the pastry, which may be of unequal thickness. With a cutter 1 in. in diameter mark an inner ring on the rounds of pastry to about half the depth, leaving a border outside the centre ring of ½ in.

3. If lids are required as for patty cases to hold savoury mixtures, roll out the scraps of pastry to ¼ in. in thickness, and cut out some small rounds with the 1 in. cutter.

4. Brush over the tops of the cases and lids, being careful not to let the egg touch the edges, which would seal them and prevent the pastry from rising.

To Bake Cases. Be certain that the oven is sufficiently hot, place the cases on a baking tin brushed over with cold water, keep them towards the middle of the tin and in the centre of the oven shelf, the heat of the oven being more uniform in the middle. Avoid opening the oven door until the pastry is well set—time required for cooking is about 20 minutes—bake the lids on a separate tin, as they require only a short time, previous to removal of the cases. If upon removal from the oven one side is higher than the other press the top down gently at once before the pastry cools and hardens.

To Fill Patty Cases.   Take out the soft centre of the case with the point of a knife and, if the patties are to be served hot, fill with the

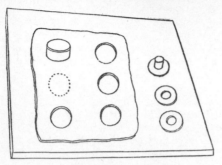

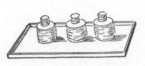

FIG. 50. METHOD OF CUTTING
OUT PATTY CASES

FIG. 51. BAKED PATTIES
READY FOR DISHING

hot savoury mixture, put on the small lids, and reheat for a few minutes.   If served cold, fill just before serving.

Use trimmings of puff pastry for jam puffs, turnovers, etc.

NOTE.   For jam tartlets, roll out the pastry not quite so thickly and without lids; use a rather smaller and fluted cutter.

"Vol-au-vent" Cases.   For a *vol-au-vent*, puff pastry requires only six turns.

1. Roll out the pastry to ¾ in. in thickness and let it cool.

2. For cutting out the case use an oval or round and deeper cutter made for the purpose, not cutting closer to the edge of the pastry than ½ in., and with a knife or smaller cutter mark a smaller oval or round on the top ; brush over the top with beaten egg, mark the small centre piece lattice fashion, and with a fine skewer pierce the pastry in the centre right through to the bottom; this tends to break bubbles of air, which would make the case rise unevenly.

3. Bake in a quick oven for about 40 minutes.

4. When baked lift off the small lid, scoop out the soft centre, and fill as directed for patties.

Vol-au-vent fillings are both savoury and sweet.

Chicken and Ham Patties (Hot).
   For Filling.

4 oz. cooked chicken.
2 oz. cooked ham or tongue.
2 tablespoonfuls white sauce.
1 tablespoonful cream.

Grated lemon rind.
Seasoning.
Pinch of nutmeg.

   For Cases.
¼ lb. puff pastry.

To Prepare Filling. Free chicken from skin and bone, chop it and the ham finely. Heat the sauce, add meat, seasonings, and flavourings, make quite hot, add the cream. Fill the patty cases as before directed. Both pastry and mixture must be quite hot if patties are served hot.

Variations. Veal and ham, game, oysters, shrimps, lobster, salmon, prawns, sweetbread, etc. These are mixed with a suitable sauce and flavourings and well seasoned.

SUET PASTRY OR CRUST

Suet crust is of considerable value in children's diet, as it is very wholesome, nourishing, and easily digested. To be easily digested suet pastry requires long and thorough cooking. Beef suet is not as hard as mutton, it is richer and of a better flavour, and is more suitable than mutton for suet puddings. Veal suet is more delicate in flavour than beef, and is often used. Suet pastry is generally boiled or steamed, but it is also sometimes baked in a moderate oven, and requires about half the time required for boiling. It is used (*a*) for lining pudding basins to enclose meat and fruit, (*b*) for roly-poly puddings, and (*c*) for dumplings. Suet for pastry should be firm and dry, it shreds and chops more easily.

Proportions of Ingredients.

½ lb. flour.　　　　½ teaspoonful salt.
4 oz. suet.　　　　Cold water to mix (about 1 gill).
1 teaspoonful baking powder.

To Make Suet Pastry.

1. Sieve flour, baking powder and salt into a basin. 2. *To chop suet.* Remove the skin from suet, dust with a little flour taken from the quantity weighed out for the pastry; this prevents stickiness while shredding and chopping. Use a long sharp-pointed knife, keep the point on the board and shred the suet finely. To chop the suet, dredge it again with a little more of the flour, hold the handle of the knife in the right hand and with two or three fingers pressing on the point to keep it on the board, work the handle up and down quickly and chop the suet until it resembles white bread-crumbs. A quicker method is to use a grater, but it is not as satisfactory, for the fine division of the suet is important as affecting the lightness, digestibility, and palatability of the pastry. 3. Mix the suet thoroughly with the flour, rubbing flour and suet lightly together with the fingers. 4. Make a well in the centre, add the water, gradually mixing the ingredients with a knife into a soft dough, which, when lightly rubbed round the basin, should leave it clean. 5. Turn on to a floured board, knead it lightly with the fingers until smooth and free from cracks. 6. Roll suet pastry out *once*, usually about ¼ in. in thickness, use as directed.

NOTE. A richer crust is made by increasing the proportion of suet. If half the quantity of flour is omitted and white fresh bread-crumbs substituted, this makes a lighter suet crust.

To Line a Basin with Suet Pastry.

1. Grease the basin.
2. Turn the prepared pastry on to a floured board, knead lightly to make it smooth as directed ; cut off one-third for the cover.
3. Roll the remainder out into a round about $\frac{1}{4}$ in. in thickness and about $1\frac{1}{2}$ times the diameter of the basin, turning the pastry round and round as it is being rolled.
4. Turn the pastry over, so that the rolled side, which is the smoothest, comes next to the basin, and line the greased basin with it. Carefully press out all the creases, otherwise bubbles of air will be entrapped between the basin and lining, and this causes the surface of the cooked pudding to have a pitted appearance.
5. Fill with the meat or fruit, adding a little liquid ; stock or water to meat, water to fruit.
6. Roll out the remainder of pastry into a round to fit the top of the basin, damp the edges of the lining, press the edges of the cover and lining together, seal well, and turn the edges slightly inwards to seal it more securely.

To Boil or Steam a Suet Pudding. Both for steaming and for boiling use a saucepan with a well-fitting lid ; for either method the water must be boiling when the pudding is put into the pan, keep the water boiling steadily all the time, and as it boils away add more boiling water. If the pudding is to be *boiled*, fill the basin quite full ; if not quite full cover the top with crusts of bread, otherwise the water will get in. Use a pudding basin, with a cloth. Dip the pudding cloth into boiling water, squeeze out as much moisture as possible, and dredge lightly with flour to prevent water from penetrating ; cover the pudding with the cloth, tie it on tightly, but leave a little room, a tiny pleat across the centre of the cloth, to allow for the expansion of the pudding. If *steamed*, the pudding basin need not be full. Cover with a greased paper and put it into the saucepan with the boiling water half way up the sides of the basin, or cook in an ordinary steamer. The time for steaming is at least half as long as for boiling.

Beefsteak and Kidney Pudding.

Ingredients.

$\frac{1}{2}$ lb. suet pastry (see page 183).
1 lb. beefsteak.
2 oz. ox kidney or one sheep's kidney.
About $\frac{3}{4}$ gill water or stock to moisten meat.

Seasoned Flour.

1 dessertspoonful flour.
1 teaspoonful salt.
$\frac{1}{8}$ teaspoonful pepper.

Gravy to serve separately.

Method. 1. Have the pan of water, basin, and greased paper in readiness. 2. Prepare the meat and toss in seasoned flour as directed for beefsteak and kidney pie. 3. Make suet pastry and follow directions already given for lining, filling and covering basin as for cooking a suet pudding.

(*a*) Well fill basin with meat, piling it up rather high in the centre to allow of shrinkage, do not pack meat too tightly or it will not cook evenly.

(*b*) A meat pudding requires long and thorough cooking ; one made in a basin of 1½ pints capacity requires at least 5 hours steady steaming.

(*c*) If the pudding is a large one, to ensure the meat being cooked and tender, the bottom of the basin need not be lined.

4. When cooked, serve the pudding in the basin with a napkin folded round it. It is necessary to serve some good gravy separately to supplement what is inside the pudding.

NOTE. A hole in the centre of a meat pudding is not necessary as in a pie, for pastry is porous and allows the steam to escape.

Fruit Pudding.

| ½ lb. suet crust (see page 183). | Sugar. |
| Fruit. 1–1½ lbs. | Water. |

Method. 1. Prepare fruit in the ordinary way for cooking. 2. Make the suet pastry and proceed as for beefsteak pudding.

(*a*) Fill up the basin with the fruit and the necessary sugar, *press* the fruit *down* well ; the shrinkage of fruit is greater than that of meat and of soft fruit very considerable.

(*b*) Add a little water and the sugar, the amount of water and sugar varying with the juiciness and acidity of fruit.

3. For a pudding made in a basin of 1½ pints capacity, allow at least 3 hours steady steaming. 4. When cooked, remove paper, let the pudding stand for a minute or two, for it to shrink from the sides of the basin, turn on to a hot dish and serve.

OTHER USES OF SUET PASTRY

I. For Roly-Poly Puddings, ½ lb. suet crust.

The pastry may be spread with jam, marmalade, lemon curd, mincemeat, syrup, and bread-crumbs (3 tablespoonfuls bread-crumbs to ½ pint syrup flavoured with lemon juice and the grated rind) and other mixtures.

Method. 1. Roll out the pastry into an oblong about ¼ in. thick, keep the edges even and uniform in thickness. 2. Moisten the edges and spread evenly with the jam or mixture to within about an inch of the edge of the pastry all round. If the jam is liquid, add a few crumbs to it. 3. Roll up, seal the edge and ends well together, roll in a greased cloth; leave a little room for expansion, tie the ends tightly with string. 4. The pudding may be boiled, steamed, or baked. A roly-poly made with ½lb. flour, requires to be steamed for about 2½ to 3 hours, the slight wrinkling of the cloth is an indication that the pudding is shrinking and is sufficiently cooked. If *baked*, less time for cooking is required, about 1 hour; place the pudding on a greased tin with the join downwards, and bake in a *moderate* oven.

II. **For Treacle or Jam Layer Pudding.**   Use ½ lb. suet crust and jam or syrup mixture as for roly-poly.

Method. 1. Roll out the pastry into three or four round pieces, each rather larger than the other. 2. Put a little jam or syrup mixture into the bottom of the greased basin, cover with the smallest round of pastry, continue until the basin is full, with a layer of pastry on the top. 3. Cover with greased paper and steam, following directions for fruit pudding.

III. **For Currant, Sultana or Raisin Duff.**   Use same proportions of suet and of flour, add sugar and fruit and a pinch of spice.

Method. 1. Mix ingredients together with water; the consistency should be rather softer than that of suet pastry used for lining basins. 2. Steam in a basin, serve with a sweet white sauce.

BOILED OR STEAMED PUDDING MIXTURES MADE WITH SUET

The foundation of these, as of suet pastry, consists of flour and of finely chopped suet, which are used in the ordinary proportions of half the quantity of suet to that of flour. They are made in a large variety by using different combinations of ingredients, and may be quite simple or rich, according to the proportion of suet and eggs used, the degree of lightness varying with the number of eggs. These pudding mixtures are lighter if made with half flour and half bread-crumbs, and light mixtures are more generally steamed in a greased basin or mould, covered with a greased paper ; the basin or mould should not be more than two-thirds or three-quarters full to allow the mixture to rise. The consistency should be that of a stiff batter dropping easily from the spoon. The time required for cooking varies ; the richer and softer the mixture, the longer time it takes to cook, but all require a considerable time and *thorough* cooking. A Christmas pudding should *boil* steadily for at least 7 to 8 hours, or steam for 12 hours, but for an ordinary mixture of medium richness, such as ginger pudding, the recipe and method of which are given as being typical of these pudding mixtures, 2½ hours *steady steaming* should be allowed.

AVERAGE PROPORTIONS OF INGREDIENTS FOR SUET PUDDING MIXTURES

Ingredients.	*Quantity.*
Flour	8 oz.
Sugar	3 to 4 oz. according to taste and other ingredients used.
Suet	3 to 5 oz.
Dried fruits	
(a) Currants, raisins, sultanas .	3 to 6 oz.
(b) Figs and dates . .	4 to 6 oz.
Jam or marmalade . .	3 to 4 tablespoonfuls.
Liquid.	
(a) Eggs ; (b) Milk . .	1 to 3 eggs, milk as required.
Syrup	4 oz. when used alone, if with sugar, then sufficient for necessary sweetness.
Ginger and spice . . .	2 level teaspoonfuls ground ginger— ½ level teasp. spice to ½ lb. flour.
Baking powder . . .	2 level teaspoonfuls to ½ lb. flour.
Bicarbonate of soda . .	1 level teaspoonful to ½ lb. flour.

Ginger Pudding (Typical Mixture).

Proportions.

4 oz. flour.	2 level teaspoonfuls ground ginger.
4 oz. bread-crumbs.	1 level teaspoonful bicarbonate soda.
4 oz. suet.	1 egg.
4 oz. golden syrup.	1 gill milk.
Pinch of salt.	Syrup sauce (see SAUCES, page 73).

Method. 1. Sieve flour, soda, salt, and ginger ; chop suet very finely, add it and the bread-crumbs to the flour. 2. Warm the syrup slightly ; if warmed it blends more readily with the liquid, mix with the milk and beaten egg, add to the dry ingredients and beat well together, the consistency being that of stiff batter. 3. Put into a greased basin, which should be about two-thirds full, cover with greased paper, and steam steadily for at least 2½ hours. 4. Serve with the sauce poured round.

Some Variations of Above. Marmalade, fig and date puddings.

For these, use the same proportions of flour, bread-crumbs, and suet, and more milk when necessary. Omit ginger, golden syrup, and bicarbonate of soda, substituting for it 1 teaspoonful baking powder. Add the special ingredients for the particular pudding (see table above).

RAISED PIE CRUST

Contrary to the important rule of keeping short, rough puff, flaky and puff pastries *cool* during preparation, the success of raised pie crust depends upon keeping it *warm*. When making this pastry, which is sometimes called " hot water crust," the utensils and ingredients must be warmed before use, and the pastry must be kept quite warm during the processes of mixing and shaping or moulding, otherwise it becomes hard and brittle and is difficult to manipulate.   On the other hand, if the paste is too hot, it is too soft and not sufficiently stiff and tenacious to support its own weight when raised.

Raised pies are served cold, and to eat pleasantly the contents should cut rather solidly : after the pies are baked, good stock is added, which fills up all the interstices and sets in a jelly.

Hot-water crust is used for raised pork, veal and ham, and game pies.

Proportions of Ingredients.

½ lb. flour.   1 gill liquid to ½ lb. flour.
2 oz. fat ; lard, or butter.   (Half milk and half water.)
               ¼ teaspoonful salt.

Method.   1. Sieve flour and salt into a warm basin. 2. Boil fat and liquid together, do not let it reduce, pour it at once into the middle of the flour and mix rapidly with a wooden spoon, the paste being too hot to handle just at first.   3. Then very quickly knead with the hand until quite smooth, add a few more drops of boiling liquid if required.   If too moist, the pastry is over-soft ; if too dry, it is hard and inelastic and brittle, and in both cases it is difficult to raise or to shape.   4. Use it at once and as quickly as possible, while it is still warm.

NOTE.   For game pies a richer crust is used, always butter or butter and lard, and 1 yolk of egg to 1 lb. flour worked into the warm crust.

Methods of Shaping the Crust for a Pie.

1. By joining a strip and round of pastry together to form a case.
2. By moulding it with the hands.
3. By moulding it into shape over a tin or jar.
4. By lining a special mould with the paste (see page 190).

Raised Pork Pie.

Raised Pie Crust.   *Filling.*

¾ lb. flour, etc. (see recipe   ¾ lb. lean pork.
     for   ingredients   and   Mixed herbs or powdered sage.
     proportions).   ½ teaspoonful salt.
Beaten egg for glazing.   ¼ teaspoonful pepper.
                                               2 tablespoonfuls water or stock.

NOTE.   As the pastry must be handled when hot, prepare the meat first.   Cut the pork into dice, sprinkle with the seasoning and herbs, mix well, and moisten slightly with water or stock.

Prepare the hot water crust as directed.

To Shape the Pie.   (*Method* 1.)

1. Knead the prepared pastry lightly and quickly on the floured board, cut into two equal portions, and divide one into two pieces. Put one of the quarters back with the half portion into the basin, cover with a cloth, and keep it warm over hot water.

2. Roll out the quarter into a round about 6 in. in diameter, and turn it up ¼ in. all round to form the bottom of the pie.

3. Roll out the half portion of pastry into a strip 4 in. wide, and long enough to encircle the round, keep it even at the edges.

4. Brush over the turned up edge of the round with white of egg and also one edge of the strip, encircle the round of pastry with the strip, press it on well, join the ends of the strip neatly and securely, one slightly overlapping the other. Pin a piece of kitchen paper round; this assists the mould to keep its shape while it is being filled and in the oven until the pastry has set.

5. Pack the meat into the mould, pressing it down well, keep it in the centre level with the edge of the pastry, but slightly depressed all round at the sides, brush the edge of pastry with egg.

6. Cover with the remaining portion of pastry, press the edges well together, and decorate them or leave plain.

7. Make a hole in the centre, brush over with beaten egg and ornament as for meat pie with leaves, cut out of pastry trimmings.

8. Bake in a hot oven for 1½ hours, lower the heat after the first half-hour, test with a skewer to see whether the meat is done.

9. Through the hole in the centre add some good well-seasoned veal or pork stock.

Alternative Fillings for a Raised Pie.

(a) ½ lb. veal, 2 oz. fat bacon, seasoning, parsley, herbs, hard-boiled egg.

(b) 1 young rabbit, ½ lb. pickled pork, seasoning, parsley, herbs, hard-boiled egg.

To Mould the Pie with the Hands.

Cut off a quarter of the pastry and keep it warm. Knead the rest quickly into a round flat cake, then, with the back of the hand, press out the middle to about ⅜ in. in thickness and about 4 in. in diameter. Using both hands work the thick part of the paste evenly upwards to form the case for the meat. Trim the edge if necessary and proceed as directed above.

FIG. 52. MOULDING A PORK PIE WITH THE HANDS

To Mould the Pie Over a Jar or Tin.

1. Use a smooth stone jar or tin, invert and flour thickly.
2. Cut off one-quarter of the paste, put aside and keep hot.

3. Form the remainder into a flat, round shape, flour the knuckles of the right hand, and with them press the paste out from the centre until it is rather larger than the jar or tin.

4. Flour the centre well, place on the inverted jar or tin and work the paste evenly over the edges and downwards to the depth required, keeping the paste of uniform thickness.

5. Trim the edges, if required, with a sharp knife, invert the jar or tin, and lift off the moulded pastry.

6. Proceed then as in previous method.

Raised Veal and Ham Pie (using Special Mould).

Raised veal and ham and game pies are made and baked in a special mould. This is provided with a detachable bottom; it opens with a hinge, and the sides are secured by means of small skewers.

Ingredients.

¾ lb. raised pie crust.
Filling. Ingredients and proportions as for veal and ham pie.

To Line the Mould. 1. Grease the mould with butter. 2. Divide the prepared hot water crust into portions as for pork pie ; roll out one quarter into an oval shape rather larger than the bottom of the tin, turn up the edges about ¼ in. and fit into bottom of tin. 3. Roll out the half portion of paste into a piece long enough and wide enough to line the sides, fix the lower edge to the pastry lining the bottom, using white of egg, press the pastry well on and into the mould to take its shape, trim the top edge, brush over the bottom and the sides with white of egg to prevent the meat juice from penetrating. 4. Fill the meat in as for pork pie. 5. Roll out remaining portion of pastry, cover the top of meat with it, seal the edges, make a hole in the centre, and decorate as for pork pie or more elaborately, and brush over with egg. 6. Tie a threefold band of paper round the tin, projecting about 3 in. above the top, this to protect the edges. 7. Bake in a hot oven for about 2 hours, test to see whether the meat is done with a skewer.

To Unmould. Let the pie stand for a short time to allow shrinkage ; take out the skewers and remove the pie from the mould. Fill up with a little good, well seasoned stock as for pork pie.

Genoese Pastry (see CAKES, page 264).

Choux Pastry (see ÉCLAIRS, page 262).

Cheese Pastry (see CHEESE COOKERY, page 222).

CHAPTER 20

BATTERS

BATTER is a mixture of flour and of some liquid: water, milk, oil, or melted butter, with the addition of eggs ; these ingredients must be *smoothly* mixed and *well beaten*. The success of a batter depends upon its *lightness*, which is determined by the amount of cold air entangled in it previous to cooking, the volume of steam given off and upon a *high temperature for cooking*.

The principles upon which the method of making batter is based are—

1. The expansion of gases when heated. Cold air (a mixture of gases) is introduced by beating, by making the batter under cool conditions and by leaving it to stand in a cool place for a time before cooking it, also by the addition of stiffly whisked white of egg.

2. Starch grains absorb water and swell, and when heat is applied, they are more readily gelatinized, hence another reason for allowing batter to stand previous to cooking.

3. Egg proteins coagulate on heating. As soon as heat is applied the entangled air begins to expand, but it will escape if the heat is not great enough to swell the starch grains quickly, whereby the liquid is absorbed, the batter mixture being converted by reason of the peculiar property of the gluten in the flour and by the coagulation of the egg into a cohesive mass, which is able to retain the expanding air. Therefore, unless the cooking temperature is sufficiently high, a batter is heavy and sodden ; this occurs when it is *baked* in a cool oven, *fried* in fat insufficiently hot (pancakes) or *cooked* in or *steamed* over water below boiling point (steamed batter).

Method of Preparing Plain or Pancake Batter.

1. Sieve the flour with the salt into a basin *or* pass it lightly through the fingers.

2. Make a well in the centre of the flour, test the egg for freshness, and drop it unbeaten into the flour, add about 1 tablespoonful of the milk and begin to mix the flour in very *smoothly* from the sides with a wooden spoon, using half of the quantity of the milk ; if the batter is kept rather thick in the early stage of mixing there is less risk of lumps forming.

3. Beat thoroughly for about 5 minutes, mix in the remainder of the milk, cover the basin and leave the batter to stand in a cool place for about half an hour or longer.

4. Bake batter mixtures in a Yorkshire pudding-tin, or pie-dish, with sufficient melted dripping in it to well cover the bottom ; steam batters in a greased tin or basin. Allow from 2 to 2½ hours for steaming batter.

5. Cook batters at a high temperature. An upper shelf of the oven is most suitable for baked batters, water must be kept at boiling point for boiling or steaming, and a faint blue smoke must rise from the fat when frying batter.

Yorkshire Pudding.

Ingredients. ½ pint batter. 1 oz. dripping.

Method. Heat dripping in tin or pie-dish, pour in the batter, bake in a quick oven for 25 to 30 minutes, cut into squares and dish.

Variations.

(*a*) Toad-in-the-hole. (*b*) Fruit in batter. Use ½ pint batter, melt dripping in tin or pie-dish, put in meat or fruit, pour batter over and bake.

(*a*) *Toad-in-the-hole.* 2 oz. dripping for the tin. ½ lb. meat cut into neat pieces, or ½ lb. sausages, each one divided into four.

VARIETIES OF BATTER AND THEIR USES

Kind.	Proportions.	Uses.
I. Plain or pancake . .	1. 4 oz. flour ½ pint milk 1 egg Pinch of salt	(*a*) *Baked* — Yorkshire pudding, toad-in-the-hole, fruit in batter. (*b*) *Fried*—Pancakes.
	2. 5 oz. flour ½ pint milk 1 egg Pinch of salt	(*c*) *Boiled or Steamed Batters.* *Note* larger proportion of flour necessary for cooking batter by moist heat.
	3. 4 oz. flour 1 gill milk pinch salt 1 egg	(*d*) *A simple coating* for fried fish and plain fritters used without egg, a very plain coating for fish. *Note* proportion of flour.
II. Coating or fritter batter .	4. 2 oz. flour ½ gill of tepid water 1 dessertsp. oil 1 whisked white of egg Pinch of salt	For coating fried food ; for fritters ; and for batter cases to hold various savoury mixtures.

NOTE. For lighter and rich pancake batter an extra egg, and less its equivalent in liquid, may be used. Sugar tends to make batter heavy. To supply the necessary sweetness dredge with sugar after cooking (e.g. Fruit in batter and sweet fritters).

(*b*) *Fruit in Batter.* ½ lb. fresh fruit, sweeten slightly ; or 1 oz. currants or sultanas. Dredge batter with sugar when baked.

Steamed Batters.

See table for proportions. Add a few currants or sultanas, if liked. Pour prepared batter into a greased basin, cover with greased paper, steam steadily for 2½ hours.

Pancakes.

Ingredients. ½ pint batter. Castor sugar. Lemon.

For pancakes to be light, they must be fried quickly. Some of the success in frying depends upon—

The Frying Pan. Use one suitable in size for the pancakes, which should be fairly small. A perfectly clean pan, with a smooth and level surface, is essential ; if new, or if the pan has not been in recent use, it should be seasoned or the first pancake fried will probably stick. To *season* frying pan put a little lard into the pan and heat it until it turns brown, but it must not burn ; pour off the lard and wipe out the pan with a clean cloth or paper. If the pan is dirty, heat a little salt in it and rub it round the pan ; empty out the salt and wipe the pan with a clean cloth. After using a pan either for pancakes or omelets, it should only require to be wiped with a clean paper or cloth. Washing should only be necessary when the pan is burnt.

To Fry Pancakes. 1. Melt some lard in a small saucepan, keep hot and at hand. Well clarified dripping can be used, but lard being free from salt is preferable, as salt causes anything fried in shallow fat to stick. 2. Pour a little lard into the frying pan and heat it until it smokes; it must not brown, then pour it off back into the saucepan, leaving the frying pan well greased. 3. Pour enough batter into the pan to cover the bottom thinly. If the fat is hot enough, and the bottom of the pan is level and standing level on the stove, the batter flows evenly over the bottom almost immediately ; the pancakes are too thick and stodgy if too much is poured in. 4. When the pancake has set (it takes about ½ minute), and while it is frying, gently shake the pan and loosen the pancake round the edges with a broad-bladed knife, and fry quickly a golden brown. If fried slowly it will be tough. 5. Either toss the pancake or slip the knife beneath it and turn it over and fry on the other side. 6. Turn on to a sugared paper, dredge lightly with castor sugar, and sprinkle with a little lemon juice, roll up neatly, and keep hot. 7. Heat a little lard in the frying pan and proceed as before until all the batter is used. 8. Serve very hot, garnish with small pieces of lemon, one piece to each pancake, or serve lemon separately.

Variations. (*a*) Spread with some suitable warm jam, raspberry or apricot, and roll up. (*b*) Sprinkle each pancake with grated vanilla chocolate mixed with a little sieved icing sugar. Dish the pancakes flat, one on the top of the other, dredge the uppermost with sugar only. Serve with custard or chocolate sauce, or cream.

(c) Currant pancakes. Allow about 2 oz. to ½ pint batter. Scatter a few over each pancake as it is beginning to set; if added to the batter they sink to the bottom.

COATING OR FRITTER BATTER

Characteristics. A coating batter must be very light, sufficiently thick to coat the food well without running off, and it must be crisp when fried. Oil affords crispness, and the whisked white of egg gives additional lightness to the batter, which is also sometimes called " Kromeski " batter.

Ingredients.

2 oz. flour.	½ gill tepid water.
Pinch of salt.	1 white of egg.
1 dessertspoonful salad oil.	

Method. 1. Sieve the flour and salt, make a well in the centre, add the oil and tepid water, mix smoothly. 2. Beat well and leave in a cool place for 30 minutes. 3. Just before the batter is required, fold in very lightly the stiffly whisked white of egg and use at once for fritters—kromeskies (see VEAL KROMESKIES, page 127), etc.

Fritters.

A " fritter " or " beignet " is a term which is in general applied to something which is coated in batter and then fried in deep fat.

Fritters may be sweet or savoury, the foundation may consist of fruit, of vegetables divided into small pieces, small strips of bread or stale cake, which is usually moistened with flavoured milk, or of small portions of some preparation, either sweet or savoury, such as kromeski or rissole mixture. The foundation mixture of some fritters is similar to choux pastry, e.g. cheese aigrettes and beignets soufflés, and the method of frying such is the same as for the ordinary fritter mixture coated with batter (see page 266).

How to Fry Fritters.

1. The fat must be absolutely clean and sufficient (2 to 3 in. deep) to float the fritters.

2. It should not be as hot as for frying food coated with egg and bread-crumbs, but the heat of the fat must be great enough to cause the fritters to expand, and for the outside to become crisp and golden brown in colour. As soon as a slight blue vapour rises from the surface of the fat, it is hot enough ; to test the heat, drop a small portion of the batter into the fat, if sufficiently hot it will rise almost at once to the surface and the fizzling will be vigorous ; if too cool, it sinks to the bottom.

3. Dip one piece at a time into the batter, remove with a skewer or spoon, allowing the superfluous batter to drain away, and drop it into the fat.

4. Avoid putting too many fritters in at one time; this not only

cools down the fat, but sufficient room is not left in the pan for their expansion. Remove small loose pieces of batter; these quickly burn.

5. Remove with a perforated skimmer or slice, let the fat drain off over the pan and then drain the fritters on paper.

6. After the removal of one quantity, bring the fat up again to the correct frying temperature before putting more into it.

7. Dredge with sugar, serve very hot and quickly; fritters soon lose their crispness after removal from the fat, and also from the condensed steam, if they are kept covered.

FRUIT FRITTERS

Apples. Peel, core, and cut into slices about $\frac{1}{4}$ in. thick.

Oranges. Divide into sections, remove pith and pips, make a small hole, squeeze the pips out without escape of juice.

Bananas. Scrape and cut into neat pieces.

Tinned Fruits. Drain well before dipping in the batter to prevent thinning down of batter.

Beignet is a term often used to describe a "fritter," but the beignet proper is not coated with batter; it is made either with (a) a foundation of panada (cheese aigrettes) or with choux pastry (beignets soufflés). See pages 223 and 266.

CHAPTER 21

MILK AND MILK PUDDINGS

MILK

Composition and Food Value. The fact that milk is the natural food of all young mammals during the period of most rapid growth, indicates its value in the diet. Milk contains lime salts (calcium) necessary for bone formation, and certain vitamins which are essential to healthy growth : these are Vitamins A and D, and, of the B vitamins, riboflavin and nicotinic acid Vitamin C, of which there is a small amount in milk, is readily destroyed by heat and exposure to light. Starch is not present, but milk is rich in "lactose," a sugar which is comparatively free from sweetness, protein (casein), and fat. The rest consists of water, 87 per cent, and over, which makes milk a very bulky or dilute food. After the early stages of infancy, milk, although containing all the food constituents, starch excepted, is unsuitable, and unable if used as the sole food in the daily diet to supply sufficient of these constituents for the growth and upkeep of the body. The absence of starch makes milk to be a suitable food to be used in combination with cereals and their products.

Average Composition of Cow's Milk.

Protein	.	.	.	3·5%	Lactose . . . 4·75%
Fat	.	.	.	3 to 4%	Water . . . 87·25%
	Mineral matter	.	.	0·75%		

The protein (casein) is held in solution by the lime salts, and the fat is in the form of a very fine emulsion, which floats to the surface as cream after the milk has been standing for a time. It is upon the percentage of fat present that the quality of the milk depends, for the calcium, lactose, and casein vary little, and the amount of water differs only slightly unless the milk is adulterated. Milk as sold must not contain less than 3 per cent fat and 8·5 per cent solids not fat.

    Digestion of Milk. Milk passes into the stomach as a fluid, but the "rennin" (the enzyme or ferment) of the gastric juices causes the casein of the milk, which the lime salts hold in solution, to separate and to coagulate, and to become solid, forming a clot. The ease or difficulty of digesting milk is determined by the density and size of the clot formed and the ease with which it can be broken up by the digestive juices. On account of this clotting of milk in the stomach, it is advisable to sip rather than to drink milk in long draughts, and for people with weak digestion to take it with bread or biscuits or cooked with other ingredients, bread, rice, etc. This prevents the formation of large clots. Diluents, such as barley or lime water, taken with the milk (see INVALID COOKERY, page 242), and its *aeration* and dilution with aerated water, e.g. milk and soda, prevent the formation of such solid clots and makes the milk more digestible.

The Clotting and Curdling of Milk are Two Distinct Processes. When milk clots, the casein undergoes some internal change, but when it curdles, the casein is simply precipitated or thrown down as curds without any further change.

Clotting (Junket). The clotting or coagulation of milk takes place in making junket. Rennet used for this purpose is a preparation of the ferment " rennin " and is derived from the membranous lining of the stomach of the calf. This, when added to the warmed milk, causes the casein to coagulate or to form a clot, and as this happens the fat is entangled, also some of the sugar of the milk is present. If left for a time after the clot has formed, it will begin to shrink, and the liquid which exudes, or is squeezed out, is the " whey."

Curdling (Curds and Whey). Milk curdles naturally, or may be artificially curdled.

The natural curdling is due to the action of certain " souring bacteria " present in the air, which, acting upon the milk sugar (lactose), produce lactic acid, and the acid causes the casein, which is held in solution by the lime salts, to separate and to be simply thrown down without undergoing any further change, in a flocculent mass as " curds." The liquid, termed the " whey," contains some mineral matter, sugar, and a little protein, and is easily digested.

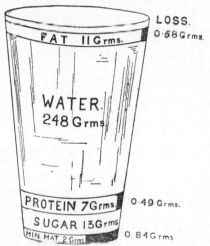

FIG. 53. ACTUAL COMPOSITION OF A TUMBLERFUL OF ORDINARY MILK, AND PERCENTAGE OF LOSS FROM NON-ABSORPTION

(By courtesy of Messrs. Edward Arnold & Company)

Curds and whey are produced artificially by the addition of a mild acid such as lemon juice or wine (see INVALID COOKERY).

Storage of Milk in the Home. Scrupulous cleanliness in relation to milk is most essential ; it is a medium in which bacteria, both harmless and disease-producing, flourish. Milk should be kept in the cool or in a refrigerator, in the bottles in which it is delivered, as they have been sterilized, or in perfectly clean, wide-mouthed vessels, these being easily kept clean; it should be covered to protect it from flies and dust, and being very absorbent, milk should be kept away from any food with a strong flavour and odour. Scald and rinse very thoroughly all vessels used for milk, and never add a fresh supply to an earlier one.

As milk is so absorbent of flavours and also readily burns. a scrupulously clean pan, either a single or double saucepan, should be kept exclusively, if possible, for heating milk.

Skim Milk is of very considerable nutritive value, for it contains the whole of its casein, lactose, and mineral matter, but is deficient in fat, only about 1 per cent being present.   After the removal of the cream from the surface of milk which has been standing, the fluid left is skim milk.

When using skim milk for milk puddings, supply the deficiency of fat by the addition of butter or suet.

Separated Milk contains a still lower percentage of fat, which is removed mechanically by a centrifugal separator.

Butter Milk is the fluid which escapes when churning cream for butter; it is very deficient in fat, but otherwise is nutritive, like skim milk, and is easily digested.   The sour flavour is due to the presence of lactic acid, and its presence is the reason for using butter milk or sour milk for mixing scones.   The acid of the milk acts upon the bicarbonate of soda (alkali), which is added to the flour and produces the raising agent, carbon dioxide (see SCONE MIXTURE, pages 259–60).

Boiled Milk.   Heating milk to a high temperature is necessary to sterilize it and to prevent souring.   In boiled milk there is an alteration in flavour and in some of its properties.   When boiled in an open pan, a " skin " forms on the top, which consists partly of lactalbumin, another protein in milk, whereby some of its nutritive value is lost.   In hot weather, if necessary, scald milk, and cool rapidly by placing jug in cold water; the more rapid the cooling the longer the milk will remain sweet.

Boiled milk does not make a firm junket, a fact which is attributed to some change in the casein.   As heat reduces the Vitamin C content in milk, it is necessary that infants fed with pasteurized milk should be given orange juice, one source of Vitamin C.   For ordinary household purposes the boiling of milk is a safeguard, but heating to 212° F. and for a prolonged time causes change in flavour and colour and in some of its properties.

STERILIZATION AND PASTEURIZATION OF MILK

As milk is so largely used in the diet of sick persons, infants, and young children, its purity is of supreme importance, and to avoid any risk it is advisable to use either sterilized or pasteurized milk.

The micro-organisms found in milk are—

1. Those which produce souring.
2. Pathogenic bacteria which convey disease.

Souring bacteria and the disease-bearing bacteria can only be destroyed by *sterilization*; in this process the milk is heated in sealed bottles *beyond* boiling-point, to 230° F., and kept at that temperature for 30 to 40 minutes. Such milk is sterile, and will keep for a considerable time, but the taste is altered, and there is also loss of Vitamin C.

Pasteurization. By this process the disease-bearing bacteria are destroyed and the action of those producing souring is arrested for a time. The method generally employed is the high-temperature, short-time method, in which the milk is heated to 161° F., maintained at that temperature for 15 seconds and then rapidly cooled to a temperature no higher than 50°F.

MILK PUDDINGS

Food Value. The ingredients of milk puddings—milk and cereal products, sugar, with or without the addition of eggs—supply in part all the necessary constituents for building up the body. If well made, milk puddings are both nourishing and digestible, but the *thorough cooking* of the farinaceous or starchy substance is very important. A simple baked milk pudding, such as rice, is, if well made, neither stiff nor sloppy, but creamy in texture, the rice having absorbed the greater part of the milk during the slow and gentle cooking.

Ingredients.

(*a*) *Milk.* Pure fresh milk makes the best and most nourishing pudding. To supply the deficiency of fat in skim milk, if used, add ½ oz. butter or finely shredded suet to 1 pint of milk and lessen or omit the sugar if using sweetened condensed milk.

(*b*) *Eggs and Their Addition.* Eggs improve the flavour and increase the food value. Never add them until the starchy matter is thoroughly cooked, otherwise the heat necessary to cook it will curdle the eggs; also, for the same reason, let the pudding mixture cool slightly before their addition. They may be added whole or the yolk and white separately, the latter being stiffly whisked. The mixture must then be reheated, baked in the oven, or cooked in a pan over the fire to cook the egg.

(*c*) *Farinaceous Substances, Method of Cooking, and Time Required.*

1. *Whole Grain* (rice) or large granules (tapioca and sago) should be soaked for a short time in the milk before they are used : these require long and gentle cooking.

(*a*) Cook the grain in the milk, carry out the whole process of cooking by baking the pudding in a *slow* oven until the rice is soft : allow at least 2 hours for a rice pudding made with 1 pint of milk.

(*b*) Stew the grain (tapioca or sago) in the milk over gentle heat until thoroughly cooked, then finish in a greased pie dish in the oven to brown the surface.

2. *Small Grains*, such as sago or semolina.   Boil these in the milk over moderate heat for 15 to 20 minutes until the grains become soft and transparent, and the mixture thickens, stirring the whole time to prevent burning.   After addition of sugar and egg, bake in a greased pie-dish in a *moderate* oven for 20 to 25 minutes.

3. *Powdery or Crushed Products*, such as cornflour, arrowroot, ground rice.   Boil these in the milk for at least 10 minutes, stirring the whole time to prevent lumpiness and burning.   Add sugar and egg and bake in a *moderate* oven about 40 minutes.

Varieties of Milk Puddings.

1. Those baked in a pie-dish and eaten hot or cold.
2. Shapes or Moulds. The cooked mixture is poured into a mould or basin : when cold it is set and firm, and takes the shape of mould or basin when turned out.

Proportions of Ingredients for Milk Puddings.

1 pint milk.	1 egg—if eggs are used.
1½ oz. farinaceous ingredient.	Flavouring.
1 oz. sugar.	

Preparation of Milk Puddings.

1. Grease pie-dishes and rinse moulds with cold water to prevent the pudding mixture from sticking.

2. Use a casserole or a pan with a *thick* enamel lining, thin enamel quickly burns; a double saucepan is an advantage for the long method of cooking. The mixture then requires little attention beyond an occasional stir.

FIG. 54. MILK AND PORRIDGE SAUCEPAN

3. Always rinse the saucepan with cold water before heating milk in it, and, after boiling the milk, rinse it again before cooking the pudding mixture in it—this prevents burning.

4. Add sugar at the last to preparations cooked on a boiling ring; sugar gives them the tendency to burn.

5. Wipe the edge of the pie-dish before baking the pudding, this prevents unsightly discoloration of the rim.

Baked Rice Pudding (Whole Grain).

Ingredients.

1 pint milk.	Fat for greasing dish.
1½ oz. Carolina rice.	1 oz. sugar.
Pinch of salt.	Nutmeg.

Method. 1. Wash rice, place it with the sugar and salt in a greased pie-dish, cover with the milk, mix well, and leave to soak for 1 hour if possible.

2. Grate a little nutmeg on the top and bake in a moderate oven for 2 hours.

Semolina Pudding (Small Grain).

1 pint milk.	1 egg.
1½ oz. semolina.	Some flavouring.
1 oz. sugar.	

Method. 1. Heat the milk, *sprinkle* in the small grain to avoid its collecting in lumps, bring slowly to boiling point. 2. Simmer for 15 to 20 minutes, stirring the whole time. 3. Remove from fire, add sugar; when slightly cooled a little vanilla essence and the whole egg or the yolk and white separately, the latter stiffly whisked. 4. Pour into a buttered pie-dish, place the pie-dish in a tin and bake in a moderate oven for 20 to 25 minutes to cook the egg and to brown the surface.

Cornflour Pudding (Powder).

1 pint milk.	1 egg.
1½ oz. cornflour.	Flavouring; lemon rind, vanilla pod,
1 oz. sugar.	or essence.

Method. 1. Mix the cornflour smoothly with a little of the pint of milk, boil the rest with the flavouring and pour on to the cornflour, mixing it smoothly. 2. Put the mixture back into the rinsed pan and *boil* for 10 minutes, stirring the whole time. 3. Proceed as for semolina pudding.

COLD SHAPES OR MOULDS

The ingredients are the same and the methods of cooking them (except baking in the oven) are identical with those for milk puddings. The proportion of starchy matter to milk is rather more for shapes and moulds, as there is less evaporation by cooking in moist heat than by the dry heat of baking.

Proportions of Ingredients.

1 pint milk.	1 egg (if used).
1½ to 2 oz. farinaceous substance.	Flavouring.
1 oz. sugar.	

Method.   1. Cook the starchy matter in the milk until the latter is nearly absorbed.   Allow 1 hour at least for rice or tapioca ; 20 to 25 minutes for small granules (semolina) and 10 minutes for powdery or crushed farinaceous products (cornflour, etc.).   2. Add sugar and flavouring essence *after* cooking, but infuse solid flavourings such as bay leaf, lemon rind, vanilla pod with the milk, and leave it in until the mixture is cooked.   If these cold sweet dishes are enriched with cream or egg, add these at the last, but *reheat* the mixture after the addition of the egg to cook the latter.   3. Pour the sweetened and flavoured mixture quite *hot* into a *wet* mould.   4. When firm turn out of the mould.

Accompaniments.   Boiled custard, jam, stewed or tinned fruit.

Junket.

1 pint milk.	1 teaspoonful castor sugar.
1 teaspoonful essence of rennet.	Nutmeg.

Method.   1. Warm the milk to blood heat, pour it into a glass bowl, add the sugar and rennet and stir lightly.   2. Leave it undisturbed and out of a draught until set, then grate a little nutmeg on the top.

NOTE.   For the principles of the clotting of milk, which underlie the making of junket, see MILK, page 197.

(*a*) To promote the activity of the rennet, which is an " enzyme " or ferment, a low heat is necessary ; if the milk is cold the " enzyme " is inactive, if too hot it is destroyed.   (*b*) As a clot of milk shrinks after standing for a time, with the exudation of the liquid " whey," make a junket only a short time before it is required.   (*c*) For the formation of a firm clot, leave the milk undisturbed after the addition of the rennet and out of a draught, warmth being conducive to the full and continued action of the rennet and to the formation of a denser clot.

CHAPTER 22

EGG COOKERY AND CUSTARDS

Composition and Food Value. Eggs are a valuable food, and being rich in protein are an excellent substitute for meat. They contain the same constituents as meat, but are, as compared with it, richer in fat and not so rich in protein, and their nourishment is in a concentrated form. On account of the absence of starch, eggs should be combined with farinaceous foods; these also give the bulk so necessary when using a concentrated food.

The White of Egg consists mostly of water and of egg albumen in solution, which is contained in infinitesimally minute cells.

The Yolk contains less water than the white, is richer in fat, which is in a state of very fine emulsification, for which reason yolk of egg is easily digested; and on account of the mineral matter, calcium salts, iron, phosphorus, and Vitamins A and D, it is valuable in the food of children. Eggs are also sources of nicotinic acid and riboflavin.

The egg shell is porous, the weight of an average hen's egg is about 2 to 2¼ oz.

Freshness. New-laid eggs are the most nourishing and easily digested, and eggs, for whatever purpose they are used, must be fresh. The shell of a freshly-laid egg is slightly

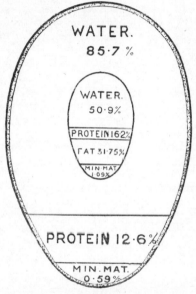

FIG. 55. PERCENTAGE COMPOSITION OF THE WHITE AND YOLK OF AN EGG
(*By courtesy of Messrs. Edward Arnold & Company*)

rough: if held towards the light it should be translucent, with no trace of a black speck.

Test. A fresh egg should feel heavy, it sinks in a 10 per cent solution of salt (2 oz. salt to 1 pint water); one that is less fresh is suspended, and a very stale egg floats. This is due to the difference in weight, the result of loss of water by evaporation through the porous shell, the water being replaced by air, which is lighter:

203

with the air, bacteria enter, causing the decomposition of the organic matter and the evolution of hydrogen sulphide.

Relative Digestibility of Eggs. A raw egg is the most easily digested; the digestibility of one that is cooked depends upon the rate and ease of digestion, which are determined by the condition of the egg, whether soft or hard ; e.g. a hard-boiled egg, if finely divided (as in a sandwich) and well masticated, is digested, but at a slower rate. Eggs are particularly useful in invalid dietaries, as they are quickly absorbed, leaving little residue, but on account of the lime salts present they have a directly opposite effect to that of laxative foods, such as brown bread and fruit.

Preservation of Eggs. Eggs to be preserved should be fresh, not more than three to four days old : they should be wiped, but not washed, unless absolutely necessary, as this removes a thin natural varnish provided by nature to exclude the air.

They are preserved by two methods—

1. At a temperature below that at which bacteria flourish, as in cold storage.

2. By the exclusion of air. Pack with the pointed end downwards :

(*a*) In some perfectly dry substance, bran or good sawdust, which will allow of tight packing, is not favourable to germ development, and will not impart flavour to the egg.

(*b*) Coat with fat, paraffin wax, or pure lard.

(*c*) Immerse in water-glass or in a solution of lime, and keep covered.   For lime solution pour 2 gallons boiling water over 1 lb. fresh lime in a zinc or tin vessel ; when cold add the salt ($\frac{1}{2}$ lb.).

(*d*) Dip in a commercially prepared solution, which leaves a wax-like coating on the shell.

Egg Substitutes. These preparations do not contain any egg, and are practically of no food value, but are useful.   They consist mostly of starch (over 80 per cent) with flavouring and colouring matter, and are used for " boiled custard " ; some preparations for cakes also contain a raising agent.

Principles which Underlie the Cooking of Eggs.

1. *Egg albumen* is soluble in cold liquid, water, or milk (often given to invalids), but it *begins to coagulate when heat is applied,* and then becomes opaque and firm, its firmness or toughness being determined by the degree of heat applied and the length of time in cooking, e.g.—

(*a*) Put an egg into water a few degrees below boiling-point and keep it at that temperature for 7 to 8 minutes—the white becomes soft and creamy and the yolk thickens—if this is continued for an hour the white becomes solid and adheres to the skin, and the yolk is very hard. (*b*) Put an egg into boiling water for 3 or 4 minutes, the white is free from the shell, but is firmer than when cooked by method (a). (c) Cook an egg at a high temperature ; as, in frying, the outside edges quickly become leathery.

2. In whisking white of egg, the covering of the cells containing the albumen is ruptured and air is entangled; the larger the volume entrapped and the colder the air, the greater the expansion when heated, and the lighter will be the mixture to which it is added. Hence the reasons for (a) whisking white of egg under cool conditions, also for the addition of a pinch of salt, which slightly lowers the temperature of the egg white, and for whisking it only just before it is required ; (b) for folding it lightly into the mixture and at the last to avoid expelling the entrapped air ; (c) and for applying heat *at once* to coagulate the egg albumen, and thus to prevent the escape of air. The methods of making and cooking *soufflés, meringue mixtures*, and *puffed omelets* are based upon this principle.

Uses in Cookery.

1. Eggs simply cooked and served as an individual dish, or in combination with other foods and ingredients, constitute very nourishing dishes. They are the basis of large varieties of preparations, savoury and sweet, and in each course of the menu they can be utilized. 2. On account of the entanglement of air in a beaten egg, of the richness of the yolk, and of the coagulating properties of the proteins, an egg affords lightness, richness, and cohesiveness to all mixtures to which it is added. 3. Beaten egg is also a protective covering for fried foods, and a binding medium for such preparations as forcemeat, croquette mixtures, etc.

SIMPLE METHODS OF COOKING EGGS

Boiled Egg.

New-laid eggs are the best for boiling and poaching. Before boiling an egg which has been preserved in water-glass, make a small puncture in the shell, as the solution closes the pores, and the shell will crack from the expansion of air inside when the egg is cooked.

Methods of Boiling an Egg. The water must completely cover the eggs, otherwise they cook unevenly. Slip them in gently off the spoon to avoid cracking.

(a) Put them into boiling water and boil for 3 minutes; if very fresh or if individual taste requires the white to be fairly firm, allow ½ to 1 minute more.

(b) Place in boiling water ; when the water boils again, put on the lid, remove the saucepan to a place on the stove where the water will keep hot, and leave for ten minutes.

(c) Place in cold water, bring slowly to boiling-point, and remove immediately the water boils.

Eggs are " lightly boiled " by methods (*b*) and (*c*). If an egg is to be boiled and happens to be cracked, rub the shell over with lemon juice, or lay a piece of gummed paper over the crack ; the egg albumen is thereby quickly coagulated by the acid, or sets before the paper comes away.

Poached Egg.

1 egg.	Vinegar or lemon juice.
Salt.	Round of buttered toast.

Method.   1. Half fill a frying pan with water, add a little salt and two or three drops of vinegar or lemon juice ; the acid hastens the setting of the white, but over much discolours it and is unpleasant

FIG. 56. EGG POACHER

in flavour.   2. Break the egg into a cup, and, when the water is gently boiling, drop the egg in carefully at the side of the pan, draw the white gently together with the spoon, and baste the top of the egg with water ; if the egg is new laid the yolk is covered with the white.   3. Cook for 2 or 3 minutes until the white is set without being hard.   4. Lift out with a fish slice, allowing the water to drain off, trim the edges, and dish on the hot buttered toast.

Various Uses.   (*a*) With fried bacon or with dried haddock. (*b*) Served on spinach, macaroni, rice, or potato.   (*c*) As an accompaniment to réchauffés of meat, mince, and hash, to increase the nutriment of the dish.

NOTE.   (*a*) Only very fresh eggs poach really well.

(*b*) An egg poacher is a convenience or small rings placed in the pan prevent the whites from spreading unduly.

Scrambled or Buttered Egg.

Proportions of Ingredients.   To each egg allow $\frac{1}{4}$ oz. butter and 1 tablespoonful milk and seasoning, and a strip or round of hot buttered toast for each.

Method.   1. Beat the eggs, add the milk and seasoning.   2. Melt the butter in a small saucepan, add the eggs, and stir steadily and evenly, but quickly, over a moderate heat until the eggs begin to set and the mixture is of a creamy consistency. 3. Remove at once and dish on the toast.

Variations. The addition to the beaten eggs of chopped parsley, mixed herbs, chopped ham, grated cheese, tomatoes, etc. Allow ½ oz. of grated cheese or chopped ham to each egg.

Hard-boiled Eggs.

These are used for a variety of purposes, for garnishing, and for numerous egg dishes : for salads, curries, fricassees, for sandwiches, etc.; they are also stuffed with different savoury ingredients and used as savouries, but their appearance is often spoilt for certain purposes through want of care in boiling.

Method. 1. Put the eggs into boiling water, bring to boiling-point and cook steadily for 15 minutes. If put into cold water the yolk is inclined to drop to one side. 2. Put at once into cold water; the shell then comes away more easily To remove it tap it gently with the back of a knife; cracking it on the table damages the white.

If the yolk is over-cooked, or is not put into cold water and the shell then removed, a black ring appears between the yolk and the white; this also happens if the egg is stale.

Curried Eggs.

2 hard-boiled eggs.	1½ gills curry sauce.
2 oz. Patna rice.	Strips of chilli skin, chopped parsley and crimped lemon for garnish.

Method. 1. Make the curry sauce (see CURRY OF FRESH MEAT, page 115). 2. Boil the eggs as directed and cut each into four or more pieces. 3. Place eggs in the hot sauce and follow directions for currying cooked food (see CURRY OF VEAL, page 115). 4 Dish the eggs in the centre of a border of cooked rice and garnish, or serve rice separately.

Fricassee of Eggs.

2 hard-boiled eggs.
1½ gills good well-seasoned white sauce.
Chopped parsley for garnish.

Method. 1. Make the sauce, divide the hard-boiled eggs into sections or slices, and reheat in the sauce without breaking them up. 2. Garnish with parsley.

Stuffed Eggs.

To prepare hard-boiled eggs for filling, cut them in half and a small piece from the bottom of each half, so that they may stand firm; pound the yolk with the butter and the other ingredients. Season fillings well.

Anchovy Eggs.

2 hard-boiled eggs.	2 anchovies.	Cayenne.
1 oz. butter.	½ teaspoonful anchovy essence.	Small rounds of buttered toast.

Method. 1. Prepare whites as above directed, wash and dry them. 2. Pound the butter, yolks, anchovies, and essence together, add cayenne and rub through a nylon sieve. 3. Fill the centres of the whites with the mixture; it is easier to use a forcing bag and small rose forcer for this; then decorate with small roses of the forced mixture or with any other suitable garnish. 4. Dish on small rounds of buttered toast.

Some Variations for Fillings.

(*a*) Grated cheese.
(*b*) Sardine paste and sardines, or any other suitable fish paste.
(*c*) Chopped ham.
(*d*) Chutney or curry paste.
Allow ½ oz. of cheese or ham to 2 eggs.

CUSTARDS

The freshness of the eggs and milk is important, and the aim in cooking is to apply just the degree of heat which will cook the mixture without curdling it. New-laid eggs make the finest steamed and baked custards, those made with skim milk are neither as rich nor as firm as those for which whole milk is used.

Varieties. 1. Baked. 2. Steamed. 3. The erroneously termed " boiled custards." All are largely used in the preparation of hot and cold sweet dishes.

Consistency and Texture. The thickness of a boiled custard and the firmness of the baked or steamed varieties depend upon the proportion of eggs to milk, and of yolks to whites. The yolks afford

AVERAGE PROPORTIONS OF INGREDIENTS FOR CUSTARDS

	Kind.	Eggs.	Milk.	Castor Sugar.
Baked	Economical	2	1 pint	1 oz.
	Richer	3	,,	,,
Steamed	Plain	2–3	½ pint	¾ oz.
	Richer	4 yolks 2 whites	,,	,,
Boiled	Economical	1	,,	½ oz.
	Rich	2 or 3 yolks and 1 white	,,	,,
Royal	(Steamed)	1	1 tablesp. milk or stock	

greater richness of flavour and smoothness of texture, while the whites contribute in a greater degree to the consistency of a custard. A steamed custard, made with more yolks than whites, is richer in flavour and smoother in texture, but there is greater risk of it cracking when turned out of the mould than when an equal number of whites and yolks are used.

Proportion of Eggs is determined by the richness required and the method of cooking. One egg to ½ pint of milk is just sufficient to thicken a boiled custard or for a baked custard to set, but for a steamed custard, which must support its own weight when turned out of the mould, more are necessary—3 to the ½ pint of milk. For a custard used as a garnish for soup, which is cut into fancy shapes when cold, 1 tablespoonful milk and stock only to 1 egg. (Royal custard.)

Flavourings. Vanilla essence for steamed or baked custards and for the " boiled " variety, also the solid flavourings, bay leaf, vanilla pod, etc., these being cooked in the milk and egg.

Cooking Temperature. Whether the custard is baked, steamed or " boiled," slow cooking and gentle heat, well below that of boiling point, are essential. Too great heat causes the coagulated egg protein to harden. As the hardening increases, shrinking of the protein takes place, and the egg mixture breaks up into flocculent masses and liquid—the curdled custard. If properly cooked, a boiled custard should be smooth and one baked or steamed should be smooth, firm, and without holes.

To Prepare Eggs and Milk for Making Custards.

1. Beat eggs sufficiently to mix the yolks and whites thoroughly, but not until " frothy," thereby air is entrapped; this expands and causes holes in a baked or steamed custard, and the custard to rise in the cooking

2. Beat the sugar with the eggs; it dissolves more rapidly.

3. Strain egg and milk to remove thread from egg and any pieces of egg albumen which may have escaped fine division; if not removed they set as small solid white specks throughout the custard.

NOTE. Grease a pie-dish for a baked custard and the basin or tin and the paper to cover for a steamed custard.

Baked Custard.

2 or 3 eggs to 1 pint milk.
1 oz. sugar.
Nutmeg—vanilla essence (optional).

Method. 1. Beat eggs with sugar, add heated milk and vanilla essence, if used, strain into a greased pie-dish, grate nutmeg on top, wipe edge of dish. 2. Place on the middle shelf of a slow oven, and bake for about 60 minutes until firm to the touch—if necessary, place for a few minutes on the top shelf to brown the surface.

To prevent too rapid cooking, place the pie-dish in a tin half filled with water; this must never boil; replenish it when necessary.

Some Variations. Bread-and-butter pudding, macaroni pudding, custard baked in a sandwich tin or flan ring lined with pastry.

Steamed Custard.

2 to 3 eggs to ½ pint milk.
¾ oz. castor sugar.
1 teaspoonful vanilla essence.

Method. 1. Prepare eggs and milk as for baked custard, strain into a basin or tin, well greased with clarified butter to prevent sticking, cover with greased paper. 2. Steam gently for about 30 minutes until firm in the centre. Use either a steamer, or steam the custard in a pan with gently simmering water in it to the depth of 1 to 1½ in. Place the tin on something to prevent it from coming into contact with the bottom of the pan and on the side of the pan away from the greatest heat. This precaution should be taken for all light steamed puddings. 3. Allow the custard to stand a few minutes before turning out.

Caramel Custard.

The same ingredients as above, using 4 yolks and 2 whites of eggs to ½ pint milk, or 3 whole eggs and—

3 oz. sugar
¾ gill cold water } for caramel.
pinch of cream of tartar.

Method. 1. Dissolve sugar in water, add cream of tartar. 2. Boil quickly without stirring (to prevent crystallization) until a light coffee colour. 3. Pour the caramel immediately into a *clean, dry, hot* "soufflé" mould, run it quickly over the mould, covering it completely To avoid burning the fingers wrap a cloth round the tin. 4. Beat eggs with sugar, add milk and vanilla essence, strain into the mould, and follow directions above for steaming. 5. Serve hot or cold.

" Boiled " Custard.

For proportions, see table.

Method. 1. Beat the egg with the sugar, rinse a pan with cold water, heat the milk, pour on to the eggs, rinse the pan again to prevent the custard from burning, and strain egg and milk into it. 2. Cook over a moderate heat until the custard thickens and coats the back of the spoon, stirring the whole time. Do not allow it to approach boiling point. 3. Add the vanilla essence, use as required, and when slightly cooled pour it into a glass dish or custard glasses, grate nutmeg on top or decorate according to taste.

To Check Curdling. If there is the slightest suspicion of curdling, turn the custard quickly into a clean basin and whisk rapidly, strain through muslin if necessary. Stirring a custard gently until quite cool prevents a skin from forming on the top.

PUDDINGS OF THE CUSTARD TYPE, BAKED OR STEAMED

These are made with milk and eggs (custard), the foundation being of stale bread or of some sponge-like cake, cut into slices or dice, and with or without additions which may be either distributed throughout or added in layers. The pudding is either baked in a pie-dish, as for an ordinary baked custard, or steamed in a basin or tin, and turned out and served with a suitable sweet sauce.

INGREDIENTS

Foundation		Additions.	Custard.	Flavouring.
Stale bread or cake		Jam or Marmalade	½ pint milk	Vanilla essence or other flavouring
Slices of bread and butter	3–4 oz.	Dried or *glacé* fruit	1 to 2 eggs	
Cooked macaroni			¾ oz. sugar	

General Method of Making. 1. Grease pie-dish or the basin or tin and paper for covering with butter. The tin or basin may be decorated or not with raisins or *glacé* fruit. 2. Put the bread or cake lightly in ; when the pudding is to be baked, it should nearly fill the pie-dish ; when steamed the tin should be only ½ or ¾ full. 3. Pour on sufficient custard (beaten eggs, sugar, and milk) to fill dish or tin and leave to soak for ½ hour. 4. Steam gently until pudding is firm to the touch, or bake in a moderate oven until it is firm and nicely coloured.

Some Examples. Bread-and-butter pudding. Cabinet pudding.

Cabinet Pudding.

½ pint milk.
2 eggs.
3 to 4 oz. bread or cake, in dice or small pieces.

¾ oz. castor sugar.
2 oz. stoned raisins or *glacé* cherries.
1 gill jam sauce (see SAUCES).

Method. Follow directions given above. Serve pudding with sauce poured round the dish.

CHAPTER 23

OMELETS AND SOUFFLÉS

OMELETS

OF all dishes an omelet is the most quickly prepared and cooked. For this reason and because of its nutritive value, it is most useful as an " emergency" dish. Eggs are generally to be found in the larder, also scraps of food which can be utilized; these afford extra nutriment and bulk to the omelet.

The three kinds are—

1. Plain or French omelets, the most general.
2. Filled omelets, either plain or puffed, the filling being either sweet or savoury.
3. Puffed omelets.

For most, the method of preparation is similar, and their success depends mostly upon *rapid cooking* in hot butter over a brisk heat, and also upon quick and deft manipulation of the egg mixture as it is setting. A well-made omelet is quite set, but moist, no part being distinctly liquid and raw ; the texture throughout should be soft and creamy, and should in no way resemble that of scrambled eggs or of pancakes. Omelets, like *soufflés*, should be dished quickly and sent to table at once.

The Omelet Pan should have a smooth and level surface, and must be absolutely clean to prevent the omelet from sticking, it is therefore advisable to keep a pan solely for this purpose. A pan, suitable in size to the number of eggs, should be used, otherwise the omelet is either over-thick and under-cooked, or too thin and tough and leathery ; for two or three eggs use a pan about 5 in. in diameter. Eggs are inclined to stick in an enamelled pan ; aluminium, steel, or copper tin-lined are the best ; failing these an ordinary clean iron frying-pan with a smooth surface will answer the purpose. A pan with a sloping or bevelled side is the best shape, as the omelet is more easily loosened, and the uncooked parts of the egg mixture flow in more readily from the sides to the centre. For loosening an omelet, use a flexible palette knife or one with a rounded blade.

To " Prove " or Season the Omelet Pan (see PANCAKES). Provided the pan is quite clean, the butter sufficiently hot and the omelet is fried quickly, the pan after use should only require to be rubbed round with kitchen paper and then with a clean dry cloth. Wash an omelet pan only when absolutely necessary ; washing tends to make the omelet stick. If any egg adheres to the pan and is difficult to remove, rub it clean with dry salt, being careful to remove all the salt.

Ingredients.

Eggs. 2 or 3 are sufficient for a small omelet ; 3 eggs for 2 persons ; 6 to 8 for a large omelet. A large quantity is difficult to manipulate in the pan.

Beat up the eggs, just sufficiently to mix yolks and whites together, but not to a froth. For puffed omelets, the whites are stiffly whisked and added to the yolks and other ingredients just before the mixture is put into the pan.

Butter. If possible, use fresh butter ; unless clarified, salt butter is one of the causes of an omelet sticking to the pan. Allow about ¼ oz. butter to each egg; only sufficient is required to be absorbed by the eggs in cooking and to prevent them from sticking to the pan. Too much butter makes an omelet greasy and unpalatable. For sweet omelets butter is used only for well greasing the pan.

FIG. 57. OMELET PAN

Addition of Water to the Eggs. One tablespoonful to 3 eggs is frequently added ; this makes the texture of an omelet *soft.*

Plain Omelet (Savoury).

Proportions of Ingredients.

3 eggs.
¾ oz. butter fresh, or clarified
  salt butter.
1 tablespoonful tepid water.

Pepper, salt.
1 teaspoonful chopped parsley.

Parsley for garnish.

How to Fry, Shape, and to Turn Out a Plain Omelet.

Have in readiness everything required for mixing, frying, and dishing the omelet.

To Fry Omelet.

1. Beat the eggs, add seasonings.
2. Heat the butter in the proved omelet pan ; when quite hot it will cease to splutter, the moisture having been driven off.
3. Stir the beaten eggs and pour gently into the pan.
4. Hold the handle of the pan in the left hand, and by an up-and-down or " lifting " movement (not round-and-round as in scrambling eggs) of a fork or metal spoon held in the right hand, begin at once to rapidly but *gently* break up the cooked surface, which sets immediately upon coming into contact with the hot pan ; this allows the still liquid portions from the sides and top to flow in beneath and to set. Repeat this as it is necessary, and with the left hand keep the pan gently moving ; this assists in the rapid and uniform setting of the whole of the mixture.

To Shape.

1. As soon as the eggs are set, and the whole is soft and creamy and still moist, but not liquid on the surface (the frying of a small omelet should not take more than a minute, if the heat is right), smooth the top and loosen the edges by shaking the pan, or with a round-bladed knife, by slipping it beneath the omelet.

2. Tilt the pan and carefully roll the omelet towards the farther edge, folding it and pressing it lightly with the knife, so that it takes an oval shape, slightly curved and thick in the centre.

3. Hold the pan over the fire or gas for a moment to slightly brown the omelet and turn out at once.

To Turn Out.　　In the left hand, hold the hot dish, hold the handle of the pan in the right hand, with the palm underneath ; bring the outer edge of the pan close to the centre of the dish and quickly slip the omelet from the inverted pan on to the dish.

Garnish with parsley, serve *immediately* and *very hot*.

If kept hot in the oven or allowed to stand, an omelet soon becomes heavy.

Variations of the Plain Omelet.　　Use the method for making a plain omelet and the same proportions of eggs and of butter with additional ingredients, all of which, excepting herbs, must be cooked before they are added.

These ingredients are added—

(*a*) Either to the beaten eggs previous to cooking the omelet.

(*b*) Or as filling after the omelet is cooked.

Additions.

1. Different herbs ; thyme, marjoram, parsley, chervil, tarragon, or a mixture of several.

2. Minced meat, poultry, game, ham, bacon, sweetbread, kidney, flaked fish, grated cheese, vegetables, tomato, mushroom, etc.

The filling *must* be hot, the ingredients for which are either simply fried or *sautéd* in a little hot butter, seasoned and flavoured, or if already cooked, they should be reheated in a little well-seasoned thick sauce, white, brown, or curry sauce.　　For sweet omelets hot jam or fruit *purée* is used.

For a 3 *Egg Omelet allow—*

1½ to 2 oz. cooked meat, poultry, game, vegetables, etc.

1 large or 2 small sheep's kidneys.

1 oz. finely grated cheese.

Kidney Omelet (Filled Omelet).

Ingredients as for plain omelet, plus the filling.

> 1 sheep's kidney.
> ½ oz. butter.
> Seasoning.

Method. 1. Wash, dry and skin kidney, remove core and cut into dice, sauté in the butter for about 10 to 12 minutes. 2. Prepare a plain omelet, place the hot kidney in the centre, fold over or roll up.

PUFFED OMELETS

The texture of an omelet is very much lighter if the white is stiffly whisked and added to the rest of the ingredients, just before the omelet is cooked. In making an omelet of this type, stir the egg mixture in the pan over a brisk heat, about *three* times ; this is to *mix* in the *butter,* then place the omelet in a moderate oven for 8 to 10 minutes. When the omelet is cooked, it should be set throughout, well risen, slightly browned, and just firm to the touch.

Fish Omelet (Puffed).

Ingredients and proportions same as for plain omelet *and*

1 tablespoonful milk or cream instead of water.
2 oz. cooked fish.
1 teaspoonful chopped parsley.
Parsley and crimped lemon for garnish.

Method. 1. Flake the fish. 2. Beat the yolks of eggs, add the milk or cream, seasonings, and fish, fold in the stiffly-whisked whites of the 3 eggs just at the last. 3. Pour the egg mixture into the hot butter in the omelet pan, stir it over the heat three times, and put it into a moderate oven for 8 to 10 minutes until set. 3. Fold in two and garnish.

Sweet Omelet.

2 eggs.   1 tablespoonful warm jam or fruit *purée.*
Vanilla essence.   1 dessertspoonful castor sugar.

Method. 1. Well grease a proved omelet pan with clarified butter. 2. Cream the yolks of eggs with the sugar until of the consistency of cream, add the vanilla essence or any other flavouring and fold in the stiffly-whisked whites, then follow directions for fish omelet. 3. When ready to remove from the oven, turn on to a sugared paper, place the hot jam or fruit *purée* in the centre, fold in two, and dredge with castor sugar.

NOTE. An omelet soufflé is made exactly like sweet omelet, the difference being the addition of another white and 1 teaspoonful flour to the creamed yolks and sugar.

SOUFFLÉS

A *soufflé,* which may be either sweet or savoury, is an exceedingly light mixture, its lightness being due to the addition of stiffly-whisked white of egg. Cream, an ingredient of meat and fish soufflés, also contributes to their light and spongy texture, and this is whipped before its addition to very light cold soufflés, such as a mousse.

The Component Parts of a Soufflé are—

1. The foundation or *panada*, the average proportion of ingredients being 1 oz. flour, 1 oz. butter to 1 gill of liquid. For sweet soufflés milk is used and milk or stock—as may be suitable—for meat, poultry, fish, cheese, pulse, etc.

2. *Eggs.* For very light soufflés, three to four eggs are usually allowed to 1 gill of panada, one more white than yolk (e.g. vanilla soufflé). For the more substantial mixtures of meat, game, fish, etc., the eggs are sometimes added whole, with the addition of cream, or the whites are added separately, these being less in number than the yolks used.

3. *Flavourings and Additions.*

(*a*) For flavouring sweet soufflés an essence such as vanilla is suitable, or some tinned or preserved fruits (2 oz. to 1 gill panada) are added.

(*b*) For savoury soufflés of meat, game, poultry, or fish, which may be either raw or cooked ; this is reduced to a pulp by " pounding," and is sieved with the panada. To 1 gill of panada the proportion varies from 4 to 8 oz. according to the kind of meat and whether

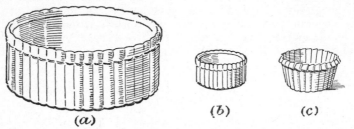

(*a*)

(*b*)   (*c*)

China Soufflé Dish. Small China Soufflé Case. Paper Soufflé Case
FIG. 58

cooked or raw, and to other ingredients which may be added. Finely grated dry cheese (3 oz. to 1 gill panada). Vegetables and pulse are also used for soufflés.

Two Methods of Cooking.

(*a*) *Steaming.* The soufflé mixture is cooked in a greased soufflé tin. For sweet soufflés (vanilla soufflé), which are exceedingly light, the sauce is poured round the dish : savoury soufflés (veal soufflé) are coated with a sauce unless several whisked whites have been used, the texture of such a mixture being too light when cooked to bear the weight of a coating sauce.

(*b*) *Baking.* A baked soufflé is cooked in a greased fireproof dish, in a fireproof china soufflé dish or in small china or paper cases.

Principle Underlying the Making of Soufflés. The expansion of air entrapped in the whisked white of egg is the *raison d'être* of a light soufflé, and the aim is to introduce a certain quantity, to retain it in the mixture, and to cook the soufflé at that temperature which will make it rise steadily and become firm.

Essentials to Success in Making Soufflés.

1. Use clarified butter for greasing the tin to prevent a steamed soufflé from sticking.

2. *A well-cooked panada* as affecting the lightness of a soufflé. Melt the butter in a white-lined pan, add the flour all at once, cook for a few seconds, add the liquid, and beat well over heat until the panada leaves the sides of the pan. If over-cooked it becomes greasy and heavy, and will not blend with the other ingredients. When making the panada for a soufflé to which several whisked whites of eggs are added the pan must be sufficiently large to permit of the whites being easily and lightly folded in, otherwise there is risk of expelling the entrapped air.

3. Add the yolks or whole eggs one at a time, and beat them in well.

4. Whisk the whites very stiffly just before they are required, fold them at once carefully and lightly into the mixture, not to expel the air. Pour into a dish or soufflé tin, either of which should be only about half full on account of the great expansion.

5. Bake or steam at once. Apply moderate and steady heat to cook the soufflé mixture, which should rise steadily, not over-rapidly, and become firm. At this point, when it is firm in the centre to the touch, the soufflé has risen to its highest, and should be immediately removed from steamer or oven, otherwise, if cooking is continued, it will begin to shrink. If a very light soufflé, made with a large quantity of whisked white of egg, cooks too rapidly, it rises equally rapidly, but without becoming firm, and will sink before the mixture is thoroughly cooked.

6. Dish quickly and serve at once : soufflés lose their lightness if kept hot ; all shrink as they cool, particularly the very light variety.

Preparation of Tin for a Steamed Soufflé.

1. For very light mixtures made with 1 gill of panada and with a large proportion of whisked white of egg, e.g. vanilla soufflé, a soufflé tin of $1\frac{1}{2}$ pints capacity is necessary, as the soufflé rises very high. For meat and other soufflés, to which whole eggs (or only a small quantity of whisked white) are added, and which do not rise so much, a smaller tin is suitable.

2. To prevent a steamed soufflé from sticking, the tin must be absolutely clean and dry and greased with clarified butter.

3. To support the soufflé as it rises above the level of the tin,

and to prevent it from falling over the sides, wrap a threefold band of white kitchen paper round the tin ; it should be sufficiently deep to extend 3 or 4 in. above the top and reaching to the middle of the tin.   Grease this band and also a piece of paper to cover the soufflé, for the prevention of steam condensing upon the surface. For a meat or fish soufflé, to prevent discoloration of the food, put a round of greased paper in the bottom of the tin.

To Steam a Soufflé.   Either use an ordinary steamer or place the tin in a saucepan, which should be filled to a quarter of its depth with gently simmering water.   Let the

soufflé-tin stand on an inverted saucer or plate, and away from the side of the pan where there may be the greatest heat ; this is to avoid any risk of too rapid cooking.

To Turn out a Steamed Soufflé.   Remove paper and string, and allow the soufflé to stand for two or three seconds to shrink slightly away from the sides ; if necessary, ease it away gently with a slight pressure of the flat of a knife or of the fingers.   Turn on to a hot dish.   When turning out a very light steamed soufflé, draw the tin up and off lightly

FIG. 59. PREPARED
SOUFFLÉ TIN

and gently, being very careful not to let it rest heavily upon the soufflé.

STEAMED SOUFFLÉS

Steamed Meat Soufflé

Suitable Meat.   White meat, veal, chicken, rabbit ; also game.

Garnish.   Crimped lemon and parsley.

Panada.	½ lb. fillet of veal.
1 oz. flour.	2 eggs.
1 oz. butter.	1 tablespoonful cream.
1 gill white stock or milk.	Lemon juice.
	1½ gills white coating sauce.

Method.   1. Grease a small soufflé tin, cover the bottom with buttered paper.   Make the panada with the flour, butter, and liquid. 2. Cut the meat into pieces, pass twice through the mincer, pound well, add the cooled panada, pound again, mix in the two yolks and 1 white of egg. 3. Season, add the lemon juice and cream, lightly fold in the one whisked white of egg. 4. Put the mixture into the prepared tin and steam at a moderate rate for 45 minutes until firm to the touch. 5. Turn on to a hot dish, coat evenly with the sauce, and garnish.

Steamed Fish Soufflé (Whiting).

1 skinned whiting	½ gill cream.
(4 oz. fish).	2 small eggs
Panada.	Cayenne and salt.
{ 1 oz. flour.	1½ gills white coating sauce.
{ ½ oz. butter.	Lemon juice.
{ ¼ gill fish stock.	Crimped lemon and parsley for garnish.

Method. 1. Grease a half-pint soufflé tin with clarified butter, place a round of greased paper in the bottom of the tin, grease paper for covering. 2. Make the panada and let it cool. 3. Cut up the fish and sieve it, add the cooled panada to it, also the eggs whole, and one at a time, pound well together. 4. Season, add lemon juice, and stir in the cream. 5. Put mixture into prepared tin, cover, and steam gently for about ¾ hour until firm (follow directions given). 6. Turn out, remove any grease from surface with paper, coat with the sauce, and garnish.

Variations. 1. Any white fish is suitable for a fish soufflé. 2. The white of egg may be whisked and added, the texture of the soufflé being much lighter, the sauce is then poured round. 3. The same mixture may be baked.

Steamed Sweet Soufflé (Vanilla).

Proportions.

Panada.	1 dessertspoonful castor sugar.
1 oz. butter.	1 teaspoonful vanilla essence.
1 oz. flour.	3 yolks and 4 whites of eggs.
1 gill milk.	Jam, custard, or any suitable sweet sauce.

Method. 1. Prepare the soufflé tin as directed, and have saucepan for steaming soufflé in readiness ; separate the whites from the yolks. 2. Make the panada. 3. Remove from the heat, add sugar and vanilla essence and the yolks one at a time. 4. Fold in the stiffly whisked whites very lightly, pour the soufflé mixture into the prepared tin, cover with the greased paper. 5. Steam steadily and gently for about 30 to 40 minutes, until the soufflé is firm to the touch in the centre. 6. Remove paper and string, and turn out as before directed. 7. Pour the sauce round the dish.

Variations. Follow the directions for making vanilla soufflé with the following additions—

(*a*) Chocolate (2 oz.) ; dissolve it in the milk used in making the panada.

(*b*) Other flavouring essences.

(*c*) Finely chopped preserved or tinned fruit, e.g. ginger or pineapple. Add these after the yolk of eggs, and use syrup or juice as part of the liquid for the panada.

BAKED SOUFFLÉS

Many soufflé mixtures are suitable both for steaming and for baking.

1. The same method of preparation is used except that for a baked soufflé a smaller proportion of flour to liquid is used in the panada (¾ oz. to 1 gill), there being greater evaporation of moisture in baking.

2. Grease the fireproof dish or soufflé-dish or cases, and fill about three-quarters full.

3. Avoid opening the oven door until the mixture has set.

For large soufflés allow about 30 to 40 minutes, for those baked in small cases, 10 to 15 minutes.

Baked Chocolate Soufflé.

Ingredients and Proportions. The same as for vanilla soufflé except ¾ oz. flour instead of 1 oz., and the addition of 2 oz. of finely grated chocolate.

Method. 1. Dissolve the chocolate in the milk, use this liquid for making the panada, then proceed as for steamed vanilla soufflé.

2. Put the mixture into a greased fireproof dish or china soufflé case.

3. Bake in a moderately quick oven until set and well risen—time about 30 minutes.

CHAPTER 24

CHEESE AND CHEESE COOKERY

Composition of Cheese. Cheese, one of the products of milk, consists of the fat and casein of milk, and roughly speaking may be said to be composed of $\frac{1}{3}$ fat, $\frac{1}{3}$ nitrogenous matter and $\frac{1}{3}$ water. Cheese is an example of a concentrated food : 1 lb. of Cheddar cheese contains *all* the casein and *nearly all* the fat of 1 gallon of milk, the approximate percentage of the constituents of Cheddar cheese being—

Protein	.	.	.	33·4	Water .	.	.	.	31·7
Fat	.	.	.	26·8	Mineral matter	.	.	3·9

The richness in fat is determined by the percentage of cream in the milk, for cheese is made from whole milk plus cream, from skimmed milk and from cream only.

Use in the Diet. As a substitute for meat cheese is most valuable in dietaries when economy is a necessity, and in those of persons

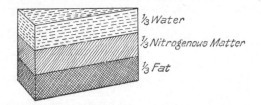

Fig. 60. Approximate Composition of Cheese

who are engaged in strenuous manual labour. 1 lb. of cheese has about twice the nutritive value of 1 lb. of beef, but for it to be a cheap substitute for meat, the cheap variety, which is equal in nutriment to the more expensive kind, must be used. Cheese is a good source of calcium and Vitamin A ; meat is deficient in the latter and has a low content of the former.

The two classes of cheese are : (*a*) Hard cheeses, (*b*) Soft cheeses, which contain a higher percentage of water, and are *relatively* less rich in protein and fat.

Manufacture. Cheese is prepared by heating the milk, and by the coagulation of the casein by the addition of rennet or of an acid ; a low degree of heat produces a soft cheese which ripens quickly, while a higher temperature causes a firmer curd, which ripens more slowly. The whey is extracted and the cheese pressed. High pressure produces a hard cheese, a soft cheese results from a less

221

degree of pressure. After pressure it is put aside in a cool place, but exposed to the air to " ripen."   This ripening is a fermentative process brought about by the action of certain bacteria present in the air, and also by the introduction of cultivated moulds. Chemical changes take place, and the particular flavour imparted to the cheese varies with the bacteria or mould which have had access to it. Skim milk cheeses ripen very slowly ; in cream cheeses the fermentative action is greater and more rapid.

Digestibility. A hard and slow ripening cheese can be more readily digested than the soft variety, but cheese is not one of the most easily digested foods ; the chief reasons for this are—

(*a*) The concentrated form of the food.

(*b*) The large amount of fat which forms, as it were, a waterproof coating round the casein, and so prevents the ready access of the digestive juices.

(*c*) Fatty acids developed in the ripening process, which are irritating to the digestive organs.

(*d*) The age, texture, composition, imperfect mastication of cheese, and faults in the preparation of cheese dishes are frequently the causes of difficulty in digestion.

Use of Cheese in Cookery. Excluding its use as a substitute for meat, cheese, on account of its distinctive and agreeable flavour, is used largely as an ingredient, and also to give additional nutriment to farinaceous dishes prepared with milk and eggs, e.g. such as macaroni cheese and cheese pudding ; for small and inexpensive savouries (cheese straws, etc.), for a flavouring to dishes prepared *au gratin*, and to some soups.

How to Render Cheese Dishes more Digestible.

1. Serve in small quantities and particularly at the end of a meal, when it is used only as a relish or savoury.

2. Finely divide it by grating, hard cheese being most suitable.

3. Mix with starchy foods—flour, sauce, potatoes, macaroni, etc.

4. Avoid over-heating and over-cooking, which further hardens the casein.

Cheese Pastry (Straws or Biscuits).

3 oz. flour.	Cayenne and salt.
2 oz. butter.	½ whole egg to bind.
1 oz. finely grated Parmesan cheese.	
1 oz. „ „ Cheddar cheese.	

Method. 1. Prepare as for short crust. Rub the butter into the flour, add the cheese and seasoning, and mix to a stiff paste with egg. Work free from cracks. 2. For straws. Roll out into a strip about 2½ in. wide and ¼ in. thick, trim the edges, and cut into strips about ¼ in. wide—should make 60 ; out of the remainder cut some rings using 1½ in. cutter and one two sizes smaller. 3. Place the straws on a baking tin, and bake in a moderate oven for 7 to 10 minutes. 4. Arrange the straws in the rings and serve hot or cold. Should give 12 bundles, i.e. 5 straws per ring.

For biscuits.   Stamp out some rounds about 1½ in. in diameter, prick and bake.

Cheese Soufflés.

Panada.

½ oz. butter.	2 yolks of eggs.
¼ oz. flour.	2 whites of eggs.
½ gill milk.	1½ oz. finely grated Parmesan cheese.
	Cayenne and salt.

Method.   1. Grease some small china or paper soufflé cases.   2. Make a panada or sauce with the ingredients given.   3. Cool it slightly, beat in the yolks, add the cheese and seasonings, and fold in the stiffly-whisked whites.   4. Put the mixture into the small cases.   5. Bake for about 12 to 15 minutes in a moderately quick oven until well risen and nicely browned.   6. Serve at once.

Cheese Aigrettes or Fritters.

Panada.

2 oz. flour.	1 egg, an extra yolk if necessary.
½ oz. butter.	1½ oz. grated Parmesan cheese.
1 gill water.	Cayenne, salt.

Method.   1. Warm and sieve the flour.   2. Bring water and butter to boiling point, draw the pan aside, add the flour immediately and all at once ; beat until smooth and cool slightly.   3. Add egg, cheese, and seasoning, and beat well.   4. Drop the mixture in small teaspoonfuls into a pan of fat which is just beginning to smoke and fry a golden brown (for details see HOW TO FRY FRITTERS, page 194).   5. Drain well.   6. Sprinkle with grated cheese and serve very hot.

CHAPTER 25

JELLIES AND CREAMS

JELLIES

THESE attractive cold sweets afford scope to artistic skill in decoration. Jellies are sweet and savoury: aspic and meat jellies belong to the latter class. They may be further classified as—

(a) Cleared or transparent, such as lemon, wine, and aspic jellies.
(b) Uncleared or opaque, e.g. egg or port wine jellies.

The ordinary cleared lemon and wine jellies are the most generally popular in the sweet course, lemon jelly being also much used for lining moulds, and for decorating creams and other cold sweets.

Jellies and creams set attractively in jelly-lined and decorated moulds are giving way to the vogue of individual portions served in glasses. This saves time and facilitates easy and quick service. Such sweets need not lack in attractiveness; they also lend themselves to skill and imagination exercised in the scheme of decoration.

Excluding jellies made by boiling the juice of fruit and sugar together, gelatine is the important factor in making all others, for upon this ingredient their consistency depends. Transparent or cleared jellies are solutions of gelatine in water with the addition of flavourings. The characteristics of these are a *brilliant transparency* and their *consistency*, which should be only just sufficiently stiff to support their own weight when turned out of the mould.

Chief Ingredients of Cleared Jellies.

Liquid	Water, wine, fruit juice.
Stiffening agent . . .	Gelatine, isinglass, agar-agar.
Clearing agent	White of egg.
Loaf sugar . . .	Makes a purer and brighter jelly.

Value of Jellies in the Diet. An uncleared jelly made with milk or eggs is nourishing; a cleared or transparent jelly, of no appreciable nutritive value, is of dietetic importance. It is easily digested, refreshing, and stimulating on account of the wine.

Gelatine. Commercial gelatine is prepared from the bones, tendons, sinews, etc., of animals, and is purified by various processes;

for culinary processes it should be of good quality, for an inferior gelatine has a decided flavour, and its stiffening properties are of less strength. The three kinds are—

(a) Strip gelatine must be soaked for 2 to 3 hours before use.

(b) French leaf gelatine, of good quality, is thin and brittle, dissolves readily and is preferable to the strip variety.

(c) Powdered gelatine dissolves readily. Gelatine is soluble in hot water, and a 1 per cent solution will set upon cooling.

Dissolve gelatine slowly and by gentle heat ; over-heating or boiling in a small quantity of water makes it sticky and unusable. When dissolved in milk, the liquid must not boil on any account, otherwise it will curdle, this being due to the acid used in the refining process of the manufacture of gelatine.

Isinglass is prepared from the swimming bladder of the sturgeon, it is the finest form of gelatine, has great stiffening power, and is tasteless ; for the latter reason it is useful in sick room cookery ; but its dietetic value is just the same as that of ordinary gelatine.

Gelatine from Calves' Feet. This is a very fine form of gelatine derived from boiling calves' feet in water, it is very pure and delicate in flavour, and on that account is largely used for invalids, but a jelly made with calves' feet has no more nutriment than one stiffened with ordinary gelatine.

Agar-agar prepared from seaweed, used in vegetarian cookery. Its stiffening properties much greater than those of gelatine.

Average Proportions of Stiffening Agents.

French leaf gelatine	1¾ to 2 oz. to set 1 quart of jelly.						
Powdered	,,	1¾ to 2	,,	,, ,,	,,	,,	,,
Strip	,,	1½ oz.	,, ,,	,, ,,	,,	,,
Isinglass	,,	1 oz.	,, ,,	,, ,,	,,	,,
Agar-agar	,,	¼ oz.	,, ,,	,, ,,	,,	,,

Too large a proportion of gelatine makes a jelly difficult to clear. The exact amount varies slightly with quality of gelatine.

The Clearing Agent, white of egg, if used in too large a proportion, impoverishes the flavour of a jelly.

Proportion. 2 whites of eggs to clear 1 quart of liquid.

In the action of whisking, the minute capsules containing the egg albumen are ruptured, and the contents are released. These, tiny particles of albumen coagulate in the liquid as it heats, and being lighter than it, they rise to the surface carrying with them the insoluble impurities, which constitute the " head " or " scum." This is the filter through which the jelly first passes as it is strained through the cloth, the liquid being passed and repassed until it is clear and brilliant.

Ingredients and Proportions for Typical Cleared Jellies.

Lemon.	Wine.	Aspic.

1½ pints cold water ⎫
½ pint lemon juice ⎬ 1 qt.
6 oz. loaf sugar. ⎭
	1¼ pints cold water ⎫
	½ pint sherry ⎬ 1 qt.
	¼ pint lemon juice ⎭
	6 oz. loaf sugar.
		1½ pints stock
		¼ pint sherry
		½ gill mixed
		  vinegars
		  (malt, tarra-
		  gon, chilli)
		½ gill lemon juice
			1 qt.

Lemon.	Wine.	Aspic.

1½ to 2 oz. gelatine.
2 whites and 2 shells of
  eggs.
Rind of 2 lemons.
2 cloves.
½ in. cinnamon.
	1½ to 2 oz. gelatine.
	2 whites and 2 shells of
	  eggs.
	Rind of 2 lemons.
	2 cloves.
	½ in. cinnamon.
		2 to 2½ oz. gelatine.
		2 whites and 2 shells of eggs
		Rind of 1 lemon.
		1 onion, piece of carrot and
		  sprig of parsley.
		½ teaspoonful salt ; 10
		peppercorns.

Method. 1. *Lemon.* Follow directions below. 2. *Wine.* The same as for lemon jelly. 3. *Aspic.* The same as for lemon jelly, but allow aspic to stand 20 minutes before straining it to extract more fully the flavour of the ingredients. Use stock for making the jelly when the aspic is one of the important ingredients of a dish, e.g. fish in aspic. When it is required for garnishing purposes only, water can be used, but such a jelly is very poor in flavour.

Method of Making a Cleared Jelly (Lemon). To ensure clearness and brilliancy use scrupulously clean, scalded utensils, etc.—pan, whisk, and jelly cloth. The pan should be white-lined, deep, and large, as the jelly rises very considerably when it boils up.

1. Put the water and gelatine into the pan, wash the lemons and peel off the rind very thinly ; wash the egg-shells and crush them ; these act as a filter in straining the jelly. Add these and all the other ingredients to the water.

2. *To Clear the Jelly.* Add the two whites and begin at once to whisk steadily and briskly over a low heat. If the whisking is insufficient or intermittent the egg albumen is not thoroughly broken up and distributed throughout the liquid, and if heat is applied too rapidly the albumen quickly coagulates and there is a smaller bulk of light " froth " to carry up the impurities to the surface, consequently the jelly will not be so clear.

3. Cease whisking well before boiling point is reached, its approach is indicated by the heaving of the " head " or " scum."

4. Remove the whisk and allow the jelly to boil up well to the top of the saucepan. Remove from heat, then repeat this process twice.

5. Draw the pan gently aside, half cover with lid, and leave the jelly to settle for 5 minutes.

6. *To Strain the Jelly.* A jelly stand is a convenience, but an inverted kitchen chair with a cloth tied over the legs to form a bag, answers the purpose. Use a chair without bars, then there is

no risk of disturbing the jelly in the cloth when removing and replacing the basins. Have two basins and a kettle of boiling water in readiness. Avoid shaking the jelly in the pan or in the cloth, this causes it to be cloudy.

(*a*) Pour some boiling water through the cloth and heat the basins with it, this prevents the jelly from cooling rapidly and setting in the cloth before it has passed through.

(*b*) Pour the jelly very gently, and without shaking the pan, into the cloth and let it run through.

(*c*) Very gently remove the basin beneath the cloth, replace it with another heated one and return the cloudy jelly to the cloth to run through again.

(*d*) Repeat this if necessary until the jelly is clear and sparkling.

(*e*) Cover the jelly and chair with a blanket to protect it from a draught, and to prevent rapid cooling, then leave it until all has passed through. If some should set in the cloth, as it may in cold weather, half fill a small basin with boiling water and place it in the middle—this is apt, however, to make that portion of the jelly cloudy, as the weight of the basin may force through some of the scum.

7. *To Mould.* When the jelly is cold, but still liquid, pour it gently to avoid air bubbles into a scalded wet mould. If moulded when hot the jelly is apt to be cloudy.

8. *To Unmould* a jelly *or* a cream.

(*a*) If the mould has been in a refrigerator or upon ice let it stand for a few minutes, it unmoulds more easily. Dip the mould for a second, immersing it completely, in a basin of water hotter than the hand can comfortably bear ; a china mould requires longer.

(*b*) Wipe the top with a clean cloth, and invert the mould on the hand.

(*c*) Give one sharp shake with an up-and-down movement, and slip it on to the dish, gently withdraw the hand and carefully draw the mould off.

If the mould used is too large for the hand to cover, place a dish over it, invert it, and give one or two sharp shakes to free the jelly or cream.

Moulds for Jellies and Creams. Copper moulds, tin-lined, are the best, or aluminium or tin moulds; the designs are sharper and more varied, and the jelly or cream is more easily unmoulded than when set in earthenware.

To Line and Decorate a Mould with Jelly. For this purpose lemon jelly is used. It must be quite liquid, but must have no appreciable heat ; to keep it at this temperature while using it place the basin of jelly in tepid water.

To Line a Mould. (*a*) Rinse the mould first with hot water to remove any trace of grease, then with cold, and leave either filled with cold water or upon the ice, if you have some, until required. To just coat the bottom of a flat mould (soufflé tin) and to decorate simply does not take long, and the whole will set without ice, given sufficient time and cool conditions; but for masking a mould entirely with jelly, and to decorate elaborately, ice is required.

(*b*) To coat the bottom only of a plain mould, pour in sufficient liquid jelly to cover the bottom $\frac{1}{8}$ to $\frac{1}{4}$ in. in thickness, leave it to set and decorate (see directions following).

(*c*) To mask the mould completely with jelly. Leave the mould on the ice and have a tin or basin with some broken ice ready. Pour a little liquid jelly gently into the mould to avoid air bubbles, two or three tablespoonfuls, the amount varying with the size of the mould. Revolve the mould slowly upon the ice until it is evenly coated with a thin layer of jelly, then leave to set. Repeat if a thicker layer is required.

To Decorate a Mould. As soon as the lining of jelly has set, the mould can be decorated. A rather bold design is the most effective. The arrangement should be symmetrical and the colours harmonize, or contrast.

Preserved fruits cut into small shapes, nuts sliced or cut across, etc., and for fruit creams small pieces of the fruit should be included.

For arranging the decorations use two hatpins, and dip the underside of each piece into liquid jelly to keep it in place. Leave the decorations to set, then secure by a thin coating of liquid jelly.

To Chop Jelly for Decorations. This should be rather firm. Turn it on to a wetted paper and chop it coarsely, but evenly ; if finely chopped it loses its brilliancy. It may also be put into a forcing bag, and forced out as a decoration to a sweet dish.

To Blanch Almonds and Pistachio Nuts. Drop them into boiling water, leave for a couple of minutes, remove skins by pressing between the thumb and first finger, then dry in a cloth.

Calves' Foot Jelly.

This jelly is stiffened by the gelatine which is extracted from the feet by prolonged boiling.

Proportions.

$$\left.\begin{array}{l}\text{2 calves' feet} \\ \text{5 pints water}\end{array}\right\} \text{For stock.}$$

To Make Stock for Jelly. The stock should be made the day before, so that it may get perfectly cold. This ensures easy and complete removal of fat from the surface.

1. Wash and scrape the feet thoroughly, and cut each foot into 4 or 5 pieces, remove marrow and fat, and wash thoroughly in warm water.

2. Blanch the feet ; put them into a pan, cover with cold water, and bring to boiling point. Pour away the water, and rinse the feet.

3. Put the feet into a white-lined pan, cover with 5 pints of cold

water, bring slowly to boiling point and simmer for 5 to 6 hours until reduced to about a quart.

4. Strain through a fine nylon sieve or muslin, and leave until cold, when it should be quite firm and stiffer than the finished jelly, to allow for its dilution with wine and lemon juice. If too stiff a little water can be added, or if insufficiently so, a little gelatine may be necessary.

To Make the Clear Jelly.

To a pint and a half of stock allow—

1 gill lemon juice.	6 oz. loaf sugar.
1 gill sherry.	4 cloves.
1 tablespoonful brandy.	1 in. cinnamon stick.
Rind of 2 lemons.	The whites and crushed shells of 2 eggs.

1. Remove every particle of fat from the surface of the jellied stock with a metal spoon, then wipe it over with a clean scalded cloth. 2. Put all the ingredients, except the brandy, into a large, deep, white-lined pan, and proceed as for lemon jelly. Add the brandy after the jelly has run through the cloth for the first time.

UNCLEARED OR OPAQUE JELLIES

Milk, Egg, and Orange Jellies.

NOTE. Those made with milk and eggs require less gelatine.

Proportions of Ingredients.

Milk Jelly.	Egg Jelly.	Orange Jelly.
1 pint milk.	2 eggs.	½ pint water.
	Juice of 2 lemons.	½ pint orange juice.
	Cold water.	Juice of 2 lemons.
½ oz. gelatine.	¾ oz. gelatine.	1 oz. gelatine.
1½ oz. castor sugar.	6 oz. loaf sugar.	3 oz. loaf sugar.
Strip of lemon rind.	Rind of 2 lemons.	Peel of 3 oranges.

Milk Jelly. 1. Heat the milk with the lemon rind and leave it to stand for a few minutes to extract the flavour. 2. Add the gelatine and sugar and stir gently until dissolved. 3. Strain into a basin and stir occasionally until the liquid begins to thicken, otherwise it separates into a thick and thin layer. 4. Pour into wet moulds.

Egg Jelly. 1. Wash the lemons and rub the sugar on the rind to extract the flavour, squeeze out the juice, strain and make up to *one pint* with cold water. 2. Beat the eggs and put all the ingredients into a pan and stir until the liquid thickens, it must not boil. 3. Strain into moulds rinsed with cold water.

A gill of sherry may be used instead of part of the water.

Orange Jelly. 1. Put the water, sugar, orange rind, and gelatine into the pan, stir until the gelatine is dissolved, then cover and leave it to stand for 10 minutes to extract the flavour of the rind.

2. Strain into a basin, add the strained orange and lemon juice, and pour into wet moulds.

CREAMS

The more economical foundation of these sweets consists of whipped cream and custard in equal quantities. This, however, can be varied by increasing or decreasing the proportion of cream to custard according to the richness desired. Various flavourings and additions, such as essences, preserved fruits, fruit *purée*, fruit syrup, etc., are combined with the foundation of cream or custard ; the whole mixture is stiffened with gelatine, and set in a mould lined with jelly and simply or elaborately decorated, or set in glass dishes. A cream mixture may be moulded in a tin lined with biscuits, as in a Charlotte Russe, and is also used as a foundation for a variety of sweet dishes.

Varieties of Cream Mixtures.

1. The very rich mixtures, composed entirely of cream.
2. Those composed of custard and cream.
3. Fruit creams made with fruit *purée* and cream, or, more economically, partly with cream and custard.

For lining moulds with jelly and decorating (see JELLIES, page 227).

Important Points in Preparation of " Creams."

1. Pure fresh cream is necessary : double cream, that which has stood on the milk for 24 hours, is the best for whipping. *Half whip* the cream, this gives a sponge-like texture to the mixture (for directions for whipping cream, see CAKES, page 253).

2. The correct proportion of gelatine and its careful addition to the cream mixture. The quantity required is small, therefore measure **very accurately and dissolve thoroughly so that none is** left in the saucepan or strainer, otherwise the cream may not set, but one that is too stiff is unpalatable. A little more may be required in very hot weather, and when ice is not available, or for a cream mixture which contains neither fruit nor fruit *purée* ; rather less may be used in very cold weather or when the cream is set in very small moulds. The average quantity is—

¼ oz. of powdered gelatine dissolved in ⅛ gill water to set ¾ pint of cream mixture.
About ⅛ oz. of French leaf gelatine to set ¾ pint of cream mixture.

NOTE. The ¾ pint of cream mixture includes the water in which the gelatine is dissolved (see RECIPES).

Add the gelatine when warm ; if too hot the cream is not so light in texture, if insufficiently hot it sets in tiny lumps or small specks throughout the cream, and the cream will not set.

3. To ensure a smooth texture, the cream, custard, and *purée* should, as far as possible, be of the same consistency, so that they may mix readily ; if one is thicker than another add the thinner to the thicker.

4. When all the ingredients are added, stir the mixture very gently until it is just beginning to set creamily, and until the fruit, if any is used, is just suspended, as in ginger cream, then pour at once into the prepared mould. If there is any sensible warmth in the mixture it will dissolve the thin lining of jelly and disturb the decorations. If too cold before it is moulded it will not take the shape of the mould, and small holes will appear on the surface and throughout the mixture.

5. Unmould very carefully (see directions, JELLIES, page 227), and decorate dish with chopped jelly.

Vanilla Cream (Plain).

¾ pint
{
1 gill custard.
1 gill cream.
½ gill milk.
½ gill water.

Vanilla essence.
1 oz. castor sugar.
¼ oz. (rather more) powdered gelatine.
Lemon jelly (1½ gills)
Glacé fruit or Pistachio nuts
} Decoration.

Method. 1. Line a mould with jelly and decorate it. 2. Dissolve the gelatine in the water. 3. Half whip the cream, add the sugar and ⅛ gill of milk, and add the custard to the gelatine. 4. Stir the custard and gelatine into the cream, add vanilla essence to flavour. 5. Stir till beginning to set and pour into the mould or glass dish. 6. Unmould and decorate dish with chopped jelly. 7. If the cream is set in a glass dish, when firm, decorate and coat surface lightly with jelly.

Apricot Cream (Fruit Purée).

¾ pint
{
1 gill apricot *purée*.
½ gill apricot syrup.
¼ gill cream.
⅓ gill custard.
½ gill water.

1 teaspoonful lemon juice.
1 oz. castor sugar.
¼ oz. powdered gelatine.
Pistachio nuts
Pieces of apricot
Lemon jelly 1½ gills
Carmine.
} Decoration.

Method. 1. Line a mould with jelly and decorate it. 2. Sieve the apricots, half whip the cream, dissolve the gelatine in the ½ gill water. 3. Mix apricot *purée*, custard, sugar, and lemon juice together. 4. Stir the gelatine into it, add cream and a few drops of carmine. 5. Stir till the mixture begins to set creamily; proceed then as for vanilla cream.

Ginger Cream (Fruit added in pieces *not* as a purée).

¾ pint
{
1 gill cream.	1 oz. preserved ginger.
1 gill custard.	Ginger essence.
½ gill ginger syrup.	1½ gills lemon jelly ⎫
½ gill water.	Pistachio nuts ⎬ Decoration.
¼ oz. powdered gelatine.	Preserved ginger ⎭

Method. 1. Line a mould with jelly and decorate it. 2. Dissolve the gelatine in the water, add the ginger syrup to it. 3. Half whip the cream, add the custard, sugar, and ginger cut into small dice. 4. Stir the gelatine into the mixture and add ginger essence if required. 5. Stir gently until it begins to set and the ginger to be suspended. 6. Proceed as for vanilla cream.

Charlotte Russe.

8 to 10 Savoy finger biscuits. 1½ oz. castor sugar.

¾ pint
{
1 gill cream.	1 teaspoonful vanilla essence.
1 gill custard.	¼ oz. powdered gelatine.
½ gill milk.	1½ gills lemon jelly ⎫ Decoration.
½ gill water.	Cherries and angelica ⎭

Method. 1. Mask the bottom of a pint soufflé-tin with liquid jelly and let it set. Decorate, and set the decorations with another layer of jelly. 2. Split the biscuits, trim the sides and one end of each, and arrange these closely round the tin, there must be no interstices between the biscuits. 3. Half whip the cream, add milk, sugar, and vanilla essence. 4. Dissolve the gelatine in the ½ gill water, add the custard to it and stir in the cream. 5. Proceed in the usual way and pour the cream mixture into the mould. 6. When set, trim the biscuits to the level of the mixture, dip the bottom of the mould into warm water, turn out, and serve with chopped jelly.

Variations. Any cream mixture or a fruit cream may be used as a filling.

CHAPTER 26

BEVERAGES

TEA, COFFEE, AND COCOA

Tea and coffee are of dietetic value on account of their stimulating effect upon the nervous system, while cocoa possesses some nutritive value in addition to being a mild stimulant.

The chief constituents of these are—

Tea.	Coffee.	Cocoa.
Caffeine.	Caffeine.	Theobromine.
		An astringent similar
Tannin.	Tannin.	to tannin.
		Fat.
Volatile oil.	Volatile oil.	Starch.

Tea and coffee are " infusions," that is, liquids in which the leaves and the ground berries of the plant are steeped *without boiling*. The stimulating action of tea and coffee is due to caffeine.

The aroma and fragrant flavour peculiar to tea and to coffee are due to the presence in each of an essential oil, which is also stimulating in effect. The constituent tannin is an astringent body, and is more powerful in tea than in coffee; during the prolonged infusion of tea, more tannin is extracted, giving a bitter flavour. If taken in large quantities, digestion of starch and meat proteins may be affected.

Both coffee and tea tend to retard digestion, but if taken in moderation are useful in the diet. In excess they seriously affect the nervous or digestive system. Both beverages supply to the body part of the water required daily. Coffee is a stronger stimulant than tea, it stimulates not only the nervous system, but also the heart, and makes the body more resistant to extreme cold than tea.

The Principle of Making Tea and Coffee is to extract their pleasant flavour and aroma with their stimulating properties, but without the astringent or bitter ones.

TEA

The Water for making tea should be freshly drawn, as it is better aerated. Water which has been boiled, allowed to get cold and reboiled, or that which has been simmering or boiling for a long time, is flat and insipid ; as the gases have been driven off, the flavour of tea made with it is poor. Therefore freshly-drawn water, which should be used directly it has reached boiling point, is very important.

Moderately hard water makes the best tea; very hard water, on account of the lime salts present, prevents the ready extraction of the properties of the tea. Tea made with very soft water is astringent in flavour, owing to the too ready extraction of its bitter properties.

The Teapot must be kept perfectly clean. To prevent any deposit on the inside, wash, rinse, and dry it each time after use.

Amount of Tea depends upon the blend, the hardness of the water, and upon individual taste. Allow upon an average 1 teaspoonful to ½ pint of boiling water ; for a small number 1 teaspoonful for each person and 1 teaspoonful over, but less in proportion is required for a larger number.

Infusion. Tea must be infused, *never* boiled.

Some of the volatile constituents are only properly extracted at boiling point, therefore—

1. Heat the pot thoroughly by *half* filling it with *boiling* water, not with a *small* quantity of hot or warm water.

2. Pour the water directly it reaches boiling point on to the tea in the heated teapot.

3. Infuse for 3 to 4 minutes only, according to the kind of tea used, and keep it as warm as possible during infusion for the ready extraction of its stimulating and fragrant properties.

4. Pour out the tea at once after the necessary time for infusion, or pour it off the leaves into another heated teapot. This stops any further extraction of bitter properties, and prevents the dissipation of the essential oil to which tea owes its fragrance, and which occurs by too prolonged infusion.

COFFEE

Coffee, like tea, is an infusion, and the aim in making is the same. For the beverage to be good, the coffee must be of good quality and fresh, the blend being a matter of taste ; a mixture of Java and Mocha makes a good breakfast coffee. For household use buy coffee in small quantities, and freshly roasted and ground. If a coffee grinder is available grind the coffee as it is required. It must be perfectly clean, any stale coffee left in the grinder will spoil the flavour of the fresh. Ground coffee quickly deteriorates, and readily absorbs flavours, therefore it should be kept in perfectly air-tight bottles or jars, and away from foods with a strong flavour. For reasons of economy and on account of individual taste, a small amount of chicory (the dried and ground root of the plant) is frequently added to breakfast coffee, the usual proportion being 2 oz. of chicory to 1 lb. of coffee, but black coffee must be made with pure coffee only. Chicory imparts a slightly bitter flavour and a darker colour. It can easily be detected, as it sinks in cold water, while pure coffee floats.

Moderately Hard Water is better than soft water for making coffee, the latter extracts the strong and bitter properties, which overpower the delicate flavour and aroma.

Proportions. Coffee to be good must be strong, but not bitter. The quantity is a question of economy, of individual taste, and whether the coffee is for breakfast or to be served as *café noir*. For good breakfast coffee, the usual proportions are 2 tablespoonfuls of coffee to 1 pint of boiling water, but when economy has to be considered the proportion must be less—3 tablespoonfuls to 1 quart of water. A pinch of salt and of mustard added to the dry coffee develops its flavour.

To Make Good Coffee.

1. Use a good blend of fresh coffee and *not* sparingly.
2. Make it in a perfectly clean and hot earthenware utensil; either in a jug, or simple coffee-pot, or in a fireproof eathenware pot—the cafetière. The flavour of coffee made in a metal utensil is not as good as that which is made in an earthenware pot.
3. Use freshly-drawn water which has just reached boiling-point.
4. Infuse as directed.
5. Strain carefully.
6. Serve *very hot*, with hot milk. Scald the milk in preference to boiling it, boiled milk alters in flavour and affects that of the coffee. Allow an equal quantity of milk and of coffee or $\frac{2}{3}$ milk and $\frac{1}{3}$ coffee.

To scald milk. Heat it thoroughly, but *not quite* to boiling point.

To Make Coffee in a Jug.

1. Heat the jug thoroughly with boiling water; heat the coffee, with a pinch of salt and of mustard, either in the oven or before the fire, or in the hot jug, stand the latter in the oven, near the stove, or in a pan of simmering water. Heating the coffee aids in the extraction of its aroma and flavour, and the salt assists in developing it.
2. Pour freshly boiling water on the coffee, stir with a spoon, cover tightly, and stand it by the side of the stove or in a pan of simmering water for 10 minutes to infuse. After the coffee has been standing for a few minutes pour about a gill into a *hot* cup and return it to the jug, this helps to clear the coffee and to settle the grounds.
3. Strain through muslin into a hot coffee-pot or jug and serve very hot.

To Make Coffee in the Fireproof Earthenware Cafetière. The *cafetière* consists of an upper part, or strainer, through which the liquid coffee filters into the lower one. The strainer must be perfect, otherwise the coffee will be thick and not clear.

1. Heat the coffee as before directed and heat the *cafetière*, both the upper and lower part with boiling water.
2. Put the heated coffee with a pinch of salt into the upper part or strainer.

3. Pour the required amount of freshly boiling water *very slowly* on the coffee which *filters* or drips through into the lower part. While this is proceeding place the coffee-pot in a shallow pan of simmering water so that the liquid is kept very hot. By this method of making coffee, by the gradual steeping of the coffee in the strainer and by the slow percolation, the flavour is more thoroughly extracted.

4. When all the liquid coffee has passed through, serve it at once.

The ordinary coffee-pot can be fitted with a ring to which is attached a muslin bag, the latter acts as the strainer of the *cafetière*. Coffee may also be made in a percolator.

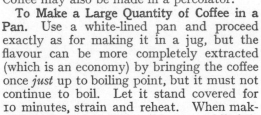

FIG. 61. A CAFE-TIÈRE

To Make a Large Quantity of Coffee in a Pan. Use a white-lined pan and proceed exactly as for making it in a jug, but the flavour can be more completely extracted (which is an economy) by bringing the coffee once *just* up to boiling point, but it must not continue to boil. Let it stand covered for 10 minutes, strain and reheat. When making coffee in a large quantity, throw in a little cold water while it is infusing. This clears it; the cold water, being heavier, sinks to the bottom of the pan, carrying the grounds with it.

Black Coffee should be very strong and clear, but not bitter. Make it in a jug or coffee-pot as directed, using rather more than one tablespoonful of the best pure coffee to ½ pint of boiling water. Strain carefully and serve very hot with coffee sugar.

COCOA

Cocoa not only stimulates, but has some nutritive value on account of the fat and starch present in its composition, and when made with milk and plenty of sugar it is a very valuable food.

The important constituents of the cocoa-bean, from which cocoa is manufactured, are (a) theobromine, which is similar to caffeine, but because it is present in such a small amount, cocoa is much less stimulating than either tea or coffee, (b) an astringent body similar to tannin, (c) fat (cocoa-butter) two-thirds of which is removed in the preparation of cocoa, but left in chocolate; for this reason chocolate is more nourishing, but less easily digested than cocoa, (d) a certain amount of starch.

Cocoa is *not* soluble in water, but cocoa is a powder which is so finely crushed and ground that it will remain in suspension in water—some powders are treated with an alkali which assists suspension.

To Make Cocoa. Follow the directions given with the special kind used.

The average proportion is 1 good teaspoonful to $\frac{1}{2}$ pint of liquid, using milk or half milk and half water. Mix the cocoa with a little of the cold milk, boil the rest, and when boiling pour on to the cocoa, stirring all the time. The flavour is improved, and there is more body in the cocoa if it is then boiled. The starch in it slightly thickens it and makes it smooth in texture.

CHAPTER 27

INVALID AND CONVALESCENT COOKERY

It is not within the scope of this book to deal with Dietetics and Dietaries, but every housewife should be able to select, prepare, and serve food suitable for an ailing or sick member of her family.

No food requires greater care and accuracy in the preparation than that for the sick and convalescent, for the feeding of a sick person is frequently no mean factor in retarding or hastening the recovery. In providing food for sick people, the object is to—

(a) Choose food suitable to the illness or ailment which will supply the necessary nutriment to replace normal or excessive wastage ; this should be in comparatively small bulk, as an invalid's appetite is usually slender.

(b) To select those articles of food which are the most easily digested, and to prepare them in the most digestible manner, so that there is no risk of unduly taxing the often already weakened digestive system, which in illness is usually more or less impaired. A complete dietary for a sick person must be well balanced, containing all the necessary constituents and in the correct proportions. But often the proportion of some constituents may have, according to the nature of the illness, to be more or less modified or almost or entirely eliminated, e.g. animal protein, starch, and sugar. In these cases strict adherence to, and scrupulously careful preparation of, the special diet is essential. In cases of serious illness the food, either stimulating or nourishing, is given in a liquid form, such being milk, raw eggs, beef tea, barley water. Convalescents pass on to light and easily digested solid food, which as convalescence proceeds is increased in variety and amount.

This section deals only and briefly with general suggestions as to the preparation of invalids' food, with a few of the most ordinary items in the dietary, which, though simple, are not always well prepared.

With a knowledge of food values, of how to cook food in the most digestible manner, and to retain the greatest amount of nutriment, which the recipes throughout are selected to illustrate, some of these can be used or easily modified or adapted to the requirements of invalid and convalescent fare.

Essentials in the Preparation of Food for Sick People.

1. Absolute freshness and food of the best quality, especially that which is of a very perishable nature : milk, eggs, fresh vegetables, fruit, meat, and fish.

2. Scrupulous cleanliness of hands and of all utensils, and freedom

from any flavour of food which has been previously handled or cooked in them, for the palate of an invalid is particularly sensitive to any flavour foreign to the food or to the slightest trace of burning. Milk and farinaceous foods prepared with milk are very absorbent of flavour.

3. Preparation in small quantities to avoid unnecessary waste, for invalids' food is not the least expensive ; the reappearance of the same food often creates a distaste for it; an invalid's appetite is frequently capricious.

4. Endeavour to supply the necessary nutriment in a relatively small bulk, this facilitates the digestion of the food. Milk, which may often be a large item in a sick person's diet, is a very bulky food, which if taken in a considerable quantity daily is another strong reason for the avoidance of " over bulkiness " in other forms of nourishment.

5. If there are definite and strict instructions from the doctor as to the food and its preparation, adhere strictly to them.

6. Variety in the food, in the method of cooking as far as is consistent with digestibility, and in serving. Attractive dishing in small dainty portions and little surprises will often tempt a capricious and slender appetite. Soup or broth in tiny marmite-cups, the use of small china shells and soufflé cases, jellies, etc., moulded in small darioles, are all more attractive and often more conducive to stimulating the appetite than when served in larger quantities.

7. Seasoning and flavouring must be delicate. Pepper should not generally be used ; vegetables, which tend to create flatulency, should be used judiciously and sparely, either for flavouring or for serving separately. Over-sweetening is likewise to be avoided.

8. Avoid greasiness; it is most objectionable both to palate and eye, and causes indigestion. Remove every particle of fat from beef tea, broth, and soup.

9. The simplest method of preparation, and the most digestible methods of cooking, and those whereby the most nutriment is retained are the most suitable—steaming, stewing, grilling; the food should never be accompanied with rich, highly-seasoned sauces. Steamed fish must often be served without a sauce, as the latter cannot be digested, and hinders the digestion of the former.

Prepare the food preferably by steaming or stewing ; frying is to be avoided except when convalescence has advanced.

10. Cook all food thoroughly, it must be neither under- nor over-cooked.

11. In cases of severe illness always have some nourishment or a beverage in readiness, such as broth, beef tea, jelly, barley water, lemonade, etc.

12. Serve food for an invalid punctually at the time expected, and let hot food be perfectly hot. Serve daintily on a tray covered with a spotless cloth, and with shining silver and sparkling glass.

BEEF TEA

The old-fashioned but erroneous idea that beef tea which set in a firm jelly was a most nourishing food for an invalid has long been exploded. Beef tea, however carefully made, cannot be considered of any great value as a *food*, but it is most useful in a sick-room on account of its *stimulating* effect, and if properly prepared is of some value as a nutrient.

The *underlying principle* upon which the method of making beef tea is based is that meat protein coagulates at about 140° F.

The kind of meat used is of importance, but the real nutritive value of beef tea is determined by the temperature at which it is cooked. The object in its preparation is to extract as much as is possible of the soluble protein in a *digestible* form and to retain this, otherwise the beef tea is of little use, beyond that of a stimulant.

Composition of a Cup of Beef Tea. If a cup of beef tea is properly prepared and allowed to get cold, two distinct layers are seen, an upper one of clear liquid brownish in colour, and a lower one composed of a light flocculent mass of brownish coloured particles. The latter represents the coagulated protein in minutely fine flakes, which can be easily digested; the liquid is simply a solution of gelatine, meat extractive, and mineral salts, the fat having been removed.

(*a*) If the beef tea is kept *well* below boiling point while it is being prepared, and then strained through a *coarse* strainer, a certain proportion of the lightly coagulated flakes of meat protein is retained in the liquid, which, in addition to being stimulating, has also a percentage of nutrients in it.

(*b*) If the beef tea, after it is made, is strained through muslin or a *fine* strainer, most of the coagulated protein is retained in the muslin or strainer, and the liquid possesses little more than stimulating properties.

(*c*) If the beef tea is allowed to *boil*, the heat hardens the tiny particles of protein; these adhere to the fibres and are removed with them in the strainer—such beef tea is of still less nutritive value.

Suitable Meat for Beef Tea. Juicy meat of the best quality is the best ; rump steak, beef steak or topside, gelatinous parts, such as shin of beef, are unsuitable. If beef tea sets in a jelly, it is a proof that either the wrong kind of beef has been used or that it has been carelessly prepared.

Since beef tea can never be thoroughly cooked, not more than a supply for 24 hours should be made at one time.

Average Proportions.

Ordinary Beef Tea.	Quickly-made Beef Tea.	Raw Beef Tea.
1 lb. lean juicy beef	1 lb. lean juicy meat.	2 oz. lean juicy beef.
1 pint cold water.	1 pint cold water.	2 tablespoonfuls cold water.
Pinch of salt.	Pinch of salt.	Pinch of salt.

By increasing the proportion of beef, a stronger beef tea can be made.

Ordinary Beef Tea.

Method. 1. Remove skin, gristle and fat, and cut the meat in the direction of the grain into thin strips and scrape them with a knife: this separates and breaks down the fibres which contain the nutriment from the connective tissue, and the solvent action of the water has greater power.

2. As the meat is shredded put it into a clean basin containing the water and pinch of salt : stir with a wooden spoon, cover with the lid or a greased paper, and let it stand for 30 minutes ; the solvent action of the cold water extracts part of the meat juices.

3. Place the basin in a deep pan containing sufficient cold water to reach half way up the outside of the basin.

4. Bring the water in the pan up to boiling point and leave it simmering gently for 3 hours. While cooking, stir the beef tea occasionally, pressing the meat against the sides of the basin to aid in extracting the meat juices.

5. At the end of this time the liquid will be brown in colour ; strain through a *coarse* strainer, and remove every particle of grease by passing kitchen paper over the surface.

6. When it is served, *reheat* only, do not let it boil.

NOTE.—(*a*) Beef tea may be cooked in the oven, but it has then a strong savoury flavour, and is not so suitable for a person who is seriously ill. (*b*) It may be made more nourishing and more of the nature of a soup by the addition of a yolk of egg or by groult (finely crushed) tapioca, cornflour, or arrowroot (using 1½ teaspoonfuls to ½ pint). The farinaceous matter must be cooked first in a little water and then added to the beef tea. When using a yolk of egg, strain it into the beef tea and heat gently to cook it. (*c*) *Mutton and veal* tea are made by the same method—use juicy meat of the best quality.

Quickly-made Beef Tea.

This is used when required in an emergency.

Method. 1. Prepare the meat as before, and put it and the water and a pinch of salt into a white-lined pan, cover and leave for 10 to 15 minutes. 2. Stir over a gentle heat, pressing the meat against the sides of the pan occasionally until the meat looks white and the liquid is brown, the raw appearance and taste having been removed. 3. Strain through a *coarse* strainer, remove fat, and serve at once.

Gruel.

Proportions.

1 dessertspoonful fine oatmeal or " patent groats."	½ pint water, or milk and water. Sugar or salt to taste.

Method.   1. Mix the oatmeal or groats smoothly with a little of the cold liquid.   2. Boil the rest.   Add to the oatmeal or groats.   3. Rinse the pan, return the oatmeal or groats to pan, boil from 15 to 20 minutes, stirring all the time.

Cup of Arrowroot.

Proportions.

½ pint milk ;   1 teaspoonful arrowroot ;   ½ teaspoonful castor sugar.

Method.   1. Mix arrowroot smoothly with a little of the cold milk, boil the remainder and mix with the arrowroot.   2. Boil for 7 to 10 minutes, stirring the whole time—add the sugar and serve.

NOTE.   Both gruel and arrowroot must be of a liquid consistency, and *not* thick, and free from lumpiness.

Barley Water (Clear).

NOTE.   Barley water keeps fresh only for a few hours, and should be kept covered in a cool place.   When made it should not be heated to boiling point again, this tends to set up fermentation.

Proportions.

1 oz. pearl barley.	A thin strip of lemon rind.
1 pint boiling water.	Sugar to taste.

Method.   1. Wash and blanch the barley and strain it : blanching cleanses it and keeps the barley water a good colour and clear. 2. Put the barley, lemon rind, and sugar into a jug, and pour the boiling water on it, cover closely, and strain when cold.

If to be served with milk omit lemon rind, also sugar if desired.

Barley Water (Thick).

Thick barley water is used to dilute milk. Barley contains a considerable amount of *mucilage*, a substance which acts mechanically upon the casein of milk, by separating the particles of casein during coagulation in the stomach, and preventing them from forming solid clots or curds—thus the milk is rendered more digestible.

Proportions.

2 oz. pearl barley to 1 pint of water, sugar optional.

Method.   1. Wash and blanch the barley.   2. Put it into a white-lined pan (or the colour will be spoiled) and boil very gently until reduced to two-thirds ; strain.

CHAPTER 28

MEATLESS COOKERY

It is altogether outside the scope of this book to discuss the arguments, physiological and economic, for or against vegetarianism. The custom is growing in many households of substituting more or less frequently other dishes for meat, and the question of "meatless dishes" is one that confronts most housekeepers. When providing these dishes it is of the highest importance that they should be equivalent in nutriment to those composed of meat for which they are substituted, otherwise they do not supply the necessary nourishment. On this account a comprehensive knowledge of food values is even more important for the preparation of meatless dishes than in the arrangement of the ordinary fare.

Food Constituents and Food Value of Meatless Dishes.

1. Whether the single dish or a whole meal is to be meatless or not, all necessary food constituents must be present, and, as in the ordinary diet, in the right proportions and suitably combined, viz.

Protein (body-building material), fat, carbohydrates (sugars and starches) producing energy, and mineral matter, water, and vitamins.

2. In preparing a meatless dish, there is no difficulty as to the provision of fat, carbohydrates, and mineral matter, the sources of which are plentiful, but the great danger is in not providing the necessary amount of body-building material to replace the protein of meat.

The protein is supplied by : (*a*) pulse foods, (*b*) by nuts (these also contain in addition a large percentage of oil and are very nutritive) ; (*c*) farinaceous products, macaroni, vermicelli, and semolina, which contain protein, but in a very small quantity. These, with the addition of the important protein foods, milk, cheese and eggs, supply necessary protein in meatless dishes.

3. The deficiency of fat and protein in pulse, in farinaceous foods, and in vegetables, is supplied by the addition of cream, milk, butter, cheese, yolk of egg, and oil.

4. Fresh vegetables and fruits are the chief sources of mineral matter and supply certain vitamins.

5. Suitable combination to supply the proper proportion of nutrients is very important, otherwise the dish will have too much of one constituent and too little of another, and be lacking either in nutritive value or in digestibility ; e.g. in preparing a dish with a foundation of rice (mainly starch) the deficiency of fat and of body-building material must be supplemented by the use of foods rich in these constituents, such as milk, eggs, cheese, butter.

APPROXIMATE PERCENTAGE OF IMPORTANT CONSTITUENTS OF

Constituent.	Nuts.	Lentils.	Semolina.	Macaroni.	Rice.
Protein	15–20	23	10–11	10	8
Fat	50–60	2	Less than ¼%	about 5%	0.3
Carbohydrate	9–12	58	73	76	76

Foods Used for Meatless Dishes. Vegetarians, excepting the most rigid, use milk, cream, cheese, butter, and eggs very freely, either alone or as additions to foods of vegetable origin. From these it is not difficult to make a variety of nourishing and palatable dishes suitable both for ordinary and for vegetarian fare.

(a) Eggs cooked and dressed in various ways : stuffed or curried or in fricassees ; in mayonnaise, in salads ; as omelets, plain or filled.

(b) Farinaceous foods: macaroni, rice, semolina, etc., with additions of cheese, eggs, butter, milk, cream.

(c) Vegetables including pulse: in pies, curries, salads, soups, and in mixtures for cutlets, croquettes, etc.

Preparation and Cooking. These meatless dishes require, as a rule, a longer time to prepare and more careful attention, e.g. compare the baking of a leg of mutton with the preparation and cooking of lentil cutlets.

1. Cook pulse, cereals, and vegetables thoroughly, the latter, when suitable, in a small amount of water to preserve mineral salts and to prevent an increase of bulkiness ; grate nuts finely.

2. Season and flavour well. Pulse and cereals are insipid in flavour, and vegetables possess fewer and less powerful " extractives " than meat.

3. Avoid sloppiness and bulkiness, which are frequent faults. Remember that rice absorbs about five times its own weight of water in cooking, macaroni and vermicelli absorb about three times their weight, vegetables a considerable amount, and pulse in soaking and cooking a very large quantity.

4. Variety is very essential—meatless preparations soon become monotonous, thus creating a distaste for this class of food.

5. Serve when suitable with the usual accompaniments to meat— fresh vegetables and a gravy or sauce.

NOTE. Should the dish be required for a strict vegetarian—use vegetable fat for pastry or for frying, vegetable stock and marmite for gravies.

Building up of Recipes for Meatless Dishes. By following and adapting the various methods given for dealing with the different foods, including those suitable for this purpose, a large variety of recipes can be evolved. Space permits to give one only as a " type " of meatless dish, with pulse as its foundation.

Lentil Cutlets.

Ingredients.	*For Dishing and Accompaniments.*
½ lb. red lentils.	½ lb. small grilled tomatoes.
1½ oz. butter.	Brown sauce or gravy made with veget-
2 eggs.	able stock or marmite.
1 dessertspoonful chopped parsley.	
1 teaspoonful minced onion.	
3 oz. mashed potato.	
Bread-crumbs.	
Seasoning.	

Method. 1. Soak lentils overnight in 1 pint of cold boiled water. 2. Cook them in the water in which they have been steeped, add the onion, cook until soft, and beat over the fire until smooth and dry. 3. Add the butter, potato, herbs, parsley, and sufficient beaten egg to bind to a smooth stiff paste; season well, if too moist add a few crumbs. 4. Shape into cutlets, coat with egg and crumbs and fry in deep fat (see MEAT CROQUETTES). 5. Arrange as for mutton cutlets, pour the sauce round, and serve the tomatoes separately.

NOTE. See FOOD VALUE, PREPARATION AND COOKING OF PULSE, pages 154-5.

CHAPTER 29

BREAD AND CAKES

As the result of present-day conditions of living, the making of bread has ceased to be an essential duty of the housewife, even in the more remote country districts. But " how to make and to bake a loaf of white bread," which is the simplest form of " fermented dough," may be of use at some time, and, if bread-making is understood' the preparation of any cake mixture raised with yeast is no difficult matter.

As regards cake making, it is convenient and it is frequently cheaper in the end to buy some of the more elaborate types of cake, but putting aside all consideration of economy and of extra trouble, there is no comparison between the flavour, purity of ingredients, and nutriment of the simple home-made cakes and the bought variety. For children the home-made, plain and well-baked cake is a nourishing and wholesome item of food.

As in all branches of cookery, the building up of individual recipes is greatly a matter of proportion and of good judgment, and an enormous variety of cakes, from the simplest to the most elaborate, can be evolved from a few foundation recipes, provided the methods of combining, using and mixing ingredients are understood.

Ingredients. The flavour of bread and of the simplest cake mixture is spoiled if the ingredients are not fresh and good in quality.

Flour. Use household flour for the white loaf and for all ordinary purposes, but it must be fresh, dry, and sieved. For fancy bread and for cakes of a very light texture, the best pastry flour should used; before sieving it is necessary to dry it to remove any moisture. For cakes a small quantity of cornflour or of rice flour is often added to the ordinary flour as these afford greater lightness and shortness to some mixtures, but on account of the absence of gluten, which gives cohesiveness to flour, these cannot be used alone.

Butter. As for very light pastry, fresh butter is best for very light mixtures and for cakes which are to be kept for a considerable time. If very salt butter is used, wash it in cold water to remove the salt, and dry in a floured cloth ; any rancid flavour in inferior butter becomes more pronounced when heated. If economy is a consideration, use for the plainer mixtures, margarine, lard, and vegetable fats or oils. Mixtures of fats, as for plain pastry, make excellent plain household cakes.

Eggs. Must be perfectly fresh ; preserved eggs, if good, are quite suitable. Always break each egg separately into a basin to avoid any risk of adding a stale one. Add one at a time to the other ingredients, beating in well ; several added at one time often cause a cake mixture to curdle. If this occurs mix in a little flour and the curdled appearance will disappear.

Milk. The addition of too much milk tends to make a cake mixture heavy, and gives to a large cake a flat-topped appearance when baked. As the proportion of eggs and butter increases, that of milk decreases. Water is often substituted for milk, as it has a less toughening effect.

Fruit. It is necessary to wash currants and sultanas and remove the stalks by rubbing them in a cloth or on a sieve or in a colander. Dry washed fruit thoroughly first in a cloth and then in a warm place, and allow it to get quite cold before it is used; warm and wet fruit makes a cake heavy. Dip candied peel and crystallized fruit in boiling water to remove the sugar, then dry.

Raising Agents. The lightness of a cake mixture is based upon the principle of " the expansion of gases when heated." This lightness is due to the presence of air, or of carbon dioxide, which is introduced into the mixture before it is baked.

Air is entangled in several ways : by sieving the flour, by adding whole beaten eggs, by beating the mixture, and by the addition of stiffly-whisked whites of eggs.

The gas, carbon dioxide, is introduced by various " raising agents," the principal of which are—

1. Yeast, which has a fermentative action with the production of carbon dioxide.
2. Baking powder.
3. Cream of tartar and bicarbonate of soda used separately.
4. Buttermilk and sour milk with bicarbonate of soda.
5. Vinegar or lemon juice with bicarbonate of soda.

Bicarbonate of ammonia is used commercially, but it is apt to impart an unpleasant flavour.

1. *Yeast* is a form of plant life consisting of microscopically minute cells (see MICRO-ORGANIC GROWTH, page 21), its property as a "raising agent " being due to a ferment or enzyme which it contains, the process of " fermentation " taking place when bread and cakes are raised with the yeast. The conditions for the rapid multiplication and growth of the yeast cells are gentle heat, about 75° to 90° F. (the degree of heat required varying with the prevailing temperature), moisture and the presence of sugar. If the temperature is allowed to vary when fermentation is in progress, this proceeds unevenly ; extreme heat kills and cold retards or hinders the growth of the cells, hence the great importance of using warm utensils, of warming ingredients to which yeast is added, and of not exposing any yeast mixture either to draughts or to a high degree of heat during the process of fermentation.

Fermentative Action of Yeast Upon Flour. Yeast cells require a food to feed upon—this is sugar—and the fermentation of dough (flour mixed with water) is rendered possible because of the presence of some sugar in the dough. There is a small quantity of sugar in wheaten flour, and more is produced in the dough by the action of the enzyme or ferment, termed diastase, which is present in wheaten flour, and this body is able by chemical action to convert part of the starch of the flour into sugar (maltose), this provides the necessary food for the yeast. To stimulate or to hasten the growth and activity of the yeast, it is " creamed " or blended with a little sugar, and this is diluted with tepid liquid and added to the warm flour, so, under the conditions of the presence of sugar, warmth, and moisture, the activity of the yeast commences. Enzymes in it attack the sugar present in the dough, a chemical action takes place, and the sugar is finally split up by the enzyme zymase, carbon dioxide and alcohol are produced, and the process is termed fermentation.

As fermentation proceeds, the gas collects in small bubbles throughout the dough, these expand with the heat, and cause it to swell and to rise. When the dough or cake mixture is put into the oven, the alcohol, which is very volatile, is driven off by the heat, and the gas bubbles expand, which results in the further expansion of the loaf or cake. Meanwhile the loaf or cake sets and becomes firm, and the texture becomes porous or spongy, which is due to the cavities left by the gas as it passes off.

Three Kinds of Yeast. Of the three "Compressed Yeast," "Brewer's Yeast," and "Dried Yeast," the first is the most convenient and most reliable to use. Yeast must be perfectly fresh; it does not keep well, and spoils quickly in close or hot weather; if stale the fermentation is not so rapid, and the flavour of the bread is unpleasant. This is caused by other fermentations taking place, the result of impurities in the yeast. Fresh yeast has a pleasant smell, is of a pale greyish colour, crumbles easily, and "creams" readily with sugar. The quantity of yeast required depends upon several conditions; the larger the amount of yeast the shorter the time required for rising, but if too much is used the bread is very "crumbly," and the flavour not so pleasant. The liquid added to yeast must be only lukewarm, the temperature most favourable to its growth. If too hot the yeast is killed. If the yeast does not "cream" readily (see METHOD OF MAKING WHITE BREAD), it is not fresh: this is the most certain test of freshness.

Proportions of Yeast to Flour.

> 1 oz. yeast is sufficient to raise flour up to 3½ lbs.
> 2 oz.   ,,   ,,   ,,   ,,   ,, 7 ,,
> ½ oz.   ,,   ,,   ,, any quantity below 1 lb.

2. *Baking Powder* consists of an acid salt or acid (e.g. cream of tartar or tartaric acid), and an alkaline carbonate (bicarbonate of

soda), used in the proportion of twice the amount of acid to alkaline carbonate, with the addition of some starchy ingredient such as ground rice, which absorbs any moisture and also prevents the baking powder from getting lumpy; hence the reason for keeping baking powder closely covered. Immediately it is moistened the alkaline carbonate and acid combine to form a salt, and the gas, carbon dioxide, is given off. Tartaric acid is double the strength of cream of tartar, therefore when used, it and bicarbonate of soda must be in equal proportions; the advantage of cream of tartar is that hardly any gas is generated before heat is applied, and its lightening power is consequently greater. In commercial baking powders, the acid salt used with bicarbonate of soda gives a delayed chemical action, so that there is little reaction in the cold, but in the presence of heat a good volume of gas is produced. Thus scone and cake mixtures containing baking powder do not require to be baked immediately after mixing. A batter or very light mixture, to which baking powder is added, should be baked at once, since the gas produced can more readily escape from it in the cold.

Too much baking powder makes small cakes and biscuits dry, and gives to large plain cakes a disagreeable flat taste. This is due to a residue which is left after the action of the baking powder has ceased.

Proportions of Baking Powder to Flour.

For plain mixtures (scones, etc.) 4 level teaspoonfuls to ½ lb. flour when fat is ½ that of the flour.
For richer mixtures 1 level teaspoonful to ½ lb. flour when fat is ¾ that of the flour.
For rich mixtures usually none.

Home-made Baking Powder. *Ingredients.* 4 oz. cream of tartar, 2 oz. bicarbonate of soda, 2 oz. rice flour.

Dry each ingredient, crush out lumps with a rolling pin, mix well together, and rub twice through a fine nylon sieve. Store in air-tight tins in a dry place. To *test* put a very little in a glass and add a little water. If fresh the baking powder will effervesce vigorously.

3. **Cream of Tartar and Bicarbonate of Soda.** These are used separately, the lightening power being relatively greater than when incorporated with rice flour as in baking powder, hence their use for making scones rise rapidly. Great care is necessary to mix them thoroughly with the flour.

Proportions. 2 parts of cream of tartar to 1 of bicarbonate of soda. Soda in excess imparts an unpleasant soapy flavour and a dark colour to scone mixtures.

4. **Buttermilk and Sour Milk with Bicarbonate of Soda.** Sour milk need never be wasted, it is excellent for scones. The lactic acid in the milk reacts upon the bicarbonate of soda, and carbon

dioxide is given off. When using buttermilk or sour milk for mixing, reduce the cream of tartar by half.

5. **Vinegar, with bicarbonate of soda,** is often used for a plain mixture, the egg being omitted.

1 tablespoonful vinegar to $\frac{1}{2}$ lb. flour.

$\frac{1}{2}$ teaspoonful bicarbonate of soda.

Bicarbonate of ammonia is used commercially by confectioners, but the flavour of cakes made with it is apt to be unpleasant.

Classification of Cake Mixtures. According to the ingredients used, their character and method of combination with other ingredients, they may be for convenience grouped as—

1. Those in which fat is *one* of the principal ingredients, the proportion varying with the type and richness of the mixture. The fat may be added by three different methods—

(*a*) By rubbing it into the flour when a comparatively small proportion of fat to flour is used, as in scone and other simple mixtures.

(*b*) By creaming the fat with the sugar. By this method a larger proportion of fat can be more easily and thoroughly incorporated than by rubbing it into the flour, this method being used for rich fruit and Madeira cake mixtures.

(*c*) By melting the fat. In gingerbread and parkin mixtures the fat with the sweetening agents, sugar and the heavy liquid treacle or syrup, are heated together, and by so doing all are more readily and evenly mixed with the other ingredients.

2. Those of a very light and spongy texture, such as sponge cakes, Genoese pastry, and Swiss roll. In these (except Genoese pastry) butter is entirely omitted, and the quantity of sugar exceeds that of the flour, which ingredient is small in quantity in proportion to the number of eggs used, to which these sponge-like mixtures owe their lightness. The eggs are added by :

(*a*) Whisking the whole eggs with the sugar, as for sponge cake and Genoese pastry, which is the most common method.

(*b*) Whisking the whites separately and adding to the whisked yolks and sugar.

(*c*) Making a syrup with the sugar and water, and whisking the eggs with the syrup as in the preparation of some sponge cake mixtures.

3. Yeast cake mixtures, the foundation of which is ordinary dough, to which milk, eggs, butter, and fruit may be added, as for Vienna bread, doughnuts, savarin, Yorkshire teacakes, etc.

4. Those in which whisked white of egg and a large proportion of sugar are the characteristic ingredients, yolks of eggs are omitted and flour used in a very small quantity. Such include meringues, coco-nut pyramids, and macaroons.

5. Cakes for which choux pastry is used as a foundation, e.g. éclairs.

6. Biscuits which are characterized by their dryness and crispness,

and by the absence of, or very small quantity of butter except in the fancy sweet, or wine variety.

AVERAGE PROPORTIONS OF CHIEF INGREDIENTS IN TYPICAL CAKE MIXTURES

NOTE. Quantities in ounces except when otherwise specified.

Ingredient.	Scone Mixtures.	Plain Mixtures for small and large Cakes.	Richer.	Very Rich.	Ginger-bread.	Short-bread.	Sponge Cake.
Flour	8	8	8	8	12	6	$1\frac{1}{2}$
Fats	$1\frac{1}{2}$	3–4	5–6	8	4	4	—
Sugar	$\frac{1}{2}$–1 teasp.	3–4	5–6	8	4	2	2
Eggs	—	1–2	2–3	4–5	2	—	2
Milk	1 gill	1 gill	A little	—	2 tablesp.	—	—
Fruit	None or 1 oz.	2–3	4–8	8–24	—	—	—
Candied Peel	None or $\frac{1}{2}$ oz.	1–$1\frac{1}{2}$	2	3–4	—	—	—
Treacle	—	—	—	—	8	—	—
Baking Powder	4 level teasp.	4 level teasp.	1–2 level teasp.	—	—	—	—

Allow 2 level teaspoonfuls ground ginger to $\frac{1}{2}$ lb. flour.
  ,,   1 dessertspoonful caraway seeds ,,   ,,   ,,
  ,, $2\frac{1}{2}$ to 3 oz. coco-nut   ,,   ,,   ,,
  ,,   2 level teaspoonfuls cream of tartar and 1 level teaspoonful bicar-bonate of soda to $\frac{1}{2}$ lb. flour.
  ,,   1 level teaspoonful bicarbonate of soda to $\frac{1}{2}$ lb. flour for gingerbread.

Necessary Preliminary Preparations. Before the actual mixing is commenced all utensils and requisites should be at hand, ingredients weighed out and prepared, attention given to have the oven in readiness and cake tins lined or greased according to requirements. This is particularly necessary when preparing cake mixtures to which white of egg has been added, or very light spongy mixtures, which must go in to the oven immediately they are mixed.

Preparation of Cake Tins. For plain mixtures the tins need only be greased, but for those which are delicate and light in texture, and for rich cakes, they should be lined with paper greased with clarified butter. This prevents discoloration and burning.

(a) *Flat Baking Tins* for rock cakes, scones, and similar mixtures: grease lightly or dredge with flour.

(b) *Small Cake Tins for Light Mixtures.* Grease lightly with clarified butter; they may also be dusted with flour and sugar.

(c) *Sponge-cake Tins.* When using a large tin or mould, tie a double band of paper round the outside to protect the mixture as it rises; the paper should be broad enough to extend 3 to 4 in. above

the top.   Brush over the inside of the tin and the paper with clarified
butter, and coat with the sugar and flour.

Coating for Sponge-cake Tins.   Sieve together an equal quantity
(1 tablespoonful) of castor sugar and of flour.

Put the coating into the greased tin, turning the tin round and
round until it is evenly coated, invert tin and shake it to remove
what does not adhere.   This coating gives a crisp and smooth
appearance to the outside of the sponge-cake.   Small sponge-cake tins
are coated in the same way.

To Line a Round Cake Tin.   For lining use a double thickness of
white kitchen paper, but for a rich cake, which is 3 or 4 hours in
the oven, 3 or 4 thicknesses are necessary.   Cut 2 rounds of paper
the size of the tin and grease with clarified butter, also a double
band of paper 2 or 3 in. broader than the depth of the tin, and an
inch or two longer than its circumference.   Fold over one of its
edges to the depth of 1 in., make a sharp crease, unfold, and grease,
then cut the narrow part up to the crease, the cuts being about 1 in.

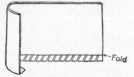

Notched Band of Paper for Lining Tin   Tin Lined with Paper

FIG. 62.   HOW TO LINE A ROUND CAKE TIN

apart.   Line the tin smoothly with the band of paper, let the ends
closely overlap and the notched part lie flat on the bottom of the
tin, then place the greased rounds in the bottom.

For a very rich cake the paper is not greased, and a lining of brown
paper next to the tin prevents it from catching so readily.

To Line a Baking Sheet for Swiss roll, etc.   Use one thickness of
paper, fit it well into the tin by snipping it at the corners and grease.

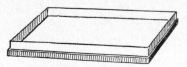

FIG. 63.   SWISS ROLL TIN LINED WITH PAPER

To Clarify Butter for Greasing Tins.   This is to remove the salt.
Heat the butter in a small pan and water until it ceases to bubble,
remove the scum, and strain the liquid butter gently off, leaving the
sediment at the bottom of the pan.

In cake making certain methods of blending and of preparing
ingredients are constantly used, such as—

1. **Creaming Butter and Sugar.**   Put the butter into a basin, and

with a wooden spoon work or beat it until it is of a creamy consistency; for a large quantity use the hand or an electric mixer, and in cold weather it may be necessary to slightly warm the basin or the butter before using it, but it must not be allowed to become "oily"; this makes a cake heavy. Sieve the sugar, add to the butter, and work together until the mixture is white and creamy in appearance and falls lightly from the spoon or the beater. Thorough creaming of the butter and sugar is essential to the lightness of a mixture in which fat is added by this method.

2. **Creaming of Yolks and Sugar.** Work the sieved sugar and the yolks together with a wooden spoon until the mixture becomes pale in colour and light and frothy. When whisking whole eggs and sugar together, whisk the former a little first, by so doing greater bulk is obtained. (Genoese pastry.)

3. **Whipping Whites of Eggs.** For the whites to come up well, the eggs must be perfectly fresh; coolness also contributes largely towards good results. For this reason keep the eggs cool before use, whisk in a cool place if possible, use perfectly clean, dry, and

FIG. 64. WIRE EGG WHISK

cool utensils, and add a pinch of salt to the whites, this slightly lowers the temperature. Separate the white carefully from the yolk, the presence of any of the latter prevents the former from whipping satisfactorily. If one or two whites only are required, put them on a plate, and with a light horizontal and upward movement of the hand, using a round bladed knife, whip them with steady strokes until they are white and stiff enough to adhere to the plate when it is inverted. For a larger quantity use a clean, dry whisk, a rotary whisk or an electric mixer. When sufficiently whisked the whites will adhere to the basin when inverted, or to the whisk without dropping off.

To Whip Cream. Keep cream for whipping cool, and use clean, dry, and cool utensils. For a small quantity use a fork, for a larger amount a whisk. Whip more slowly as the cream begins to thicken and add flavouring and sugar; at that stage it thickens very rapidly, and if over-whipped it loses its smooth texture. If these additions are made at the commencement the cream is apt to curdle. For piping, the cream should be stiff enough to stand up in little points when the whisk is drawn up and out.

General Directions. Successful results in cake making depend upon *accuracy* as to details in method and of measurement of ingredients. This refers particularly to those which are used in small quantities, such as raising agents, and flavourings ; upon the *mixing* and *consistency*, and finally upon the *baking* ; for a cake, like pastry, is often spoiled in the oven.

1. Mixing. (*a*) Thorough blending of fat, when used, with the other ingredients.

(*b*) Careful mixing of baking powder, cream of tartar, and of bicarbonate of soda with the flour and other ingredients.

(*c*) Addition of fruit at the last. If dredged with a little of the weighed flour, it does not stick together, mixes more readily and evenly with the other ingredients, and does not sink to the bottom.

(*d*) When adding flour to a very light mixture fold it in as lightly as possible with a metal spoon, avoid beating a cake after the flour is added, this makes it heavy.

(*e*) Fill cake tins two-thirds full, let the mixture sink down well into the tin ; make a hole with the spoon in the centre of a large cake, this prevents it from rising in a high point in the centre while baking.

2. Consistency of Mixture. (*a*) For scones and small cakes such as rock cakes, which are not baked *in* tins, the mixture should be just stiff enough to handle, then, provided the heat is correct, the cakes should neither lose their shape nor spread much on the tin.

(*b*) A mixture baked in a large tin should not be slack, but just stiff enough to require a slight shake for it to drop from the spoon.

3. Baking. Careful and continuous attention to the oven is very necessary. When baking a rich or very light sponge cake, the oven should, if possible, be used for that purpose only.

(*a*) It is most important that the oven should be at the right heat required for the particular type of cake, when it is put in and that a steady heat should be maintained during the time necessary to allow the mixture to rise and to set, so that it may be cooked through to the centre. A moderate steady heat is the average temperature which most cake mixtures require, but the degree of heat and the time in the oven depend upon the texture and type. If the oven is too hot when the cake goes in, it quickly browns on the surface, a crust forms, and as the mixture expands and rises, which it does rapidly, it breaks through the crust and spoils the appearance of the cake. If carefully baked, the surface of a large cake should be almost flat. Place cakes on the centre of the oven shelf and on a middle shelf, the heat there being more uniform.

For Small Cakes, Scones, etc., which require a short time to cook, rather a hotter oven is required, an upper shelf being suitable.

Richer and Softer Fruit Mixtures. Put these into a moderately quick oven at first, otherwise the fruit sinks to the bottom before the mixture has set, then reduce the heat or remove the cake to a cooler shelf. Cakes which contain a large amount of sugar easily burn. Large ones require careful watching.

(*b*) Time for cooking. For scones and small cakes this varies from 12 or 15 minutes to 20 and 30 minutes.   For cakes made with a foundation of ½ lb. of flour and baked in *one* tin 1¼ to 1½ hours.

For a rich cake a longer time is necessary.   The heat should be very considerably reduced during the last hour in the oven to allow the cake to cook through.

(c) Avoid slamming the oven door, open and close it gently. An inrush of cold air checks the rising, and may cause the mixture, if it is a very light one, to rise unevenly.   Moving or shaking a large cake before it has set will cause it to sink in the centre.   Avoid, if possible, opening the oven door for at least 5 minutes after small cakes have been put in, and for 15 to 20 minutes when richer and larger cakes are being baked.

(d) Test when done.   Small cakes are just firm to the touch when lightly pressed with the finger, and if light in colour they should be evenly coloured on all surfaces.   To test a large cake, heat a bright skewer and run it into the centre of the cake ; if it comes out quite clean and bright the cake is cooked: running a cold knife into a hot cake is apt to make it "sad."   A large rich cake shrinks from the sides of the tin when it is cooked.

(e) Cooling.   Before removing cakes from the tins, let them stand for a minute or two, then turn on to a cake rack or wire sieve so that the air may circulate round and the moisture evaporate; if allowed to cool in a draught, or in a very cold place, cakes are apt to be heavy.

(f) Never store until perfectly cold, then put into air-tight, dry tins.   Wrap a large rich cake in greaseproof paper.   Biscuits lose their crispness if kept in the same tin as cakes.

WHITE BREAD

Proportions for a Quartern Loaf.

3½ lb. flour.	1 teaspoonful castor sugar.
3½ teaspoonfuls salt.	1½ pints tepid water.
1 oz. yeast.	

Method.   1. Sieve the flour and salt into a *warm* basin and place it near the fire to heat it slightly.

2. Cream the yeast and sugar together in a basin, that is, work them together with the back of a spoon until liquid, add the tepid water.   *Tepid water* consists of 1 part of boiling water and 2 parts of cold water.

3. Make a well in the centre of the flour, pour the yeast and water into it, and sprinkle a little flour over the liquid.   This accelerates activity of yeast.

4. Cover the basin with a cloth and put it to rise in a *warm* place, protected from a draught, for about 20 minutes until the surface is covered with bubbles as it should be if the yeast is fresh and fermentation vigorous ; the length of time depends upon the temperature.   This process is termed " setting the sponge."   A

quick method, when using a small quantity of flour, is to omit the process of " setting the sponge." Mix all the flour with the liquid, knead thoroughly to distribute the yeast, form into a loaf, and leave in a warm place until it has risen to double its original size, then bake.

5. Mix in all the flour with the hand, adding more tepid water if necessary, some flours being more absorbent than others, the dough must be firm but elastic.

6. Knead lightly but thoroughly, this is to distribute the yeast evenly throughout the dough. If sufficiently kneaded at this stage the dough should not adhere to the fingers, and the baked loaf will be of uniform texture, full of tiny holes of equal size, and not permeated with large ones.

7. Make two transverse cuts across the surface, *cover* and leave it in a warm place for another $1\frac{1}{2}$ to $1\frac{3}{4}$ hours until well risen, the dough should then be twice its original size. Covering the dough during "sponging" and "rising" prevents evaporation from the surface. If the dough is allowed to get too hot during this stage the surface becomes dry and cracked, and the loaf is close in parts and has dark streaks.

8. Turn on to a floured board and knead "lightly" to redistribute the yeast through the dough; over-kneading expels the gas and makes the dough close; if insufficiently kneaded the loaf will be perforated with large holes irregularly distributed.

9. Divide into two. Fill the bread tins, which should be warm and floured, two-thirds full with the dough, press it well into the corners, and set in a warm place away from draughts to " prove " for 15 minutes. This is necessary to continue the fermentative action which has been retarded by removal from warmth and by kneading. When the dough has risen to the top of the tins, or has increased by one-third of its bulk, it is ready for the oven. If over-proved the bread is sour and coarse in texture, and if greatly over-proved the bubbles of gas expand until they break through the dough and it collapses, a heavy loaf being the result.

NOTE. Dough which is shaped and not baked in tins must be rather stiffer: prove shaped loaves for the same time on warm floured baking sheets. For cottage loaves, shape a small and a large round, place the smaller on the top of the larger, and run the floured handle of a wooden spoon through the centre.

10. Baking. Put bread into a quick oven (about 450° F.) at first, this stops the further growth of the yeast. When well risen and slightly browned, reduce the heat and put on a cooler shelf so that the loaf may cook through to the centre.

The time depends upon the size of the loaf. For a half-quartern loaf allow about 1 hour to $1\frac{1}{4}$ hours, for small loaves and rolls less time in proportion.

11. When sufficiently baked the bread should be light in

weight and well risen, with a crisp and nicely browned crust, and when tapped sharply on the side it should ring with a hollow sound.

12. Remove from the tins at once, place the loaf on its side on a rack for the evaporation of steam.

Brown Bread.

Proportions.

14 oz. wholemeal flour.	½ teaspoonful castor sugar.
14 oz. wheaten flour.	½ pint tepid water, or milk
1¾ teaspoonfuls salt.	and water.
1 oz. yeast.	

Method. Fine, coarse, or medium wholemeal may be used, a lighter loaf is made with half wheaten and half wholemeal flour, and the bread may be made by setting a sponge, or by the following method *without* a sponge.

1. Sieve flour and salt into a warm basin, add the wholemeal : cream the yeast and sugar, add the tepid liquid, pour this into the flour. 2. Mix and knead thoroughly until smooth. 3. Set to rise for 1 hour, then knead slightly on a floured board. 4. Form into two loaves and put into warm floured tins, prove in a warm place for 15 minutes. 5. Bake in a hot oven for about 45 minutes.

"Unfermented" or Baking Powder Bread.

½ lb. flour.	½ teaspoonful salt.
4 level teaspoonfuls baking powder.	Milk or water.

Method. 1. Sieve flour, salt, and baking powder together. 2. Add sufficient liquid to *mix* to a *soft* dough. 3. Handle as quickly as possible, shape neatly and turn on to a floured baking tray. 4. Bake in a hot oven (450° F.) for 30 minutes.

NOTE. This is not as digestible as fermented bread, but it is useful in an emergency, and is a pleasant change to bread raised with yeast.

RICHER DOUGH MIXTURES

Such are Vienna bread, Yorkshire teacakes, buns, savarin, and others; these are enriched with butter, eggs and also fruit, which in a very rich mixture such as savarin or in a bun mixture are beaten into the dough after it has risen. The richer the dough, the softer it is and the longer it takes to rise. Being less tenacious than a plain dough, large bubbles of gas are less likely to collect, and for this reason it requires less kneading. The mixture is worked well with the hand or beaten with a wooden spoon in the basin until it no longer sticks to the hands or basin.

Vienna Bread.

1 lb. flour.
1 oz. butter.
2 level teaspoonfuls salt.
1 egg.

2 level teaspoonfuls castor sugar.
½ oz. compressed yeast.
⅓ pint milk.

Method. 1. Sieve flour and salt into a warm basin and rub in the butter. 2. Cream the yeast and sugar, warm the milk, add the beaten egg and mix with the yeast, pour into the flour, mix and

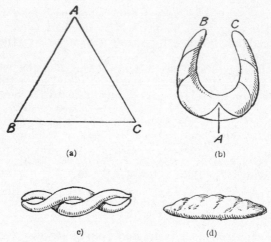

(a)   (b)

c)   (d)

FIG. 65. FANCY SHAPES OF VIENNA BREAD

beat to a smooth dough with the hand, or large wooden spoon, until the dough leaves the sides of the basin clean. 3. Cut dough across the top, cover with a cloth, and set to rise in a warm place for about 1 hour. 4. Turn on to a floured board, knead lightly, and form into fancy shapes, rolls, twists, horseshoes, etc. For a horseshoe, roll out the dough to about ¼ in. in thickness and cut it into the triangular pieces as in Fig 65 (*a*). Take the corners *B* and *C* and roll each piece up so that the point *A* turns over as in Fig. 65 (*b*). 5. Put the bread on a greased and floured tin, and set it to prove in a warm place for 15 minutes. 6. Brush over with beaten egg and bake in a hot oven (450° F.) for about 20 minutes; when sufficiently baked the rolls should be nicely browned and feel light.

YORKSHIRE TEACAKES

12 oz. flour.   1 oz. butter.
½ teaspoonful salt.   1 egg.
½ oz. yeast.   1½ gills of milk.
1 teaspoonful castor sugar.

Method. 1. Sieve flour and salt into a warm basin and heat slightly. 2. Melt the butter in a small pan, add the milk, and warm till tepid. 3. Cream sugar and yeast in a warm basin. 4. Beat the egg, add the tepid milk and mix it with the yeast. 5. Pour this into the flour and beat well with the hand. 6. Turn on to a floured board, divide into two pieces, knead each until smooth into a round and drop into greased tins or rings. 7. Cover and keep in a warm place until the dough has well risen. 8. Bake in a hot oven (450° F.) for about 15 minutes, brush over with milk and sugar immediately upon removal from the oven.

SAVARIN

¼ lb. flour.   1 gill milk.
½ oz. yeast.   4 eggs.
½ level teaspoonful castor sugar.   2 oz. butter.

Method. 1. Grease a border mould and dust with rice flour. 2. Cream yeast and sugar in a warm basin, warm the milk and add to the yeast. 3. Sieve flour into a warm basin, pour the liquid into the centre of the flour, mix well and beat until the mixture no longer sticks to the fingers. 4. Put it in a warm place and leave until it is twice its original size. 5. Beat in the eggs, one at a time, and the butter in small pieces, working all well together. 6. Fill the mould three parts full, leave in a warm place until the mixture has risen to the top. 7. Bake in a hot oven (450° F.) for 15 minutes, reduce to 375° F. for 30 minutes, then turn out on to a sieve or rack.

To dish. Pierce the savarin in several places with a skewer, pour a good syrup over it, fill the centre with preserved fruit and decorate with split blanched almonds.

SCONE MIXTURES

Characteristic. The small amount of fat.
Essential to Lightness. Rapid mixing to a "soft" dough, quick and light handling, and baking in a quick oven.

Afternoon Tea Scones.

½ lb. flour.   1½ oz. butter.
¼ teaspoonful salt.   Milk, about 1 gill.
4 level teaspoonfuls baking powder.

Method. 1. Sieve flour with salt and baking powder. 2. Rub in butter, mix the dry ingredients with sufficient milk to form a soft dough. 3. Turn on to a floured board, work rapidly and very lightly with the hands to free dough from cracks. 4. Roll out to ¼ in. in thickness, stamp into small rounds, and place on a slightly greased baking tin. 5. Brush over the tops with milk to glaze, and bake in a hot oven (450° F.) for 8 to 10 minutes.

Variations

1. *Currant or Sultana Scones.* Same ingredients and proportions with addition of 1 oz. sugar and 2 oz. sultanas or currants. Form dough into a round about ½ in. thick, cut into rounds or flatten slightly, place on a tin, cut across with a sharp floured knife into 8 or 12 divisions, bake for 15 minutes.

2. *Wholemeal Scones.* Use half wheaten flour and half wholemeal. Shape as for currant scones, and bake for 15 to 20 minutes.

3. *Soda Scones.* Same ingredients and proportions as for afternoon tea scones. For the baking powder substitute 2 level teaspoonfuls cream of tartar, and 1 level teaspoonful bicarbonate of soda. If sour milk or buttermilk is used for mixing, reduce the quantity of cream of tartar by half. Stamp out into small rounds or shape into one large round, and cut into 4, and either bake in a quick oven or on a slightly greased girdle till well risen and a light brown on the under side, then turn gently and cook on the other side until the centre is dry.

FRUIT AND MADEIRA CAKE MIXTURES

For these the butter is added by the two methods of—

(a) Rubbing it into the flour for plain mixtures, when the quantity of butter is less than half that of the flour.

(b) Creaming the butter with the sugar for richer mixtures, when the weight of butter is equal to or exceeds half that of flour.

Plain mixtures which are baked in a single tin or in little heaps on a tin should be fairly stiff, richer ones with a larger proportion of butter and eggs should be of the consistency of a thick batter. The quantities given in the recipes are average proportions for typical mixtures, which may be varied by different additions, e.g. sultanas, raisins, currants, candied peel, glacé cherries, ginger, coco-nut, caraway seeds, almonds, spice, ground ginger, lemon rind, and essences.

Plain Fruit Cake (Currant).

8 oz. flour.
3 oz. fat.
4 level teaspoonfuls baking powder.
1 egg.
3 oz. sugar.

2 to 3 oz. currants.
½ level teaspoonful mixed spice (optional).
1 gill milk (about).

Method. 1. Prepare oven and ingredients, grease cake tins.
2. Sieve flour with baking powder and spice, beat egg with the milk.
3. Rub fat into the flour, add sugar and fruit. 4. Mix the dry
ingredients thoroughly with the milk and egg to rather a stiff consistency, the mixture should just fall off the spoon when shaken.
5. Fill the greased tin three parts full. 6. Place on a baking sheet
and bake in a moderately hot oven (375° F.) for about 1¼ to 1½ hours,
reducing the heat (355° F.) after the first 30 minutes. 7. Test if done
and cool as directed.

Some Variations.
   (*a*) Seed cake, for currants substitute ½ oz. caraway seeds.
   (*b*) Coco-nut, 2 to 3 oz. and more sugar.
   (*c*) Rock cakes. Mix to a stiffer consistency and with two forks
place the mixture in rough heaps on a greased baking sheet. Bake
in a hot oven (425° F.) for 12 to 15 minutes. Instead of currants
substitute coco-nut, caraway seeds, sultanas, or lemon rind.

Moderately Rich Mixture (Sultana).

8 oz. flour.	4 oz. fruit.
4 oz. butter.	2 oz. candied peel.
4 oz. sugar.	2 eggs.
2 level teaspoonfuls baking	Grated lemon rind to flavour.
powder.	Milk if necessary.

Method. 1. Line a tin with greased paper (see DIRECTIONS FOR
LINING TIN, page 251), shred candied peel, prepare fruit and sieve
flour and baking powder. 2. Cream the butter and sugar with lemon
rind, beat in each egg separately. 3. Stir in the sieved flour and
baking powder, add fruit, add a little milk if the mixture is too stiff.
4. Put in the lined tin, bake in moderately hot oven (355° F.) for
about 1½ hours, reducing the heat after the mixture has set. 5. Cool
as directed.

Rich Fruit Mixture.

8 oz. flour.	3 large eggs.
6 oz. butter.	1 oz. almonds
6 oz. sugar.	4 oz. currants.
6 oz. sultanas.	2 oz. glacé cherries.
2 oz. peel.	

Method. 1. Cream the butter and sugar, beat in the eggs, each
one separately, add the flour and lastly the fruit and almonds.
2. Put in a tin lined with paper. 3. Bake for about 2½ hours in a
warm oven (325° F.). After the mixture has set, reduce the heat
(300° to 290° F.) and cover with a paper when necessary.

Madeira Cake Mixture.

8 oz. flour.	Grated rind of 1 lemon.
5 oz. butter.	Slice of citron peel.
5 oz. castor sugar.	2 level teaspoonfuls baking powder.
4 eggs.	

Method. 1. Cream the butter with the sugar and lemon rind, add the eggs one at a time, beating them in well, stir in the flour and baking powder very lightly. 2. Put the mixture into the lined tin and bake in a moderate oven (355° F.) for 1½ hours. After the cake has been in the oven for about 20 minutes, and when the surface of the cake is set (not before) lightly place the citron on the top. When cooked, the centre of the cake should feel firm. Test with a heated bright skewer.

Some Variations.

1. Cornflour Cake.

6 oz. cornflour.	3 eggs.
2 oz. flour.	2 level teaspoonfuls baking powder.
6 oz. castor sugar.	Vanilla or lemon essence.
6 oz. butter.	

Follow method for Madeira cake.

2. Chocolate Cake.

4 oz. flour.	1 level teaspoonful baking powder.
3 oz. grated chocolate.	2 eggs.
3 oz. castor sugar.	Vanilla essence.
3 oz. butter.	

Follow method for Madeira cake. Dissolve chocolate slowly in a basin over hot water, add to the creamed sugar and butter.

NOTE. Bake these mixtures in a large tin or in small ones.

3. Victoria Sandwich.

4 oz. butter *or* margarine.	4 oz. flour.
4 oz. castor sugar.	A pinch salt.
2 eggs.	½ level teaspoonful baking powder.
	Flavouring as desired.

Method. 1. Cream fat and sugar thoroughly. 2. Beat in eggs. 3. Sieve flour, salt and baking powder. 4. Mix lightly into creamed mixture. 5. Divide mixture evenly between 2 greased and lined sandwich tins (6–7 in. diameter). 6. Bake in moderately hot oven (350° to 355° F.), until firm to touch, for about 30 minutes. Cool as directed.

SHORTBREAD (*Butter Rubbed in*)

4 oz. flour.	4 oz. butter.
2 oz. rice flour.	2 oz. castor sugar.

Method. 1. Sieve the flour and rice flour and sugar into a basin and rub in the butter, working all together with the hand until the consistency of the mixture is that of short pastry. 2. Press

it into a shortbread mould or form it into a neat round shape with
the hand, place it on a greased tin, and prick the top well. 3. Bake in
warm oven (335° F.) until it begins to colour, and cook until it is
crisp and nicely coloured, the time required is about 1 hour.

The mixture can be rolled out thinly and stamped into small
rounds and baked.

GINGERBREAD (*Fat Melted and Added*)

12 oz. flour.	1 level teaspoonful bicarbonate of soda.
8 oz. treacle.	2½ level teaspoonfuls ground ginger.
4 oz. brown sugar.	½ gill milk.
4 oz. butter.	2 eggs (small).
2 oz. candied peel.	

Method. 1. Sieve flour, ginger, and soda, and shred peel finely
and add to flour. 2. Heat butter, sugar, and treacle in a small
pan gently until dissolved. 3. Add the treacle, well beaten eggs
and milk to the flour and mix thoroughly. 4. Pour the mixture
into a tin lined with a greased paper, and bake in a moderate oven
(350° F.) for about 1½ hours.

NOTE. Almonds and preserved ginger may be added to the
mixture to vary it.

SPONGE CAKES AND SPONGE-LIKE MIXTURES

Sponge cakes.

2 eggs.	Grated lemon rind.
2 oz. castor sugar.	2 oz. flour.

Method. 1. Prepare tins as directed for sponge cakes (see page
251). 2. Dry the flour for a few minutes in a moderate oven, then
sieve three times. 3. Beat the eggs and sugar in a basin over hot
water until frothy, if too hot the mixture becomes sticky and heavy.
4. Fold in the sieved flour with the lemon rind, if used, lightly.
5. Half fill the tins and dredge the tops of the spongecakes with castor
sugar, this to give a crisp, smooth appearance. 6. Bake in a moderate oven (350° to 375° F.) for about 15 to 20 minutes until firm to
the touch and slightly coloured. 7. To remove from the tin, run the
point of a knife round the edge of the tin, lightly tap it on the table
and turn the sponge cakes on to a sieve or cake rack.

NOTE. If a larger quantity of the mixture is made, use a large
tin or mould and prepare as directed, dredge the top with sugar,
and bake in a moderate oven for about 20 to 25 minutes.

Swiss Roll.

3 oz. flour.	1 tablespoonful hot water.
3 oz. castor sugar.	2 to 3 tablespoonfuls warm jam.
3 eggs.	

Method. Line a Swiss roll tin with paper as directed (see LINING CAKE TINS, page 251). A warped tin or an uneven oven shelf causes the mixture to spread unevenly, and not to be of uniform thickness when baked.

1. Sieve flour three times. 2. Whisk eggs and sugar until thick and frothy. 3. Fold in the flour lightly with a metal spoon, adding the hot water, if required, to make the mixture spread more easily. 4. Pour the mixture into the prepared tin, spread it evenly with a knife, if more than ¼ inch thick it does not roll well, if it is thin at the sides the mixture is apt to become crisp and it cracks in rolling. 5. Bake in a hot oven (425° F.) for about 7 to 10 minutes. 6. Turn on to a sugared paper with a damp cloth beneath it, this assists in the rolling. Trim the edges with a sharp knife, spread quickly with the warm jam, hold one end of the paper and roll it up quickly, press the paper round it for a few seconds, this keeps the roll a round shape. 7. Place on a cake rack to cool and dredge with sugar.

NOTE. This is also used in a variety of ways for sweet dishes.

GENOESE PASTRY

This is a richer sponge mixture, a considerable portion of butter being an ingredient ; it is used as a foundation for fancy iced cakes or as a richer mixture for Swiss roll.

4 oz. castor sugar.	3 oz. flour.
4 eggs.	3 oz. butter.

Method. 1. Prepare a shallow baking tin as for a Swiss roll. 2. Warm flour, sieve it three times, and clarify the butter. 3. Whisk the eggs slightly, then add sugar and whisk together over a pan of hot water for about 20 minutes and until the mixture is thick and frothy, but *not* sticky (which is caused by over-heating), then remove and whisk again until cool. Have flour and butter the same temperature. 4. Fold in the butter and flour gradually and quickly, adding them alternately to the eggs. 5. Pour it into the lined tin and bake in a moderate oven (350° F.) for about 30 minutes. Turn on to a sugared paper covering a cake rack and leave to get cold, and use as directed for small iced cakes, etc. If to be rolled, proceed as for Swiss roll.

Foundation Mixture for Iced " Layer Cakes."

8 oz. flour.	4 oz. butter.
8 oz. castor sugar.	4 eggs.
2 level teaspoonfuls baking powder.	

Method. 1. Whisk the eggs and sugar over hot water until thick and frothy, as for Genoese Pastry. 2. Fold in the melted butter and sieved flour and baking powder alternately and very lightly.

3. Pour into two shallow tins lined with buttered paper and bake in a moderate oven (350° F.) for about 30 minutes. 4. When cold, split the cakes in halves, spread each layer with some suitable filling and coat with royal, butter, or chocolate icing.

(See pages 268–71 for filling, decorations, and icings for cakes.)

MERINGUES

This mixture consists of 2 ingredients only, castor sugar and white of egg, in the proportion of 2 oz. of sugar to 1 white of egg.

For filling.

2 whites of eggs.   Whipped cream, sweetened
4 oz. castor sugar.   and flavoured.

New laid eggs do not retain the air as well as those that are two days old.

Essentials to Good Results.

(*a*) Very stiffly-whisked white of egg. Whisking should cease as soon as the white of egg stands up in points; if continued it loses its smoothness and lightness and becomes heavy in texture.

(*b*) Thorough and prolonged drying in a very cool oven; if too warm the surface cracks and the meringues colour too much.

Method. 1. Prepare the baking sheet, which should have a smooth, even surface, brush with oil, or clarified margarine, dredge with flour, then shake off any surplus.

2. Sieve the sugar, put the whites into a moderately large bowl, add a pinch of salt, and whisk to a very stiff froth or whisk in an electric mixer.

3. Mix in the sugar lightly but thoroughly.

4. *To shape the meringues—*

(*a*) Put the mixture into a forcing bag with a large rose or plain forcer and force the mixture out in fancy shapes on to the baking sheet; or—

(*b*) Shape with 2 dessertspoons. With a wet spoon take up a spoonful of the mixture, smooth it with a palette knife, bringing it up into a ridge in the centre and pointed at each end ; scoop it out with the other spoon and place it on the baking sheet, leaving a small space between each meringue.

5. Dredge with castor sugar.

6. Place in a cool oven (290° F.) until dry and crisp and delicately coloured.

7. Remove the meringues, slipping a knife beneath them, and press in the soft centres.

8. Put back in the oven until the inside is dry.

9. Fill the cases with the whipped cream, put two together and decorate the edges (or not) with piped cream.

To colour meringues add a little carmine to the egg mixture.

CHOUX PASTRY (FOR ÉCLAIRS)

This is used for various purposes in confectionery, e.g. for éclairs and also as a savoury preparation, vanilla essence then being omitted.

Éclairs.

2 oz. flour.	Pinch of salt.
1 oz. butter.	Vanilla essence.
1 gill water.	1 egg (large).

Method. 1. Dry and sieve the flour. 2. Put water, butter, and salt in a saucepan, bring to boiling point and draw the pan aside immediately so as not to reduce the liquid. 3. Add all the flour at once, not gradually, and beat in the flour vigorously; return to the heat and cook for a few minutes until the mixture is smooth and comes away from the pan. If over-cooked it becomes greasy and heavy. 4. When cool add the egg and vanilla essence, and beat the mixture well, add a little more yolk if necessary.

To Make and Bake the Éclairs.

1. Put the choux pastry mixture into a forcing bag fitted with a ½ in. plain pipe and half fill the bag.

2. Hold the bag with the nozzle of the pipe obliquely against the (greased) baking sheet, and force out the mixture into strips about 3 in. long: draw the bag slightly back as the mixture is forced out and cut the strip of pastry off close to the pipe.

3. Proceed as before, allowing about 2 in. between each strip for expansion of the pastry.

4. Bake the éclairs in a moderately hot oven (350° to 375° F.) for about 30 minutes, until crisp and lightly coloured.

5. When cold, split open along one side and fill with sweetened and flavoured cream. Ice on the top with chocolate or coffee glacé icing (see CAKE ICINGS, page 268).

BISCUIT MIXTURES

Milk Biscuits.

4 oz. flour.	1 level teaspoonful baking powder.
½ oz. butter.	¼ gill milk.

Method. 1. Sieve the flour and baking powder together, melt the butter in the milk, with it mix the flour to a smooth paste. 2. Turn on to a floured board, roll out very thinly, prick the surface, and stamp out into rounds. 3. Place on a slightly greased tin and bake in a moderate oven (355° F.) for 15 to 20 minutes.

Oatcakes.

½ lb. medium oatmeal.	Pinch of bicarbonate of soda.
Pinch of salt.	Boiling water.
¼ oz. fat (bacon fat, dripping, or lard).	2 oz. fine oatmeal for rolling.

Method. 1. Mix bicarbonate of soda with the medium oatmeal. 2. Add about ¼ gill of boiling water to the fat, when melted stir quickly into the oatmeal. 3. Turn out on to a board dredged with the fine oatmeal, knead well, avoid the edges cracking, rub the fine oatmeal in to give it a white appearance, then roll it out very thinly into a round, rub over with the oatmeal and cut into 6 or 8 pieces. Cook on a heated girdle until the edges begin to curl up, then place in the oven or before the fire until crisp and quite dry.

Sweet Fancy Biscuits (Rich Mixture).

6 oz. flour.	Flavourings : various : essences, lemon rind,
4 oz. butter.	ground ginger and cinnamon, etc.
3 oz. castor sugar.	A few currants add to the variety of biscuit.
Yolk of egg or whole egg.	

Method. 1. Beat the sugar and butter to a cream, add the flour and flavouring and sufficient egg to mix to a stiff paste. 2. Roll out to about ¼ in. in thickness, prick and stamp out into small rounds or into fancy shapes. 3. Bake on a greased tin in a moderate oven (355° F.) for 15 to 20 minutes.

CHAPTER 30

CAKE ICINGS AND DECORATIONS
HOW TO USE THEM

To most housekeepers some knowledge of " how to ice a cake " is a convenience and often a considerable economy, particularly in relation to the large family Xmas and birthday cakes. With average manipulative skill, a cake can be quite quickly iced and smartly ornamented by simple " piping " or with some other decorations, but for the very elaborate piped designs, greater skill and practice and often special appliances are necessary.

Icings most generally used are—Almond paste or icing, glacé, royal, butter, and American icings.

Essential Points in Preparation of Icings.

1. Use dry and scrupulously clean utensils.
2. Always sieve icing sugar. If it is in hard lumps, first crush it, and then rub through a dry and fine nylon sieve.
3. Flavour delicately (see FLAVOURINGS).
4. Avoid strong colouring, which gives a cheap and inferior appearance to iced cakes.
5. The correct consistency of icings both for coating and for piping is important (for details see PARTICULAR ICINGS).
6. The amount of liquid used for mixing varies slightly some sugars being more absorbent of moisture than others.

Flavourings. Use the best essences, which are very concentrated, therefore add gradually and use sparingly, an overpowering flavour in icing is very unpleasant. Replace the cork in the bottle immediately after use, essences are very volatile. Fruit juice, liqueurs, chocolate, and coffee are other general flavourings.

Colourings are in liquid, powder and paste forms. To use a paste, mix a little with a few drops of cold water and strain through muslin.

To obtain shades of violet, use carmine and a few drops of liquid blue ; for shades of apricot and orange, use carmine with yellow ; for shades of brown, dissolve a little chocolate without water and add to the icing.

Decorations. Glacé fruit, angelica, ginger, nuts, almonds, browned and sliced, or pistachio nuts sliced or chopped, coco-nut, fruits dipped in caramel, crystallized violets and rose leaves; and piped designs in royal icing, white or coloured.

Simple decorations and a bold design in piping are, as a rule, the most effective, the colours used should harmonize or contrast well. If the top only of the cake is to be iced, the sides may be

268

brushed over with a little white of egg, sieved apricot or raspberry jam and sprinkle with chopped nuts or coco-nut. If a large fruit cake is iced on the top *only*, a cake frill may be tied round it. A ribbon to secure it gives an attractive finish.

GLACÉ ICING

This is a coating icing and is one of the easiest to make. It should be soft, not brittle, and very glossy.

Proportions.

8 oz. icing sugar.	Flavouring and colouring
½ gill tepid water (about).	suitable for cake.

Method. 1. Sieve the sugar, put it into a small white-lined pan, add the water very gradually, and stir with a wooden spoon over the fire until it is warm and the sugar has dissolved ; over-heating makes glacé icing dull and hard. 2. Add the colouring and flavouring and beat till it is smooth and glossy and will coat the back of the spoon. If too thin, stir in a little more sieved icing sugar, let it dissolve and beat well ; if the consistency is too thick, add a few drops of tepid water.

(*a*) **Coffee Glacé Icing.** For liquid use sufficient strained strong black coffee to flavour, or coffee essence and a little water if necessary.

(*b*) **Orange or Lemon Glacé Icing.** Flavour with the strained juice of an orange or lemon and a few drops of water if required, colour pale yellow.

(*c*) **Chocolate Glacé Icing.**

8 oz. icing sugar.	2 oz. grated unsweetened chocolate.
½ gill water (about).	¼ teaspoonful vanilla essence.

1. Let the chocolate dissolve in the water, then boil for 2 minutes till smooth.

2. When cold, add vanilla and sieved sugar

3. Beat till glossy, add a few drops of *tepid* water if too thick for coating.

NOTE. If over-heated, or if boiled after the sugar is added, chocolate icing is dull and speckled in appearance.

How to Coat Cakes with Glacé Icing.

(*a*) *Large Cakes ;* sandwich and layer cakes. Place the cake on a pastry rack with a dish beneath. If the top only is to be coated, pour sufficient icing rather quickly on the cake, so that it may spread from the centre evenly and smoothly just to the edges. If the whole of the cake is to be iced, pour on sufficient icing to cover both top and sides completely. Should any places be left uncoated, dip a palette knife into warm water and quickly lift up the icing which has run off into the dish and cover the bare places with it.

(b) *Small Cakes.* When icing a quantity, let the pan which contains the icing stand in a basin of warm water, if kept warm the icing will be at the right consistency for using ; should it become too thick, heat very slightly and beat well until smooth again.

Place the small cake on the top of a palette knife, hold it over the pan, and with a spoon pour sufficient icing over it to coat it entirely.

Decorations must be put on while the icing is still soft; if it becomes firm, fix them with a little white of egg.

BUTTER ICING

This is used for coating and for decorating both large and small cakes, and as a filling for "layer cakes." On account of its richness butter icing should be used sparingly.

Proportions.

½ lb. icing sugar.   ¼ lb. fresh butter.
Flavouring and colouring.

If fresh butter is not obtainable, wash salt butter thoroughly and dry it.

Method. Cream the butter, sieve the sugar, and work it gradually into the butter, add the flavouring and colouring and mix well. This icing must be perfectly cold and firm before it is used, particularly in hot weather, and when used for piping.

Mocha Icing. To the creamed butter and sugar add 1 dessertspoonful of coffee essence, using more or less according to taste, or use instant coffee to flavour.

Chocolate Butter Icing. Dissolve 1½ oz. of unsweetened chocolate in 1 tablespoonful of water or milk ; when cool add it with a few drops of vanilla essence to the creamed butter and sugar.

Orange Butter Icing. Grate the rind of an orange very finely, mix it with the butter and proceed in the usual way, colour yellow.

To Use Butter Icing. (a) *As a filling*, spread each layer of cake thinly with the icing. (b) *For coating* spread the icing very thinly over the top and sides. If the cake has a filling of butter icing and it is also used for decoration, it is better then to use the less rich glacé icing for coating. (c) *For piping*, the icing must be rather firmer than the coating or as a filling, and the forcing bag must be handled lightly and quickly before the heat of the hand softens the butter, the icing spreads as it is forced out and the shape of the design is imperfect.

Fillings for Cakes. A large variety of fillings can be made by varying the flavourings and additions, such as chopped glacé fruits and nuts, to the foundation. The following are some of the most generally used foundations, either with or without additional ingredients—

1. Butter icings.
2. Whipped cream, sweetened and flavoured.
3. Lemon curd.
4. Sieved jam.
5. Almond paste.
6. Confectioner's custard alone or with whipped cream.

NOTE. A few cake-crumbs may be added to lemon curd, jam and confectioner's custard to give consistency and greater bulk.

Confectioners' Custard.

½ pint milk.
2 yolks of eggs.
⅜ oz. cornflour.

1 oz. castor sugar.
Vanilla essence.

1. Mix the cornflour with the milk to a smooth paste, stir over the fire until it boils, simmer for 10 minutes, stirring the whole time. 2. Cool slightly, add the yolks of eggs and the sugar, and reheat until the custard thickens, add the vanilla essence. 3. When cool, use as directed, either as a cake filling or as an economical filling for éclairs.

ALMOND ICING (PASTE)

The ground almonds must be absolutely fresh. If stale the paste has a rancid flavour.

Proportions.

1 lb. ground almonds.
¼ lb. icing sugar.
¼ lb. castor sugar.

3 eggs.
Flavourings : lemon juice, brandy, vanilla, ratafia, maraschino.
Colouring if desired.

Mix the sieved sugar with the almonds, add flavourings and sufficient egg to bind ingredients together, and knead well with the hands until smooth. Add the egg gradually as the paste becomes soft with working. If colouring is used, work it well into the paste. Mix either with whole eggs, with yolks only, or with whites only ; the yolks give a deeper colour and richness, while a paste mixed with white of egg only is not so moist and is of a paler colour.

Almond Paste—Boiled.

1 lb. loaf sugar.
¼ pint water.

12 oz. ground almonds.
2 whites of eggs.

Method. 1. Dissolve the sugar in the water slowly, over a low heat. 2. When dissolved, bring to boiling point, skim well and boil to 240° F. 3. Remove from heat and stir briskly until syrup becomes cloudy. 4. When slightly cooled, add the almonds, then the egg whites. 5. Stir well and turn on to a marble slab or an enamel surface. 6. Work with a palette knife until mixture is cool enough to handle. 7. Knead with hands until smooth.

NOTE. If the almond paste is not to be used at once, wrap it in greaseproof paper and keep in an air-tight jar.

AMERICAN ICING

For this icing a saccharometer (a thermometer for sugar boiling) is useful, the results being more certain when it is used.

Proportions.

1 lb. loaf sugar. 2 whites of eggs.
¼ pint water.

Method. 1. Put the sugar and water into a white-lined pan, let the sugar dissolve without boiling, this is necessary to prevent it from crystallizing. 2. Bring to boil, skim well and cover the pan with the lid for 2 minutes, the steam will dissolve any crystals that may have formed on the sides of the pan. 3. Boil to 240° F., or if not using a saccharometer, boil until the syrup, when dropped from the spoon, forms a long thread. While the syrup is boiling, skim it well and occasionally brush down the sides of the pan with a clean brush which has been dipped into cold water, this is also to prevent the formation of crystals on the sides of the pan. 4. Whisk the whites stiffly and pour the syrup gradually on to them. Whisking the whole time, continue to whisk until the icing is of a coating consistency. 5. Pour *immediately* over the cake. The icing thickens very rapidly at the last, and if the whisking is continued only a few seconds too long, it will set in ridges and not smoothly.

Fondant Icing, which is the foundation of many sweetmeats, is, on account of its high gloss, largely used by confectioners for coating, but, as its method of preparation is more elaborate, it is not so suitable for home-made cakes.

ROYAL ICING

This is a hard white icing which is used for coating large fruit cakes and also for " piped " decorations.

Proportions.

2 lb. icing sugar. 1 tablespoonful lemon juice *or*
2 or 3 whites of eggs. 8 drops of acetic acid.

Method. 1. Sieve the sugar into a basin. 2. Whisk the white of egg *very* slightly and add the sugar gradually. The exact amount is determined by the dryness of the sugar and the size of the white. Work them together with a wooden spoon, adding the lemon juice, and beat for 5 to 10 minutes until the icing is quite white and perfectly smooth and glossy. A drop or two of liquid blue improves the colour of white icings. 3. Cover the basin with a damp cloth, which must not touch the icing. The cloth prevents evaporation and the drying and hardening of the surface. 4. Beat up the icing each time before use and after removing any, then cover at once with the damp cloth. 5. Keep and use royal icing if possible in a cool atmosphere.

Consistency of Royal Icing for " coating purposes " should be sufficiently soft for the icing to be easily spread over the surface of the cake with a knife, but too thick to flow over the top and down the sides, unless, as it may be sometimes, thinned down expressly for this purpose, but such a coating is thin and takes a long time to dry.

For " piping consistency " see How to Pipe a Cake with Royal Icing.

FORCING BAGS AND PIPES FOR ICING

For decorating cakes with piped icing, a small bag and small pipes are required. The nozzles of the pipes are made in various designs to give different shapes to the icing as it is forced from the bag and through the pipe. Bags and pipes are sold separately or together in sets with a screw ring, which fits into the neck of the bag, the pipes being screwed into the ring. The bought bags are made of stout white fabric, of nylon, or of some waterproof material, but they can be

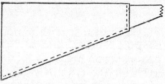

Fig. 66. A Forcing Bag made of Material

easily made at home. Some stout white material is required on account of the pressure upon the bag when using it.

To Make a Forcing Bag. Fold the material selvedge-wise, cut to the shape as in Fig. 66—the neck of the bag should be just large enough for the screw ring to fit tightly into it sew the seam and the raw edges firmly. For a beginner the bag with screw and pipes is the easiest to use, but after a little practice, the paper bag of greaseproof paper is more convenient, more comfortable to handle, and easier to manipulate. When paper bags are used, pipes made without a "collar" are required ; those with a collar are for use with a screw ring.

To Make a Paper Forcing Bag. Cut the paper into pieces of a triangular shape, the length of the base being about 11 in., then twist the paper into the form of a cornet ; cut off a small piece at the narrow end and drop in the pipe to be used. A paper bag should be fairly small. If large it breaks very readily from the pressure used in forcing out the icing. When all the icing in it has been forced through, throw it aside and use another, it cannot be refilled.

To Keep Forcing Bags and Pipes in Good Condition.   After use put bags and pipes to steep separately in tepid water, wash, rinse, and dry thoroughly.   Use a small, fine brush, if necessary, for the pipes. If carelessly handled when removing the icing from the nozzle the pattern of the pipe is injured, and the design will be defective.

An icing syringe with pipes is used by some, but the bag is the most practical.   With the bag and 3 or 4 small, sharply-cut pipes all kinds of simple but effective designs in roses, dots, or scroll

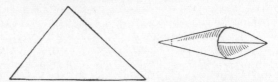

FIG. 67. HOW TO MAKE A PAPER FORCING BAG

work can be carried out, but elaborate traceries, lattice, and similar designs require practice and considerable dexterity.

HOW TO ICE A FRUIT CAKE

(a) To cover it with almond paste.

(b) To " coat " and to " decorate " it with royal icing.

Preparation of Cakes for Icing.   Rasp away any burnt parts and brush off the crumbs carefully.   The smart appearance of an iced cake is spoilt unless the surface is quite flat, the shape symmetrical, and the edges perfectly sharp and even.

1. If the cake is not to be covered first with almond icing, but simply with a coating of royal icing, cut the top level, if necessary, and turn the cake upside down ; the under surface is flat, and the cake is therefore a better shape when coated.

2. When the cake is to be covered with almond paste before the royal icing is used, it is wasteful to cut off a slice from the top to level it, it can be levelled with the almond paste, as directed, or turned upside down.

To Cover with Almond Paste.   For ease in handling the paste, dredge the board lightly with sieved icing sugar or cornflour.

(a) To Cover the Top.   Lay on small pieces of almond paste where required to make the surface level, then cover with a rather thick piece rolled out to the size of the cake.   Make the surface smooth and the edge even and sharp with a wetted knife, the layer of almond paste should be flush with the sides of the cake beneath.

(b) To Cover the Sides.   Roll out a strip of almond paste, the edges must be even and the length and width those of the circumference and depth of the cake ; if the cake is a very large one, it is easier to put the almond paste on in two pieces, but the joins must be smooth. Brush over the sides of the cake with *white of egg* or *apricot marmalade* (2 tablespoonfuls jam, 1 tablespoonful water, heated together and sieved). Press the almond paste firmly on to the sides of the cake, join the ends neatly, and with a knife make the top and bottom edges as smooth and as sharp as possible.

To Coat with Royal Icing. (*a*) If a covering of almond paste has been used, this must be quite dry and firm before the cake is coated with royal icing. (*b*) A revolving cake-stand is a great convenience for icing and decorating a cake ; if this is not available place the cake on the bottom of an inverted cake tin, which should be rather smaller than the cake, and stand the tin on a plate or dish. Fix the cake on the stand or cake tin with a little of the icing.

Quantity of Icing. For a cake about 6 in. in diameter, about 1 lb. of royal icing is required for coating the whole cake, and rather less than $\frac{1}{2}$ lb. for the top only.

To Coat the Top only of a Fruit Cake. Put sufficient icing on the top of the cake to cover it. With a palette knife dipped into cold water spread the icing evenly over it, and make it quite smooth by passing the knife in *one* direction only across the surface and smoothly over the edge.

FIG. 68. PALETTE KNIFE

To Cover the Sides. After covering the top, spread some icing on roughly all round the sides with the knife, then holding it vertically against the side of the cake, sweep the knife round the whole circumference of the cake. This will level the icing and make it smooth, and at the same time remove what is superfluous.

(*a*) Let the icing dry in a cool place.

(*b*) If a second coating is necessary, proceed as before when the first is quite *dry* and *firm*.

To Use Royal Icing for " Piping."

1. The icing must be stiff enough to stand up in little points or for the wooden spoon to remain upright in it, also it *must* be perfectly smooth. The smallest rough particle of dried sugar will block the nozzle of the pipe and cause the icing to be forced out in imperfect shapes. To avoid this it is most necessary to beat the icing well just before and immediately after removing any from the basin, and to keep it well covered with a damp cloth (see DIRECTIONS FOR MAKING ICING).

2. Use a clean forcing bag fitted with the pipe required.

3. Beat up the icing and drop sufficient into the bag to fill it rather

more than one-third full; a very full bag is awkward to manipulate.
Press the icing well down, and twist the open end of the bag from left
to right until the icing is in a compact firm mass within, and just
showing at the nozzle of the pipe.   Test the consistency of the icing
first by forcing a little out; if correct, proceed to use.

4. Hold the bag in a vertical position in the right hand with
the nozzle low down and close to the surface of the cake; with the
pressure of the fingers and thumb force out the icing.   To free the
nozzle from the icing as each small shape is forced out, give the bag
a slight and quick twist with a slightly downward pressure, this
prevents the icing from standing up in small points.

5. As a guide in piping a large design, it is of assistance to prick
or pencil the outline lightly on the surface of the cake.

6. If using several pipes for one design, let those not in immediate
use rest with the nozzle downwards on a damp cloth and keep
covered, this prevents the icing from drying in the nozzles.

CHAPTER 31

PRESERVATION OF FOOD

Methods of Preserving Food. The changes which take place in food that is kept for some time are due to the growth of micro-organisms, the conditions favourable to their propagation being *warmth, moisture,* and the *access of air.* Avoidance of these conditions, exclusion of air, the complete sterilization of the food and of the vessels containing it, and the preservation of food in or by some medium which is not favourable to the growth of bacteria, are the bases of the various methods employed. Such are—

1. The maintenance of a very low temperature as in the " freezing " and " chilling " of food that is transported and long in transit and storage ; such being meat, fish, poultry, eggs, etc., for at this temperature bacterial growth does not develop.

2. The removal of as much moisture as possible. This by the methods of dehydration (dried vegetables and milk), by evaporation (condensed milk), and by smoking, which is also antiseptic in effect.

3. Sterilization and exclusion of air, as in canning and bottling; these principles are the bases of the household processes of making jams, jellies, and pickles, and of bottling fruits and vegetables.

4. The addition and use of certain harmless preservatives, which. are unfavourable to micro-organic growth. Such are salt, brine, sugar, spice, alcohol, vinegar, oil, e g. the preservation of mincemeat, made with animal fat and with uncooked fruits (apple) is due to the preservatives, sugar, spice, lemon juice and alcohol.

5. The use of various chemical preservatives.

Home-preserved Food. The preservation of fruit and vegetables and of other foods was in generations past an important duty of the housewife, and was successfully performed, although the scientific reasons for the methods may not have been fully understood. This custom, however, has fallen largely into disuse ; one reason for this is the rapid development of the commercial industry of " Food Preservation"; the present-day housekeeper benefits in no small degree from this by the large variety of frozen, bottled and canned foods on the market, which are often a great convenience, particularly in a sudden emergency.

Now the only foods preserved in the average household are fruits and vegetables (mainly fruits), which are preserved (*a*) in the form of " jams, jellies, and pickles," and (*b*) by the process of " bottling." In country districts, where there may be an abundance or even a glut of garden produce, a wastage of these foods can be avoided by " drying " such as are suitable, e.g. apples and plums. "Drying" is a very simple process, entailing no expense for preservative ingredients, and the dried produce requires very little room for storage, but space does not permit of more than reference to this process incidentally in the drying of herbs, of which a few of the most common are grown, even in small town gardens, for winter use.

The making of jams and jellies and bottling fruit are very simple processes, and an adequate supply of jams, etc., for use during the year well repays the housewife for a little extra expenditure of time and labour.

Points in Favour of Home-made Jams, etc.

1. They are cheaper than the bought variety of good quality.
2. The ingredients are good as to quality, fresh, and free from adulterations (e.g. glucose in jams and jellies).
3. The flavour is superior, and jams and jellies are more nutritious.
4. In children's dietaries, good jam made with pure cane sugar is of considerable value as a source of energy, and is useful for other reasons.

CANNED FOODS

Now that the use of certain harmful chemicals for the preservation and colouring of canned foods has been prohibited by law, the risk of eating them has been reduced to a minimum. The real disadvantage of and objection to the use of canned food is the partial loss of nutrients and certain vitamins in some, but its consumption, if occasional, and in moderation, is attended with the minimum risk of ill-effects to persons in normal health, provided the food has been properly preserved and care has been observed in using it. The absolutely fresh and sound condition of the food before it is preserved, scrupulous cleanliness in all the processes, the use of lacquer-lined cans to prevent any action of the food acids upon the metal, complete sterilization of the can and its contents, and sealing hermetically are essential to ensure the wholesomeness of the food canned. Select a good and reliable brand. Avoid cheap brands. Examine the can carefully; the slightest "bulge" indicates that gas is being produced by the decomposition of the food inside. Empty the contents of an opened can immediately into a dish, and look for any small pieces of solder in the bottom, which in sealing the can may have dropped inside. Open canned food only shortly before it is required, and avoid as far as possible *having* left-overs of canned animal food.

Store cans of food in a cool place.

JAMS AND JELLIES

Fruit which is preserved in the form of jams and jellies is sterilized by boiling it with the preservative, sugar ; by the exclusion of air it is protected from the action of micro-organisms (yeasts, moulds and bacteria) during storage.

Pectose. The setting of either jam or jelly is due to the presence in the fruit of a certain body which corresponds to gelatine in substances of animal origin, and which enables fruit or fruit juice when boiled with a solution of sugar, to set. This body termed " pectose " belongs to the carbohydrate group. It is of a gum-like nature, and varies as to kind and quantity in different fruits. It is more abundant in some fruits (plum, gooseberry, apple) than in others (strawberry or peach) and is less in dead ripe fruit than in that which is just under-ripe. Its presence is seen in the gum-like matter which exudes from a baked apple, or is found as a deposit upon a ripe plum.

Pectose which is present in fruit in the unripe stage is insoluble, but as the fruit ripens, this body undergoes a change, and the fruit enzymes convert it into "pectin," which is soluble in water, and causes the jam or jelly to set when cold. Acid is also essential and is the reason for the addition of acid fruit or its juice to certain fruits — such as the strawberry—which otherwise do not set so readily when made into jam.

Fruit. Any kind of fruit is suitable. Jam made with mixed fruit of two or more kinds is often an economy, and the flavour is excellent. To eke out the quantity of a more expensive fruit such as strawberry, raspberry, or black-currant, a small quantity of another less expensive, such as rhubarb, is often added. This is delicate as to flavour, and does not overpower that of the fruit with which it is mixed. Apple is used with blackberry. Dried fruits such as apricots, peaches, and figs, and wild growing fruit and hedgerow berries, crab-apples, whortleberries, blackberries, hips and haws as well as grapes and vegetable marrow, are all used for jam.

Condition of Fruit. It should be perfectly sound and uniformly ripe, firm, dry, and fresh. Fruit for preserving is best if freshly gathered with the early morning sun upon it, and it should be made into jam soon after it is picked, these conditions being only possible when fruit is home-grown. Jam made with unripe fruit neither sets so readily (see PECTOSE), nor is it as full in flavour and colour as that which is just ripe. The flavour of fruit, particularly the soft juicy kinds, if gathered wet or in the rain is not so full, and jam made with it does not keep well. If it is desired to keep the fruit whole in the jam, it should be of uniform ripeness and size.

Preparation of Fruit. It must be clean, and stalks, leaves, and hulls should be removed. The harder kinds, such as plum, gooseberry, etc., may be washed and dried in a cloth. If it is an absolute necessity to wash soft fruit to free it from dust or grit, put it into a colander and gently move it up and down in a basin of water, drain the fruit well and then toss it lightly in a cloth in order to dry it.

Sugar. Pure cane sugar is the best and also the most economical, if crushed it dissolves more readily.   Jam made with inferior sugar is not so good in colour nor in flavour, it does not keep so well and throws up more scum, which is wasteful.   The quantity of sugar varies with the pectin content and acidity of the fruit.

The Average Proportion is ¾ to 1 lb. of sugar to 1 lb. of fruit. Some fruit requires a larger quantity.   If too small a quantity of sugar is used the jam does not keep so well, while too large an amount causes it to crystallize.

The *heating* of sugar before its addition to the fruit lessens the time of cooking slightly, and is an advantage when the colour of the fruit is a consideration.

Water and Fruit Juice.   For soft juicy fruit, water is not necessary, and should not be used, but for those varieties which are harder, rather dry, and have thick skins, such as the apple, gooseberry, cranberry, etc., just a little at the bottom of the preserving

FIG. 69.   PRESERVING PAN

pan—2 pints to about 5 or 6 lb. of fruit—assists in softening it and in extracting the juice before the sugar is added.   The addition of a little juice of another rather more acid fruit not only helps to set the jam, but is often an improvement, as it imparts a pleasantly sharp flavour to a fruit which may be slightly flat in taste otherwise.

When using the fruit juice be careful to allow for an extra quantity of sugar.   1 lb. to each pint of juice.

For strawberries use ½ to ¾ pint red-currant juice to about 6 lb. of fruit.
For cherries   ,,   1 pint of rhubarb or gooseberry juice, or the juice of 3 lemons, to about 6 lb. of fruit.
For black-currants,,   1 pint of rhubarb or gooseberry juice to about 6 lb. of fruit.

To Prepare the Fruit Juice.   If rhubarb is used, it should be young and juicy, cut it into small pieces ; bruise gooseberries or currants and put the fruit into a jar with just sufficient water to moisten the bottom, cover and cook slowly in the oven or in a pan of water over the fire until the juice is extracted.   Strain and use as directed.

The Preserving Pan (or large white-lined saucepan answers the purpose) should be of thick metal to prevent burning, scrupulously clean, dry, and in good condition—a chipped enamel-lined pan is fatal to good results.   A pan of copper or brass destroys some of the

Vitamin C content in jam. Aluminium or stainless steel pans are suitable, or an iron pan lined with thick, hard enamel, but jam burns more readily in it. Use a large wooden spoon—iron spoils the flavour and colour of the fruit. Greasing the pan slightly with *fresh* butter or glycerine tends to prevent jam from burning. The preserving pan should not be over full, otherwise stirring is difficult and the jam cannot boil vigorously.

Method of Making Jam.

The fruit is first gently heated in the preserving pan until tender, either alone or with water to extract the juice, the method used for the harder and firmer fruits. The sugar is then added and the whole boiled together.

Essential Points in Boiling Jam.

1. Jam burns readily, therefore the pan may be put on an asbestos mat.

2. The sugar must be completely dissolved before the jam begins to boil, otherwise it may crystallize. It should be stirred while dissolving.

3. The removal of the scum (impurities) is necessary if the jam is to be clear and good in colour. To begin to skim too soon is wasteful, as more rises to the surface. As a rule, scum is removed only when the making of the jam is completed.

4. Stir jam occasionally while it is boiling, and gently if the fruit is to be kept whole.

5. Boil jam briskly and steadily, the whole of the surface should be bubbling. Jam quickly cooked is a better colour and flavour. For this reason it is better not made in a very large quantity—the pan should not be too full to prevent easy stirring.

6. The time is upon an average from 20 to 25 minutes after boiling point has been reached, but it depends upon the method, the kind, and softness of the fruit and the rate of cooking. A watery fruit such as the strawberry often requires a longer time than one that is firm. If boiled too long the jam is sticky, not good in colour, and the flavour of the fruit is spoiled ; if insufficiently boiled the jam quickly ferments.

To Test if Jam is Sufficiently Boiled. Put a little on a cold plate ; if ready to be removed from heat it quickly wrinkles on the surface and round the edges, and sets or "jells" in a minute or two. Thermometer Test. Boil jam to 220° F.

Covering and Tying Down Jam. However carefully the jam may have been prepared, the possibility of it keeping well or not is largely determined by the care taken in covering and tying down the pots. Success depends upon the exclusion of air, which is the means by which micro-organisms productive of moulds and fermentative activity gain access. To prevent this, jam should be removed from the heat immediately it is ready and when very hot, and should be poured at once into the prepared jars. Thus the hot vapour rising thickly from the surface of the jam will prevent the cold air from gaining access to it, and if the jars are covered and tied down immediately as directed the risk of "spoiling" is reduced to a minimum. To ensure these conditions it is essential, before removing the jam from the fire, to have all necessaries ready and close at hand. If the jam is well made, covering it when cold should not affect its keeping qualities. When jam contains whole fruit, e.g. strawberries, it should be allowed to cool before pouring it into the jars, as the fruit will then be held in suspension.

Glass Jam-pots are preferable to stone-ware—the condition of the contents can be examined more easily. The jars must be sound, clean, dry, and heated when the jam is poured in.

Covers should be air-, dust-, and moisture-proof. Various methods of covering and covers are used. Cellophane or ordinary vegetable parchment papers, with the smaller rounds of waxed paper, are reliable and convenient. One side of these covers should be dipped in cold water before use.

To Cover and to Tie Down the Jam-pot. Fill the pot to within $\frac{1}{4}$ in. of the top and remove any drops on the side immediately with a scalded cloth. 2. Place a round of the waxed paper in direct contact with the surface of the jam. 3. Cover the jar with the parchment paper or Cellophane damp side uppermost, and press it tightly and smoothly over the top and round the edge. This is very necessary in covering jams and jellies for, however, minute the folds or creases, air will penetrate. Tie securely with string or affix a rubber band. 4. Affix a label to the side of the jar with the name of jam and the date.

Storage. Store both jams and jellies in a cool, dry, well-ventilated room or cupboard. Dampness and bad ventilation cause both to become mouldy ; warmth and dampness cause fermentation, and much heat makes the sugar crystallize.

JELLIES MADE WITH FRUIT JUICE AND SUGAR BOILED TOGETHER

Most fruits can be used, those of the juicy and soft berry variety, the red-currant, blackberry, black-currant, and loganberry ; and others such as the apple, crab-apple, and green gooseberry, in which pectin is abundant, are particularly suitable.

Fruit jellies, like jam, owe their consistency or setting power to the pectin in the fruit, acid and sugar, and the general rules for making jam and for storing it apply to jellies, which differ from jams in that the juice of the fruit is first extracted and then strained and boiled with the sugar. The aim in making them is that they should be clear and set well.

How to Prepare the Fruit Juice.

1. By slow and gentle cooking of the fruit, which may be slightly bruised first for the more ready extraction of the juice. Put hard fruit, such as apple, cranberries, gooseberries, into a preserving pan, cover with water; soft fruit, with or without water; and cook until the fruit is tender and broken, but *not* in a *pulp*.

2. To strain the juice, pour the fruit into a jelly cloth and let the juice drip through overnight. Avoid pressing by squeezing the juice through the cloth, this makes the jelly cloudy.

3. Measure the strained fruit juice.

Proportion of Fruit Juice and Sugar.

1 pint of fruit juice.　　　　1 lb. of preserving sugar.

Sometimes a little less sugar is possible, but a jelly made with too little sugar is tough in texture ; too much makes it thin.

Method. 1. Put the fruit juice and sugar into the preserving pan, heat gently and stir until the sugar is thoroughly dissolved. 2. Bring to boiling point and boil steadily ; as in jam-making, the shorter the time for boiling the better the colour and the more pronounced the flavour of the fruit. 3. Boil for about 20 to 30 minutes until the jelly sets; test as for jam. 4. Remove scum, pour into clean, dry, warm pots, and tie down immediately.

CHAPTER 32

BOTTLING, PICKLING AND FREEZING

FRUIT bottling is a simple process, but scrupulous cleanliness and minute attention to detail are very essential.

The Underlying Principles are—

(a) Thorough sterilization, that is the destruction of any micro-organisms which may be present in the fruit, water, or jar and which would be productive of moulds and fermentation. This is effected by applying heat gradually until the temperature inside the glass jar is sufficiently high and is maintained long enough to destroy any micro-organisms, the exact degree of heat varying with the different fruits.

(b) The exclusion of air after sterilization by sealing the jar immediately and while still hot, so that no micro-organisms can gain access during cooling or afterwards.

The old-fashioned method of bottling fruit in ordinary glass jars and sealing with fat, paper covers, etc., is by no means unsuccessful, but it is more laborious and there is always the risk of an imperfectly sealed jar. The *Fruit Sterilizing Outfit* economizes both time and labour, and reduces the risk of failure to a minimum. This consists of a deep pan with a stand for holding the patent bottles, or vacuum jars, which is provided with a false bottom to prevent the bottles from coming into immediate contact with the heated pan. In the lid there is a socket in which a thermometer is fixed, so that the bulb is at the same level as the middle of the sides of the bottles. Always test the thermometer before using it. Put it into a pan of cold water with the mercury about 3 in. below the surface, bring the water to boiling point (212° F.) and if the thermometer registers above or below this degree, calculate accordingly when using it. The advantage of a thermometer is that the exact temperature at which the fruit should be removed can be ascertained, and the results are more certain.

General Directions. The methods vary slightly, but the general rules are applicable to all.

1. *The fruit* must be clean, dry, sound, and rather under- than over-ripe, but ripe enough for the flavour of the fruit to be fully developed ; the skin of over-ripe stone fruit cracks very easily during sterilization, and this spoils its appearance. By grading the fruit as to size and ripeness, space in the bottles is economized, and all pieces of fruit are equally sterilized and alike in appearance. Prepare fruit in the usual way for cooking—use only green gooseberries for bottling Wash the fruit if necessary ; handle soft

284

juicy fruits as little and as gently as possible ; examine raspberries and loganberries for grubs. Peel, core, and halve or quarter apples and pears, and drop into slightly salted water (2 oz. salt per gallon) to prevent discoloration while they are being prepared : rinse the fruit before filling the bottles. For bottling, use only young rhubarb, wipe it and cut it into pieces of equal length. Apricots, peaches, and nectarines, unless small, should be divided, use a stainless steel or silver knife for this, remove the stones, blanch some of the kernels and mix in with the fruit : the halves of fruit should be arranged in the bottle closely and evenly overlapping.

2. Use perfectly clean, wide-necked bottles, free from flaws and cracks.

3. Well fill the bottles (see details under DIFFERENT METHODS). Pack the fruit closely and firmly ; this is to prevent it from rising in the bottles, as it shrinks during sterilization. Care must be taken not to crush the fruit. Fill the bottles with syrup (see page 288).

4. *Heat* the water in the sterilizing utensil *slowly,* so that the fruit is heated gradually. Perfect sterilization depends not only upon the degree of heat but upon the rate at which it is applied. Rapid heating causes the bottles to break, the skin of fruit to crack, and the fruit to collect in a mass and to rise in the bottles.

5. Glass expands when heated, and is also a bad conductor of heat ; if one side of a thick glass bottle is heated it expands before the other part has had sufficient time to get hot and to expand, this inequality of expansion causes the glass to crack. For these reasons bottles must never be exposed to sudden extremes of temperature ; a cold bottle must not come into contact with a hot surface such as an oven shelf, neither must a hot bottle come into contact with a cold surface or be allowed to cool in a strong draught. To protect the bottles in either case, place a piece of wood, cardboard, folded paper or duster beneath.

6. The removal of *one* bottle *at a time* from sterilizer, or oven, and *immediately sealing* while still very hot is most *important* to prevent access of air and of micro-organisms. Neglect in this respect is a frequent cause of failure in bottling.

TO BOTTLE FRUIT—USING STERILIZING OUTFIT WITH VACUUM JARS AND THERMOMETER

Principle of the Patent Bottle or Vacuum Jar. The patent glass jar or vacuum bottle has a rubber band and a glass cap, also a metal screw-down ring or steel clip, which keeps the cap tightly fixed on the bottle and thus when the glass cap is bedded on the rubber band a perfect seal is formed between it and the jar. In the process of sterilization the air in the bottle expands and some is expelled. As the contents cool and the screw is tightened, a partial vacuum inside the bottle is formed, and by the contraction within, and by the atmospheric pressure without, the bottle is hermetically sealed, and the contents will keep indefinitely, as micro-organisms cannot exist in a vacuum. In bottles provided with a steel clip, the spring in the clip allows of the expansion within, and of the escape of some of the air, and as the bottle and its contents cool, the clip or spring is tightened by atmospheric pressure and the jar is sealed.

To Test Soundness of Bottles. Failure when using these bottles is sometimes due to infinitesimally minute defects in bottle or glass cap, the result of imperfect moulding, or in the rubber band, which

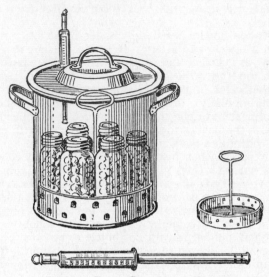

FIG. 70. FRUIT STERILIZING OUTFIT

allow air to enter quickly or very gradually. To prevent the risk of new bottles cracking before using them put them into cold water, bring slowly to boiling point and keep at that temperature for 5 minutes. To test for defects (*a*) run the thumbnail round the neck of the bottle and rim of glass cap ; remove any minute projection with a fine file ; if both surfaces are smooth the lid should not rock when placed on the bottle; (*b*) reject any rubber bands which are not elastic and perfectly smooth at the edges when pulled out.

Sterilizing in Vacuum Jars.

1. Sterilize bottles, caps, and rubber bands in boiling water ; this also makes the latter softer and more pliable.

2. Pack the bottles tightly with fruit, which should not fall out when the bottle is inverted, but avoid crushing. Shake soft juicy

fruit down.   For hard fruits two smooth sticks, blunt at one end, are useful for arranging in layers and for packing closely.

3. Cover the fruit with cold syrup or water, filling the bottles to overflowing.

4. Slip on the rubber ring, the glass cap, and ring.   Screw the latter up, then loosen by giving a half turn back, this to allow for expansion, otherwise the bottle will burst.

5. Place the bottles in the sterilizer and *cover completely* with cold water.   This is very important for uniform sterilization in every part of each bottle.

6. Heat the water slowly to the required temperature in $1\frac{1}{2}$ hours.

7. When the maximum temperature required is reached, keep the water at that for 10 to 30 minutes ; the time depends upon the kind of fruit, its quality and ripeness.

APPROXIMATE TIME AND TEMPERATURE

	Time.	Temperature.
(a) Soft fruits—raspberries, straw-berries, loganberries . . .	$1\frac{1}{2}$ hrs.	165° F. Keep at this for 10 minutes.
(b) Hard fruits, plums, damsons .	$1\frac{1}{2}$ hrs.	180° F. Keep at this for 15 minutes.
(c) Apples (solid pack) and plums (halved)	$1\frac{1}{2}$ hrs.	180° F. Keep at this for 15 minutes.
(d) Pears	$1\frac{1}{2}$ hrs.	190° F. Keep at this for 30 minutes.

8. Remove one bottle at a time from the sterilizer, screw up the ring as tightly and as quickly as possible.   It may require to be tightened 2 or 3 times as the glass contracts during the cooling process, otherwise the air would be drawn in.

9. The next day, when perfectly cold, remove the ring or clip and test if the seal is perfect ; if imperfect when the bottle is lifted by the cap, the latter will become loose.   If the seal is perfect the rings are no longer necessary, and they should not be left on damp, as they rust, and are then difficult to remove.   If the bottles are not perfectly sealed, no vacuum has been formed ; air will enter and the fruit will not keep, and must, therefore, be resterilized. Examine the rubber rings for any defects, place the bottles in the sterilizer and bring the water up to the temperature required.

10. Always store bottled fruit in a cool, dry place and away from the sunlight to prevent fading of colour.   Examine it occasionally : if a bottle is drawing air, minute bubbles are seen running up towards the lid and round it.

11. *To Open Patent Glass Jars.*   Place the bottle in a pan of warm water and heat gradually, the expansion of air inside fills up

the vacuum and loosens the glass cap ; or insert the point of a knife between the glass cap and rubber ring and the inrush of air will release the cap.

NOTE. Bottled stone fruit, such as plums, may require to be cooked slightly before use.

To Bottle Fruit in Syrup. Make a syrup; allow ½ lb. to 1 lb. sugar to every pint of water; boil for 1 minute, strain and when cold use instead of water. Fruits should be bottled in syrup. It improves their flavour and colour, but a disadvantage is that the fruit tends to rise in the bottles.

Substitute for Sterilizing Outfit. Any large pan will answer the purpose, provided the depth is sufficient for the bottles used to be covered with water, or for the water to come to the shoulder of the bottles. For a false bottom, which is absolutely essential, tack some small strips of wood together lattice-fashion to form a rack, or put a folded cloth or some straw at the bottom. For the thermometer an ordinary bath- or dairy-thermometer can be used. Pierce a hole in the cover of the pan, and, to keep the thermometer in place, make a hole in a piece of rubber, cork, or cardboard; this will grip the thermometer and keep it in place when inserted in the lid.

Fruit may be sterilized in a pressure cooker after packing the bottles and filling them with *boiling* syrup. By this process the time is reduced considerably because of the high temperature reached. Generally 5 to 10 minutes is taken to build up the pressure in the cooker and the pressure is maintained for 1 to 15 minutes, according to the fruit used. Instructions given with pressure cookers should be followed.

HOW TO BOTTLE FRUIT IN ANY GLASS JAR

This is done without a thermometer, in an ordinary large utensil with some arrangement for a false bottom, and sealing by the ordinary methods.

Jars or Bottles must be wide-necked, clean, and without cracks or flaws.

Seals (*a*) with parchment covers or with 2 or 3 layers of foolscap or note-paper. To strengthen the covers and to seal more effectively, brush over the top of each cover, as it is put on, with gum, tie down or gum on to the sides of the bottle. When this method of sealing is used, and to avoid any risk of the covers becoming damp and the seal imperfect, the bottles must not be too full, and in moving them care is necessary to prevent the liquid from touching the covers.

(*b*) With the sealing wax mixture (see PICKLES, page 291) cut out some rounds of stout linen, brush over with the hot mixture, cover the jar at once with it while it is hot, press it on well and tie securely.

Method I. In a Pan of Water. 1. Pack the jars tightly with fruit, but only *just* to the *shoulder* of the jar or bottle—fill with hot syrup or water. 2. Put into the pan, add sufficient cold water to come up to the level of the fruit in the bottles. 3. Heat very slowly to simmering point, maintain for required length of time, e.g. soft fruits, 2 minutes; stone fruits (whole), 10 minutes; pears, 40 minutes. 4. Take one bottle at a time from the pan. Cover at once by one of the methods given.

Method II. In the Oven. 1. Fill the bottles *almost* to the top with tightly packed fruit and fill an extra bottle for replenishing. 2. Place in a very moderate oven (250° F.) on a board or piece of cardboard and heat very gradually, so that the heat may penetrate steadily to the centre of the bottles; when the fruit cracks and shrinks the bottles can be removed, but the cracks alone do not denote thorough sterilization, the fruit *must* also shrink. 3. Remove *one* jar *at a time*, fill up with fruit from extra jar, cover the fruit at once with boiling syrup or water, and seal immediately.

NOTE. The patent jars are often used for this method, then the rubber bands (sterilized) must be adjusted when the bottles are removed—the dry heat of the oven would cause them to perish.

FRUIT PULP

This is prepared by boiling fruit *without* the preservative, sugar, to a thick pulp ; most of the water is driven off, and there is consequently a very great reduction in bulk, which is a consideration in storage.

Pulping fruit is on this account an easy and economical method of using surplus fruit from the garden or orchard when, on account of the expense of bottles and of limited storage accommodation, bottling in large quantities may not be possible. Reduction as to bulk varies with the firmness and juiciness of the fruit—about 3 lb. of rhubarb will boil down, in from ¾ to 1 hour, into sufficient pulp to fill a 1 lb. jar.

Method. 1. Prepare the fruit in the usual way as for jam ; place it in the pan with the addition of very little, if any, water ; the amount varies with the firmness and juiciness of the fruit, only sufficient is required at the bottom of the pan to start the cooking of the fruit. 2. Cook slowly, stirring constantly until the fruit is soft. 3. Bring slowly to boiling point, and boil until the fruit is reduced to a *thick, stiff* pulp, stir the whole time, for as the pulp thickens it easily burns : continue boiling until the pulp leaves the bottom of the pan, when the spoon is drawn through it. 4. Have in readiness some dry, hot vacuum glass jars. Fill and cover one jar at a time. 5. The pulp must be *boiling* when put into the jars—fill a jar with the boiling pulp to within about ½ in. of the top, pressing it down well with a sterilized wooden spoon. 6. Cover immediately and proceed in the same manner with the next jar to be filled. Immerse the bottles in a pan of hot water (fitted with a false bottom), bring to boiling point and boil for 5 minutes. Remove, cool and test for seal.

NOTE. The pulp can be made later into jam as required or used for other purposes.

To Make Fruit Pulp into Jam.

1 lb. fruit pulp.	1¼ lb. sugar.
½ pint water.	

Heat the fruit pulp with water, add the sugar, let it dissolve, bring to boiling point and boil for 10 minutes.

NOTE. 1 lb. of fruit pulp produces two 1 lb. pots of jam.

TO BOTTLE VEGETABLES

The bottling of vegetables in the home is not to be recommended, as they may be contaminated by soil organisms, many of which are very resistant to heat. A temperature of 240° F. is necessary to destroy them. If they are not destroyed during sterilization they may produce a toxin, which can cause fatal food poisoning. The effects of the toxin may not be apparent on examining the bottle or its contents.

A reliable pressure cooker is essential if vegetables are to be sterilized by bottling and its management thoroughly understood.

General instructions are given here with a few examples of vegetables particularly suitable for bottling. The majority of vegetables can be bottled, but those that have a short or comparatively short season when they can be purchased fresh, are most often chosen, e.g. asparagus, celery, French beans.

All vegetables must be young, fresh and in excellent condition. They are prepared according to kind, washed and *scalded in boiling water*.

Examples.

Asparagus. Trim, after grading according to thickness; wash thoroughly, scald for 2 to 4 minutes, and dip into cold water.

French beans. Wash, string if required, scald for 2 to 3 minutes and dip in cold water.

Celery. Do not use outer stalks; scrub remainder thoroughly to remove earth and any insects, trim to fit size of container, scald for 5 minutes and dip into cold water.

Vegetables are covered in brine (proportion ½ to 1 oz. salt to 1 quart water).

Vacuum bottles in perfect condition must be used. Vegetables are packed firmly into the bottles and covered with brine. If bottles with screw-bands are used, the screws are given a quarter turn back to permit escape of air, before putting them in the cooker. The bottom of the cooker must be covered with water to a depth of 2 in. and the bottles must stand on a false bottom, e.g. a metal rack. They must not touch each other nor the side of the cooker, to prevent risk of cracking.

After the lid of the cooker has been fixed, the control valve must be left open until the steam issues from it and it must remain open for 8 to 10 minutes to ensure that all air is expelled. The valve is closed and the pressure is brought up to 10 lb. (240° F.) and maintained constantly at that pressure for the required time for sterilizing the vegetables being bottled.

Example.

Asparagus, celery. 30 minutes.
French beans. 35 minutes.

(These times are for bottles of 1 pint capacity; those of 2 pint capacity need an additional 5 minutes.)

When processing is completed, the cooker must cool *very slowly* until pressure is reduced to 0 lb. (212° F.), when the valve is opened and the lid removed. The bottles are taken out one at a time, placed on a wooden surface and the screwband tightened at once.

When cold, the bottles are tested by removing the screwband and lifting by the lid. If they are not sealed, they must be resterilized, or the contents used at once.

Directions for bottling vegetables are included in books relating to the use of pressure cookers and others.

PICKLES

Pickles can be bought so cheap that few housekeepers make them, but when time, opportunity, and material are available it is worth the trouble, for the home-made pickle is superior in every way. The quality of the ingredients is of the best, and there is no risk of ill-effects from the use of deleterious substances to fix the colour and to make the vegetables crisp, which may occur in the manufactured pickles. The dietetic value of pickles is not to be entirely ignored. Eaten in excess they are harmful, but in moderation they are not, and also act as a stimulant to the digestive activity and so indirectly assist digestion.

Pickles consist of vegetables and of fruits which are preserved by boiling in vinegar with spices and other ingredients, and are sour, salt, sweet, and pungent combined.

Directions for Preparation.

Vegetables and fruit for pickling must be perfectly fresh, sound and dry, and *not over-ripe*. If the vegetables are wet the pickle does not keep. To clean the vegetables or fruit, rub them with a clean, damp cloth, then with a dry one ; vegetables to be boiled in vinegar may be washed first, but they must be dried also. Fruits such as cherries, plums, and damsons should not be over-ripe. A pickle made with very ripe fruit is not so bright in colour.

Preservatives. Use fresh spices, good sugar, and the best malt vinegar. Inferior vinegar is crude in flavour and discolours the vegetable. White wine vinegar is more expensive, but is the best for preserving the colour of white vegetables.

Utensils. Use perfectly clean, dry vessels and utensils—an enamel-lined pan or basin, or a stoneware jar placed in a pan of boiling water for boiling the vinegar, and a wooden or silver spoon. Never boil vinegar in a copper vessel, the acid acts upon the metal and the results are dangerous.

Storage. Use wide-necked bottles or stoneware jars with a glazed lining, the former are preferable, it being easier to ascertain the condition of the contents during storage. Unglazed stoneware is not so suitable, being porous, and there is now no risk of lead poisoning from the glaze. The capacity of jars or bottles should be sufficient for a usable quantity, pickles do not keep so well when once opened. Fill pickle jars only to within 1½ in. of the top, so that the vinegar may completely cover the pickle and without the risk of coming into contact with the cover, which if of parchment would become moist and not airproof and if of metal would affect it. Store in a cool, dry cupboard or room. Most pickles require to be kept from 6 to 12 weeks before they are ready. Some improve with keeping, while others, such as red cabbage, deteriorate after a short time.

To Cover Pickles. The aim of all methods of covering, as for jam, is the exclusion of air, and, as vinegar very readily evaporates, *some* methods are for this reason more reliable than others.

1. The patent screw top bottle is the most efficient of all, and is the easiest.

2. The patent tin clip cover is reliable. This should be brushed over on the inner side with melted paraffin wax to prevent the acid from coming into contact with the metal.

3. Large corks or bungs, which must fit the neck of the bottles well. As cork is porous, fit a small round of paper inside the neck of the bottle, this also prevents the pickle from touching the cork, then insert the cork and cover with parchment paper, or coat with paraffin wax or sealing wax.

To Coat Corks with Paraffin Wax. Melt the wax, invert the bottle and dip the cork and the neck of the bottle to the depth of ¼ in. into the wax.

A good Sealing Wax is made by melting together in a jar, placed in a pan of boiling water, ½ lb. of resin, 1 oz. of tallow, and 1 oz. of beeswax. Apply in the same way as paraffin wax.

4. Parchment covers as for jam, using 2 or 3 pieces ; to further strengthen paper, brush over the top of each, as it is put on, with gum.

Causes of Softening of Vegetables. 1. The use of an inferior and crude vinegar. 2. Leaving them for too long a time in the brine. 3. Heating them too long in the vinegar after they have been already cooked.

Brine for Vegetables. For ordinary purposes the brine should be strong enough to float an egg (2 oz. salt to 1 pint of water). For a strong brine necessary for walnuts use 3 oz. salt to 1 pint of water.

Spiced Vinegar for Pickles.

2 pints good malt vinegar.	½ oz. allspice.
½ oz. black peppercorns.	¼ oz. chopped shallots.
½ oz. whole bruised ginger.	2 cloves of garlic.
½ oz. mace.	3 small bay leaves.
½ oz. cinnamon bark.	

Put the spices in a small muslin bag, boil spices and other ingredients for 15 minutes, skim, strain, and use hot or cold as required. Cover pan when boiling and until vinegar is strained.

The shallots, garlic, and bay leaves may be omitted if preferred.

To Dry Herbs for Winter Use. Herbs are at their best just before flowering, then their flavour and perfume are finest. Gather herbs after the dew has dried off them and on a fine day ; if dry when picked they are a better colour. Cut off the roots, cleanse well from grit and soil, divide into small bunches. Dry fairly quickly to preserve their colour and flavour, either in the sun, in a cool oven with the door ajar, or on the rack over the stove. As soon as dry, pick off the leaves, rub them to a powder between the palms of the hands, and then through a fine sieve to remove small stalks. Put the powdered herbs into glass bottles with tight-fitting corks or stoppers, and store in a dry place.

Herb.	Time for picking.
Thyme, lemon thyme, marjoram, mint.	July.
Chervil.	May, June, July.
Parsley.	June, July, August.
Sage.	August and September.
Savory.	July and August.

To Dry Parsley for Garnishing. For this purpose choose freshly gathered large curly parsley, divide it from the larger stalks into small sprigs, wash thoroughly. For convenience, put the parsley into a frying basket, and immerse it in slightly salted boiling water and boil for 2 minutes. Remove from the water, drain well, and place parsley on a sheet of paper. Dry thoroughly, but quickly, in a cool oven or on the rack over the stove. Store in a bottle with a wide mouth and a tightly fitting cork or stopper, and keep in a dry place. When required, soak what is necessary in warm water for 2 or 3 minutes, shake to remove moisture and use for garnish.

Herb Vinegar. Mint, tarragon, basil, thyme, and marjoram are all used, separately or mixed, for flavouring vinegar.

Method. Pick the herbs when young, remove the leaves, wash and dry in a cloth and fill wide-necked bottles about three parts full with the herb ; fill up the bottles with good vinegar, cork tightly and leave for 2 or 3 weeks to extract the flavour of the herb. Then strain off the vinegar into small, clean, dry bottles and cork tightly.

DEEP FREEZING

Deep freeze cabinets are available for domestic use, and fruit and vegetables (and other foods) can be successfully preserved in them.

The food is placed in the deep-freezer, which is at a temperature of between 0° F. and 10° F., in the coldest part—against the side. After 6 to 7 hours it will have frozen, but it will not reach a temperature of 0° F. until 24 hours later.

Low temperatures render micro-organisms and enzymes inactive but do not destroy them; hence when food is removed from the deep-freezer it should be used without delay and never be refrozen.

It is an advantage to make up packages of fruit and vegetables that could be used at one meal.

Containers may be polythene bags, waxed boxes or tubs, or suitable wrapping material may be used. They must be moisture-proof, and liquid must not be able to leak out. No flavour should pass from one food to another. Square or rectangular boxes are more economical in space for stacking in the freezer. All containers should be clearly marked with contents and weight for identification, and the date shown.

When bags are used they can be sealed by twisting and then tied with soft string or a plastic fastener, or the open ends can be folded over twice and heat-sealed with a warm iron.

When packing, as much air as possible should be excluded and when there is liquid in the package, room must be allowed for its expansion on freezing.

Fruits may be frozen sweetened or unsweetened, though the former is usually preferable.

Method I. Place fruit and sugar together in a bowl, stir lightly until sugar begins to dissolve in the juice.

Method II. Cover fruit with a cold syrup. Prepare syrup before-hand by dissolving sugar in water and bringing it to boiling point. Strain if necessary. Cover while cooling to prevent evaporation.

Proportion.

½ pint syrup.   1 lb. fruit

The strength of the syrup is usually determined by the fruit to be frozen. All fruit must be perfectly sound.

Proportions.

Soft fruits.	1 lb. sugar.	1 pint water.
Stone fruits.	½ lb. sugar.	1 pint water.
Sliced apples.	¼ lb. sugar.	1 pint water.

1. Prepare fruit according to kind (removing stems, etc., when necessary) and wash in very cold water. 2. Drain well and mix with sugar or cold syrup. 3. Pack into containers, expelling as much air as possible. 4. Allow room for expansion of syrup. 5. Seal the containers. 6. Freeze quickly. 7. On removal from the deep-freezer, thaw in the unopened container.

During freezing, the ice crystals formed damage the tissue of soft fruits, that have a high water content, and on thawing they become soft and lose their appearance; hence these fruits should not be completely thawed before serving.

Stone fruits, which discolour quickly in the atmosphere, should be thawed quickly.

FREEZING VEGETABLES

Vegetables should be young and in excellent condition. They are prepared as for cooking and immersed in boiling water. This process helps to maintain the colour of the vegetables and to prevent undesirable flavours developing in them.

Asparagus (thick) immersed in boiling water for 4 minutes.
   ,,   (thin)   ,,   ,,   ,,   ,,   ,, 2 ,,
Brussels sprouts   ,,   ,,   ,,   ,,   ,, 3 ,,
Green peas   ,,   ,,   ,,   ,,   ,, 1 to 2 ,,
Carrots   ,,   ,,   ,,   ,,   ,, 5 ,,

It is advisable to scald only small quantities at a time. After scalding, immerse at once in ice-cold water, drain well and pack into containers. Containers must be filled to the top, but when vegetables, e.g. peas, can be packed very closely, a space must be left and as much air excluded as possible. Vegetables should be frozen quickly.

When they are removed from the deep-freezer they should *not* be thawed before cooking. As they have been scalded, cooking-time is less than with fresh vegetables. The vegetables are removed from the package and in the frozen state are put into boiling salted water ($\frac{1}{2}$ pint water to 1 lb. vegetables). Since they are frozen, the temperature is reduced and cooking time, usual a half to one third of the normal time, is estimated from the time the water comes to boiling point again.

ACCELERATED FREEZE-DRYING

This commercial process of freezing foods has the advantage that the foods are dried and a deep-freezer is not necessary for storing them. They can be stored in a cool, dry cupboard.

The principle is that the moisture in the food freezes and then passes to the vapour state *without* going through the liquid stage, i.e. sublimation, thus the food is dried without the ice having melted.

After being quick-frozen, the food is placed in a vacuum oven on expanded metal trays between heating plates. The rate of evaporation is so great that the food remains frozen. The tissues, comprising solids and fluids are immobilized, and at temperatures below freezing point the water is removed by sublimation.

On evaporation, the food is left as an open honeycomb of dry tissue. With the addition of water the microscopic tissues become perfused and the food returns to its original condition. This process is stated to change neither the flavour, texture nor nutritive value of the food.

CHAPTER 33

ARRANGEMENT OF THE FAMILY'S MEALS

THE menu for the formal luncheon or dinner, with many and more or less elaborate dishes, is a different matter from the arrangement of the daily meals for a family of fairly moderate means, which meals include breakfast, the midday meal or luncheon, tea and the evening meal—supper or simple dinner.

It is of much assistance to think out meals, or at least the chief items in them for several days ahead ; this often saves considerable mental fatigue and worry, it economizes time, material, and money, and allows food needed for a midday meal to be delivered on the day it is required in time for it to be *thoroughly* cooked.

The daily inspection of the larder is important, so that surplus food may be utilized if necessary for the day's meals.

As regards the actual provision of food—

1. The meals must provide a well-balanced daily diet, in which the constituents of food necessary to the healthy maintenance of the body are present and in the proper proportions; and the foods selected must be so combined that they supply the required daily nutriment in the most digestible form, and suitable to the season of the year and weather.

2. Variety is very essential. Variety also affords a wider selection of foods, and thereby greater facility and more certainty as to the supply of the necessary nutrients and in the right proportions.

3. Fresh food, animal and vegetable, is very important ; stale and canned foods lack or are deprived of some of the substances vital to the health of the body.

4. Cater with a view to ample sufficiency, to reducing the amount of reheated food to a minimum, particularly for children, and to the possibility of reheating the surplus, if any, by a digestible and appetizing method. Avoid a surplus from those foods and dishes which are less digestible and less palatable when reheated, e.g. vegetables, boiled fruit and meat puddings, batters, etc.

5. The individual requirements of the members of the household, which vary with age, habits, occupation, health, and with any idiosyncrasy of digestion. The meals of young and growing children and of those of adolescent age require special attention. In addition to the necessary materials for body-building—protein and mineral salts, it is most essential that there should be a liberal supply of those foods which produce energy, of which there is an enormous expenditure in childhood and youth. Foods rich in easily-digested fats and in sugars should be well represented in their diet ; fat in suet puddings, in milk, cream, butter, and dripping; sugar in fruits, honey, jam, and syrup. Also the vitamins which are so essential to normal and

healthy growth and which are found in green stuffs, in wholemeal flour, and bread, in unpolished rice, and in fresh fruits and vegetables, milk, eggs, etc.

6. The time of year and the foods in their season, this being when they are at their best and cheapest, must determine the suitability and choice of foods for the different meals.

7. The selection must also be regulated by the capacity of the housekeeping purse, and by the type of household.

NOTE. For other details in relation to the provision of food for the family, see *Manual of Nutrition* (H.M.S.O.).

Breakfast Dishes. 1. Breakfast, being the first meal of the day, should be nourishing and digestible, and for most people it requires to be of a fairly substantial nature, for the interval between breakfast and the next meal is usually long, and a considerable amount of strenuous work, physical and mental, is performed both by adults and by children of school age. With adults the character of this meal is a matter of individual taste and requirement.

2. As far as possible, and particularly if the meal is taken at an early hour, breakfast dishes should not necessitate much time and labour in preparing and cooking them in the morning ; when they can be partially prepared the day previous it is of great assistance.

3. The dishes and adjuncts to the breakfast table must depend upon the type of household, customs and habit, and upon the season. Usually porridge (in winter) or its equivalent, and one hot or cold dish according to the season are provided; jam, marmalade, and toast are the usual adjuncts, but wholemeal bread and fresh fruit, if possible, should find a place in the breakfast menu.

Supper Dishes. As in planning all meals, variety is sometimes a problem, but with forethought and a little resourcefulness many suitable and appetizing supper dishes can be prepared, and with no very great expenditure of time and of labour.

1. As regards the kind of food, the season must be considered, and it must be suited to the circumstances of the family and to its requirements as a whole, or to those of individual members.

2. Supper is often a fairly late meal, for which reason, if it must be fairly substantial, it must also be light and digestible.

3. The preparation of supper dishes, when it is possible, in the earlier part of the day is a convenience as to time and labour, and often economizes fuel.

4. The selection of dishes should be a means of utilizing perishable food left over from a previous meal and which spoils rapidly in hot weather.

CONSTRUCTION OF THE MENU

The courses of a complete dinner comprise the following—Hors d'oeuvre — Soup — Fish — Entrée — Remove — Rôti — Entremets — Dessert—Coffee.

The style of dinner depends upon the social position of the host or hostess, upon the occasion, whether of a formal character or not, upon the number of guests, and upon the season of the year; but the less elaborate type of dinner, with elimination of double courses, is coming more into favour, and for a small informal dinner it is very general to leave out two or more courses.   As in planning simple meals, a luncheon or dinner menu should be well balanced in relation to food values.   When making out a menu, the following are a few points of outstanding importance.

1. Avoid repetition particularly in close sequence in the menu of (a) food, (b) method of preparation, (c) colour, (d) flavour; e.g. it would be unsuitable for green pea *purée* soup to be followed by green peas as the vegetable entremet; for fried fish to precede fried lamb cutlets; for fish with Cardinal sauce to be preceded by tomato soup, or for a game entrée to precede venison in the remove course. Distribute hot and cold dishes evenly on the menu.

2. Variety in colour and in dishing and decoration.

For luncheon menus, the courses are more limited, but the same rules apply to them.

Hors d'oeuvre. This course has become increasingly popular and to the exclusion often of another course in a small dinner.   This consists of appetizers or small morsels of cold food ; oysters, caviare, small mixed salads, sardines, anchovies, olives, thin slices of sausage, etc.

Soup or Potage. There is often a choice of soups. If one only is to be served a clear soup is preferable, particularly in hot weather.

Fish or Poisson. This may be either plainly boiled—then it is accompanied with boiled potatoes—or in the form of a fish entrée, e.g. fish soufflé.

Entrée. This term is applied to all made dishes, which may be hot or cold ; they should be smartly dished and garnished, all the accompaniments forming a part of the dish itself.   If there are two entrées on the menu, the simpler should precede the more elaborate and the hot the cold.

The Remove or Relevé is the substantial dish in the menu, and consists of a joint, which is roast, boiled, or braised ; it is accompanied with potatoes and with one other vegetable.

The " Sorbet " is a half frozen water ice, which in an elaborate and ceremonial formal dinner is served immediately after the Remove.

The Rôti consists of roast poultry or game, accompanied with chipped potatoes and a salad.

Entremets. These include (a) a dressed vegetable, (b) sweet entremets, hot and cold, (c) the savoury.

Dessert consists of various fruits with petits fours or small sweet fancy cakes, etc.

Coffee. Black with cream.

How to Estimate Quantities and Portions for the Family's Meals.
The inexperienced housewife may at first find some difficulty not
only in knowing how to buy economically, but also how to estimate
the weight or quantity of food and the suitable size of portions which
when cooked will be sufficient for the number of persons, or it may
be in purchasing a joint how to choose one which will suffice for
two or more meals as the case may be. In raw foods, meat, fish,
vegetables, and fruit as purchased, and even after preparation and
cooking, there are certain inedible parts which mean *wastage*, and
must be taken into account as regards weight when buying. This
is not the only wastage: there is the loss of weight in cooking, which
is very considerable in relation to meat, which is the most expensive
source of protein, and also in fish.

It is not within the scope of this book to discuss catering in detail or for large numbers, but the following should be taken into
account when buying food and catering for the family—

(a) The approximate loss in the preparation and cooking of meat
and fish.

(b) The quantity or size of an average portion of meat, fish,
vegetables, etc.

(c) The number of portions that a given quantity of the most
common food preparations or dishes when cooked will yield.

The loss or wastage in the preparation and cooking of animal
food (meat and fish) is not uniform, but differs in every instance
according to the variety of meat or fish, the quality, the cut, and the
method of cooking.

In a cut of solid meat, such as rumpsteak, which is of the first
quality, there is practically no waste in preparation, and very little
loss in cooking, and it is therefore easy to estimate the amount
required, but with a joint it is different, this may be of inferior or
of only medium quality, or may have a considerable amount of
bone (e.g. ribs of beef), sinew, gristle, or fat, and more judgment
is required as to the weight, otherwise the dish will be not only far
from economical, but the amount of cooked meat will be insufficient
for the number of portions or yield portions too meagre. For an
adult the average approximate weight of portions is—

Cooked meat from 2 oz. to an average of 3–4 oz. per portion.
Cooked fish from 4–5 oz. (without bone) and 6–8 oz. (with bone) per portion.

The weight of portions and size of helpings must obviously depend upon the age, digestion, health, and occupation, also upon the
weather and season, upon the accompaniments served and the
substantial nature or otherwise of other items on the menu.

The following examples illustrate the difference of weight between the raw and the cooked food, which point the housewife
should bear in mind when marketing. This difference applies also
to vegetables and fruit, in some of which there is much loss of weight

in the preparation before cooking, e.g. green-leaved vegetables, such as spinach and greens, peas, apples, etc.

EXAMPLE I.

1. A family of 4 adults.
2. Rib of beef purchased, weight 5 lb. Percentage of bone high in this joint.

Loss: (a) of weight in bone, gristle, etc. } approximately 45 per cent of
(b) of weight in cooking } weight of uncooked joint.

$\therefore$ Loss of 45 per cent of 5 lb. $= 2\frac{1}{4}$ lb.

Weight of cooked meat $= 5$ lb. $- 2\frac{1}{4}$ lb. $= 2\frac{3}{4}$ lb., or 44 oz.

Yield of cooked meat $= \dfrac{44}{4}$ $= 11$ portions of 4 oz. each.

For a family of 4 adults, 5 lb. of rib of beef will be sufficient to provide for 2 meals, allowing portions of 4 oz. each with a surplus of approximately $\frac{3}{4}$ lb. to be used for some other dish.

EXAMPLE II.

1. Family of 4 adults.
2. Piece of cod purchased, weight $2\frac{1}{2}$ lb.

Loss of weight after preparation and cooking $= 25$ per cent of weight of raw fish.

$\therefore$ Loss of 25 per cent of $2\frac{1}{4}$ lb. $= 10$ oz.

Weight of fish cooked with bone $= 2\frac{1}{2}$ lb. $- 10$ oz. $= 30$ oz.

Yield of fish served with bone $= \dfrac{30}{4}$ $= 4$ portions of $7\frac{1}{2}$ oz. each.

For a family of 4 adults, $2\frac{1}{2}$ lb. of cod will be sufficient for *one* meal, allowing portions of $7\frac{1}{2}$ oz. of fish served with the bone.

QUANTITIES AND NUMBER OF PORTIONS OBTAINABLE

Food.	Quantity.	No. of Portions.
Meat— Baked joint . . .	1 lb. after preparation and cooking	4 portions of 4 oz. 5 portions of 3 oz. 8 portions of 2 oz.
Stewed meat . . .	1 lb.	4
Meat pudding . . .	1 lb. steak, 4 oz. kidney, $\frac{1}{2}$ lb. flour	5–6
Meat pie . . .	1 lb. steak, 4 oz. kidney, $\frac{1}{4}$ lb. flour	5–6

Food.	Quantity.	No. of Portions.
Roast fowl . . .	2½ lb. prepared for oven	4–5
	3½–4 lb. prepared for oven	8–9
Liver and bacon . .	1 lb. liver, 4 oz. bacon	4
Fish		
Boiled fish (cod) . .	2 lb. uncooked	4
		(of 6 oz. with
		bone)
Filleted fish . . .	1 lb. uncooked	3–4
Boiled salmon . . .	2 lb. uncooked	6–7 portions
Whiting	One	1
Oysters	Four	1
Soup		
As one course in a menu		
of several . . .	1 qt. when finished (no surplus)	8
As a substantial item in a		
meal	1 qt. ,, ,,	4–5
Vegetables		
Potatoes . . .	1 lb.	3–4
Green peas (good yield) .	2 lb.	3
Runner beans . .	1 lb.	3–4
Greens (broccoli, etc.) .	2 lb.	4–5
Spinach	2 lb.	4–5
Asparagus . . .	6 heads if large, 8–10 if small	1
Globe artichoke . .	1	1
Jerusalem artichokes .	1 lb.	4
Sweets		
Baked rice pudding . .	1½ pt. milk	4–5
Baked custard . .	1 pt. milk	3–4
Moulds	1 pt. milk	4
Boiled fruit pudding .	½ lb. flour, 1½ lb. fruit	4–5
Fruit pie . . .	6 oz. flour, 1½ lb. fruit	4–5
Steamed suet mixtures .	½ lb. (flour and bread-crumbs)	5–6
Pancakes . . .	½ lb. flour, 1 pt. milk	5–6
Omelet	4 eggs	2
Porridge . . .	5 oz. oatmeal, 1 qt. water	5–6

Cooking Utensils for Small Households of 4 to 6 Persons. The quantity and type of some of the utensils will depend upon the number in family, the space available, and the style of living. For more elaborate cookery, particular utensils and requisites are essential. This list includes only those which are necessary for good plain cookery required by the average household, and for the sink-work and general clearing up which cooking necessitates.

Pans and Kettles—
3 heavy enamel (ground base) sauce-pans (different sizes).
1 set of four aluminium or stainless steel saucepans.

1 lipped saucepan.
1 double saucepan.
1 steamer with graded base to fit different sizes of pans.
1 preserving pan.

Pans and Kettles (contd.)—
1 deep fat fryer with basket.
1 meat double baking tin with grid.
or 1 self-basting tin.
1 large kettle.
1 small kettle.
1 frying pan.
1 omelet pan.
1 pressure cooker (optional).

Small Utensils and Requisites—
1 meat saw.
1 meat chopper.
1 set of skewers.
1 steel or knife sharpener.
1 trussing needle.
1 potato masher.
1 egg slicer.
1 rotary whisk.
1 whisk.
1 funnel.
1 tin opener.
1 corkscrew.
1 pair of scissors.
2 strainers.
1 lemon squeezer.
1 grater.
1 flour dredger.
1 sugar dredger.
1 fish slice.
1 wire spoon.
1 graduated measure 1 pt.—$\frac{1}{4}$ pt.
1 colander.
1 box of round cutters.
1 mincing machine.
1 electric mixer (optional).

Tins —
1 Yorkshire pudding tin.
2 baking sheets for oven use.
1 Swiss roll tin.
2 round cake tins, 6 in. and 7–8 in.
12 patty pans.
12 small cake tins.
1 bun or cake sheet.
2 sandwich tins.
6 dariole tins.
3 or 4 aluminium jelly or pudding
    moulds.
1 cake rack.

Turnery—
1 pastry board.
1 meat or chopping board.
1 rolling pin.

1 pastry brush.
1 egg brush.
3 or 4 wooden spoons.
1 nylon sieve.
1 wire sieve.
1 vegetable presser.
1 bread board.

Knives, etc.—
2 French cook's knives.
1 vegetable knife (stainless).
1 potato knife (stainless).
2 kitchen forks.
2 nickel tablespoons, dessertspoons
    and teaspoons.
Pepper and salt casters and mustard
    pot.

China—
2 or 3 casseroles.
2 flameproof dishes.
2 fireproof glass dishes.
1 set of jugs.
2 large jugs.
Set of pudding basins (six).
2 or 3 mixing basins.
3 plates.
3 dishes.

Brushes—
1 vegetable brush.
1 saucepan brush.
1 mop for washing up.
1 pan scourer.
1 sink brush.
1 scrubbing brush for floors.
1 scrubbing brush for boards.
1 nail brush.
1 long-handled broom.
1 hand brush and dustpan.

Cloths—
2 oven cloths.
1 floor cloth.
2 dish cloths.
2 pudding cloths.
6 kitchen towels.
Dusters.

Miscellaneous—
1 Clock.
1 garbage pail and cover.
1 sink basket.
1 hand bowl for sink.
1 polythene washing up bath.
2 polythene basins.

QUESTIONNAIRE

I

1. WHAT do you understand by "conservation of energy." How can you apply this principle in relation to teaching and practice of cookery?

2. Your own "Domestic workshop" may not be one of the most convenient—by means of a moderate outlay and a little rearrangement, how would you suggest that it might be brought more up to the standard of convenience of a kitchen constructed and arranged upon the modern "labour-saving" lines?

3. When placing heavy and any fixed kitchen equipment in position, what are the chief points to bear in mind?

4. What suggestions would you make to a young housekeeper as to the selection of small equipment?

5. When fixing a gas stove, what points do you consider are of importance as affecting its efficiency?

6. How can you ascertain the amount of (a) gas and (b) electricity consumed for cooking? What economies in the use of boiling rings and oven would you observe to check wasteful consumption of gas or of electricity?

2

1. Why is the keeping of accounts and of records in relation to cookery important as affecting economical household expenditure?

2. In the purchase of food which is stored in larder and storeroom, and in "marketing" generally, what points do you consider important? What are the advantages of personal selection?

3. When is buying in bulk an advantage and advisable and when the reverse?

4. How is the card index system, as applied to the collection of receipts and of culinary methods, an aid to efficiency?

3

1. What are the functions of food in the body? Name the chief constituents of the body and of its food. What are the three most important constituents of food which are necessary for its functions in the body?

2. Why is water as a beverage important in the diet? Which solid foods supply most to the system? What are the chief sources of mineral matter? Why is mineral matter such an essential constituent of food? How can "extractives" and "cellulose" be said to assist in digestion?

3. What foods are the chief sources of vitamins? Why are these bodies so necessary to the growth and health of the child and to the health of the adult? Under what conditions is the activity of vitamins destroyed or lessened?

4. Compare the nutritive and dietetic value of the proteins. In which foods are proteins most abundant?

5. Protein is the most important and at the same time the most expensive constituent of food—what facts in relation to the various foods rich in protein would guide you in supplying the necessary amount of this constituent in the daily diet?

6. In a diet that is frugal from necessity, which one of the three chief constituents of food is likely to bulk too largely and what is the result? Suggest some of the cheaper sources of protein and of fat.

7. How is energy conserved in the body? From what foods, how, and in what form is the reserve energy stored? How is the energy value of a food measured?

8. How does the refuse or waste in a food affect the real cost, and how would you estimate the nutritive and economic value of foods in relation to their money value?

9. The nourishment of the body does not depend upon the amount of food consumed. This is determined by other factors: what are they? What conditions affect the quantity and kind of food required daily by the individual?

10. In the economical planning of meals, what points, based upon the principles of nutrition, are most important?

4

1. What are the micro-organisms which cause the deterioration of food? How may food be contaminated in transit, by storage in larder or storeroom, and in the preparation for the table?

2. What are the conditions favourable to bacterial growth, and why is the destruction of these organisms more difficult than that of moulds and yeasts?

3. What conditions are essential to the growth of yeast cells: how may their activity be destroyed or retarded?

4. What conditions are favourable and unfavourable to the growth of moulds? How are they utilized in relation to the preparation of food?

5. What are the essentials of a good larder? In its management and supervision, how would you guard against deterioration or waste of food?

5

1. What is the difference between a physical and a chemical change? Give some examples of these changes in food when it is cooked.

2. What effect has heat upon proteins generally? How are starch, sugars, and fats affected by heat?

3. What are the objects in view in applying heat to meat and by what methods of cooking are these best obtained?

4. Why is it necessary to hang meat, and what change takes place during the period of hanging? Explain how the nature of the fibre and the cutting or carving of the meat affect its tenderness?

5. How can you account for a sirloin of beef, the wings of poultry, and the legs of feathered game being more tender than shin of beef, legs of poultry, and wings of game?

6. What constituents of meat and conditions affect its flavour? Upon what does the nutritive value of meat depend and what factors determine its digestibility?

6

1. What are the differences between roasting and or grilling?

2. A piece of grilled steak may be tough and hard when cooked; to what errors in the choice, preparation, and cooking of the meat may this be due?

3. What is the difference between boiling and steaming? Why is "boiled meat" a misleading term?

4. For what reasons is stewing an economical method of cooking meat? What parts and cuts are suitable and why do you select these?

5. Explain how you would treat very tough meat which is to be stewed. What are the advantages of using a casserole for stewing purposes?

6. Frying is the quickest method of cooking—why is this possible? Criticize the expression "frying in boiling fat." What is the difference between frying and sautéing?

7. What is the object of coating food which is to be fried? What coatings are used?

8. Why does the composition of a fat affect its suitability for frying purposes? Why are clarified fat and oil best for deep fat frying and butter unsuitable?

9. To ensure success in steaming food, what points claim particular attention?

10. For what reasons is steaming preferable in some circumstances for meat and fish?

7

1. In cookery, accuracy of measurement is important: in relation to what classes of ingredients is this particularly essential?

2. What points would you emphasize in the use of seasonings and flavourings?

3. A dish may be perfectly well cooked and appetizing in flavour, but the reverse in appearance; to what faults in dishing may this be due?

4. What is the object of garnishing? How may a dish be spoiled by the garnish?

5. Supposing you had a meal to cook, how would you set about it and proceed so as to ensure neither waste of time, labour, nor fuel, and punctual and efficient dishing?

8 AND 9

1. What principles underlie the making of stock and of meat soups? What kind of meat is suitable for first stock; what proportions of meat and bone and of water would you use, and how would you make this stock?

2. What ingredients are unsuitable for the stock-pot?

3. Why is soup a useful and important item in the diet? How do clear soups compare with broths and thickened soups as to nutritive value? By what additions can the nutritive value of a soup be increased?

4. What are the general characteristics of a well-made soup?

5. What are the approximate proportions of meat pulse and vegetables to liquid for mutton broth, lentil soup, and tomato soup respectively? What points require particular attention in making mutton broth?

6. What faults in preparation and cooking cause (a) greasiness, (b) lack of brilliancy, (c) poor flavour of a *consommé*?

7. What is a *liaison*, and of what may it consist? For 1 pint of soup, what proportions of ingredients would you use for the various *liaisons*?

8. What are the causes of (a) curdling of a cream soup, (b) greasiness and thin consistency of a soup thickened with brown roux, (c) separation of the sieved part from the liquid and lack of smoothness in a *purée*?

9. What faults in preparation and cooking would affect the colour of a white vegetable soup or of green pea *purée*?

10. Soup is a bulky food—how can you increase the nutriment and decrease the bulk of a broth made for an invalid?

10

1. What are the functions of sauces in relation to the dishes they accompany? What are the characteristics of any well-made sauce?

2. How are sauces thickened? What is roux and what proportions of ingredients are used in making it? How does white

differ from brown roux? What is the cause of brown roux becoming thin and of the fat separating from the flour?

3. What are the proportions of ingredients for (*a*) a flowing sauce, (*b*) a coating sauce?

4. A plain white sauce may have the following faults: (*a*) poorness of colour, (*b*) lumps, (*c*) lack of smoothness, (*d*) a raw and insipid flavour, (*e*) lack of gloss. To what are these faults due?

5. How can the following be avoided: (*a*) Lumpiness when a sauce is reheated, (*b*) a skin forming on the top when it is removed from the fire?

6. How are the following ingredients added to a sauce: butter, cream, eggs, lemon juice, vinegar and essences? Give reasons for the methods of addition.

7. What are essential points in making brown sauce, to avoid greasiness, to obtain a full and pleasant flavour, glossiness, and a good and uniform colour?

8. What is meant by "tammying," and what is the object of tammying sauces?

9. What faults in the preparation of (*a*) apple sauce, (*b*) bread sauce, would cause discoloration, a wrong consistency (stodginess or a too liquid consistency) and lumps?

10. What are the characteristics of a chaudfroid sauce?

II

1. How do fish and meat compare (taking an equal weight of each) as to nutritive and economic value? Why is fish not an economical food?

2. How do white-fleshed, oily and shellfish differ as to nutritive value and digestibility? What are the reasons for these differences? When economy in diet is necessary, what fish would you select for a meal as supplying the most nutriment for the least money?

3. What general points do you look for in choosing fish? How may you be misled as to its freshness?

4. What are the most digestible methods of cooking fish and by what methods is the most nutriment preserved?

5. When cleaning fish, why is it important not to leave it soaking in water? What fish are exceptions to this rule? How would you clean, skin, and fillet a sole?

6. Why is the method of steaming preferable to boiling, and when is it particularly suitable? What is the curd-like substance which is present between the flakes of boiled, steamed, and lightly baked fish, and what does its absence indicate?

7. What are the indications that boiled fish is sufficiently cooked? What difference in method is necessary when boiling (*a*) salmon, (*b*) salt fish, (*c*) mackerel?

8. A dish of fried fillets of fish coated with egg and crumbs may

be sodden and greasy. To what errors in preparation and frying is this due?

What points require particular attention when frying fish which is coated with batter?

9. If whitebait is not crisp and the fish are not separate when cooked, to what faults in preparation and frying may this be due?

10. What are the indications of freshness and of age in lobsters and oysters? What parts of a crab are inedible? How would you dress a crab?

12

1. A joint or cut of meat may be cheap as to price, but what factors determine its real economy?

2. Compare beef, mutton, lamb, and pork as to digestibility and nutritive value.

3. What are the indications that meat is in good condition and of good quality?

4. What are the best cuts of beef, veal, mutton, and lamb, and the best methods of cooking each?

5. When buying the following: (a) a piece of sirloin, (b) ribs of beef, (c) mutton for cutlets, what would guide you in your choice?

6. Why is silverside not so suitable as topside for roasting or baking. Why is rump steak suitable for grilling; and shin of beef for stews and stock?

7. It is sometimes more economical to buy a whole neck of mutton and a large leg of mutton; under what conditions would you do this and how would you divide and cook the joints?

8. What parts of beef, mutton, lamb and veal would you choose for stewing and braising?

9. In the use of internal parts, what points in preparation and cooking are essential to ensure wholesomeness and digestibility?

10. How can you test the freshness of a gammon of bacon or of a ham? What are the best cuts of bacon for broiling and boiling?

11. How can you distinguish pork which is in good condition and young? What joints are most suitable for roasting and boiling?

13

1. What are the principles upon which the cookery of meat is based?

Why is the temperature of the flesh in the middle of a roast leg of mutton or of a boiled joint, while they are cooking, much below that of the oven or of the surrounding water?

2. To obtain good results in oven roasting, what points are of importance?

How would you prepare a frozen or chilled leg of mutton for the oven? What is the difference in the method of cooking frozen and home-killed meat?

3. What is "roasting in a stewpan"? What is the advantage of this method and when is it most suitable?

4. For what reasons do veal, lamb, and pork require a longer time for cooking than beef and mutton?

5. How would you prepare and grill kidneys? What are the usual accompaniments to grilled meat?

6. Why is boning a joint an economy? In the process of boning a joint, what points require particular care?

7. What is the difference in methods of boiling fresh and salt meat? A piece of bacon may be hard, salt, and strong in flavour, to what faults in preparation and boiling may this be due?

8. What are the average proportions of meat and of liquid for a brown stew? What faults in the preparation and cooking of a brown stew would cause (a) greasiness, (b) too dark or too pale a colour, (c) an insipid or burnt flavour, (d) thin consistency of sauce?

9. What cut of mutton would you choose for cutlets? If the mutton is large, how would you trim the cutlets to avoid unnecessary waste? What points require care in frying cutlets?

10. Why is braising a very savoury method of cooking? What is a "mirepoix"? What are the characteristics of a well-prepared dish of braised meat?

14

1. Why is the preparation of reheated food an important branch of cookery in relation to (a) the economy of food, (b) the health of the household?

2. What is the essential point in the preparation of food which has been already cooked?

What other points are important in preparing a palatable and digestible réchauffé of meat or of fish?

3. Suggest several ways of reheating the remains of a cold joint of mutton, and of utilizing scraps of poultry, game, rabbit, ham, etc.

4. How would you make a curry, using cooked veal? What faults would cause a hash or mince of meat to be greasy, insipid in flavour, and the meat to be tough?

5. What is a panada, how is it made, and what are its uses? What proportion of panada is required for making croquettes and cutlets of (a) cold meat, (b) cold fish? Of what consistency and texture should such preparations be?

15

1. How does poultry compare with meat as to nutriment and digestibility?

2. What are the indications that poultry is young and in good condition? How can you distinguish that which has been in cold storage during transit?

3. In drawing and trussing a fowl, what points require special attention? Of what do the giblets consist; how are they prepared and for what purposes are they used?

4. Which kind of fowl is the most suitable for (*a*) roasting, (*b*) boiling?

5. How would you prepare an old fowl or turkey that is intended for roasting? For what purposes is old and foreign poultry most suitable?

6. How would you bone a fowl for a galantine? What are essential points to success in boning poultry?

7. In selecting rabbits, what points in relation to freshness and age would you look for? How does the flesh of the wild rabbit compare with that of the tame variety?

8. Why are soaking and blanching of rabbits preparatory to cooking so necessary? In what constituent is the flesh of rabbit deficient and how is this deficiency supplied in cooking?

16

1. How does feathered game compare with butcher's meat and poultry as to nutritive value and digestibility?

2. Why is it more difficult to judge the age and condition of game than of poultry? In selecting game, what are the indications of age and of good condition?

3. How may foreign game be distinguished from English? Why is game hung longer than poultry? Is there any exception?

4. What are the general accompaniments to game? How would you prepare, cook, and serve a roast pheasant?

5. How would you skin and paunch a hare?

17 AND 18

1. What is the value of vegetables in the diet? Why is vegetable food not as digestible as some other foods? How is the deficiency of fat supplied?

2. What changes do vegetables undergo in cooking? What is the aim in cooking them and what are the most frequent faults in boiling vegetables?

3. For what reason should soda not be used in boiling green vegetables? How can the colour of white and of green vegetables be preserved? Vegetables, as a class, are a bulky food—in preparation and cooking what tends to increase their bulkiness?

4. What are the most economical methods of cooking potatoes, and why?

5. Compare the food value of pulse with vegetables generally. In what constituent is it particularly rich?

6. For what reasons are pulse vegetables not very readily digested? In what constituent are pulse foods deficient and what are important points in cooking this type of food?

7. Why are salads of importance in the diet? How may salads be an economical method of utilizing "left-overs"?

8. What are essential points in the preparation of a green salad? What are the characteristics of a well-made salad dressing?

9. Why is fruit of so much value in the diet? What are the advantages derived from cooking fruit? For what reason is ripe, raw fruit of importance in the dietary? Which fruits are particularly wholesome for children, and why?

19

1. What constituent of flour renders it possible to make a paste or dough with flour mixed with water? Why is household flour more nutritive than fine pastry flour?

2. Explain the principles that underlie the methods of making pastry? What are the methods of incorporating the fat with the flour?

3. In the preparation and rolling out of pastry, what is the aim, and what points require particular attention as affecting its lightness and even rising, when baked?

4. What is the approximate quantity of water required to mix flour into a paste? Why and when may the amount vary? What is the result of making pastry too moist or too dry?

5. Which is the best position in the oven for baking pastry? After pastry is removed from the oven what may cause it to become heavy?

6. What points in making short crust and in the manipulation of the pastry when using it to cover a fruit pie, are important?

7. How is the fat incorporated with the flour in making (a) flaky pastry, (b) rough puff pastry? To what is the lightness and flakiness of these pastries largely due? Explain the method of rolling out rough puff pastry.

8. Why are suet crust and suet puddings very suitable for growing children? What careless faults in preparation and cooking would render suet crust indigestible?

9. Why is the proportion of fat to flour less for hot-water crust than for other pastries? In making hot-water or raised pie crust what is essential to good results? To what faults are brittleness or a too soft consistency due?

10. How many times is puff pastry rolled and folded? Why is this necessary, and for what reasons are the edges left unsealed after the pastry is folded?

20

1. What factors in the preparation and cooking of a batter determine its lightness? How is smoothness obtained?

2. What principles underlie the making of batter mixtures?

3. What are the proportions of flour to liquid for (a) pancakes, (b) steamed batter, (c) pancake batter used for coating purposes?

4. Should a steamed batter be heavy, to what may this fault be due?

5. To which points in preparation and frying would lack of attention make pancakes heavy and tough?

6. What are the characteristics of a coating batter? For what reasons are oil and white of egg used? Give ingredients and proportions for making Kromeski batter.

7. In frying fritters, what points require particular attention? Are there any differences of method in frying food: (a) coated with batter, (b) coated with egg and crumbs?

21

1. Which constituent of the carbohydrate group is present in milk, and what is its peculiar property? Why is milk a bulky food?

2. Upon what constituent does the richness of milk depend, and what is the average percentage? What changes take place when milk enters the stomach, and how is its digestibility determined?

3. Compare the nutritive value of whole new milk with that of skim milk and of separated milk.

4. What ingredient should be added to milk puddings made with skim milk? Why is this necessary, and in what proportion should it be used?

5. What changes take place when milk is boiled?

6. When boiling or heating milk, and in cooking farinaceous mixtures made with milk, what precautions would you take to avoid burning? How can you lessen the risk of souring of milk and of its contamination after delivery and before use?

7. How is junket made, and to what is its formation due? What are its component parts and of what do these consist? Why does boiled milk not make a firm junket?

8. How is curdling of milk brought about: (a) naturally, (b) by artificial agents? How does "curdling" differ from "clotting?"

9. What is of most importance in making any kind of milk pudding? How long is required for cooking (a) whole grain—rice, (b) small grain—semolina, (c) powdered products—cornflour?

10. How can the nutritive value of milk puddings and of shapes or moulds be increased, and when are these ingredients added? Why is the proportion of starchy matter greater for shapes and moulds than for baked milk puddings?

11. What is the object of sterilizing milk? How is the process carried out, and what changes take place during sterilization? How does pasteurization differ from sterilization? Why should orange juice be given to infants fed upon pasteurized milk?

22

1. How does the yolk differ from the white of an egg in relation to its constituents and food value?

2. What are the indications of freshness of eggs? Exclusive of cold storage, how are eggs preserved and upon what principle are the methods based?

3. What principles underlie (a) the methods of cooking eggs, (b) their utilization for various purposes in cooking?

4. Upon what principle is the use of whisked white of egg based? How is its expansion of bulk during whisking and cooking brought about?

5. What are the causes of boiled eggs cooking unevenly, and of the yolk of a hard-boiled egg setting towards one side of the shell? Why should vinegar or lemon juice be added to the water in which an egg is poached?

6. How would you cook an egg for it to be what is termed "lightly boiled," or sufficiently hard to be used for sandwiches or for savoury eggs, etc.?

7. What determines the consistency and texture of a custard? Why is fresh milk preferable to boiled or skim milk for custards?

8. What are the proportions of egg and milk for baked, boiled, and steamed custards, and why do the proportions vary? Should a boiled custard show a tendency to curdle, how may this be checked, and if only slightly curdled, how may the smoothness of texture be restored?

9. What faults in preparation and cooking would cause a baked or steamed custard to be pitted with holes or curdled?

23

1. Why is an omelet a useful emergency dish? Upon what does the success of an omelet mainly depend?

2. How would you prove or season an omelet pan; why and when is this necessary?

3. What is the reason for the addition of water, cream, or milk to the beaten eggs? What is the general proportion of butter to each egg? What faults in frying render an omelet tough?

4. How does a sweet omelet differ from an omelet soufflé? How does the cooking of a puffed omelet differ from that of the ordinary savoury omelet and how does it differ as to texture?

5. What is the principle which underlies the method of making soufflés? What are the component parts of a soufflé?

6. Which ingredient of the panada is less in a baked than in a steamed soufflé? To ensure lightness of texture what points require particular attention in the preparation and cooking of soufflés?

7. Why should a soufflé case or dish be only half or three parts filled with the mixture? What is the object of tying a band of paper round the tin containing a soufflé mixture, which is to be steamed? What may cause a steamed soufflé to stick when it is turned out?

8. What is the indication that a soufflé is sufficiently cooked? What directions would you give for turning out a light steamed soufflé? What are the causes of a steamed or baked soufflé collapsing and shrinking during cooking or immediately upon removal from steamer or oven?

24

1. What is the average composition of cheese? How do these constituents vary in hard and soft cheeses? Upon which constituent does the richness of a cheese depend? How are certain flavours in cheese produced?

2. What is the value, nutritive and economic, of cheese in relation to meat? As an economical substitute for meat, what kind of cheese would you choose?

3. Why is cheese not a readily digested food? How does the method of manufacture affect the nutritive value and digestibility of cheese?

4. What are the various purposes for which cheese is used in cookery? In the preparation and cooking of cheese dishes what would you do to facilitate their digestion?

5. What points require care when mixing and baking cheese pastry?

25

1. What is the dietetic value of jellies? Which is the more nutritive, a cleared or an uncleared jelly, and why? What should be the consistency of any jelly?

2. From what substances are the following stiffening agents prepared: gelatine, isinglass, agar-agar? How do they vary as to degree of stiffening power?

3. What are the average proportions of gelatine and of white of egg necessary for making one quart of cleared jelly? What is the result of using too large a proportion of either gelatine or white of egg?

4. What is the principle involved in the clearing of a jelly?

5. What faults in preparation of ingredients and in boiling and straining a jelly would cause it to be cloudy?

6. What is the effect of moulding a cleared jelly when still hot? When lining a mould with jelly, what would cause the coating to be of unequal thickness, bubbles to appear in the jelly, and the decorations to be disturbed?

7. For what reason should aspic jelly stand longer than lemon jelly after it has boiled up?

8. What proportion of gelatine is required to set a cream mixture —how may this proportion vary? What precautions are necessary when dissolving gelatine and adding it to any mixture?

9. What faults in preparing a cream would cause (a) roughness of texture, (b) fruit, if used, to sink in the mould, (c) small specks or threads to appear throughout the mixture? What are essential points in moulding a cream?

10. How would you unmould a jelly or cream?

26

1. What are the chief constituents of tea and coffee and the characteristic properties of each?

2. How do tea and coffee respectively affect the digestive and nervous systems?

3. What is an infusion? What is the aim in making tea and coffee?

4. What effect has the hardness or softness of water used for making tea and coffee? Why is it essential to use freshly drawn water and to make tea and coffee with water as soon as it boils?

5. By what errors in making and how may the characteristic properties of the constituents of tea and coffee be affected?

6. How does cocoa differ in composition and as to dietetic and nutritive value from tea and coffee? Why should boiling cocoa improve the flavour and texture of this beverage?

27

1. What principles underlie the process of making beef tea? How are the digestibility and nutritive value of beef tea affected by the kind and quality of the meat used and the temperature at which the beef tea is made? Beef tea is a stimulant rather than a nutrient. Why is this?

2. What factors determine the choice of food for invalids or convalescents?

28

1. Why is the knowledge of food values of particular importance in relation to meatless cookery?

2. What foodstuffs substituted for meat can most efficiently supply the body-building constituent of meat?

3. In the cooking and serving of meatless dishes, what are the most general faults?

4. To avoid these faults, how would you prepare and cook the following: vegetables, pulse, nuts, and cereals?

5. Suppose that a meatless dish is to consist either of (a) pulse, (b) nuts, or (c) some cereal, and is to be the substantial item in a simple meal of two courses: (a) what ingredients would you combine respectively with these foodstuffs, (b) what accompaniments would you serve with each dish, (c) what pudding or sweet would you suggest as being suitable to follow the dish in the first course, in order to provide a well-balanced meal in each case?

29

1. Explain the principles upon which the lightness of bread and of cake mixtures is based? What are the various raising agents used?

2. What is meant by "fermentation?" What conditions favour, delay, or destroy the fermentative action of yeast?

3. Describe the growth of yeast and its fermentative action upon flour. What proportion of yeast is used to raise a quartern loaf of bread?

4. Of what is baking powder composed, and what are the proportions of its ingredients? How is the activity of baking powder brought about? How does cream of tartar differ from tartaric acid? What is the advantage to be gained from using the ingredients of baking powder separately and not blended ready for use?

5. How would you proceed when adding (a) flour to a light mixture, (b) baking powder and fruit to a fruit cake, (c) whipped white of egg? What conditions are necessary to obtain the maximum bulk when whipping white of egg?

6. What should be the consistency relatively of mixtures for the following: (a) scones, (b) rock cakes, (c) a plain currant cake, (d) a rich fruit-cake? What is the result of making a mixture which is to be baked in a tin too soft or too dry?

7. What are the differences in oven temperatures when baking (a) rock cakes, (b) a plain sultana cake, (c) a rich Christmas cake? How would you manage the oven to maintain or to regulate the heat necessary throughout the baking?

8. What would cause a cake mixture (a) not to rise and to be close and heavy, (b) to fall in the centre?

9. What are essential points in making and baking meringues?

10. Should sponge cakes be close and heavy when baked, to what faults in preparation and cooking is this due?

11. What faults in preparation and cooking will cause choux pastry to be heavy?

30

1. What points are common to and important in the preparation of cake icings generally?

2. What are the characteristics of glacé icing? How would you prepare it and what faults would render it brittle and dull?

3. What should be the consistency of glacé icing, and how would you coat a large cake and small cakes with this icing?

4. What proportion of chocolate to sugar is required for chocolate icing? What faults in preparation render it dull, speckled, and rough in appearance? Should this icing be too thick or too thin, how would you correct this?

5. For what purpose is butter icing used? What are the proportions of butter and of sugar, and how is this icing prepared?

6. What are the ingredients and their proportions for royal icing? How can you test that the icing is of the right consistency for piping? What faults in preparation will affect its smoothness and glossiness?

7. When covering a cake with (a) a layer of almond icing, (b) a coating of royal icing, what points require special attention in order to keep the cake a good shape and for the outer coating to be smooth and uniform as to thickness?

8. To obtain satisfactory results when piping, what precautions would you take as regards (a) the bag and forcing pipes, (b) attention to the icing while using it?

31

1. What are the objections to canned foods? What precautions should be taken as to their use?

2. What principles underlie the methods of preserving food? What are these methods?

3. What is the body in fruit which enables the latter when boiled with sugar to set in a jelly? What is the result of making jam with fruit, which is either under- or over-ripe? Why is the addition of the juice of some acid fruit an improvement to and useful in making some kinds of jam?

4. For what reasons is cane sugar preferable for making jams and jellies? What are the average proportions of sugar and of water, if any, to each pound of fruit for making jam?

5. What are the reasons of the following faults in jam: (a) not setting, (b) consistency too liquid, (c) over-stiffness, (d) poorness of flavour and of colour, (e) cloudiness, (f) crystallization.

6. To ensure that jams and jellies neither ferment nor become mouldy when stored, what precautions are necessary when putting them into pots and covering?

7. What are the proportions of fruit juice and sugar necessary for making fruit jellies? What is the method of obtaining the

juice from the fruit? What faults in straining the juice and in boiling it with the sugar would render a jelly cloudy?

32

1. What are the principles which underlie the methods of bottling fruit and vegetables?

2. What should be the condition of fruit used for bottling? Why are the following general points in bottling fruit of importance: (a) packing the fruit closely, (b) covering the fruit completely with cold syrup or water, (c) heating the bottles and their contents gradually?

3. What is the principle upon which the patent or vacuum jars are constructed? How can you test for defects in the jars, glass covers, and rubber rings, and why is the detection of flaws important? Why should the metal ring not be screwed on too tightly while the sterilizing process is proceeding?

4. What are the causes of (a) the fruit rising in the bottles, (b) the fruit becoming "mushy," and (c) the skin of some fruits cracking badly? What is the general indication that the fruit is sufficiently sterilized?

5. "Glass is a bad conductor of heat." How does this property of glass affect the bottles as their contents are heating and cooling? Why is it important to remove one bottle at a time from the sterilizer or oven and to seal it at once?

6. Why is it essential to screw the metal rings of patent jars very tightly immediately after the fruit is sufficiently sterilized, and also at intervals during the period of cooling? How can you ascertain that the seal is perfect? What are the indications that air is entering the bottles during storage of fruit?

7. When bottling fruit in ordinary jars without the use of a thermometer and sterilizing it in a pan over a boiling ring, or in the oven, how do these methods differ? What is the only sure indication that the fruit is thoroughly sterilized?

8. When would you bottle fruit (a) in syrup, (b) without water?

9. Why is it necessary to use a pressure cooker to bottle vegetables? How does the method differ from that for bottling fruit?

10. What should be the condition of vegetables and fruit for pickling purposes? What effect has the quality of the vinegar upon the pickle? Why should vinegar not come into contact with metal?

11. What kind of jar is most suitable for storing pickles, and what are the most satisfactory methods of covering pickles?

12. Why can fruits and vegetables be preserved successfully at very low temperatures? How should they be treated after removal from a deep-freezer?

33

1. Taking the principles of "conservation of energy" and of "economy" as a basis, what would be of initial importance in the general arrangement for simple household meals?

2. For the food to supply all that is necessary to each individual member of a household what essential points must the housekeeper bear in mind as regards the complete daily fare?

3. When considering the menu for a small dinner of a slightly formal character, what courses would you include in the menu, and what do you consider of most importance as to the selection of dishes? What would be a suitable menu in the month of June?

INDEX